"The grass withers and the flowers fall, but the word of our God endures forever."
Isaiah 40:8

DEFENDING OLD TESTAMENT AUTHORSHIP

The Word of God Is Authentic and True

EDWARD D. ANDREWS

DEFENDING OLD TESTAMENT AUTHORSHIP

The Word of God Is Authentic and True

Edward D. Andrews

Christian Publishing House
Cambridge, Ohio

Copyright © 2017 Edward D. Andrews

All rights reserved. Except for brief quotations in articles, other publications, book reviews, and blogs, no part of this book may be reproduced in any manner without prior written permission from the publishers. For information, write, support@christianpublishers.org

Unless otherwise stated, Scripture quotations are from Updated American Standard Version (UASV) Copyright © 2022 by Christian Publishing House

DEFENDING OLD TESTAMENT AUTHORSHIP: The Word of God Is Authentic and True by Edward D. Andrews

ISBN-10: 1945757655

ISBN-13: 978-1945757655

Table of Contents

Book Description 6

Preface 8

INTRODUCTION The Destructive History of Higher Criticism 10

CHAPTER 1 The Mosaic Authorship: Debunking the Documentary Hypothesis 49

CHAPTER 2 Defending Joshua, Judges, and Ruth 106

CHAPTER 3 Defending First and Second Samuel, First and Second Kings 124

CHAPTER 4 Defending First and Second Chronicles, Ezra, Nehemiah, and Esther 143

CHAPTER 5 Defending Job, Psalm, Proverbs, Ecclesiastes, and the Song of Solomon 173

CHAPTER 6 Defending the Book of Isaiah 219

CHAPTER 7 Making a Case for the Book of Jeremiah and Lamentations 247

CHAPTER 8 Refuting the Critical Objections to the Book of Ezekiel 265

CHAPTER 9 The Book of Daniel on Trial 276

CHAPTER 10 Defending Hosea, Joel, and Amos 314

CHAPTER 11 Defending Obadiah, Jonah, and Micah 349

CHAPTER 12 Defending Nahum, Habakkuk, and Zephaniah 381

CHAPTER 13 Defending Haggai, Zechariah, and Malachi 406

Bibliography 476

Edward D. Andrews

Book Description

In a world where the veracity of the Old Testament is increasingly questioned, "DEFENDING OLD TESTAMENT AUTHORSHIP: The Word of God Is Authentic and True" serves as a timely and rigorous answer to skeptics and critics alike. This comprehensive volume not only dismantles higher criticism's skeptical claims about the Old Testament but also provides compelling evidence for its historical, theological, and moral integrity.

Staring Down Higher Criticism

The book begins by dissecting the rise and influence of higher criticism, from the late dating theories of Julius Wellhausen to the unfounded assumptions of multiple authors based on language and style. With surgical precision, the work exposes the flaws, biases, and intellectual pitfalls of this critical approach, revealing its speculative nature and the erosion it causes to Biblical authority.

A Book-by-Book Defense

Following the introduction, the book undertakes a chapter-by-chapter defense of individual Old Testament books, refuting arguments against their authenticity, authorship, and dating. From the Mosaic authorship of the Pentateuch to the historical reliability of the Books of History, from the wisdom literature to the Prophets, each chapter serves as a fortress of facts, standing firm against the tide of criticism.

Special Features

In addition to its primary content, the book also features an invaluable appendix addressing various Bible difficulties. This section offers practical principles for overcoming apparent contradictions, mistakes, and scientific errors in the Bible, thereby reinforcing the inerrancy and trustworthiness of Scripture.

An Authoritative Reference

DEFENDING OLD TESTAMENT AUTHORSHIP

Written with scholarly depth and accessible language, this book serves as an authoritative reference for pastors, seminary students, Bible scholars, and anyone committed to defending the reliability of the Old Testament. Prepare to have your faith fortified and your understanding deepened as you discover why the Word of God is, indeed, authentic and true.

"DEFENDING OLD TESTAMENT AUTHORSHIP" is more than a scholarly rebuttal; it's a clarion call to uphold the sanctity and truth of Jehovah's Word in an age of skepticism.

Edward D. Andrews

Preface

In recent times, the Old Testament has come under a torrent of scrutiny that threatens not just the trustworthiness of the text, but the very foundations of Judeo-Christian thought. This book was born out of a recognition that our faith community can no longer afford to be passive bystanders in the face of these challenges. As someone who has dedicated years to the rigorous study of the Hebrew Scriptures, I felt it incumbent upon me to put forth a thorough, systematic defense, laying bare the assumptions, inconsistencies, and biases of higher criticism that undermine the Old Testament's authenticity.

The primary goal of this book is twofold: First, to counteract the widespread misinformation about the Old Testament by dismantling the claims of higher criticism in a scholarly yet accessible manner. Second, to equip believers with the intellectual tools and evidence needed to stand firm in their faith and engage in meaningful dialogue with skeptics.

While a plethora of works exist that defend the New Testament, the Old Testament often remains an overlooked frontier. This is a glaring oversight, as the Hebrew Scriptures are not merely a precursor to the New Testament but a complete, divine revelation in their own right. Moreover, the Old Testament forms the bedrock upon which the New Testament stands; to undermine one is to destabilize the other.

To this end, each chapter of this book will focus on the authenticity, authorship, and dating of a specific Old Testament book or group of books. This methodical, book-by-book approach allows us to delve into each text with the depth and nuance it deserves, addressing the specific challenges and criticisms it faces.

The book also includes an appendix that offers practical guidance for handling Bible difficulties, thereby cementing the Old Testament's inerrancy and reliability. In a world increasingly hostile to faith, it is my sincere hope that this work will serve as both a shield and a sword: A shield to protect your faith against the arrows of criticism and a sword to cut through the web of skepticism that ensnares the modern mind.

Edward D. Andrews

Chief Translator of the Updated American Standard Version

Edward D. Andrews

INTRODUCTION The Destructive History of Higher Criticism

The Rise of Higher Criticism

As one delves into the labyrinthine complexities of biblical interpretation, there's an elephant in the room: Higher Criticism. Originating in the intellectual ferment of the 18th and 19th centuries, this approach to biblical scholarship claims to apply rigorous, scientific methods to the interpretation of Scripture. However, an incisive investigation reveals a different reality: Higher Criticism is a paradigm characterized by ideologically motivated assumptions, speculative theories, and an almost cavalier willingness to question or dismiss the authority, inspiration, and historical accuracy of the Bible.

The rise of Higher Criticism as an intellectual force coincided with broader ideological shifts that were reshaping Western thought. The Enlightenment, with its emphasis on human reason, laid the groundwork for the secular humanism and skepticism that were to follow. Meanwhile, the German idealism of the 19th century introduced a sort of philosophical subjectivism that would influence thinkers for generations. These streams of thought converged into what became the Higher Criticism, a methodology that purports to dissect the Scriptures with scientific detachment but is instead laden with a plethora of unexamined presuppositions.

Among the most notable proponents of this school of thought was Julius Wellhausen, who posited the Documentary Hypothesis—the idea that the Pentateuch was composed of various source materials, cobbled together over centuries. While seemingly academic, the hypothesis was grounded in the presupposition that the Bible could not be divinely inspired, that prophecy is implausible, and that miracles are myths. Wellhausen and his followers did not merely present these as theories but as settled fact, a dangerous presumption that has caused many to question the Bible's integrity and reliability.

This shift from reverence for the Word to an almost forensic dissection of it did not occur in a vacuum. Wellhausen's theory, and those of other Higher Critics, enjoyed a symbiotic relationship with the rising acceptance of Darwinian evolution and other naturalistic theories. Evolutionary biology seemed to provide a scientific framework within which critics could theorize about the development of Israelite religion. In other words, if species evolved, then so too could religion and religious texts, going from simple to complex. This led to ludicrous suppositions such as the idea that the Mosaic laws and priestly instructions were late innovations, even though there is no empirical evidence to support such claims.

The most damaging consequence of Higher Criticism has been its corrosive impact on the doctrine of biblical inerrancy and authority. Critics assert that the Scriptures are filled with discrepancies, anachronisms, and ideological biases, ignoring the counterarguments grounded in a holistic, historical-grammatical interpretation of the text. By highlighting supposed contradictions and casting doubt on the historical accounts, critics make it increasingly difficult for believers and skeptics alike to approach the Bible as a reliable source of divine revelation.

An additional problem lies in the selective skepticism that characterizes Higher Criticism. Critics often employ one set of criteria when examining secular ancient texts and another, far more stringent set when scrutinizing the Bible. This selective skepticism reveals a deeper ideological bias that presupposes the Scriptures' human origin and fallibility, leading to circular reasoning: the Bible is fallible because it is human, and we know it is human because it is fallible.

Ironically, despite its claim to objective analysis, Higher Criticism rarely subjects its own methodologies to critical scrutiny. Any examination from the perspective of institutional archaeology or other forms of external evidence is often dismissed or ignored, even when such evidence substantiates the biblical account. For example, archaeological discoveries have repeatedly confirmed the historical reliability of the Scriptures, from the existence of Hittite civilization to the details surrounding the fall of Jericho. Yet, these findings have done little to temper the critics' enthusiasm for dissecting the Bible along speculative lines.

In summary, Higher Criticism poses a significant challenge to the authority and reliability of Scripture. Under the guise of scholarly rigor, it has infiltrated academic and theological circles, casting doubt and fostering skepticism. However, this is not an objective, scientific approach to the Bible; it is a methodology rooted in presuppositions that reflect broader ideological systems—namely, secular humanism, Enlightenment rationalism, and German idealism. These ideologies are antithetical to the tenets of conservative hermeneutics, which affirm the inerrancy, inspiration, and historical reliability of the Scriptures.

The ultimate aim of this discourse is to expose the underlying fallacies of Higher Criticism and to offer an alternative: a conservative approach to biblical hermeneutics that is rooted in the historical-grammatical method, respects the unity and diversity of Scripture, and is committed to its authority and inerrancy. This is not merely an academic exercise; it is a bulwark against a tide of skepticism and disbelief that has been undermining faith in the Bible for far too long.

Therefore, let us engage with the text not as skeptics who doubt its every claim but as diligent scholars committed to unearthing its riches, fully persuaded that the Scriptures are what they claim to be: the inspired and authoritative Word of God.

Julius Wellhausen and the Late Dating Theory

A name that has become almost synonymous with Higher Criticism is Julius Wellhausen, the German Protestant theologian and biblical scholar whose influence on modern biblical criticism is both expansive and contentious. Although he was not the first to propose source-critical theories, Wellhausen popularized the Documentary Hypothesis in a way that has shaped and guided liberal-moderate biblical criticism for over a century. This introduction aims to critically examine the theories and methodologies introduced by Wellhausen, specifically his late dating theories, which not only distance biblical interpretation from its historical and textual roots but also erode the very foundations of the authority and inerrancy of Scripture.

The Rise of Wellhausen

Wellhausen emerged at a time when European intellectual life was awash in Enlightenment ideals, secular humanism, and German idealism. Armed with these ideologies, he embarked on an academic mission to dissect the Pentateuch (the first five books of the Old Testament) into various supposed sources, arguing that these texts were not authored by Moses but were instead compiled much later in history. His Documentary Hypothesis suggested that four primary sources—often identified by the acronyms JEDP (Jahwist, Elohist, Deuteronomist, and Priestly)—were stitched together to create what we now call the Pentateuch.

The Late Dating Theory

Wellhausen's late dating theory held that the Priestly Code, which contains much of the law and ritual instructions, was not Mosaic but was instead a product of the post-exilic period, written to serve the ideological and political purposes of a priestly class in a reconstructed Jerusalem. The implications of this theory are not just academic; they strike at the very core of the biblical claim that Jehovah gave the laws to Moses for the governance and sanctification of His chosen people.

Presuppositions and Prejudices

Central to Wellhausen's hypothesis are a series of underlying presuppositions: miracles cannot happen, prophecy is not valid, and divine revelation is an intellectual impossibility. Guided by these tenets, his methodology already anticipates the conclusions: the Pentateuch cannot be a divinely inspired text, and therefore it must be a human construction that evolved over time. The fallacy here is that

Wellhausen and like-minded critics present their speculations not merely as possibilities to consider but as settled facts that one must accept.

The Consequences

The late dating theory has wrought severe damage to the understanding and interpretation of Scripture. Wellhausen's speculative dating creates a milieu in which the Scriptures are viewed as merely human documents. As a result, the Bible becomes a fluid text, open to ideological manipulation and deconstruction, rather than a reliable source of divine revelation. Thus, higher critics, under the guise of scholarly detachment, have in fact imposed a subjective framework that disconnects the text from its original context and ultimate Author.

The Flaws in the Theory

Not only is Wellhausen's late dating theory speculative, but it is also riddled with internal inconsistencies and external contradictions. For example, while he and his disciples argue for the late development of Israelite religion based on their dating of the Pentateuch, this contradicts historical data, including the discovery of the Hittite empire, the historical context of the patriarchs, and the evidence supporting an early date for the conquest of Canaan.

Moreover, Wellhausen's theory cannot explain the thematic unity seen in the Pentateuch or the intricate foreshadowings and prophetic utterances that span centuries. This thematic and prophetic unity strongly argues for a single Author behind the text, an Author who exists outside of time and space.

A Conservative Response

As adherents of the historical-grammatical method of biblical interpretation, committed to the inerrancy and authority of Scripture, it is incumbent upon us to challenge the speculative theories and subjective biases that characterize the work of Wellhausen and other higher critics. The Scriptures, when examined through the objective lens of the historical-grammatical method, provide abundant evidence for their divine origin, coherence, and reliability. There is a growing body of external evidence, from archaeology to manuscript studies, which corroborates the Bible's historical accounts.

Julius Wellhausen, in popularizing the late dating theory and the Documentary Hypothesis, did not open a new vista for understanding the Scriptures; rather, he led a generation of scholars and laypeople alike into a quagmire of doubt and skepticism. His theories are not the result of objective, scientific analysis, but the product of ideological presuppositions that are intrinsically hostile to the Bible as the inspired Word of God.

The ultimate goal of this critique is not merely to expose the fallacies inherent in Wellhausen's methods and theories but to fortify the foundations of a conservative, objective approach to Scripture. This approach not only respects but celebrates the divine origin, authority, and inerrancy of the Bible, serving as an antidote to the corrosive skepticism that higher criticism has introduced into biblical studies. In a world increasingly awash with doubt, it is imperative to reaffirm that the Scriptures are, indeed, the very words of God, designed to guide us into all truth.

The Assumption of Multiple Authors: The 'Elohim' and 'Jehovah' Division

One of the most pernicious elements of Higher Criticism has been the persistent assumption of multiple authorship for the Pentateuch, most infamously executed through the division of texts based on the names used for God—Elohim and Jehovah. Proponents of this perspective assert that the different names for God in the Old Testament, particularly in the Pentateuch, suggest varying traditions, authors, and therefore multiple sources. This assumption is a cornerstone of the Documentary Hypothesis, popularized by Julius Wellhausen and his intellectual descendants. However, far from elucidating the text, this approach muddles understanding, undermines the authority of Scripture, and moves us further away from a true, objective comprehension of the Word of God.

The Evolution of the Name-Division Theory

The idea of dividing the biblical text based on the names used for God has roots reaching back to the Enlightenment period. As Enlightenment thinkers began to doubt miracles, prophecy, and divine revelation, they also called into question the traditional views on the authorship of the Bible. When German higher critics adopted these doubts, they turned them into a formalized approach that scrutinized the Bible not as a divine revelation but as a human-made artifact. The division based on the names Elohim and Jehovah became a key tool in their critical arsenal.

The Flawed Methodology

The presumption of multiple authorship based on the variation in divine names is fundamentally flawed for several reasons. For one, it arbitrarily imposes a modern, secular mindset on ancient, sacred texts. It presumes that the ancient Hebrews were incapable of employing literary techniques or of using various names for God to convey different aspects of His nature and character. The Documentary Hypothesis suggests that these divisions reveal separate traditions cobbled together, ignoring the much more plausible explanation that these names serve theological and literary functions.

The Ignorance of Historical Context

By insisting on the division of the text based on the names for God, proponents of Higher Criticism willfully or negligently ignore the historical context in which these texts were written. Ancient Near Eastern literature frequently employed multiple names or titles for gods, kings, and other figures to express different attributes or roles. When the Old Testament uses both Elohim and Jehovah, it's not signaling multiple authorship or conflicting traditions; rather, it's conveying a fuller picture of God's character.

Theological Ramifications

The assumption of multiple authors based on the names for God has troubling theological implications. If the text is so divided and is a product of multiple human authors with differing agendas, what becomes of its inerrancy, its coherence, its authority? The presumption of multiple authorship reduces the text to a human artifact subject to ideological manipulation, thereby eroding the bedrock of faith in the Bible as the inspired, inerrant Word of God.

The Disregard for Internal Evidence

The Bible itself offers no hint that its use of different names for God implies multiple authorship or conflicting traditions. Quite the contrary, the Scriptures portray a consistent, unified narrative and theological message. For example, the interplay of divine names within the same passages (such as in Genesis 2–3, where Elohim and Jehovah are both used) would make no sense if they were from disparate sources. This internal evidence argues strongly against the speculative nature of Higher Criticism's authorship divisions.

A Conservative Rejoinder

Committed to the historical-grammatical method and to the inerrancy of Scripture, conservative scholars reject the assumption of multiple authors based on the names for God. Not only does this perspective lack objective, textual support, but it also contradicts the extensive evidence affirming the divine inspiration and coherence of Scripture. Through objective methods and an unswerving commitment to the authority of the Word of God, conservative scholars affirm that the different names for God serve to enrich our understanding of His multifaceted character rather than to signal multiple human authors.

The division of biblical texts based on the names Elohim and Jehovah represents one of the most flawed aspects of Higher Criticism. It is not based on objective analysis but is heavily influenced by Enlightenment skepticism and German idealism. This method has not enhanced our understanding of Scripture; instead, it has sowed seeds of doubt and eroded the faith of many. As proponents of an objective, conservative approach to the Bible, it is our duty to challenge these speculations, to expose their biases, and to reaffirm the unity, inerrancy, and divine authorship of Scripture. As a warning to the faithful, we must remember that these critical methods serve to undermine confidence in the Bible, rather than to elucidate its truths. Our ultimate aim must always be to uphold the Bible as the inspired and authoritative Word of God, presenting a consistent, reliable guide for faith and life.

The Rejection of Historical Accounts: Jacob and Esau as Allegory

A particularly damaging aspect of Higher Criticism is the propensity to allegorize or demythologize historical narratives in the Bible. This trend results in a reductive interpretation of the biblical text, undermining the inerrancy and historical reliability of Scripture. One vivid example is the interpretation of the account of Jacob and Esau as mere allegory rather than historical narrative.

Historical Genesis of the Allegorical Method

The trend toward allegorizing biblical texts did not emerge in a vacuum but is rooted in Enlightenment skepticism. It was subsequently developed during the 19th century by German higher critics who sought to understand the Bible primarily as a product of human culture rather than as divine revelation. These approaches imbued Scripture with Enlightenment presuppositions such as anti-supernaturalism and rationalism, transforming the Bible from a historical account into mere symbolic narrative.

Methodological Flaws

The allegorical interpretation of the story of Jacob and Esau involves several flaws. First, it disregards the intent of the original authors who clearly presented these accounts as historical events. Whether discussing Jacob's birthright, the divine revelation at Bethel, or the reconciliation with Esau, the narratives maintain a consistent historical tone. They contain concrete details—names, locations, and temporal markers—that argue for a historical interpretation.

The Consequences of Denying History

When one reduces these rich narratives to allegory, the Bible's history becomes plastic, mutable, and subject to the interpreter's whims. Moreover, it raises unsettling theological implications. For instance, if Jacob and Esau are allegorical figures, what does that say about God's covenant with Jacob and, by extension, the nation of Israel? Such an approach threatens the integrity of the biblical metanarrative, which traces God's covenantal relationship with His people.

Scriptural Consistency

The allegorical interpretation also dismisses the consistent portrayal of Jacob and Esau throughout Scripture. Later books like Malachi and Romans refer back to the twins as historical figures in God's sovereign plan. This consistency argues for their historicity and underscores the problem with relegating them to the realm of allegory.

Erosion of Doctrinal Foundations

When the accounts of Jacob and Esau are reduced to allegory, foundational doctrines such as election, grace, and divine providence also become vulnerable. The hermeneutical shift from literal-historical interpretation to allegorical interpretation opens the door to subjective reinterpretation of key doctrines, eroding the very foundations of the Christian faith.

Ideological Underpinnings

Higher critics often assert that their methods are neutral and scientific, but this is hardly the case. Their allegorical approach is influenced by philosophical commitments to rationalism, anti-supernaturalism, and sometimes even socio-political agendas. These ideological underpinnings further distance biblical interpretation from an objective pursuit of truth.

A Conservative Counterpoint

A conservative hermeneutical approach, committed to the historical-grammatical method, honors the text's self-presentation as historical narrative. It recognizes that the authority of the Bible lies in its divine inspiration, unified message, and historical reliability. Accordingly, the conservative method rejects allegorizing tendencies, opting for a straightforward reading that respects the text's genre, context, and evident meaning.

The allegorical interpretation of Jacob and Esau's account serves as a glaring example of the destructive capabilities of Higher Criticism. This approach not only distorts the intended meaning of the text but also poses a risk to foundational Christian doctrines. Such critical methods claim objectivity yet are marred by ideological commitments alien to the biblical worldview.

By adopting the historical-grammatical method and holding to the inerrancy and authority of Scripture, conservative scholarship offers a robust alternative to the subjective, ideologically-driven practices of modern biblical criticism. Therefore, it is paramount for serious students of the Bible to equip themselves with conservative exegetical principles and methods. This not only allows for a correct understanding of the Bible but also serves as a safeguard against the corrosive influences of Higher Criticism, which have undermined the faith of many and distorted the Word of God.

Let this serve as a warning: The floodgates opened by Higher Criticism have washed away the confidence many had in Scripture, leaving behind a desolate landscape where the Bible's authority is questioned and its message diluted. This is why a commitment to conservative, objective hermeneutical methods is not merely an academic exercise—it is a defense of the integrity, authority, and divine origin of the Holy Scriptures.

The Delegitimization of Israel's Religious Institutions: The Ark and Tabernacle

One of the more audacious facets of Higher Criticism's assault on the biblical text involves the delegitimization of Israel's religious institutions, specifically the Ark of the Covenant and the Tabernacle. This approach, tainted by skeptical presuppositions, aims to relegate these critical elements of Israel's religious history to the realm of myth or political agenda, thus undermining their historicity and divine significance.

The Emergence of Skepticism Towards Israelite Institutions

The skepticism regarding Israelite religious institutions traces its roots back to Enlightenment thought, where reason was elevated above revelation. During the 19th and 20th centuries, German critics, heavily influenced by rationalistic assumptions, began to dissect the Pentateuch and historical books of the Old Testament. They assumed these texts were not accounts of divine revelation but rather the concoctions of various redactors seeking to centralize religious power or formulate a national identity.

The Ark of the Covenant Under Scrutiny

Critics have sought to explain away the Ark as a political or cultural symbol rather than an actual object associated with Jehovah's presence and covenant. They cast doubt on accounts like the fall of Jericho's walls or the Ark's return from Philistine captivity, dismissing these as folklore rather than real divine intervention. However, this assumption fails to consider the detailed, consistent narrative of the Ark's construction, purpose, and history found within the biblical text.

Deconstructing the Tabernacle

Similarly, the Tabernacle, with its intricate design and sacrificial system, has been portrayed as a later religious invention, with critics arguing that such a complex structure could not have been constructed during the Israelites' sojourn in the wilderness. This critique ignores the text's explicit statements regarding the Tabernacle's materials, measurements, and divine instructions for construction.

Methodological Concerns

Such critiques often employ a form of criticism called "source criticism," aiming to dissect the biblical text into multiple, often conflicting, sources. However, this methodology is speculative at best, ignoring the unified narrative presented in the text and failing to consider the divine inspiration that ensures the Scriptures' coherency and reliability.

Consequences of Delegitimizing Israel's Religious Institutions

By casting doubt on the historicity and function of the Ark and Tabernacle, Higher Criticism not only undermines the text but also has severe theological implications. It implicitly questions Jehovah's covenantal relationship with Israel and, by extension, His providential involvement in human history. This, in turn, disrupts the foundational doctrines of God's holiness, omnipotence, and faithfulness.

Ideological Biases

Higher critics claim that their methods are objective, but the truth is their methodologies are heavily laden with ideological biases. Secular humanism, Enlightenment rationalism, and German idealism pervade their analyses, effectively transforming what should be a scholarly enterprise into a platform for promoting skeptical and secularist agendas.

A Conservative Approach

In contrast, the conservative, historical-grammatical method seeks to honor the Bible's self-presentation as a reliable historical document. It takes seriously the text's own claims about the Ark and Tabernacle, interpreting them in the immediate and broader context of Scripture, thus respecting their complexity, historical placement, and divine significance.

The move to delegitimize the Ark of the Covenant and the Tabernacle by Higher Criticism has far-reaching consequences, not just for the interpretation of biblical history but also for foundational doctrines concerning God's nature and His dealings with humanity. This approach is not merely flawed but perilous, as it shakes the very pillars of faith, reducing God's acts to human fabrication and theological concepts to mere constructs of cultural evolution.

For this reason, it is imperative to reclaim a conservative approach to biblical interpretation, rooted in the historical-grammatical method and committed to the inerrancy of Scripture. This is not an academic exercise of preserving traditionalism but a critical endeavor to maintain the integrity and authority of the Word of God.

So let this be a warning and a call to action: Higher Criticism has unleashed a torrent of skepticism that has eroded people's confidence in the authority and inerrancy of Scripture. We must arm ourselves with the truth and the proper hermeneutical tools to safeguard the Bible against these corrosive influences. The stakes are not merely academic—they are spiritual, affecting our understanding of God, His Word, and His redemptive plan for humanity.

Flawed Principles: Repetition and Style as Criteria

Higher Criticism has entrenched itself in biblical studies with its audacious methodologies that claim scientific objectivity. However, these methods are inherently flawed, often driven by a commitment to rationalism, secularism, and other ideologies that originated in the Enlightenment. One significant area where this flawed approach manifests is in the principles of "repetition" and "style," which critics employ to justify a complex array of source theories and redactions.

Repetition as a Criterion for Source Division

One common argument from Higher Critics is that repetition in narrative or legal texts implies multiple sources. For instance, critics point to the two accounts of Creation in Genesis 1 and 2 as evidence of two different traditions. However, repetition can serve various functions within a text, such as emphasis or presenting different facets of an event. According to a conservative, historical-grammatical approach, the first chapter of Genesis describes the creation account in a broad scope, while the second chapter offers a detailed focus on humanity. It is not an issue of contradictory sources but rather a matter of perspective.

Style as a Criterion for Source Division

The criteria of "style" have also been heavily employed. Critics argue that variances in vocabulary, syntax, or thematic focus must indicate different authors or sources. For example, they point to the different names for God—Elohim and Jehovah—as evidence of different traditions fused together. This style-based argumentation is not only methodologically flawed but also ignores the rich literary tapestry woven by the biblical authors under divine inspiration. Using different names for God serves to emphasize His various attributes rather than signify different authorial sources.

The German School and Its Influence

Higher Criticism finds much of its genesis in 19th-century German scholarship. Names like Wellhausen have become synonymous with source criticism, using stylistic and repetitive features to deconstruct the Pentateuch into a complicated web of multiple sources and redactions, collectively known as the Documentary Hypothesis. This approach is significantly influenced by German idealism, which, among other things, views history as a sort of unfolding idea—thus, Israel's religious history must also be an evolution from polytheism to ethical monotheism, they argue. However, this interpretation not only conflicts with the text but also imposes a foreign philosophical system upon it.

Ideological Biases

The assumption that the Bible's historical and theological claims are somehow subject to stylistic and repetitive features as evidence of multiple sources isn't a neutral scientific posture. It is embedded in the larger ideologies of secular humanism and rationalism. The claim to objectivity masks a predetermined commitment against supernaturalism and divine revelation.

A Conservative Counterpoint

In opposition to these flawed methodologies, the conservative historical-grammatical method insists on taking the text at face value unless there is compelling evidence to do otherwise. It honors the text's historical setting and recognizes that repetition and stylistic variation can be deliberate literary techniques. Instead of casting doubt upon the text's unity or divine inspiration, it seeks to understand the author's intent and the message being conveyed, within both the immediate and broader contexts of Scripture.

The High Stakes

The stakes are far from merely academic. By casting doubt on the integrity and unity of the biblical text, Higher Criticism has led many astray, sowing seeds of skepticism and diminishing people's confidence in the Bible's inerrancy. This has profound spiritual ramifications, weakening the foundation upon which faith is built.

The principles of repetition and style, as employed by Higher Critics, serve as shaky ground upon which to dissect the biblical text into an amalgam of sources and redactions. These methods are not neutral; they are riddled with ideological biases that align more with secular and rationalistic worldviews than with a respect for the text's own claims. Therefore, the conservative historical-grammatical method remains the more reliable approach, committed to the integrity, inerrancy, and divine inspiration of Scripture.

The Higher Criticism that has burgeoned over the last few centuries is not an innocent academic endeavor but an ideological onslaught against the Bible's authority. Understanding these flawed principles helps in defending the text and affirming its divinely inspired nature. It is critical that we equip ourselves with conservative exegetical methods that adhere to the Bible's own presentation of itself, thereby offering an antidote to the speculative and skewed practices of modern biblical criticism.

The Speculative Nature of Higher Criticism

In biblical studies, there is perhaps no approach more contentious, more ideologically charged, and more rife with speculation than the Higher Criticism that has taken root in the last few centuries. Presented under the guise of objective academic inquiry, it purports to offer scientific insights into the origins, composition, and redaction of the Scriptures. Yet, upon closer inspection, the speculative nature of these methodologies becomes evident, as does their ideological underpinnings. These criticisms have not only affected academic discourse but have had far-reaching consequences in eroding public trust in the authority and inerrancy of the Bible.

The Speculative Foundations

Higher Criticism, often conflated with historical-critical methods, employs a range of speculative techniques. From source criticism to form criticism and beyond, the field is littered with theoretical models that attempt to dissect the biblical text. These methodologies often go beyond the text itself, speculating on hypothetical documents, redactors, and the intentions behind them. For instance, the Documentary Hypothesis argues for the existence of multiple sources behind the Pentateuch, none of which have ever been found.

The Fallacy of Scientific Objectivity

One of the most pernicious aspects of Higher Criticism is its claim to scientific objectivity. While it dons the mantle of rational inquiry, it often leaps from evidence to hypothesis in a manner that would be unacceptable in other disciplines. The idea that different styles, repetitions, or even themes in the biblical text are grounds for separating sources or denying single authorship is more an act of academic imagination than empirical reasoning.

German Idealism and the Roots of Speculation

Much of Higher Criticism's speculative nature can be traced back to its origins in German scholarship of the 19th century. Inspired by German idealism, scholars like Julius Wellhausen assumed that religion evolved from primitive forms to more ethical monotheism. This speculative lens was then used to read the Old Testament, leading to the creation of theories that align with this evolutionary view, rather than with the text itself.

Ideological Biases Masked as Methodology

The theoretical nature of Higher Criticism becomes more troubling when its ideological commitments are brought to light. Rooted in Enlightenment rationalism, secular humanism, and a rejection of the supernatural, these methodologies are not the neutral tools they claim to be. They come loaded with assumptions that preclude divine intervention, predictive prophecy, or the very idea of inspired Scripture.

Eroding Confidence in Scripture

The speculative methods of Higher Criticism have been damaging, not just in the ivory towers of academia but in churches and among everyday believers. Many, introduced to these theories through seminaries or popular literature, have found their faith shaken and their confidence in Scripture eroded. The introduction of doubt where there was once assurance has profound spiritual ramifications.

A Conservative Alternative: The Historical-Grammatical Method

In contrast, the historical-grammatical method of exegesis offers a grounded alternative. This approach respects the text's own claims and context, refusing to impose external ideological frameworks upon it. It seeks to discover the original intent of the author and the meaning of the text within its historical setting, operating under the conviction that the Bible is a unified, divinely inspired document.

The Importance of Recognizing the Speculative Nature of Higher Criticism

It is essential for believers and scholars alike to recognize the speculative underbelly of Higher Criticism. Understanding its theoretical nature and ideological commitments allows us to be better equipped in both defending the faith and in interpreting Scripture responsibly.

Higher Criticism, despite its claims of objectivity, is laden with speculation and ideological bias. It speculates about sources, authors, and redactors without sufficient evidence and often flies in the face of the text itself. Furthermore, its methodologies are ideologically aligned with secularism, rationalism, and other Enlightenment-based ideologies. As a result, it has undermined confidence in the authority and inerrancy of Scripture, leading many into skepticism and doubt. The field of biblical studies does not need more speculation; it needs a return to sound exegetical methods grounded in a high view of Scripture. The historical-grammatical method provides this grounding, adhering to the text's own presentation of itself as a unified, divinely inspired work, and offers a bulwark against the speculative and often destructive methodologies of Higher Criticism.

The Fallacy of Evolutionary Assumptions in Biblical Criticism

In the grand arena of biblical studies, few approaches have wreaked as much havoc on the integrity and authority of Scripture as Higher Criticism. Among the numerous biases that plague this field, the evolutionary assumptions stand out as particularly egregious. This viewpoint fundamentally misrepresents the nature of the biblical text, its transmission, and its inherent unity, making a thorough examination of these fallacies vital for anyone committed to a conservative understanding of Scripture.

The Evolutionary Paradigm: A Brief Overview

The evolutionary paradigm within Higher Criticism is an outgrowth of the 19th-century intellectual milieu. Rooted in German idealism and later nurtured by Enlightenment skepticism and secular humanism, this paradigm posits that religious thought—like biological organisms—evolves over time. Scholars like Julius Wellhausen applied this framework to the Old Testament, arguing that Israelite religion developed from a crude polytheism to an ethical monotheism.

Evolutionary Assumptions in Source Criticism

One of the most visible instances of the evolutionary assumptions is found in source criticism, notably the Documentary Hypothesis concerning the Pentateuch. Under the presupposition of religious evolution, scholars dissect the text into multiple strands, each corresponding to different stages of religious and cultural development. This hypothesis, though touted as "scientific," relies heavily on these unproven evolutionary assumptions, making it a shaky foundation for biblical interpretation.

Contradiction with the Unity of Scripture

The concept of an evolving religious text is in direct opposition to the conservative understanding of the unity and divine inspiration of Scripture. The Bible presents itself not as a hodgepodge of evolving ideas but as a unified narrative, stretching from creation to the New Covenant. The evolutionary assumptions ignore or undermine this intrinsic unity, creating an artificial and fragmented view of the biblical text.

Devaluing the Historicity of Biblical Events

The evolutionary approach often devalues the historical events portrayed in Scripture. Stories of miracles, divine intervention, and prophecies are considered primitive and thereby relegated to the realm of myth or allegory. This approach not only erodes the historicity of the events but also their theological significance, often reducing them to mere cultural expressions of an evolving religious awareness.

The Theological Consequences

The implications of accepting an evolutionary paradigm in biblical criticism are severe. If the text is merely a product of its time, reflecting the evolving beliefs of the ancient Israelites, it raises serious questions about the text's inerrancy, authority, and relevance for contemporary faith. This opens the door to radical reinterpretations that are out of step with both the text and the historical faith of the community to which it was given.

Questioning the Objectivity of Evolutionary Assumptions

The purported objectivity of the evolutionary assumptions must be questioned. Far from being neutral, these assumptions often serve to validate the secular, naturalistic worldviews of those who employ them. Consequently, this raises significant questions about the scholarly integrity and objectivity of such approaches.

An Alternative: The Historical-Grammatical Method

For those committed to the authority and inerrancy of Scripture, the historical-grammatical method offers a more reliable alternative. This approach seeks to understand the text within its original historical and linguistic context, acknowledging its inherent unity and divine inspiration. By rejecting unfounded evolutionary assumptions, this method allows for a more authentic and meaningful engagement with the biblical text.

The evolutionary assumptions within Higher Criticism have been a corrosive force in biblical studies, serving not the illumination of the text but rather the propagation of a secular, skeptical agenda. These assumptions undermine the unity, historicity, and theological richness of the Bible, diverting scholars and laity alike from the true riches contained therein. The historical-grammatical method, grounded in a conservative understanding of the authority and inerrancy of Scripture, offers a far more credible and respectful approach. This method not only honors the text but also fortifies believers in their faith, countering the skepticism and secularism that so often accompany the evolutionary assumptions in Higher Criticism. Thus, recognizing and jettisoning these flawed assumptions is not merely an academic exercise; it is a safeguard for the faith and integrity of believers who hold the Bible to be the inspired Word of God.

Edward D. Andrews

Two Weak Pillars: Ritual Complexity and Source Age

One of the most challenging aspects of understanding the current landscape of biblical studies is navigating the labyrinth of Higher Criticism. For the unwary reader, the methodologies and terminologies deployed by proponents of this school can give the illusion of scientific rigor and objective analysis. However, upon closer scrutiny, several of its foundational pillars reveal profound weaknesses. Two of such dubious supports are the arguments from ritual complexity and source age. These approaches, often masquerading as neutral or objective, instead introduce a significant level of subjectivity and speculative reasoning, seriously compromising the reliability of the conclusions drawn.

Ritual Complexity as a Criterion for Dating

Higher Criticism often employs the complexity of religious rituals described in the biblical text as an indicator of their historical development. For instance, the well-structured priestly laws and rituals in Leviticus are often dated later than the simpler religious practices described in the earlier books. This methodology presupposes that religious rituals evolved from simple to complex over time—an assumption devoid of empirical verification and rooted in the socio-evolutionary theories of the 19th century. Such a premise conveniently sidesteps the possibility that complex rituals could be both ancient and divinely instituted, as the conservative approach, grounded in the authority and inerrancy of Scripture, maintains.

The Consequences of Misdating Texts

The fallacy of using ritual complexity as a dating mechanism has far-reaching implications. If one accepts that the elaborate priestly code is a late addition, it effectively dislocates the theological significance of these rituals from their historical and covenantal context. This undermines the biblical testimony itself, which presents these laws and rituals as divinely ordained from the time of Moses. Further, it questions the inerrancy and integrity of the Scriptures, attributes that are foundational for conservative hermeneutics.

Source Age: An Unreliable Pillar

Another fragile pillar of Higher Criticism is the emphasis on the age of a particular source as a measure of its reliability or theological sophistication. Critics often presume that older texts are more authentic or 'pure' and later texts are corruptions or adaptations. This premise is not only methodologically flawed but also assumes what it needs to prove. It neglects to consider that later texts can faithfully transmit, clarify, or systematize earlier teachings without compromising their integrity.

Source Age and the Canonization Process

The issue of source age becomes even more problematic when we consider the process of canonization. The books that constitute the Old Testament were recognized as authoritative not merely because of their age but also because of their fidelity to revealed truth. The conservative stance understands this canonization as a complex process guided by divine providence, not just the happenstance assembly of ancient texts. By undermining this process, the critics inadvertently attack the trustworthiness of the Scriptures as a unified, divine revelation.

Challenging the Objectivity of These Pillars

The theories based on ritual complexity and source age are often presented as objective, but they are deeply embedded in the speculative methodologies born out of Enlightenment rationalism, secular humanism, and even German idealism. They are hardly the neutral, scientifically robust principles that their proponents claim them to be. Rather, they are the offspring of broader ideological systems that have been at odds with biblical faith for centuries.

The Alternative: The Historical-Grammatical Method

The conservative exegetical method, particularly the historical-grammatical approach, offers a more objective and respectful way to study the Scriptures. By focusing on the text within its immediate historical and grammatical context, it allows for a comprehensive understanding that is faithful to the intended meaning. This method also recognizes the internal unity and consistency of the Bible, guided by a commitment to its authority and inerrancy, rather than subjecting it to external, and often hostile, ideological frameworks.

The pillars of ritual complexity and source age are not merely shaky; they are ready to crumble under the weight of their own methodological and philosophical inconsistencies. Yet, these are the foundations upon which much of Higher Criticism is built. It is high time for a reevaluation, a return to methods that respect the integrity, unity, and divine origin of the Scriptures. Only by doing so can one escape the labyrinthine maze of Higher Criticism and rediscover the enduring truths that have nourished the faith of countless believers throughout history. This return to a conservative approach is not a retreat into obscurantism; it is rather a pursuit of genuine understanding, unclouded by the ideological biases that have marred biblical studies for far too long. In this way, both the scholar and the lay reader can be equipped with the tools necessary to counter the undermining influences that have eroded confidence in the sacred text and can discover anew the Bible's transformative power.

Archaeological Evidence: A Reality Check for Higher Criticism

The interface between archaeology and biblical studies has long been a contested battleground, primarily because the former offers tangible data that can either corroborate or challenge the historical narratives contained in Scripture. A thorough review of archaeological findings offers a significant reality check to the methodologies and assumptions of Higher Criticism. Despite what critics claim, archaeological evidence often harmonizes remarkably well with a conservative reading of the Bible, thereby challenging the speculative and ideologically-driven constructs of liberal-moderate biblical criticism.

Presuppositions and Skepticism: A Brief Overview

One common tactic in Higher Criticism is to start with a skepticism toward the biblical text, demanding extraordinary evidence for ordinary claims. This approach effectively places the Bible on trial, assuming its guilt (i.e., unreliability) until proven innocent—a standard not applied to other ancient documents. This ideological commitment often results in a discounting of corroborative evidence and a highlighting of so-called discrepancies between the archaeological record and the biblical narratives.

The City of Jericho: A Case Study

Consider the case of Jericho, a city whose walls the Bible says "fell down flat" after the Israelites encircled it for seven days (Joshua 6:20, UASV). Early 20th-century excavations led by John Garstang appeared to confirm the biblical account. However, later investigations by Kathleen Kenyon challenged this view. Critics seized upon her conclusions to argue against the historicity of the biblical story. However, subsequent research and reassessment, particularly by Bryant G. Wood, found that the earlier positive assessment was more accurate. When the pottery, stratigraphy, and carbon-14 dating are carefully examined, they align with the biblical narrative. Thus, here archaeology serves as a corrective to hasty critical skepticism.

The House of David Inscription

Another notable example is the Tel Dan Inscription, discovered in 1993, which provided the first historical evidence of King David outside the Bible. Before this, critics had questioned the very existence of a Davidic dynasty, reducing it to mere mythology. The inscription dealt a severe blow to such speculative theories, vindicating the historical reliability of the biblical accounts related to David and his house.

Problems with the Minimalist Approach

Higher Criticism often aligns with what is termed the "minimalist" approach in archaeology, which assumes that the lack of evidence is evidence of lack. For instance, absence of conclusive archaeological evidence for a particular biblical event or figure is sometimes used to dismiss the Bible's historical reliability. However, this approach is flawed both logically and methodologically. Archaeology is a discipline that works with what survives the ravages of time, and absence of evidence is not necessarily a definitive argument against the Bible's accounts.

Preserving a Rational Perspective

Critics often underestimate the highly selective nature of the archaeological record. A conservative approach maintains a balanced perspective by acknowledging the limitations of archaeology. Many aspects of daily life, specific events, or even major figures may never appear in the archaeological record but that does not make them any less real or historical.

The Historical-Grammatical Method and Archaeology

The conservative exegetical approach, employing the historical-grammatical method, seeks to understand the text within its original historical context, which includes the material culture. Archaeological findings serve as ancillary data that can enrich our understanding of the text. Importantly, this method recognizes that while archaeology can provide contextual background, the authority and inerrancy of Scripture stand independently of external verification.

Archaeological evidence, when examined objectively, serves as a robust counterpoint to the presumptions and skepticism of Higher Criticism. Multiple findings have underscored the historical reliability of the Old Testament, challenging the critical methodologies that start from a position of doubt rather than one of reasoned faith. These discoveries are significant not because they "prove" the Bible—its authority is self-authenticating—but because they offer a reality check to the speculative and ideologically driven criticisms that have gained prominence in modern academia.

It is time to approach biblical archaeology without the ideological blinders that have plagued the field for so long. This will allow both scholars and laypersons to better appreciate the depth, richness, and historical grounding of the biblical text. The conservative historical-grammatical method offers a pathway for this kind of rigorous and respectful engagement with Scripture, unclouded by the prejudices that have distorted the study and interpretation of the Bible. This balanced approach provides a shield against the erosion of confidence in the Bible, fortifying our understanding and respect for its divine message.

The Appeal to Intellectuals: Aligning with Evolutionary and Rationalist Views

In the world of biblical studies, there is a distinctive magnetism that Higher Criticism exerts on the intellectual class. The methodological elements of Higher Criticism, often portrayed as the zenith of rational thought, have formed a symbiotic relationship with evolutionary theory and rationalist ideologies. This is not accidental but rather a calculated maneuver aimed at lending credence to liberal-moderate views, thus perpetuating a circle of bias that marginalizes conservative approaches grounded in the authority and inerrancy of Scripture. In the quest for academic respectability and intellectual rigor, many have strayed from a historically grounded and textually respectful methodology. The effect has been corrosive, distancing biblical interpretation from objective truth and promoting speculative theories under the guise of academic excellence.

The Quest for Academic Acceptance

There is a pervasive tendency within the academic community to seek recognition and approval from peers. This drive for acceptance has led to an unspoken alliance between biblical critics and proponents of naturalistic theories of origin and existence, particularly evolutionary thought. The implied message is that an acceptance of evolutionary theory should naturally extend to an acceptance of liberal-moderate biblical criticism as the intellectual default position.

Darwinism and Higher Criticism: An Unholy Alliance

The relationship between Darwinism and Higher Criticism has historical roots in the Enlightenment era but gained momentum during the 19th century. While Charles Darwin's work on evolution gave naturalistic explanations for the origin of species, Higher Criticism offered a similarly naturalistic framework for understanding the development of biblical texts. Critics claimed that just as species evolved through natural processes, so too did the biblical texts evolve through a series of edits, redactions, and modifications over time.

This narrative has influenced a whole generation of scholars to reject divine agency in the formation of Scripture. Texts are no longer seen as inspired, but rather as human constructs shaped by social, economic, and political forces. This aligns perfectly with an evolutionary view that removes Jehovah from the equation altogether.

Rationalism and the Demotion of Faith

The Enlightenment period birthed an ideology that elevated human reason above divine revelation. The fruit of this was Rationalism, which often manifests as an undue skepticism towards anything that cannot be empirically verified. Higher Criticism has borrowed this philosophical framework, subjecting Scripture to the rationalist scalpel, cutting away at the miraculous, the supernatural, and the divine. This practice is incongruent with a conservative approach to biblical interpretation, which respects the text's self-attestation of divine origin and authority.

A Divorce from Objective Methods

Higher Criticism claims to be objective, employing "scientific" methods in its analysis. However, this is deceptive; in aligning with evolutionary and rationalist views, it imposes ideological constraints that steer interpretation in a particular direction. This approach is incompatible with the objective historical-grammatical method favored by conservative scholars, which seeks to understand the text in its historical context, utilizing grammar and language as keys to interpretation, without the imposition of external ideologies.

The Cost of Intellectual Compromise

The entanglement with evolutionary and rationalist views has a severe cost: it leads to a skewed understanding of Scripture, one that aligns with secular humanism and diverges from the truth. The end result is a form of biblical criticism that is not just intellectually flawed but also spiritually corrosive. The distortions introduced by Higher Criticism have weakened the faith of many, and its pseudo-scholarly works have contributed to a decline in the confidence that believers and seekers alike have in the Bible.

A Call to Intellectual Integrity

The intellectual allure of Higher Criticism can be seductive, especially when it masquerades as the epitome of scholarly engagement. However, intellectual integrity demands that we scrutinize its underlying assumptions and alliances. By aligning with evolutionary and rationalist ideologies, Higher Criticism has ventured far from a methodological approach that respects the authority and inerrancy of Scripture. Instead, it has become a tool for reinforcing a naturalistic worldview that is fundamentally at odds with a conservative understanding of the Bible.

It is crucial to steer biblical scholarship back toward a methodology grounded in an unswerving commitment to the truth of Scripture. This means rejecting the ideological underpinnings that have skewed the field of biblical criticism and returning to a conservative, historical-grammatical approach that maintains the integrity of the text. Only by doing this can we restore a balanced, respectful, and truthful engagement with the Bible, fortifying our understanding and respect for its divine message. This is not just an academic imperative but a spiritual necessity, one that has profound implications for our understanding of Jehovah, His will, and His work in the world.

The Biased Rejection of Prophecy and Miracles

Among the various facets of Higher Criticism that raise concern, perhaps one of the most telling is its near-universal dismissal of prophecy and miracles in the biblical narrative. This rejection, far from being a neutral, academic stance, is predicated upon a host of preconceived ideological biases. It emerges not from a judicious evaluation of the Scriptural evidence, but from an a priori commitment to naturalistic and rationalistic presuppositions. In this context, the critic doesn't approach the text to ask if a miracle or prophecy could have occurred but operates from the assumption that such events simply cannot occur. This form of bias, steeped in Enlightenment rationalism and secular humanism, profoundly distorts the interpretive process, rendering the methods of Higher Criticism not only flawed but fundamentally incongruent with a conservative, historical-grammatical approach to Scripture.

The Ideological Roots of Denying Prophecy and Miracles

From the outset, it's crucial to understand that the rejection of biblical prophecy and miracles in Higher Criticism is ideologically motivated. The Enlightenment period laid the foundation for this, instilling a profound skepticism toward the supernatural. Miracles and prophecies are seen as relics of an unenlightened past, incompatible with modern scientific understanding. This is a form of chronological snobbery, deeming ancient accounts as unworthy of consideration due to their age and pre-scientific context.

The Fallacy of Methodological Naturalism

Central to the critical approach is a commitment to methodological naturalism, which insists that all phenomena must be explained solely through natural causes. While this method may be suitable for the natural sciences, its application to the realm of theology and biblical studies is not only unwarranted but deeply flawed. In particular, methodological naturalism refuses to countenance the idea of divine intervention in history, thereby excluding a priori one of the key claims of Scripture—that Jehovah actively engages with His creation.

Prophecy: Dismissed as Postdiction

One of the key strategies employed by Higher Critics to dismiss biblical prophecy is to argue for "postdiction"—the idea that prophecies were written after the events they purportedly predict. This approach, exemplified in the skeptical treatment of books like Isaiah and Daniel, assumes that precise predictions are impossible and must therefore be fabrications. Critics often split these books into multiple sections, attributing them to different authors over several centuries, purely to accommodate their disbelief in predictive prophecy. This dismissal is not based on textual or linguistic evidence but is a blatant manifestation of ideological bias.

Miracles: Explained Away

Higher Criticism also dismisses the miraculous events recorded in the Scriptures as either fabrications or exaggerations. Miracles are often "demythologized," interpreted as mere natural events that were misperceived or embellished over time. For example, the parting of the Red Sea is often reduced to a naturalistic explanation involving strong winds or a shallow marsh. Such interpretations not only distort the text but also strip it of its intended meaning and significance.

Undermining Scriptural Authority and Inerrancy

The biased rejection of prophecy and miracles has a corroding effect on the doctrines of Scriptural authority and inerrancy. If the Bible's accounts of predictive prophecies and miraculous events are unreliable, it follows that Scripture itself becomes untrustworthy. This leads to a spiral of doubt and skepticism, undermining the foundational beliefs of countless believers.

Consequences: Loss of Truth and Spiritual Damage

The rejection of prophecy and miracles leads not merely to academic disputes but causes spiritual erosion. It fosters a brand of biblical studies divorced from real-life faith, thereby robbing the Bible of its transformative power. It can cause lasting damage, leading believers to question their faith and weakening the church's witness to the world.

Returning to a Conservative Methodology

The Higher Critical rejection of prophecy and miracles is neither neutral nor objective; it is a deeply flawed approach influenced by naturalistic and rationalistic presuppositions. To maintain both academic and spiritual integrity, it is essential to return to a conservative, historical-grammatical methodology—one that recognizes the possibility of the supernatural and allows the text to speak for itself. Only then can the authority and inerrancy of Scripture be fully upheld, providing a robust antidote to the toxic influence of Higher Criticism. And only by doing so can scholars and laypeople alike engage deeply with the biblical text, appreciating its rich tapestry of history, prophecy, and miraculous works that point unequivocally to the divine hand of Jehovah.

The Consequences: Eroding the Foundation of Biblical Authority

Higher Criticism's trajectory in the realm of biblical studies has had severe and far-reaching consequences, most significantly in eroding the foundation of biblical authority. A professedly objective enterprise, this modern form of biblical criticism often cloaks itself in the language of academic rigor and scholarly dispassion. However, beneath the veneer lies an array of speculative methods and ideological commitments that threaten the very core of biblical trustworthiness. These consequences are not confined to the ivory towers of academia; they ripple through congregations, seep into Bible study groups, and infiltrate the minds of believers, corroding faith from within.

The Breakdown of Textual Confidence

Higher Criticism often advances hypotheses that cast doubts on the text's historical veracity, authorship, and composition. Documents are dissected into theoretical sources or redacted layers, often without compelling manuscript evidence to substantiate such claims. This speculation leads to an implicit (or sometimes explicit) distrust of the text, fostering a skepticism that poses an existential threat to the doctrine of biblical inerrancy. When Scripture's foundational reliability is questioned, it logically follows that its moral and theological claims are also suspect, which undermines the Bible's position as the final authority in matters of faith and conduct.

The Rise of Relativism and Pluralism

Another corrosive consequence of Higher Criticism is its accommodation to the spirit of the age, characterized by moral and religious relativism. This perspective harmonizes well with secular humanism, which often treats all religious texts as human products shaped by cultural and historical contingencies. Consequently, the Bible becomes just another voice in a cacophony of religious options, thereby losing its uniqueness and supreme authority. This has serious implications for exclusivist claims of biblical faith, and it often leads to theological pluralism, where the Bible is seen as one of many equally valid paths to understanding the divine.

The Shift Towards Reader-Centric Interpretation

Traditionally, conservative exegesis has employed the historical-grammatical method, focusing on discovering the text's original meaning through understanding its historical context and grammatical structure. Higher Criticism, on the other hand, often shifts focus from what the text meant to what it means to contemporary readers. While reader response can be a valuable exercise, it becomes problematic when it sidesteps objective methods of interpretation in favor of subjective or communal interpretations, further destabilizing biblical authority.

Theological Liberalism and the Decline of Orthodoxy

As the authority of Scripture is eroded, theological liberalism often fills the vacuum. With a diminished Bible, there is less resistance to heterodox teachings that contradict foundational doctrines of the Christian faith. Consequently, the scope for personal speculation, ideological manipulation, and doctrinal fluidity expands. Churches that imbibe this liberal spirit may still use the language of faith, but their core beliefs are often far removed from the historical tenets of orthodox Christianity.

The Ethical Ramifications

When the Bible's authority is eroded, so is its ethical force. If its historical narratives are unreliable and its moral teachings are culturally bound, then its ability to speak with authority into contemporary ethical issues is seriously undermined. Such skepticism often leads to a subjective, à la carte approach to biblical ethics, where individuals or communities pick and choose which commands to obey, devoid of a coherent, scriptural framework.

The Spiritual Cost: A Crisis of Faith

Perhaps the most tragic consequence of all is the spiritual toll that Higher Criticism exacts on individual believers. Once the Bible's reliability is undermined, many find it difficult to entrust their eternal destinies to its promises. The erosion of confidence in Scripture leads to a spiritual malaise that manifests in a lack of vigor in both personal spirituality and evangelistic outreach. Faith communities suffer as doctrinal divisions emerge and commitment to shared beliefs wanes.

Reaffirming Biblical Authority

As serious as these consequences are, the answer lies in a robust reaffirmation of biblical authority rooted in a conservative, historical-grammatical method of interpretation. A return to these principles is not merely a retreat to tradition but a reclamation of a hermeneutical approach that genuinely seeks to understand and articulate what the Bible consistently declares. Only then can we recover a high view of Scripture, safeguard its foundational authority, and resist the corrosive impact of Higher Criticism. This requires an unswerving commitment to the authority and inerrancy of Scripture, values that serve as the bedrock for a faithful engagement with God's inspired Word. Only by doing so can we provide an antidote to the subjective and ideologically skewed practices that have undermined faith and triggered theological chaos.

In this regard, conservative exegesis serves not just as an academic exercise but as a spiritual imperative. The stakes are eternal, making it all the more urgent to reclaim a hermeneutical approach that faithfully represents Jehovah's revelation to humankind, thus restoring the Bible to its rightful place as the ultimate authority in all matters of faith and life.

The Unfounded Assumptions of Higher Criticism and the Reliability of Scripture

Higher Criticism, with its manifold methodologies and assumptions, claims to objectively scrutinize the biblical texts. However, a careful examination reveals that it often operates on unfounded presuppositions, which not only sway its conclusions but also undermine the reliability of Scripture. To safeguard the integrity of the biblical text and to uphold the principle of its divine inspiration and inerrancy, it is critical to expose these assumptions and offer a more reliable framework grounded in conservative exegesis.

Assumption 1: Late Dating of Biblical Texts

One of the primary strategies of Higher Criticism is to assign late dates to biblical texts, particularly the books of the Old Testament. For instance, the Documentary Hypothesis posits that the Pentateuch is a compilation of various sources edited over centuries, reaching its final form only in the post-exilic period. Such dating often contradicts internal textual evidence and disregards the testimonies of early church fathers and Jewish tradition. Late dating serves the purpose of discrediting the prophetic nature of Scripture, making it easier to classify biblical prophecy as mere vaticinium ex eventu (prophecy after the fact).

Assumption 2: Multiple Authors and Redactors

Another frequent assertion is that biblical books, initially considered single-author works, are products of multiple hands and redactions. This theory relies heavily on dissecting the text into various strands, often based on speculative criteria such as stylistic variations or differing names for God, like the distinction between "Elohist" and "Jahwist" sources in the Pentateuch. Such an approach minimizes the possibility that a single author could employ a variety of styles and titles for God, depending on the context or purpose of the text.

Assumption 3: Cultural and Historical Relativism

Higher Criticism often situates the Bible solely as a product of its ancient Near Eastern context, dismissing its claims to divine inspiration and eternal relevance. This assumption aligns with Enlightenment rationalism, which sees Scripture as merely a human product, influenced by the historical and cultural circumstances in which it was written. Such a view dilutes the Bible's distinctiveness and universal applicability.

Assumption 4: Inability to Record Accurate History

A particularly egregious assumption is that the biblical authors, or the cultures they represented, were incapable of accurate historical recording. This belief often leads critics to dismiss biblical accounts of miracles or significant historical events as mere myth or allegory. This assumption blatantly disregards the care with which many biblical authors approached their work, aiming to provide careful accounts as affirmed in texts like Luke 1:1-4 or as seen in the detailed genealogies and historical records in the Old Testament.

Assumption 5: Bias Against Supernatural Elements

Aligned with the rationalistic presuppositions, Higher Criticism tends to dismiss or reinterpret the supernatural elements in the Bible. Miracles are often explained away as natural events misconstrued or as legends that accrued around a historical figure like Moses or Jesus. This bias seriously compromises the integrity of biblical accounts, which often present these supernatural events as central to their narrative and theological message.

The Reliability of Scripture: A Conservative Response

In stark contrast to the critical assumptions, conservative scholarship, grounded in the historical-grammatical method of interpretation, takes the Bible's claims seriously, beginning with its assertion of divine inspiration ("All Scripture is inspired by God," 2

Timothy 3:16). The conservative approach also respects the Bible's own internal witness about its authors, structure, and historical details, thereby building a coherent and robust framework for understanding Scripture.

The reliability of Scripture is not merely an article of faith but is supported by substantial evidence. Manuscript discoveries like the Dead Sea Scrolls affirm the integrity and preservation of the biblical text over millennia. Archaeological evidence frequently corroborates the historical accounts found in the Bible, providing an external line of verification. Furthermore, fulfilled prophecies in Scripture speak to its unique nature and divine origin.

Conclusion: Reaffirming the Conservative Approach

The conservative approach to Scripture does not blind itself to the complexities and challenges inherent in any ancient text. However, it approaches these challenges from a standpoint of trust in the Bible's divine origin and inerrancy. By rejecting the unfounded assumptions that often underpin Higher Criticism, conservative scholarship offers a more reliable and respectful approach to understanding God's inspired Word.

Thus, the task at hand is twofold: to identify and critique the speculative and often unfounded assumptions of Higher Criticism, and to robustly defend the reliability and inerrancy of Scripture through a conservative, historical-grammatical approach to exegesis. Doing so is not only an academic necessity but also a theological imperative, for the reliability of Scripture is foundational to its authority in guiding the faith and practice of believers. Therefore, by reaffirming conservative exegetical principles, we can restore confidence in the Bible as Jehovah's authoritative revelation to humanity, undiluted by the subjectivity and ideological biases of Higher Criticism.

CHAPTER 1 The Mosaic Authorship: Debunking the Documentary Hypothesis

Introduction: Setting the Stage for the Documentary Hypothesis

Introduction: Setting the Stage for the Documentary Hypothesis

In the vast landscape of biblical scholarship, few theories have generated as much debate, consternation, and indeed, skepticism as the Documentary Hypothesis. This theory, most notoriously associated with German scholar Julius Wellhausen, posits that the Pentateuch—the first five books of the Hebrew Bible—was not authored by Moses but was a compilation from various authors and sources over a lengthy period. This theory has engendered various offspring, each attempting to dissect Scripture's composition like a frog in a high school biology lab. They all share the flawed premise that the texts are not historical and divinely inspired but are instead products of later religious communities.

First, let us clarify what we mean by the "Documentary Hypothesis." Essentially, this theory proposes that the books traditionally attributed to Moses were not, in fact, his writings but were instead patched together from various sources, identified as J (Jahwist), E (Elohist), P (Priestly), and D (Deuteronomic). Wellhausen's approach sought to align Scripture with historical criticism methods and presuppositions based on broader movements like the Enlightenment and German idealism.

These presuppositions make two fatal errors. First, they begin with the premise that the miraculous elements within the text must be relegated to the genre of myth or folklore. Second, the theory considers the Bible not as a unique revelation but as a text to be sliced and diced according to secular critical methodologies, paying little heed to its internal structure, historical context, and most importantly, its claims of divine origin and unity.

Moreover, the Documentary Hypothesis is fraught with methodological problems. Take, for example, the division of texts based on the name used for God—'Elohim' in some passages and 'Jehovah' in others. Such a division seems rather arbitrary and fails to consider the nuanced usage of these terms within ancient Israelite religion. Could not Moses, a sophisticated writer, employ different names for God to convey different aspects of His character or actions? Even within our contemporary writing styles, we adjust our tone and style according to the subject matter and target audience.

Also, it is noteworthy that higher criticism, including the Documentary Hypothesis, has found little support from the field of archaeology. On the contrary, archaeology has time and again vindicated the historical claims of the Scriptures, often turning skeptical assumptions on their head. The critics frequently assume that the text could not be historically accurate because it predates by centuries the events it purports to describe. Yet archaeological discoveries have provided supporting evidence for biblical narratives time and again, discrediting the assumption that the Pentateuchal accounts are mere reflections of a much later period.

The Wellhausen school, which holds that Israel's religion was a mere product of human evolution, faces serious challenge from a conservative standpoint grounded in a literal, historical-grammatical interpretation. Wellhausen and his followers began with the assumption that the Bible was not inspired by God. In doing so, they rendered their conclusions about biblical texts not as the result of unbiased analysis but as affirmations of their presuppositions. Their approach is akin to a man who, having already decided that a building has no foundation, refuses to inspect its base and instead dedicates himself to showing how it stands through other means.

So why do intellectuals find higher criticism attractive? It is a perfect storm: the rationalism of the Enlightenment, the skepticism of German idealism, and the speculative nature of modern academia converge to create an environment where the miraculous is not merely questioned but is deemed intellectually unacceptable. To accept Mosaic authorship and divine revelation is to reject the naturalistic and humanistic ideologies that are pervasive in academia today.

One should understand that the Documentary Hypothesis and its kin are not merely academic exercises. They have profound implications for faith. When people read the Bible as a fractured, human document, its moral and theological teachings lose their weight. These critical methodologies have therefore served to undermine people's confidence in the Bible, contributing to an overall decline in the belief in its authority and inerrancy.

In light of all these considerations, it is clear that the Documentary Hypothesis, while popular in academic circles, is deeply flawed. Its popularity speaks more to its alignment with prevailing academic ideologies than to its evidential base. As we delve further into the specifics in subsequent sections, we will dissect its methodological errors and examine how a conservative, historical-grammatical approach not only affirms the Mosaic authorship of the Pentateuch but also upholds the reliability and inerrancy of Scripture.

Thus, our journey begins by setting the stage against the Documentary Hypothesis, which has been more destructive than constructive, serving as a Trojan horse that has ushered in skepticism and disbelief. This chapter will serve as a cornerstone for constructing a more faithful understanding of the Scriptures, grounded in a conservative exegesis that respects both the divine and the human elements in this sacred text. We will unapologetically stand firm on the reliability and inerrancy of Scripture, critiquing and debunking the fallacies of the Documentary Hypothesis in the process. It is a stand worth taking, for if we are to be faithful to the text, we must be honest about its origins, context, and purpose.

Julius Wellhausen and the Genesis of Higher Criticism

The figure most prominently associated with the Documentary Hypothesis and its controversial impact on Old Testament studies is undoubtedly Julius Wellhausen. His name serves as a watermark in the timeline of biblical criticism, signifying a transition from older methods of interpretation to a new wave of skepticism grounded in the ideologies of the Enlightenment and German idealism. While Wellhausen was certainly not the first to propose a composite authorship for the Pentateuch, his formulation of the Documentary Hypothesis was the most systematic and influential. He built upon the works of earlier scholars like Karl Heinrich Graf and Wilhelm Vatke, refining their ideas into the JEDP framework that has been taught in seminaries and religious studies departments across the world.

It is imperative to understand Wellhausen in his historical context. The 19th century was a period marked by radical shifts in thought, primarily fueled by the Enlightenment's emphasis on reason, skepticism, and human autonomy. A scholarly environment dominated by these ideologies was fertile ground for the rise of higher criticism. Wellhausen's work was not an isolated event but a product of these broader cultural currents. The Enlightenment ideals dovetailed neatly with German idealism, creating an intellectual climate where the acceptance of divine inspiration was readily discarded in favor of mechanistic explanations of religious phenomena.

Wellhausen's influence was compounded by his methodological finesse. His work "Prolegomena to the History of Israel" is still referenced today as a seminal text for higher criticism. In this work, Wellhausen not only proposed the existence of different sources (J, E, D, P) but also a historical reconstruction of ancient Israel's religious development. His view was that Israel's religion evolved from a simple, free-form faith into a legalistic, ritualistic system, embodied in the Priestly code. This reconstruction was deeply influenced by evolutionary theories of the time, projecting backward a progressive development that, conveniently, accorded with 19th-century European conceptions of "primitive" versus "advanced" societies.

However, one must scrutinize the foundations upon which Wellhausen built his arguments. First, Wellhausen began with several presuppositions that were clearly at odds with the biblical text. He assumed that the Israelites could not have possibly had complex laws and rituals at an early stage, thereby assigning a late date to the Priestly material. This presupposition has been largely discredited by subsequent archaeological findings that demonstrate a high degree of societal and religious sophistication in societies contemporaneous with early Israel.

Second, Wellhausen's source divisions based on the usage of divine names or stylistic differences are methodologically questionable. Ancient writers were more than capable of varying style and terminology for specific theological or rhetorical purposes. The division of texts based on such flimsy criteria should make any serious scholar pause.

Third, Wellhausen and his followers were colored by a subtle yet pronounced anti-Judaism. The evolutionary scheme proposed denigrated the Priestly laws and rituals as a degenerate form of ancient Israel's religion. This bias served to confirm prejudices held by 19th-century German scholarship and to some extent still reverberates in contemporary criticisms of "legalism" in the Hebrew Bible.

The legacy of Julius Wellhausen is thus a mixed one. While he undeniably pushed the field of biblical studies into new territories, the ideological and methodological flaws in his work have become increasingly apparent. His impact cannot be underestimated, but neither can it be uncritically accepted. He opened doors to questions about the text, but at the same time, these doors have often led scholars down a labyrinthine path of skepticism and speculative theories that have little grounding in the text itself.

Conservative scholarship, rooted in the objective historical-grammatical method, offers a more coherent and respectful approach to the text. The internal and external evidences supporting Mosaic authorship are robust and compelling when not viewed through the skewed lens of higher criticism. A responsible reading of the biblical text—attentive to its linguistic, historical, and literary context—does not warrant the dissection of the Pentateuch into multiple, conflicting sources. Instead, it reveals a sophisticated, unified narrative that bears the imprints of Mosaic authorship and divine inspiration.

Wellhausen's ideas, then, are not the inevitable conclusions of rational inquiry but the products of his environment and presuppositions. As such, they should be weighed critically, always bearing in mind that the starting point of any interpretive exercise should be the text itself, not a preconceived framework that dictates the outcomes of our study.

So as we dissect the Documentary Hypothesis and its progeny, it is important to remember that these are not neutral academic exercises. They come with significant ideological baggage that has profound implications for the faith and practice of millions around the globe. In contrast, a conservative, historical-grammatical approach to the text seeks to honor the unique nature of Scripture, viewing it not as a human artifact to be dissected, but as a divinely inspired message to be understood and obeyed. To reclaim the text from the morass of higher criticism, we must critique the historical roots and ideological underpinnings of these methods. Only then can we arrive at an interpretation that does justice to the text's historical and theological richness.

The Forefathers of Source Criticisms

To assess the validity of modern higher criticism, it is imperative to understand its historical underpinnings. In this chapter, we examine some key figures who laid the foundation for source criticism and subsequently, the Documentary Hypothesis.

Astruc, Eichhorn, and the Birth of Fragmentation

The French physician Jean Astruc is often credited as one of the first individuals to partition the Book of Genesis into separate sources based on the varying usage of divine names. Astruc's work was not intended to undermine Mosaic authorship; rather, he sought to reconcile the dual nomenclature (Elohim and Jehovah) by proposing that Moses himself used two distinct sources.

Johann Gottfried Eichhorn took Astruc's analysis further by applying it to the entire Pentateuch, thus laying the groundwork for more complex theories like the Documentary Hypothesis. Like Astruc, Eichhorn did not initially intend to question Mosaic authorship, but his methodologies indirectly paved the way for it by proposing a fragmented composition of the Torah.

Wilhelm de Wette and the Skeptical Turn

However, it was Wilhelm de Wette who steered biblical criticism into a decidedly skeptical direction. De Wette contended that the Pentateuch was essentially a post-exilic compilation, designed to legitimize the Levitical priesthood. This view undercut the historicity and reliability of the Torah, casting it as a product of religious and political agendas.

Julius Wellhausen and the JEDP Theory

Wellhausen, heavily influenced by Hegelian philosophy, proposed what would become the most famous version of the Documentary Hypothesis, suggesting the existence of four main sources: the Jahwist (J), Elohist (E), Deuteronomist (D), and Priestly (P) sources. This theory was informed by a presupposition of evolutionary development in religion, arguing that Israelite religion progressed from animism to monotheism, reflected in the supposed sources.

Critiquing the Pillars

1. **Fragmentary Approach**: The fundamental problem with these forefathers of source criticism is their fragmentary approach to the text, an approach that runs contrary to the principles of historical-grammatical interpretation. There is no compelling evidence to suggest that these texts, with their

thematic and linguistic coherence, are a mishmash of various sources.

2. **Ideological Influence**: The influence of Enlightenment skepticism and German idealism on these scholars is evident. They approached the text with the presumption that it could not be divinely inspired or historically accurate. Their methods were not neutral but laden with philosophical assumptions that were foreign to the text itself.

3. **Disregard for External Evidence**: These early theories did not sufficiently consider external evidence that supported the Mosaic authorship of the Pentateuch. The consistent affirmation of Mosaic authorship in both the Old and New Testaments, as well as among early Jewish and Christian writers, was often brushed aside.

4. **Evolutionary Assumptions**: The belief that religion must evolve from simple to complex is a 19th-century bias that has no basis in the empirical study of religions. Many ancient religions exhibit complex theologies and rituals from their inception.

Returning to a Sound Methodology

The conservative approach, guided by the historical-grammatical method, treats the text as a coherent whole and interrogates it on its terms. It considers both internal and external evidence and does not impose alien philosophical constructs on the text. Moreover, it is aligned with a high view of Scripture, taking seriously the Bible's own claims about its divine inspiration and Mosaic authorship.

Legacy and Lessons

The forefathers of source criticism have left an enduring legacy, but it is one that has led many down a path of skepticism and relativism. However, their methodologies are not the final word. A conservative approach to Scripture provides a robust alternative, offering both intellectual rigor and spiritual fidelity. By returning to the principles of historical-grammatical interpretation and affirming the authority and inerrancy of Scripture, we not only debunk the flawed premises of source criticism but also uphold the Bible's integrity as the inspired Word of God.

By understanding the flawed foundations laid by the forefathers of source criticism, we can better appreciate the need for a conservative exegetical approach. Such an approach not only honors the text but also fortifies the faith of those who look to the Bible as the ultimate source of truth, thereby providing an antidote to the destructive tendencies of modern higher criticism.

Methodological Assumptions: The 'P' and 'J' Sources

One of the most significant contributions of the Documentary Hypothesis is the notion that the Pentateuch, particularly the Torah, is a composite of various sources. Among these, the 'P' (Priestly) and 'J' (Jehovistic) sources stand out as the most frequently discussed and debated. They serve as cornerstones of higher criticism's fragmented view of the Old Testament, allegedly representing separate, almost rival, traditions within ancient Israelite religion.

The 'P' Source: A Flawed Premise

According to proponents of the Documentary Hypothesis, the 'P' source is supposedly late, written post-exilic or during the exile, reflecting a centralized, priestly tradition focused on ritual and law. This alleged source is seen as "advanced" and complex, embodying a hierarchical system that had evolved from the more "primitive" faith of early Israel.

However, this view encounters several glaring issues. First, it presupposes that the Israelites could not have had complex religious codes and rituals at an early stage, despite archeological evidence to the contrary. For example, the Nuzi tablets and the Code of Hammurabi, both from societies that were contemporaneous with the Israelites, show complex social and legal systems, casting doubt on the assumption of 'P' as a late development.

Moreover, by assuming that 'P' represents a different stratum of religion, scholars have disregarded the internal consistency within the Torah regarding law, covenant, and ritual. For instance, elements that are considered "Priestly" like the detailed instructions in the book of Leviticus, coherently align with the broader themes of covenant and sanctity found throughout the Pentateuch.

The 'J' Source: A Questionable Divide

The 'J' source, identified by the use of the divine name Jehovah, is thought to be one of the earliest sources, focusing on narrative over law, characterized by anthropomorphic descriptions of God. Yet, the division between 'J' and 'P,' based on the use of divine names or stylistic preferences, proves problematic. It's an elementary principle of hermeneutics that a single author can employ a variety of styles and terminologies to convey different aspects or themes. This is especially true in ancient Near Eastern literature, where variation in divine names and literary styles are often used purposefully within unified compositions.

So why, then, would we assume disjointed authorship based on such differences? This methodology contradicts the very nature of textual analysis, which should begin with the presumption of coherence unless compelling evidence indicates otherwise.

Underlying Assumptions: Questionable Grounds

The hypothesis leans heavily on dubious assumptions. One of these is evolutionary: the belief that religion progresses from simple to complex. This is not a neutral, academic assumption but rather a relic from 19th-century social theories. Another assumption is that of contradiction: the idea that different styles or focuses (narrative vs. law, for example) imply different sources. This overlooks the likelihood that diverse elements can coexist in a unified, intentionally composed text.

Scripture: A Cohesive Whole

In contrast, a conservative approach grounded in the historical-grammatical method starts with the assumption of unity and coherence in the text, only resorting to theories of diverse authorship or textual corruption when the evidence is overwhelming. This method allows for a more nuanced appreciation of the text, respecting its historical, linguistic, and literary complexity.

Conservative scholars argue that Mosaic authorship best accounts for the internal and external evidence. Mosaic authorship is corroborated by subsequent books of the Old Testament and the New Testament, where Moses is affirmed as the lawgiver and covenant mediator between Jehovah and Israel. Additionally, the cohesiveness in theme, language, and structure throughout the Pentateuch supports the idea of a single author or a single guiding hand, which is consistent with the traditional understanding of Mosaic authorship.

The Importance of Methodology

As we scrutinize the 'P' and 'J' sources, we must be aware that these are not neutral, objective categories but are laden with methodological and ideological assumptions. They reflect not just an academic exercise but also a particular worldview that is deeply influenced by Enlightenment rationalism and secular humanism. While such methodologies may claim to "uncover" the origins of the Old Testament, they often end up obscuring the text, casting a veil of doubt and speculation over what is, in essence, a cohesive, divinely inspired document.

By contrast, conservative scholarship, grounded in a commitment to the authority and inerrancy of Scripture, offers a more fruitful approach. When we honor the text by examining it through the lens of its historical and literary context, we find a rich tapestry that points not to a patchwork of conflicting sources, but to a harmonious, divinely orchestrated revelation. This respect for the text as a unified whole provides an antidote to the divisive and skeptical tendencies of higher criticism, allowing us to approach Scripture not as a puzzle to be dissected but as a revelation to be cherished and obeyed.

The Documentary Hypothesis ("J," "E," "D," "P," and "R")

The Documentary Hypothesis, commonly attributed to Julius Wellhausen, posits that the Pentateuch—traditionally ascribed to Moses—is actually an amalgamation of different sources or documents. These sources are typically identified as the Jahwist ("J"), Elohist ("E"), Deuteronomist ("D"), Priestly ("P"), and a Redactor ("R"), who is thought to have combined these sources into the final text.

Understanding the Components

1. **Jahwist (J)**: This source is said to be the earliest and uses "Jehovah" as the name of God. It supposedly reflects the perspective of the southern kingdom (Judah) and is characterized by a more anthropomorphic view of God.

2. **Elohist (E)**: This source is believed to come from the northern kingdom (Israel) and uses "Elohim" as the name for God. It is often considered less anthropomorphic than the Jahwist source.

3. **Deuteronomist (D)**: Identified mainly with the book of Deuteronomy, this source is linked with the religious reforms under King Josiah. It emphasizes the law and covenant.

4. **Priestly (P)**: This source is said to be concerned with rituals, genealogies, and legal matters. Scholars argue that it reflects the perspective of the post-exilic priestly class.

5. **Redactor (R)**: This hypothetical editor is believed to have brought together the J, E, D, and P sources into the final form of the Pentateuch.

DEFENDING OLD TESTAMENT AUTHORSHIP

Methodological Flaws and Assumptions

1. **Arbitrary Separations**: One of the most glaring problems with the Documentary Hypothesis is the arbitrary manner in which the text is dissected. The theory assumes, without empirical proof, that variations in style, vocabulary, or theological emphasis are indicators of different sources rather than facets of a unified work.

2. **Historical Anachronisms**: The hypothesis imposes upon ancient Near Eastern literature a modern concept of authorship and editing that is inconsistent with the practices of antiquity. Ancient writers frequently employed different styles, genres, and vocabulary depending on the subject matter.

3. **Lack of Manuscript Evidence**: No manuscripts have been discovered that represent any of the hypothetical sources (J, E, D, or P) in isolation. This is a significant absence, given the rich manuscript tradition for other ancient texts.

4. **Assumed Evolution of Religion**: The theory presupposes a developmental view of Israelite religion, from polytheism to ethical monotheism, which is ideologically driven and not universally supported by archaeological or historical evidence.

A Conservative Rejoinder

1. **Internal Consistency**: A careful reading of the text reveals a high degree of internal consistency in terms of historical details, legal codes, and theological themes. If multiple sources were combined by a later editor, we would expect to find more contradictions and anachronisms.

2. **Historical Corroboration**: External evidence, including historical and archaeological data, consistently validates the biblical account, lending credibility to the traditional understanding of Mosaic authorship.

3. **Scriptural Testimony**: Both Old and New Testaments consistently affirm Mosaic authorship of the Torah. This

internal evidence carries weight, especially when supported by the unbroken tradition of Jewish and Christian scholarship that upholds Mosaic authorship.

4. **Theological Unity**: The Pentateuch demonstrates a cohesive theological vision, from the creation account in Genesis to the giving of the Law in Deuteronomy. Such unity suggests a single, divinely-inspired author rather than a patchwork of sources.

A Return to Sola Scriptura

In conclusion, the Documentary Hypothesis is a speculative construct that does not withstand critical scrutiny. Its methodological flaws and ideological assumptions reveal an approach to Scripture that is not only academically suspect but also spiritually damaging, undermining confidence in the Bible's historical reliability and divine inspiration.

By returning to a conservative, historical-grammatical method of interpretation that respects both the text and its Author, we regain a more authentic, robust understanding of the Pentateuch and reaffirm its status as divinely inspired Scripture. This conservative approach, therefore, stands as an antidote to the corrosive skepticism of higher criticism, equipping the faithful with the tools to defend the inerrancy and authority of God's Word.

The Fallacy of Linguistic Division: Elohim vs. Jehovah

One of the cornerstones of the Documentary Hypothesis is the division of the text based on the name used for God—Elohim or Jehovah. Proponents of this hypothesis argue that the different names signify different sources, the "E" source favoring "Elohim" and the "J" source favoring "Jehovah." However, this linguistic division is fundamentally flawed for several reasons and ignores the complex nature of ancient Hebrew writing styles, narrative techniques, and theological nuances.

Textual Incongruities Under the Documentary Hypothesis

1. **Cherry-Picking Evidence**: Scholars employing this hypothesis often cherry-pick verses to support their argument, while ignoring instances where "Elohim" and "Jehovah" are used interchangeably or in close proximity. For example, Genesis 2:4 uses both names in a single verse, presenting a textual incongruity for the Documentary Hypothesis.

2. **Context Ignored**: The Documentary Hypothesis largely overlooks the context in which the names are used. In several instances, the choice of name serves to emphasize particular attributes of God. "Elohim" is often used in contexts highlighting God's sovereignty and omnipotence, whereas "Jehovah" is employed to underline God's covenantal relationship with His people.

Traditional Hebrew Writing Styles

1. **Synonymous Parallelism**: Hebrew literature is rich in employing parallelism, where similar or antithetical ideas are placed in juxtaposition for emphasis or clarification. The usage of both "Elohim" and "Jehovah" could well be a form of synonymous parallelism, serving to deepen our understanding of God's multifaceted character.

2. **Narrative Flow**: Hebrew storytelling frequently used various names and titles for God as part of the narrative flow. These were not intended to signal different sources but to provide a fuller, richer portrait of God.

Scriptural Consistency and Theological Unity

1. **Witness of Scripture**: Both the Old and New Testaments consistently affirm Mosaic authorship of the Pentateuch. If the Documentary Hypothesis were correct, it would mean that

both Jesus and the apostles were either mistaken or deceptive when they attributed the Torah to Moses.

2. **Theological Coherence**: A comprehensive reading of the Pentateuch reveals a coherent theological vision that would be hard to maintain if it were a mere patchwork of various sources. The consistent unfolding of the promises and purposes of God from Genesis to Deuteronomy supports the idea of a single, inspired author.

Ideological Biases and Flawed Assumptions

1. **Cultural Imposition**: The idea that different names must equate to different authors is largely a modern Western imposition and shows a fundamental misunderstanding of ancient Near Eastern literature.

2. **Presuppositions**: The Documentary Hypothesis often operates on presuppositions that discount the possibility of divine inspiration or Mosaic authorship from the outset. This is reflective of broader ideological systems, such as secular humanism and Enlightenment rationalism, which are imposed on the text rather than derived from it.

Upholding the Integrity of the Text

The division of the text based on the names "Elohim" and "Jehovah" is a speculative and methodologically flawed approach. When scrutinized, it fails to account for the complexities of Hebrew literature and the internal and external evidences supporting Mosaic authorship. It also presupposes a set of ideological commitments that are foreign to the text.

Adhering to a conservative, historical-grammatical method of interpretation allows for a more nuanced understanding of why different names for God might be used. It recognizes that these variations serve theological, literary, and pastoral purposes within a unified, divinely-inspired text.

By understanding the weaknesses of the Documentary Hypothesis, especially as it pertains to the fallacy of linguistic division, we can better appreciate the inerrancy and authority of Scripture. In doing so, we provide a necessary corrective to the subjective and ideologically skewed practices of modern biblical criticism, reaffirming our commitment to the truth and divine inspiration of God's Word.

Perceived Discrepancies: Exposing the Falseness

Another facet of the Documentary Hypothesis that has often been cited as evidence against Mosaic authorship pertains to the so-called "discrepancies" or "contradictions" in the text. Proponents of the Documentary Hypothesis contend that these incongruities indicate multiple authors and even diverse communities behind the biblical text. In this chapter, we will scrutinize these alleged discrepancies and offer a counter-narrative grounded in a conservative, historical-grammatical approach to interpretation.

A Critical Analysis of the Alleged Discrepancies

1. **The Two Creation Accounts**: Critics argue that the creation accounts in Genesis 1 and 2 contradict each other, suggesting separate authors. However, a careful reading reveals no contradiction but a telescopic detailing, where Genesis 1 offers a cosmic view and Genesis 2 focuses on humanity's creation. The two narratives serve to complement and not contradict each other.

2. **The Genealogies in Genesis**: Higher critics point to divergent genealogies in Genesis as evidence of disparate sources. Yet, genealogies in ancient Near Eastern literature often served various purposes such as establishing kingship, lineage, or covenant relationships. They weren't meant to be exhaustive, and gaps or variations do not necessarily indicate inconsistency.

3. **The Ten Commandments**: The slight variations in the wording of the Ten Commandments in Exodus 20 and Deuteronomy 5 are cited as another discrepancy. However, this overlooks the ancient teaching method of repetition with variation, employed to ensure memorization and comprehension. Moses was reiterating the Commandments to a new generation in Deuteronomy, so slight modifications were pedagogically and contextually apt.

4. **The Numbering of Israelites**: The census figures in Numbers are often cited as inflated or contradictory. Yet, these numbers serve thematic and symbolic roles and are coherent within ancient Near Eastern census practices and idiomatic expressions for "thousands."

Why These Are Not Real Discrepancies

1. **Unwarranted Assumptions**: Many of the discrepancies pointed out are based on anachronistic readings, where contemporary understandings of history, science, and literature are imposed upon an ancient text.

2. **Ignoring Literary Forms**: Ancient Hebrew literature often employed repetition, parallelism, chiasmus, and other complex structures that might seem redundant or contradictory to modern readers but were meaningful and purposeful to the original audience.

3. **Scriptural Harmony**: Across both Testaments, there is an internal coherence and harmony. For instance, the New Testament writers and Jesus Himself quoted the Old Testament, including the allegedly "contradictory" passages, as authoritative and consistent, affirming their Mosaic authorship.

Theological Integrity and the Authority of Scripture

1. **The Unity of Revelation**: The Bible is not merely a human book but divinely inspired. Its theological and moral message remains coherent from Genesis to Revelation.
2. **Discrepancies as Deepening Understanding**: Far from being obstacles, the so-called discrepancies deepen our understanding of complex realities. For instance, the diverse descriptions of God serve to give us a fuller understanding of His character.

The Impact of Ideological Biases

1. **Modernist Presuppositions**: Higher criticism frequently assumes naturalistic or anti-supernatural biases, which by definition exclude the possibility of Mosaic authorship or divine inspiration.
2. **Cultural and Historical Relativism**: Higher critics often analyze the Bible through a lens that prioritizes their own historical and cultural assumptions over those of the ancient Near East and the Hebrew worldview.

Upholding Scriptural Integrity

In summary, the perceived discrepancies within the Pentateuch do not hold under scrutiny when viewed through a conservative, historical-grammatical lens. Often, they can be explained by understanding the ancient literary forms, cultural contexts, and the theological depth of the text. It is imperative to approach Scripture with a hermeneutic that recognizes its divine inspiration and respects its historical and literary context.

By exposing the fallacious nature of these perceived discrepancies, we fortify our commitment to the authority and inerrancy of Scripture. This, in turn, serves to equip believers with robust tools for interpretation, standing against the tide of speculative and ideologically driven higher criticism that has sought to erode confidence in the divine origin and unity of God's Word.

The Problem of Repetition (Doublets) and the Assumed Multiple Authors

One of the most persistent arguments supporting the Documentary Hypothesis is the presence of repetitions or "doublets" within the Pentateuch. Critics propose that these doublets are evidence of multiple sources woven together by later redactors. The hypothesis posits that these doublets are conflicting, each reflecting a different theology, authorship, and historical context. In this chapter, we will address this argument by examining the role of repetition within the Ancient Near Eastern literature and the specific thematic and theological nuances that these supposed "doublets" serve in the text.

Understanding Repetition in Ancient Literature

1. **Parallelism**: Repetition and parallelism are well-established literary techniques in the Ancient Near Eastern literature, including biblical Hebrew literature. They often serve to emphasize or clarify the subject matter.

2. **Progressive Revelation**: Repetition sometimes works to offer a fuller, more detailed understanding of the same event or commandment. The principle of "progressive revelation" allows for deeper insights over the course of the narrative.

3. **Pedagogical Utility**: In an oral culture where written texts were rare, repetition aided in memorization and teaching, serving as a mnemonic device for a largely illiterate populace.

Notable Doublets in the Pentateuch

1. **Creation Accounts in Genesis 1 and 2**: These accounts are often cited as conflicting. Yet, when viewed through a

historical-grammatical lens, the first account provides a macroscopic view of creation, while the second narrows the focus to humanity. Both accounts offer a complete picture of creation.

2. **The Abrahamic Covenant**: This covenant is reiterated several times (Gen 12, 15, and 17). Each repetition adds new elements and reinforces previous promises, serving to emphasize the covenant's significance rather than suggest multiple sources.

3. **The Passover**: Critics point to the multiple descriptions of the Passover (Ex. 12, Lev. 23, Num. 28, Deut. 16) as conflicting. However, each account provides different perspectives or details, contributing to a comprehensive understanding of the event.

Counterarguments to Assumed Multiple Authors

1. **Authorial Intent**: The claim that doublets imply multiple authors dismisses the possibility that a single author might use repetition for emphasis, clarification, or deeper elaboration.

2. **Thematic Unity**: Rather than fragmenting the narrative, these doublets often serve to knit the themes more tightly together. For instance, the reiterated covenants and laws underscore the gravity and permanence of Jehovah's relationship with Israel.

3. **Doctrinal Consistency**: The so-called "contradictions" often vanish when scrutinized closely, with apparent differences reconcilable through an understanding of historical context, literary style, and language idioms.

The Logical Flaws in the Documentary Hypothesis

1. **Reductionism**: By assuming multiple authors based on stylistic differences, proponents of the Documentary Hypothesis engage in reductionism, ignoring that a single author can employ varied styles and techniques.

2. **Lack of External Evidence**: Despite a century of research, no concrete external evidence has been unearthed to substantiate the existence of J, E, D, P, or R as separate documents or traditions.

Theological Considerations

1. **The Witness of Christ**: Jesus consistently treated the Law as a unified whole, attributing its authorship to Moses.
2. **Apostolic Endorsement**: New Testament authors also ascribe Mosaic authorship to the Pentateuch, treating so-called "doublets" as harmonious elements of a singular revelation.

A Reaffirmation of Scriptural Integrity and Mosaic Authorship

In summary, the presence of doublets or repetition within the Pentateuch is not a reliable indicator of multiple authorship. When understood in their Ancient Near Eastern literary context and analyzed through a conservative, historical-grammatical lens, these repetitions serve meaningful thematic and theological functions. They affirm, rather than compromise, the unity and integrity of Scripture. By debunking the assumption that repetition necessitates multiple authors, we further assert the Mosaic authorship of the Pentateuch, upholding the Scripture's inerrancy and authority. This conservative approach is not only methodologically sound but also acts as a countermeasure to the subjective, speculative tendencies of modern higher criticism, reinforcing our commitment to the integrity and unity of Jehovah's divinely inspired Word.

The Style Argument: Shifting Narratives, Shifting Authors?

One of the cardinal arguments advanced by proponents of the Documentary Hypothesis is the perceived stylistic differences within the Pentateuch, which they suggest could only be attributed to multiple authors. The line of reasoning asserts that shifts in narrative style, tone, and vocabulary are indicative of varied authorial contributions over time, pieced together by later redactors. In this chapter, we will examine the validity of the style argument through a critical lens that adheres to the historical-grammatical method and upholds the Mosaic authorship and the inerrancy of Scripture.

The Fallacy of Equating Style with Authorship

1. **Multi-faceted Styles of Single Authors**: It is not uncommon for a single author to employ different styles for different contexts or to communicate different themes. Well-known authors in history have been known to use different styles depending on the subject matter or audience.

2. **Composite Yet Unified**: The Pentateuch itself is a composite work covering law, history, genealogy, and narrative. It would be a gross oversimplification to assume that a single author couldn't have employed various styles suitable for each.

3. **Ancient Artistry**: Ancient Near Eastern authors often used stylistic shifts as a deliberate literary device, a fact well-acknowledged in conservative scholarship. The usage of different styles was often seen as a skill, not an indication of multiple hands at work.

Specific Examples and Rebuttals

1. **First and Third Person Narration**: A shift from first-person to third-person narration does not necessitate different authors but can instead reflect a change in perspective for thematic or didactic reasons.

2. **Varying Vocabulary**: Words like "Elohim" and "Jehovah" serve specific thematic functions. Their alternation is often interpreted as markers of different sources, a claim we have previously debunked. The variety enriches the text rather than divides it.

3. **Changes in Tone**: The Pentateuch contains both legalistic texts and flowing narrative. These are not inconsistencies; they are appropriate shifts in style to match the subject matter.

Unwarranted Assumptions and Subjectivity

1. **Circular Reasoning**: Often, the argument for different styles is grounded in the assumption that different sources exist, to begin with. This is a circular line of reasoning that fails to prove the point it sets out to demonstrate.

2. **Arbitrary Criteria**: The criteria for distinguishing between supposed different authors are often arbitrary, not founded in any objective measures but influenced by ideological presuppositions against Mosaic authorship and Scriptural inerrancy.

3. **Methodological Inconsistency**: Liberal critics who argue for multiple authorship due to stylistic variations often do not apply the same reasoning to other ancient texts, revealing an inconsistency in their methodological application.

Theological Stakes and Historical Witnesses

1. **The Testament of Christ and Apostles**: Jesus Christ and the New Testament authors attributed the Torah to Moses. To suggest otherwise would require challenging the veracity of the New Testament writings and the truth claims of Christ Himself.

2. **The Tradition of Mosaic Authorship**: The consistent tradition within Judaism has been that Moses is the author of the Torah. This tradition should not be lightly dismissed without substantial evidence.

Affirming the Integrity of Scripture and Mosaic Authorship

Stylistic variety within a text is not an airtight argument for multiple authorship. When one applies a rigorous, historical-grammatical method of exegesis, it becomes clear that stylistic differences can serve various literary, thematic, and theological purposes within a single, unified work. The evidence suggests that Mosaic authorship is not only plausible but also provides a robust framework for understanding the Pentateuch as a coherent and divinely inspired work.

Through a commitment to a conservative exegetical approach that upholds the authority and inerrancy of Scripture, we are better equipped to repel the fallacies propagated by liberal-moderate biblical criticism. Our aim is to instill in readers a deepened trust in Jehovah's Word, steering them away from the speculative and often biased methodologies that have plagued modern biblical criticism. As such, we remain steadfast in affirming the Mosaic authorship of the Pentateuch, underlining the unswerving unity and divine authority of Scripture.

Dissecting the Fallacies: Archaeological Evidence

One of the core assertions often wielded against the Mosaic authorship of the Pentateuch comes from the realm of archaeology. Critics argue that the Pentateuch's historical and cultural descriptions contradict what is known from archaeological findings, thereby implying multiple authorship over an extended period. However, a conservative, historical-grammatical approach reveals that these contentions are riddled with fallacies, methodological inconsistencies, and unwarranted assumptions. This chapter aims to dissect these issues by bringing archaeological evidence into the fold of the debate.

Archaeological Evidence Supports Mosaic Authorship

1. **Ancient Near Eastern Law Codes**: One of the noteworthy archaeological discoveries that affirm the historical credibility of the Pentateuch includes ancient law codes like the Code of Hammurabi. These law codes bear striking similarities to Mosaic Law, thereby affirming the possibility of a comprehensive legal code in Moses' time.

2. **Place Names and Geography**: Archaeological findings have corroborated many of the place names mentioned in the Pentateuch. These affirmations offer strong support for its historical reliability and timely authorship, plausibly within the life span of Moses.

3. **Material Culture**: Household artifacts, pottery, and even farming tools described in the Pentateuch are consistent with what we know of the Late Bronze Age, the period traditionally ascribed to Moses.

Fallacies in the Use of Archaeological Arguments

1. **Argument from Silence**: Critics often point to the absence of direct evidence as proof against the Mosaic authorship. However, an argument from silence is fundamentally flawed. Lack of evidence is not evidence of lack.

2. **Chronological Snobbery**: Critics sometimes dismiss the historicity of the Pentateuch based on its "primitive" outlook compared to later periods. This is fallacious, as ancient does not equate to unhistorical or inaccurate.

3. **Presumption of Discrepancy**: The tendency to emphasize supposed discrepancies between the Pentateuch and archaeological findings often ignores the nuances and limits of interpreting ancient data. Critics commonly begin with a presumption of discrepancy rather than one of harmonization, betraying a methodological bias.

4. **Selective Skepticism**: The critical scholarship often applies a higher level of skepticism to biblical texts than to other ancient literature, despite the Bible's excellent manuscript evidence.

Context and Interpretation

1. **Contextual Alignment**: The Pentateuch is aligned contextually with the second millennium B.C.E., reflecting the socio-political and religious milieu of the Ancient Near East, which supports its authorship by a figure deeply entrenched in that culture, such as Moses.
2. **Textual Witnesses**: Ancient texts, including the Septuagint and Samaritan Pentateuch, uniformly attribute the Torah to Moses, further reinforcing the traditional viewpoint supported by internal biblical evidence.

Archaeology and the Integrity of the Pentateuch

When scrutinized carefully, archaeological evidence does not contradict the Mosaic authorship of the Pentateuch but instead provides supportive indications. The discrepancies touted by critics often arise from methodological biases and unwarranted assumptions, rather than a fair treatment of the archaeological data.

It is imperative to approach archaeological evidence with a balanced and consistent methodology, one that adheres to the historical-grammatical method and upholds the inerrancy and divine inspiration of Scripture. By doing so, we not only counter the speculative claims of liberal-moderate criticism but also deepen our understanding of the Pentateuch within its historical and cultural setting.

As we engage in this rigorous intellectual exercise, our ultimate aim remains to equip readers with a robust understanding of conservative exegetical principles. In doing so, we offer a staunch defense of the Pentateuch's authorship, integrity, and, above all, its divinely inspired authority. Thus, we affirm our unwavering commitment to the authority and inerrancy of Scripture, firmly refuting the fallacies and biases that have muddled biblical interpretation and led many astray. The Word of Jehovah stands the test of time and scrutiny; we do well to stand firmly with it.

Ideological Biases: Higher Criticism's Relationship with Evolution Theory

The enterprise of Higher Criticism is often heralded as a neutral, scientific approach to the Bible. However, a closer inspection reveals that it is far from unbiased. In fact, one of the clearest ideological alignments of Higher Criticism is with Evolution Theory. The relationship between these two fields has significantly influenced academic attitudes toward the Mosaic authorship of the Pentateuch, injecting a series of assumptions and biases that cast doubt upon traditional viewpoints.

The Theoretical Overlay of Evolution Theory on Biblical Criticism

1. **Assumption of Progression**: Evolution Theory posits a continual, directional change, generally marked by complexity and improvement. This assumption of progression influences Higher Criticism by promoting the idea that religious thought must have evolved over time, thus undermining the idea of a unified, divinely inspired text attributed to Moses.

2. **Historical Development of Religions**: Critics often apply evolutionary principles to trace the supposed development of Israelite religion from polytheism to monotheism, even though the Pentateuch consistently proclaims the monotheistic worship of Jehovah from the onset.

3. **Complexity Equals Multiple Authorship**: Building upon evolutionary assumptions, critics often suggest that complex or sophisticated elements within the Pentateuch must be later

additions, dismissing the possibility that a single, enlightened individual such as Moses could have penned such a text.

Contradictions Within Higher Criticism

1. **Selective Application**: Critics are inconsistent in their application of evolutionary thought. While they employ evolutionary ideas to deconstruct the Mosaic authorship, they hesitate to extend the same logic to deconstructing the evolutionary premises themselves.

2. **Circular Reasoning**: The integration of Evolution Theory into biblical criticism is often justified by arguing that the Bible must be critiqued by modern scientific theories, presupposing the very evolutionary principles they seek to prove.

3. **Ignoring Alternative Explanations**: The allegiance to evolutionary thought blinds critics to other plausible explanations. For instance, apparent inconsistencies within the Pentateuch can be understood as complementary details rather than contradictions, which is more in line with a historical-grammatical interpretation of Scripture.

Ideological Commitments Over Academic Objectivity

The conflation of Evolution Theory with biblical criticism reveals an ideological commitment that undermines academic objectivity. Far from being a neutral evaluation of biblical texts, Higher Criticism is reflective of broader ideological systems like secular humanism and the Enlightenment.

Dissecting Fallacies: A Conservative Response

1. **False Dichotomy**: The attempt to juxtapose scientific theories like evolution against religious faith creates a false dichotomy. Science and faith address different realms—how and why, respectively—and both can coexist without undermining each other.

2. **Misuse of Interdisciplinary Approaches**: While interdisciplinary research can be fruitful, the insertion of evolutionary principles into biblical criticism results in a methodological mishmash that compromises the integrity of both disciplines.

3. **Biased Critique**: By grounding their approach in evolutionary presuppositions, critics have created a self-fulfilling prophecy where the only "logical" conclusion is one that confirms their biases.

The Need for Methodological Purity and Unbiased Scholarship

As defenders of the integrity and inerrancy of Scripture, we must be vigilant in identifying and critiquing the ideological biases inherent in Higher Criticism. The uncritical adoption of evolutionary principles into biblical scholarship is not only methodologically flawed but also ideologically motivated. This taints the objectivity of scholarly endeavors and misleads many into questioning the divine authority and historicity of the Bible.

Our ultimate goal is to equip readers with the tools necessary for a robust understanding of conservative exegetical principles and methods. We aim to restore confidence in the Word of Jehovah as the authoritative, reliable, and divinely inspired text that it is. By adhering to a historical-grammatical method of interpretation, we stand on a firm foundation that not only withstands the scrutiny of critics but also honors God's revelation to humanity.

By debunking the ideological underpinnings of Higher Criticism, we offer a corrective lens through which to approach biblical texts. In doing so, we reaffirm our unswerving commitment to the divine inspiration and authority of Scripture, effectively countering the biases and speculative theories that have long plagued the field of biblical scholarship. Thus, our quest for truth remains rooted in the immutable Word of Jehovah, rather than the shifting sands of human speculation.

Theology vs. Ideology: Wellhausen's Assumptions

In examining the Documentary Hypothesis, particularly as articulated by Julius Wellhausen, it becomes abundantly clear that the foundational assumptions are not mere academic postulations; they are, in fact, ideological positions masquerading as objective analysis. Wellhausen, a figure of prodigious influence in the realm of Higher Criticism, propounded his theories in the late 19th century. The reverberations of his work continue to be felt today, shaping the contours of modern biblical scholarship. However, a critical look reveals that his assumptions are rife with fallacies and deeply rooted in ideological convictions rather than a rigorous theological approach.

A Recapitulation of Wellhausen's Prolegomena

Wellhausen is famous for his articulation of the "JEDP" theory, which seeks to divide the Pentateuch into four main sources: the Yahwist (J), the Elohist (E), the Deuteronomist (D), and the Priestly (P) source. He argued that Israel's religion evolved from a simple, free form of worship to a legalistic, cultic religion, and this evolution is supposedly reflected in these different strands of the Pentateuch.

Wellhausen's Assumptions: An Analysis

1. **Evolutionary Assumption**: In line with 19th-century evolutionary thought, Wellhausen assumed a natural evolution in Israel's religion. This teleological outlook, however, does not align with the evidence found in the text itself, which consistently affirms a monotheistic, covenantal relationship between Jehovah and His people from the beginning.

2. **Ethnocentric Bias**: Wellhausen's German Protestant background shaped his view that cultic and priestly regulations were "lower" forms of religion. This Eurocentric lens unjustifiably superimposed his cultural norms on ancient Israelite culture.

3. **Anti-Supernatural Bias**: His naturalistic assumptions precluded the possibility of divine revelation, thus skewing his interpretation from the outset. The notion of a divinely inspired text was sidelined in favor of an evolutionary, human-centric development of religious thought.

4. **Assumption of Inconsistency**: Wellhausen operated under the assumption that any differences in style, vocabulary, or theological emphasis must necessarily indicate different authors or sources. However, such variations can easily be reconciled within the framework of single authorship, provided one applies a consistent historical-grammatical method of exegesis.

Theology vs. Ideology

A genuine theological approach to Scripture requires a commitment to its divine inspiration and authority. This does not mean ignoring its human elements but recognizing that these are perfectly harmonized under the superintendence of the Holy Spirit. Wellhausen's methodology, however, elevates ideology over theology. His theories do not spring from an objective, scholarly quest for understanding but are rooted in his ideological leanings influenced by German idealism and Enlightenment rationalism.

Dissecting Fallacies: A Conservative Response

1. **Methodological Rigor**: It is crucial to bring methodological rigor to our analysis, respecting the historical and literary contexts, rather than imposing an external framework onto the text.

2. **Supernatural Acceptance**: Unlike Wellhausen, who dismissed supernatural claims a priori, a conservative approach allows for divine activity and revelation as recorded in the Scriptures, respecting their claims at face value unless there is substantial reason to do otherwise.

3. **Textual Integrity**: We must affirm the textual and theological coherence of the Pentateuch, recognizing that variations in style and focus do not necessitate fragmentary authorship.

Upholding the Mosaic Authorship

The assumptions of Wellhausen and like-minded critics fail to hold up under scrutiny and are significantly influenced by ideological presuppositions rather than sound theological principles or empirical evidence. This does not merely represent an academic debate but touches on the very integrity and authority of Scripture. As proponents of a conservative exegetical approach grounded in the historical-grammatical method, our task is to expose the speculative and ideologically motivated nature of such criticisms.

By doing so, we aim to redirect the focus towards an understanding of Scripture that is both academically rigorous and theologically sound, thereby reestablishing confidence in the Mosaic authorship of the Pentateuch. The goal is not just to argue against modernist criticism but to furnish believers with the tools to understand and affirm the divine, authoritative nature of God's Word. This sets the stage for an exegesis that honors Jehovah and upholds the sanctity and unity of His revealed will, countering the destructive tendencies of Higher Criticism to undermine these foundational truths.

The Jewish Encyclopedia's Critique of Wellhausen's Assumptions

In further scrutinizing the premises and conclusions of Julius Wellhausen's Documentary Hypothesis, it is instructive to turn our attention to the critiques presented in esteemed academic resources like the Jewish Encyclopedia. It is noteworthy that the Jewish tradition, which has preserved the Torah through millennia, has its own sets of critiques against the Documentary Hypothesis, many of which resonate profoundly with conservative Christian perspectives.

Edward D. Andrews

Context: The Jewish Encyclopedia's Position

The Jewish Encyclopedia, while not necessarily conservative in all of its theological views, remains a reputable resource that provides a comprehensive analysis of Jewish history, religion, and traditions. It offers a historical and analytical lens to the Old Testament texts, or the Hebrew Bible, that is deeply rooted in Jewish scholarship.

Critiquing Wellhausen's Assumptions

1. **Questioning the Evolutionary View**: The Jewish Encyclopedia challenges Wellhausen's evolutionary view of Israelite religion. Wellhausen's theory presupposes that religion evolved from animism to polytheism and ultimately to monotheism, fitting neatly into his 19th-century framework. Jewish scholars find this assumption flawed because it dismisses the Torah's own assertion of an original monotheism with Abraham and a consistent, covenantal relationship between Jehovah and Israel.

2. **Disputing the Historical Reconstruction**: Wellhausen proposed that the priestly code (P) came during or after the Babylonian exile. The Jewish Encyclopedia argues that this is historically implausible, given the extensive priestly systems and regulations that existed before the exile. The Temple and the priesthood were essential elements of pre-exilic Israelite religion, making it improbable that such a significant corpus of laws was formulated only during or after the exile.

3. **Challenging Source Division**: The Encyclopedia points out that Wellhausen's division of the text into multiple sources often leads to implausible and arbitrary fragmentations. These fragmentations create inconsistencies and complexities that do not naturally exist within the text.

4. **Rejecting Anti-Supernaturalism**: Wellhausen's strong leaning towards naturalism negates the idea of divine revelation. Jewish tradition, however, has always upheld the concept of divine revelation at Sinai and throughout Israel's

history. To assert otherwise is to conflict fundamentally with the foundation of Jewish (and, by extension, Christian) belief in the Scriptures.

5. **Refuting Ethnocentrism**: Wellhausen's theories are markedly Eurocentric, as he deems the primitive and folk elements of religion as "lower" stages, reflecting his own cultural biases. Jewish scholars call this out as a form of ethnocentrism that undermines the complexities and uniqueness of ancient Near Eastern religions.

Theology Over Ideology

The Jewish Encyclopedia's critique aligns with a conservative approach that places theology over ideology. It insists that the assumptions held by scholars like Wellhausen are not neutral but are driven by philosophical and ideological systems of thought alien to the text itself.

Upholding the Consistency and Unity of the Text

The Jewish Encyclopedia, along with conservative Christian scholarship, advocates for an interpretation that respects the textual and theological unity of the Pentateuch. There is a continuity in the theme, tone, and language of the Torah that is more logically explained by a unified authorship under divine inspiration than by disparate, conflicting sources.

Renewing Our Confidence in the Mosaic Authorship

Critiques such as those found in the Jewish Encyclopedia provide valuable insights that affirm the conservative position of Mosaic authorship. They remind us that the ideological presuppositions that underlie Wellhausen's theories and much of Higher Criticism are not innocuous; they shape conclusions in ways that deviate from the text's own self-presentation. Our objective should always be a hermeneutical approach that respects both the historical context and the theological message of the text. This should guide us in the development of an exegetical methodology that is committed to the inerrancy and authority of Scripture. This stand against the speculative nature of Higher Criticism serves as both an antidote to its errors and a bulwark against its attempts to undermine the Scriptures. By examining and understanding these critiques, believers can be better equipped to defend the authority and integrity of God's Word, thereby fulfilling our responsibility to "rightly dividing the word of truth" (2 Timothy 2:15, UASV).

The Shaky Foundation of Higher Criticism

The assault on the Mosaic authorship of the Pentateuch by proponents of Higher Criticism represents one of the most profound challenges to the traditional understanding of Scripture. Although Higher Criticism is often clothed in the garb of academic rigor and scientific objectivity, a closer scrutiny reveals a foundation riddled with methodological shortcomings and ideological bias.

The Siren Call of "Scientific Objectivity"

One of the first points of critique against Higher Criticism's claim to "scientific objectivity" lies in the very nature of its inquiry. Science deals with empirical data that can be tested and repeated under controlled conditions. Biblical criticism, by contrast, often involves historical analysis and textual scrutiny that do not lend themselves to empirical testing. The categorization of the Documentary Hypothesis as "scientific" is therefore not only inaccurate but also misleading.

Ideological Filters: Enlightenment Rationalism

Higher Criticism, born out of the Enlightenment's rationalistic ethos, inherently views the Bible through a lens clouded by secular humanism. This ideology presupposes the Bible to be a purely human product, dismissive of any divine interaction or inspiration. By starting with such assumptions, critics have already concluded their investigations before they have even commenced.

Textual Criticism vs. Literary Fragmentation

Textual criticism, a valid and useful tool, aims to determine the most authentic form of a text based on available manuscripts. Higher Criticism, however, extends this method inappropriately to dissect the Pentateuch into various strands of "sources" like J, E, D, and P. This fragmentation assumes that differing styles or terms within a text must be indicative of different authors, disregarding the possibility of a single author employing a variety of styles and terms.

Wellhausen's A Priori Assumptions

Julius Wellhausen, the scholar most famously associated with the Documentary Hypothesis, was burdened with a set of a priori assumptions that guided his critical endeavors. His historical reconstruction of Israel's religious evolution was not deduced from the text but imposed upon it. This reflects a profoundly problematic approach where the text is twisted to fit the theory, rather than the theory being formulated based on the text.

Disregarding Internal Evidence and Historical Affirmations

Throughout history, both Jewish tradition and Christian doctrine have affirmed Mosaic authorship. Jesus Himself attested to this (John 5:46-47, UASV). However, Higher Criticism discards these affirmations in favor of its speculative theories. This selective use of historical data violates the principles of sound historical investigation.

The Semantics of Deception: The Term "Redactor"

Higher Criticism often employs the term "redactor" to explain the compilation of the Pentateuch. This term suggests an editorial process that collates various independent sources into a single text. Such a view implicitly denies the possibility of divine inspiration and presents the Bible as a mere human product subject to human errors and inconsistencies.

Hermeneutical Inconsistencies

The proponents of Higher Criticism frequently employ a hermeneutic of suspicion that questions the text's credibility while ignoring the same level of scrutiny for their own theories. This double standard undermines the very academic integrity that these scholars claim to uphold.

Objectivity vs. Subjectivity

Higher Criticism professes to be objective, yet its conclusions are often influenced by prevailing cultural, theological, or philosophical trends. Thus, the so-called "objective" analysis is inherently subjective, colored by the personal biases and presuppositions of the scholars involved.

A Call to Unswerving Commitment to the Authority of Scripture

The shaky foundation upon which Higher Criticism stands should caution us against unquestioningly accepting its claims and conclusions. An objective Historical-Grammatical method, committed to the authority and inerrancy of Scripture, offers a more reliable approach to understanding the Bible. This conservative exegetical methodology acts as an antidote to the speculative nature of modern biblical criticism.

By exposing the fallacies and biases in Higher Criticism, we can better appreciate the robust, integrated unity of the Pentateuch and reaffirm our commitment to its Mosaic authorship. This approach does not stem from a fear of intellectual inquiry but from a respect for the text itself, acknowledging its divine origin and purpose. In doing so, we counter the assault on the Bible, strengthening our own faith and equipping ourselves to "always be prepared to make a defense to anyone who asks you for a reason for the hope that is in you" (1 Peter 3:15, UASV). Thus, we fulfill our sacred duty to uphold the Scriptures, which stand as the eternal and unchanging Word of God.

Archaeological Criticism: A Counterpoint

The field of biblical archaeology has often been cited by proponents of Higher Criticism as a tool to deconstruct traditional views on the Mosaic authorship of the Pentateuch. Yet, it is imperative to recognize that archaeological findings can equally serve as a robust counterpoint to such critical methodologies, affirming the historical reliability and integrated unity of these foundational texts.

The Ambiguity of Archaeological Data

Higher Criticism often claims archaeological findings as allies, positing that these discoveries contradict or challenge the biblical narrative. However, archaeological data is often ambiguous and open to interpretation. Importantly, the absence of direct archaeological evidence for a specific biblical event is not equivalent to evidence of absence.

The Testimony of Material Culture

A careful examination of material culture—ranging from pottery to inscriptions—reflects a reality consistent with the biblical accounts in the Pentateuch. For example, the types of pottery and household items described in the time of Moses align with what we know from excavations related to that period. This congruency adds an external line of evidence supporting the traditional view of Mosaic authorship.

Egyptian Linguistic Parallels

One of the most compelling arguments for the Mosaic authorship of the Pentateuch is the text's usage of Egyptian loanwords and idioms, which is consistent with Moses' upbringing in Pharaoh's court. Such linguistic features serve as internal evidence affirming the historical backdrop against which the Pentateuch was written.

Laws and Legal Codes

The legal codes within the Pentateuch, including the Covenant Code, Deuteronomic Code, and Holiness Code, bear striking similarities to other ancient Near Eastern legal systems, such as the Laws of Hammurabi. However, the biblical laws also demonstrate a unique theocentric character, setting them apart from mere human legal compilations and affirming a divine origin.

Historiographical Methods

The Pentateuch employs historiographical methods consistent with ancient Near Eastern practices, validating its claims of historical reporting. Critics often assume that the biblical text should conform to modern standards of historical writing, neglecting the fact that ancient historiography had its own set of conventions.

Kings and Kingdoms: The Historical Context

Names of places and rulers mentioned in the Pentateuch align with what we know from other ancient Near Eastern sources. While some critics argue that these could be later additions, the seamless integration of such names into the narrative suggests otherwise.

The Challenge of Radiocarbon Dating

Higher critics often use radiocarbon dating to assert a late date for the Pentateuchal texts. However, radiocarbon dating has its own set of limitations and should not be the sole determiner for dating ancient texts, especially when other forms of evidence point to an earlier date.

Literary Unity and Archaeology

Archaeological evidence often points to the integrated unity of the Pentateuch. For instance, themes and motifs that start in Genesis have their climax in Deuteronomy, suggesting a unified narrative structure, inconsistent with the Documentary Hypothesis which posits different authors for different sections of the text.

Archaeology as a Supplementary Tool

It's vital to understand that archaeology serves as a supplementary tool for biblical interpretation, not a dictatorial one. No archaeological find has the power to override clear textual evidence, especially when one employs a rigorous, objective Historical-Grammatical method of interpretation.

Selective Interpretation: A Caution

Higher critics often employ a selective use of archaeological data, cherry-picking findings that seemingly support their views while ignoring or dismissing those that do not. Such an approach is intellectually dishonest and violates the principles of sound research and interpretation.

Archaeology in the Service of Truth

In sum, when approached without preconceived notions or ideological bias, archaeological evidence can serve as a robust counterpoint to the claims of Higher Criticism concerning the Mosaic authorship of the Pentateuch. By adhering to a rigorous and objective Historical-Grammatical method, one can integrate archaeological findings to affirm the historical reliability, integrated unity, and divine inspiration of the Pentateuch.

Through this approach, we not only expose the shaky foundations of Higher Criticism but also fortify our own convictions about the authority and inerrancy of Scripture. This positions us to effectively counter pseudo-scholarly works that seek to undermine the Bible, fulfilling the apostolic admonition to "demolish arguments and every pretension that sets itself up against the knowledge of God" (2 Corinthians 10:5, UASV).

By grounding our beliefs in a methodologically sound and intellectually honest interpretation of both the biblical text and archaeological data, we honor God, uphold the Scriptures, and equip believers to engage with challenges to their faith in a fallen world that desperately needs the eternal truths contained in God's Word.

The Intellectual Appeal of Higher Criticism

It's crucial to recognize why Higher Criticism, which has so fundamentally challenged traditional beliefs about the Mosaic authorship of the Pentateuch, has gained so much traction in academic circles and beyond. The appeal of this methodology is not accidental but is closely linked to broader intellectual currents that have shaped Western thought over the past few centuries.

The Allure of "Scientific" Inquiry

One of the principal attractions of Higher Criticism is its purported objectivity. By presenting itself as a scientific, analytical approach to biblical texts, it gains instant credibility in an era dominated by empirical research. Critics often employ complex linguistic analysis, historical reconstruction, and even elements of social science to frame their arguments, lending an air of academic respectability.

Intellectual Autonomy

Higher Criticism resonates with the Enlightenment's emphasis on human reason and intellectual autonomy. The idea that one can arrive at "truth" by applying rational, critical methods is appealing to many who prefer human reason over divine revelation. This autonomous approach essentially places man above the text, in the position of a judge, rather than beneath the text, in a posture of submission to its divine authority.

Post-Modernism and Deconstruction

Higher Criticism has also found allies in post-modern circles that champion deconstructionism, a methodology that seeks to dismantle traditional narratives and meanings. By asserting multiple authors and sources for the Pentateuch, critics effectively disintegrate the text, allowing for a plurality of interpretations that aligns well with post-modern sensibilities.

Complexity and Nuance

To the modern academic mind, complexity is often equated with profundity. Higher Criticism, with its multiple layers of source criticism, form criticism, and redaction criticism, offers a complex framework for studying the Bible. For many scholars, this complexity appears more intellectually satisfying than "simplistic" traditional approaches that affirm Mosaic authorship and divine inspiration.

The Novelty Factor

Higher Criticism, with its novel theories about multiple sources and later redactions, offers something "new" compared to the age-old belief in Mosaic authorship. In an academic culture that often values innovation over tradition, the allure of fresh, groundbreaking interpretations can be irresistible.

Affirming Cultural and Moral Relativism

Higher Criticism provides an academic cover for those who wish to distance themselves from the moral imperatives of Scripture. By deconstructing the text and thereby diluting its authority, one creates room for a relativistic ethics that better aligns with current societal norms.

Academic Peer Pressure

Let's not underestimate the force of academic consensus or, more precisely, the perceived consensus. Once an idea gains traction within scholarly circles, the pressure to conform can be immense. The fear of intellectual ostracization often drives scholars to adopt prevailing theories, regardless of their validity.

Critique: The Fatal Flaws

Yet, for all its intellectual appeal, Higher Criticism suffers from fatal flaws. At its core, this methodology is driven by an a priori rejection of the supernatural, a naturalistic bias that automatically discounts any notion of divine revelation or inspiration.

Moreover, Higher Criticism employs a deeply flawed hermeneutic approach. In dissecting the text into various sources, critics ignore the internal and external evidence for the literary and thematic unity of the Pentateuch. By doing so, they effectively silence the text, reducing it to a mere artifact to be dissected rather than God-breathed Scripture to be revered and obeyed.

Lastly, the intellectual appeal of Higher Criticism often masks its foundational weaknesses. While presenting itself as objective and scientific, the methodology is rife with speculation. Many of its core assertions—like the identification and dating of various sources—lack concrete evidence and are often based on circular reasoning.

The Need for a Return to a Reverent Hermeneutic

As this chapter has endeavored to show, the intellectual appeal of Higher Criticism is largely rooted in broader ideological systems that are fundamentally at odds with a high view of Scripture. Our task is not merely to debunk these theories but to offer a robust alternative: a return to an objective Historical-Grammatical method that takes seriously the claims of the text itself, treating it with the reverence due to the inspired, inerrant Word of God.

By adopting such a method, grounded in a commitment to the authority and inerrancy of Scripture, we provide an antidote to the speculative, ideologically driven practices that have eroded confidence in the Bible. We fulfill our calling to be faithful stewards of the mysteries of God, "accurately handling the word of truth" (2 Timothy 2:15, UASV) and thereby equipping the body of Christ to stand firm in a culture increasingly hostile to the eternal truths contained in the Holy Scriptures.

The Inconsistencies and Weaknesses of the Documentary Hypothesis

The Documentary Hypothesis, which gained prominence through scholars like Julius Wellhausen, posits that the Pentateuch (the first five books of the Bible) is not a unified work penned by Moses but is a composite of various sources and traditions. These sources are commonly identified as J (Jehovah), E (Elohim), D (Deuteronomy), and P (Priestly). However, a careful examination reveals glaring inconsistencies and weaknesses in this theory, which we will enumerate and dissect here.

Lack of Manuscript Evidence

First and foremost, there is a distinct lack of manuscript evidence to support the existence of the alleged separate sources (J, E, D, P). No ancient manuscript of the Hebrew Bible exists that isolates these sources from each other. This absence of physical evidence weakens the foundation upon which the hypothesis stands.

Subjectivity in Source Division

Higher critics, in their attempt to break down the text into various sources, often rely on subjective judgment. For instance, the criteria for distinguishing between the J and E sources is largely conjectural. Elohim is used in passages traditionally attributed to the J source, and the name Jehovah appears in E segments. This lack of consistency undermines the credibility of the source division.

Redactional Complexity

The Documentary Hypothesis presupposes an incredible level of redactional complexity. According to this theory, numerous redactors across centuries pieced together various sources to create the Pentateuch as we know it. The logistical intricacies involved in such a complex redaction process, spanning generations and perhaps even geographical locations, strain credulity.

Literary Unity and Structure Ignored

The hypothesis dismisses the remarkable literary unity and intricate structure of the Pentateuch, aspects that argue for a single author or a closely coordinated team of writers. For example, Genesis to Deuteronomy exhibits clear chiasms and parallelisms, something difficult to reconcile with a piecemeal compilation from multiple disparate sources.

Overlooking Historical Testimony

The Documentary Hypothesis also ignores or downplays the consistent testimony of ancient historians and Jewish tradition, which unequivocally attribute the authorship of the Pentateuch to Moses. External evidence, such as references in other ancient Near Eastern literature and the New Testament, also affirms Mosaic authorship.

Theological Assumptions

The hypothesis often assumes a development from polytheism to monotheism in Israelite religion, but this does not square with the evidence. Israel's confession of faith, the Shema ("Hear, O Israel: Jehovah our God, Jehovah is one!" Deuteronomy 6:4, UASV), firmly establishes monotheism, undermining the alleged evolutionary religious path suggested by the hypothesis.

Misuse of Language and Style

Proponents claim variations in language and style as evidence for different sources. However, any skilled author can employ a range of vocabulary and styles, especially when discussing varied subject matter. To argue otherwise is to unnecessarily restrict the capabilities of a single author, in this case, Moses.

Lack of Agreement Among Critics

Interestingly, there is no uniform agreement among proponents of the Documentary Hypothesis on how to divide the text. This lack of consensus reveals the speculative and subjective nature of the methodology involved.

Discrepancies in Historical Reconstruction

The hypothesis often falls into the trap of anachronism. For instance, it argues that the Priestly source reflects a post-exilic milieu, yet numerous elements within the text suggest an environment much closer to the period traditionally ascribed to Moses.

Contradictions in Narrative Continuity

The alleged fragmentation into multiple sources often results in a choppy, disjointed narrative, something that does not bear out when reading the text in its canonical form. The continuity of the narrative suggests a far more coordinated effort than the Documentary Hypothesis allows.

The Need for a Return to Solid Ground

The Documentary Hypothesis, for all its intellectual bravado, is fraught with inconsistencies and weaknesses that render it unsuitable as a method for understanding the Pentateuch. These problems are not mere quibbles but foundational flaws that shake the very underpinnings of the hypothesis.

As students and stewards of the Bible, it is incumbent upon us to approach Scripture with the respect and reverence it deserves, employing a hermeneutic grounded in a commitment to its authority and inerrancy. This is achieved best by the Historical-Grammatical method, which seeks to understand the text within its historical context and literary structure, respecting its unity and divine inspiration.

In doing so, we not only honor the Word of God but also furnish ourselves and those we teach with a far more stable and reliable framework for understanding the Scriptures. This provides a vital antidote to the speculative, ideologically driven methodologies that have marred the study of the Bible, empowering the believer to engage with God's Word in a manner that is both intellectually robust and spiritually enriching.

What Does the Biblical Evidence from the Old Testament Report about the Mosaic Authorship?

While the tradition of attributing the Pentateuch to Moses has been subject to severe scrutiny in modern times, particularly due to the rise of higher criticism, it remains essential to grapple with the evidence within the Old Testament text itself. Weighing this evidence requires a return to an objective Historical-Grammatical approach to interpretation, wherein the very text of the Scriptures stands as a witness to its own authorship and credibility.

Internal Evidence within the Pentateuch

The most straightforward line of evidence comes from the internal textual testimony of the Pentateuch. Numerous passages explicitly state or strongly imply that Moses was the writer. Take, for instance, Exodus 17:14, where Jehovah instructs Moses: "Write this as a memorial in a book and recite it in the ears of Joshua." Additionally, in Exodus 24:4, Moses is said to have "wrote down all the words of Jehovah." These internal affirmations continue through Leviticus (e.g., Leviticus 1:1), Numbers (e.g., Numbers 33:1-2), and Deuteronomy (e.g., Deuteronomy 31:9). The Pentateuch itself, therefore, serves as the primary witness to its Mosaic authorship.

The Chain of Tradition

Following the books of Moses, the subsequent Old Testament books consistently refer to the Mosaic origin of the Torah. In the Book of Joshua, for instance, the Law is continually identified as "the Book of the Law of Moses" (Joshua 8:31, 23:6). This unbroken tradition is carried on throughout the historical books, wisdom literature, and prophetic writings. In 2 Kings 14:6, King Amaziah follows "the book of the law of Moses" in his judgments, underlining the importance and acknowledgment of the Mosaic legal code across diverse periods and leaders in Israelite history.

The Testimony of Prophecy

The prophetic tradition, which comes after Moses, also affirms the Mosaic authorship of the Pentateuch. Jeremiah 7:22 refers to "the day that I brought them out of the land of Egypt, from the house of slavery," drawing upon the Mosaic narrative and thereby affirming its divine source and Mosaic channel. Moreover, the prophet Malachi unequivocally states, "Remember the law of my servant Moses, the statutes and rules that I commanded him at Horeb for all Israel" (Malachi 4:4). The voice of the prophets, then, serves as an added layer of confirmation regarding the Mosaic heritage of the Torah.

The Consistency of Theological Themes

While not an explicit testimony, the consistent theological framework found throughout the Pentateuch offers further internal evidence. The laws, historical narratives, and covenantal principles all reflect a unified theological message that points to a single authorial source. It's hard to conceive that disparate authors across several centuries could maintain such a tightly-knit theological fabric.

The internal evidence from the Old Testament overwhelmingly points to Moses as the author of the Pentateuch. This conclusion is not only in keeping with the tradition found within the text but is also consistent with the subsequent historical, wisdom, and prophetic books of the Old Testament. To deny Mosaic authorship, therefore, is to go against the grain of the textual testimony and to replace it with speculative theories, often grounded more in modernist assumptions than in the textual data. This not only distances us from the true meaning of the Scriptures but undermines their authority and inerrancy. Therefore, any authentic understanding of the Old Testament must begin with the recognition of its Mosaic foundation, a point that serves as the bedrock of biblical authority and that equips us against the unwarranted and ideologically skewed conclusions of higher criticism.

What Does the Biblical Evidence of Jesus Christ Report about the Mosaic Authorship?

An often-overlooked area of investigation when discussing the Mosaic authorship of the Pentateuch is the testimony of Jesus Christ Himself. As Christians guided by an unswerving commitment to the authority and inerrancy of Scripture, there is no higher validation than that of Jesus. What He has said concerning the issue carries profound implications, not just for our understanding of the Torah but also for the foundation of our faith.

Jesus and the "Law of Moses"

Throughout the Gospel accounts, Jesus frequently refers to the Mosaic Law as an authoritative document. In the Sermon on the Mount, for instance, He says, "Do not think that I have come to abolish the Law or the Prophets; I have not come to abolish them but to fulfill them" (Matthew 5:17). By categorizing the Law with the Prophets, Jesus places the Pentateuch within the broader context of the Hebrew Scriptures, affirming its Divine origin and, by extension, its traditional Mosaic authorship.

Jesus' Direct References to Mosaic Legislation

In various debates with the Pharisees and in His teachings, Jesus quotes laws that are explicitly detailed in the books attributed to Moses. One of the most striking examples is His discussion on divorce. Jesus cites Genesis 2:24, a Mosaic text, as the basis for His argument: "Have you not read that he who created them from the beginning made them male and female, and said, 'Therefore a man shall leave his father and his mother and hold fast to his wife, and the two shall become one flesh'?" (Matthew 19:4-5). In doing so, Jesus not only affirms the content but validates the origin of the Law, embracing its Mosaic authorship.

Jesus' Interaction with Sadducees: Affirming Mosaic Authorship

In His dialogue with the Sadducees concerning the resurrection, Jesus referred to the account of the burning bush, saying, "But as for the resurrection of the dead, have you not read what was spoken to you by God: 'I am the God of Abraham, and the God of Isaac, and the God of Jacob'? He is not the God of the dead, but of the living" (Matthew 22:31-32). By saying "what was spoken to you by God," Jesus is upholding the divine and Mosaic authority of the Pentateuch.

Moses' Seat: Authority and Tradition

In Matthew 23:2, Jesus remarks, "The scribes and the Pharisees sit on Moses' seat." While He criticized the religious leaders for their hypocrisy, He did not question the concept of "Moses' seat" as a seat of teaching authority based on the Law of Moses. This confirms that during Jesus' time, the understanding of Mosaic authorship was not only accepted but also acknowledged by Jesus Himself.

The Unity of Scripture: Law, Prophets, and Writings

Jesus often spoke of the Hebrew Scriptures as a coherent, unified revelation. On the road to Emmaus, He expounded "in all the

Scriptures the things concerning Himself" (Luke 24:27). The expression "all the Scriptures" presupposes a recognized canon that prominently includes the Mosaic books. By taking the Pentateuch as a vital component of this redemptive-historical narrative, Jesus once again indirectly but powerfully affirms its Mosaic authorship.

When the testimony of Jesus Christ is considered, the case for the Mosaic authorship of the Pentateuch becomes compelling and, indeed, unassailable. The words of Christ not only affirm the Mosaic authorship but also, in doing so, support the reliability, coherence, and divine authority of the Pentateuch. To cast doubt upon Mosaic authorship, then, is not a mere academic exercise; it is to call into question the very teachings of Jesus and, therefore, the foundation of Christian doctrine. Thus, the authority of Jesus Christ serves not only as a vindication of Mosaic authorship but also as an antidote to the skeptical inquiries that mar the modern discourse, anchored in the subjectivities of higher criticism. Therefore, as believers committed to the truth of Scripture, affirming the Mosaic authorship of the Pentateuch is not an option; it is a necessity—a doctrinal cornerstone in the edifice of an unshakable Christian faith.

What Does the Biblical Evidence from the Apostles Report about the Mosaic Authorship?

While the testimony of Jesus Christ offers an invaluable endorsement of the Mosaic authorship of the Pentateuch, we also find compelling evidence in the writings of His apostles. Their views on the Torah are of monumental significance for several reasons: they were the ones instructed directly by Jesus, and their letters and activities shaped the beliefs of the early Christian church.

Paul's Endorsement of Mosaic Authorship

The Apostle Paul, considered the most prolific writer of the New Testament, makes frequent references to Moses and the Law throughout his letters. For example, in Romans 10:5, Paul writes, "For

Moses writes about the righteousness that is based on the Law, that the person who does the commandments shall live by them." This statement clearly reflects Paul's belief in the Mosaic authorship of the Law.

In 2 Corinthians 3:15, Paul notes, "Yes, to this day whenever Moses is read a veil lies over their hearts." This not only endorses the Mosaic authorship but also suggests that the Law of Moses held a position of continuous influence and authority in the synagogue readings and by extension, in the early church.

Peter's Affirmation

The Apostle Peter, a key figure in early Christian history, also recognizes Moses as the author of the first five books of the Bible. In the book of Acts, Peter states, "Moses said, 'The Lord God will raise up for you a prophet like me from your brothers. You shall listen to him in whatever he tells you'" (Acts 3:22). This quotation from Deuteronomy 18:15, again, reinforces the traditional view of Mosaic authorship.

James and the "Law of Liberty"

James, another prominent New Testament figure, refers to the "law of liberty" (James 1:25; 2:12), which he closely associates with the moral imperatives found in the Mosaic Law. The way James uses the Mosaic Law to develop his arguments and ethics affirms the traditional understanding that Moses is the author of the Law.

John's Testimony

In the Gospel of John, the Apostle often mentions "Moses" in a way that assumes his authorship of the Pentateuch. John 1:17 states, "For the Law was given through Moses; grace and truth came through Jesus Christ." This confirms that, like Paul, Peter, and James, John too accepted the traditional attribution of the Pentateuch to Moses.

Stephen's Defense and Martyrdom

In Stephen's defense before the Sanhedrin, as recorded in Acts 7, he extensively recounts the history of Israel, attributing the Law to "the living oracles given to us by Moses" (Acts 7:38). Stephen's respect for the Mosaic Law and his understanding of Moses as its author were so profound that they formed a central part of his final testimony before his martyrdom.

Mosaic Authorship and Apostolic Teaching

The teachings of the apostles laid the doctrinal foundation of the early church. As evidenced by the New Testament writings, these teachings include the belief in Mosaic authorship. The New Testament writers did not view the Torah as a compilation of multiple sources but as a unified work given by God through Moses. To dismiss Mosaic authorship is to question the theological and historical foundation established by the apostles themselves.

The unanimous apostolic voice on the issue of Mosaic authorship of the Pentateuch is not only consistent with the testimony of Jesus Christ but also serves as an independent line of evidence that further solidifies the case for traditional attribution. Their accounts and teachings, preserved in the New Testament, exhibit a unified commitment to the Mosaic authorship and the authority of the Torah.

In light of this, to accept the speculative theories of the Documentary Hypothesis and related forms of higher criticism is to consciously depart from the apostolic foundation upon which the Christian church is built. For believers who place their trust in the authority and inerrancy of Scripture, the evidence from the apostles offers an indispensable affirmation of the Mosaic authorship of the Pentateuch. It reassures us that our faith is not based on traditions of men but on the unchanging word of God, as recognized and endorsed by the apostles. Therefore, to uphold the authority of Scripture is to affirm the Mosaic authorship of the Pentateuch as an incontrovertible and foundational truth.

Archaeology Evidence and Mosaic Authorship

The realm of archaeology has been a battleground for scholars, apologists, and critics when it comes to validating or disputing the Bible. One area where this contention is evident is the issue of Mosaic authorship of the Pentateuch. The Documentary Hypothesis, which proposes that the first five books of the Bible were assembled by various authors and editors across centuries, is a pillar of liberal-moderate biblical criticism. However, a careful examination of the archaeological evidence yields data that supports the traditional view that Moses is indeed the author of these books.

Historical Context of the Pentateuch

The Pentateuch provides numerous historical and cultural details that fit within the timeline of Moses' life and the Israelite sojourn in Egypt. These include mentions of specific places like Pithom and Raamses (Exodus 1:11), currencies like the shekel (Genesis 23:15), and references to the Hittites (Genesis 15:20), among others. The depiction of Egyptian culture and practice in the accounts of Joseph and the Israelite enslavement align with what is known from Egyptian history. These historically accurate elements suggest that the Pentateuch comes from a writer intimately familiar with this period and locale, lending credence to the traditional view of Mosaic authorship.

The Nuzi Tablets and Patriarchal Customs

One crucial piece of evidence is the Nuzi tablets, discovered in the 20th century in Mesopotamia. These tablets describe practices that parallel the patriarchal customs described in Genesis, like adoption for the purpose of inheritance, which is consistent with the account of Abraham and Eliezer (Genesis 15:2). The Nuzi tablets date back to the 15th century B.C.E., which places them in a period that makes the practices described in Genesis believable.

Laws and Covenants

Another dimension of archaeological corroboration comes from the discovery of ancient Near Eastern law codes such as the Code of Hammurabi. These legal traditions exhibit similarities with the Mosaic Law, like the lex talionis principle ("an eye for an eye"). However, there are also clear distinctions in ethical and moral imperatives, making it implausible to argue that the Mosaic Law is merely a derivative of earlier codes. Rather, it stands as an original document that reflects its unique origin, pointing to Moses as the author who received these laws from Jehovah.

Archaeology and the Documentary Hypothesis

One of the claims of the Documentary Hypothesis is the supposed anachronisms in the Pentateuch. However, archaeological finds have often overturned these claims. For example, the mention of the Philistines in Genesis was considered anachronistic until evidence confirmed their presence during the patriarchal period. Moreover, the term "Habiru," often associated with the Hebrews, appears in Egyptian texts that date back to the time of the Exodus. These archaeological finds work against the assertions of the Documentary Hypothesis.

Writing in Moses' Time

Skeptics often argue that writing was not sufficiently developed during Moses' time to allow for the composition of such a complex work. However, the discovery of texts like the Ebla tablets, dating back to around 24th century B.C.E., confirms that writing, administration, and legal formulation were highly advanced even before the time of Moses, making it entirely plausible for him to have penned the Pentateuch.

Unity in Diversity

The Pentateuch comprises different genres, from historical narrative to poetic material like the Song of the Sea (Exodus 15). The

Documentary Hypothesis would suggest multiple authors for these genres, but archaeological finds often reveal that diverse genres could coexist within a single document. For example, the Mesha Stele includes both historical and poetic elements, much like the Pentateuch. This shows that the diversity in the Pentateuch doesn't necessitate multiple authors.

The archaeological evidence, when evaluated from a conservative exegetical standpoint, substantially corroborates the traditional view of Mosaic authorship of the Pentateuch. From historical contexts to legal formulations and ancient practices, the evidence points to an author intimately familiar with the events and settings described, undermining the speculative nature of the Documentary Hypothesis.

In the quest for truth, the conservative scholar must rely on an interpretive framework that respects the authority and inerrancy of Scripture. The archaeology of the ancient Near East, rather than posing a threat to the Bible, provides a robust platform for affirming its historical and cultural context, thereby supporting the Mosaic authorship of the Pentateuch. Far from being a series of stitched-together documents from various authors and periods, the Pentateuch stands as a unified work that accurately portrays its historical context and authorship, just as it claims. Therefore, to maintain the integrity and authority of Scripture, we must regard Moses as the author of the Pentateuch, guided by the divine hand of Jehovah, a stance fully justified by both internal and external evidences, including the field of archaeology.

CHAPTER 2 Defending Joshua, Judges, and Ruth

Authenticity, Authorship, and Date of Joshua

The Situation Confronting Israel in the Time of Joshua

The time covered by the Book of Joshua is one of transition and conquest. The Israelites are at a crucial juncture, having just emerged from 40 years in the wilderness following the Exodus. The death of Moses, the charismatic leader who had guided them since leaving Egypt, has left a leadership vacuum. More immediately, the Israelites are on the cusp of entering Canaan—the Promised Land. This land is inhabited by various tribes and nations whose religious and cultural practices are deeply opposed to the worship of Jehovah. Therefore, the situation calls for military conquest, as well as spiritual and ethical fidelity to Jehovah's commandments.

Why Joshua as Leader?

Joshua was an appropriate choice for multiple reasons. As Moses' aide and military commander, he had direct experience in leading Israelites in combat (e.g., the Amalekite battle in Exodus 17). His demonstrated faithfulness—especially as one of the two spies who brought back a favorable report from Canaan despite the odds—showed him to be a man of strong faith in Jehovah.

Moreover, Joshua had been ordained by Jehovah and was filled with the spirit of wisdom (Deuteronomy 34:9). He was not only a military leader but also a spiritual leader who could guide the nation in obeying Jehovah's laws. His leadership was not merely human governance but divine stewardship. He was keenly aware that success depended not on military prowess but on fidelity to Jehovah and His laws. His directive for the people to sanctify themselves before major events, like crossing the Jordan, signifies his understanding of the spiritual dimension of their mission (Joshua 3:5).

Why Joshua as Recorder?

Joshua is frequently noted as the author of the book that bears his name, and the internal evidence supports this. Passages like Joshua 24:26, where it mentions, "Then Joshua wrote these words in the book of God's law," clearly indicate his role as a recorder of these events. Moreover, the text contains details that someone intimately involved with the events would know. The book's military accounts, geographical descriptions, and allocation of tribal lands are thorough and precise, fitting for someone of Joshua's background and responsibilities.

Joshua's role as recorder is particularly significant because it was not just history he was documenting; it was divine history. He was writing the acts of Jehovah in history, fulfilling the covenant promises made to the patriarchs. The book serves both as a historical account and a theological commentary, outlining the fulfillment of divine promises and the consequences of obedience or disobedience to Jehovah's laws.

In summary, the choice of Joshua as both leader and recorder was profoundly appropriate. He was uniquely qualified to lead Israel through a period of military conquest and spiritual testing, being both a seasoned military commander and a man of deep faith. His role as recorder ensures the accuracy and theological integrity of the account, providing future generations with a detailed narrative that stands as a testament to Jehovah's faithfulness and the crucial importance of covenantal fidelity. Thus, through the objective historical-grammatical method, we can affirm the multi-faceted roles of Joshua, underscoring the unity and integrity of the text and the events it recounts.

The Book of Joshua is crucial for our understanding of Israel's early history as it encapsulates the account of the conquest and partitioning of Canaan. Unfortunately, skepticism surrounds the book's authorship, date, and historicity, mostly emanating from higher-critical methodologies. However, the internal and external evidence for Joshua's authorship is robust and compelling, supporting the historical-grammatical interpretation approach.

The Credentials of Joshua as Author

Joshua, the servant and successor of Moses, was both a military leader and a spiritual guide to Israel. The Scriptures portray him as an individual who exhibited an unwavering faith in Jehovah. His experience in the leadership and spiritual spheres qualifies him to pen down events he personally witnessed. Acts 7:45 and Hebrews 4:8 acknowledge Joshua, thus bolstering his historical veracity as a figure in the biblical narrative.

Internal Evidence

The book itself carries internal evidence suggesting that an eyewitness was responsible for the accounts. One of the strongest pointers is Joshua 6:25, which mentions the sparing of Rahab and her family, an incident that Joshua directly supervised. Additionally, Joshua 24:26 states, "Then Joshua wrote these words in the book of God's law." The text attributes the writing directly to Joshua, substantiating his authorship.

Prophetic Consistency

Joshua's prophetic role is evident in the curse he pronounced upon Jericho (Joshua 6:26), a curse that saw fulfillment some five centuries later in the days of King Ahab (1 Kings 16:33-34). Such long-range prophecy substantiates the book's authenticity and Joshua's prophetic role, marking him as an inspired writer.

Later Scriptural References

The historicity and authenticity of the Book of Joshua gain further validation from subsequent scriptural references. The Psalms (e.g., Psalms 44:1-3; 78:54-55; 135:10-12), the Prophets like Isaiah (Isaiah 28:21), and even New Testament figures like Paul (Acts 13:19; Hebrews 11:30-31) and James (James 2:25) refer to the events in Joshua. These references illustrate a consistent scriptural tradition affirming the book's historicity and authorship.

Timeframe and Date

The book covers a span of about 20 years, beginning with Israel's entry into Canaan in approximately 1406 B.C.E. up to around 1353 B.C.E., likely the year of Joshua's death. The book itself was probably completed shortly before Joshua's passing, around 1353 B.C.E. The timeframe is consistent with the chronological and geographical markers provided within the text, reinforcing its historical credibility.

The Name "Joshua"

The Hebrew name Yehoh·shu'a', meaning "Jehovah Is Salvation," aptly describes Joshua's role in the Israelite history. The Septuagint uses the term I·e·sous', from which the name Jesus is derived. Joshua stands as a "splendid prophetic type of 'our Lord Jesus Christ'" (Romans 5:1), as both are saviors in their respective contexts.

Joshua as a Reliable Witness

Joshua was an integral part of Israel's leadership, from serving Moses during the Exodus to leading the conquest of Canaan. In all these, he remained a steadfast worshiper of Jehovah. His competence in leadership, military prowess, and above all, his spiritual insight makes him a reliable witness. He penned down events and teachings that would fortify faith in Jehovah, and consequently, his account warrants trust and acceptance.

The Book of Joshua is more than a historical chronicle; it's a theological narrative that emphasizes Jehovah's faithfulness in fulfilling His promises. The book exhibits internal consistency and is corroborated by subsequent scriptural narratives, thereby affirming its authorship and historicity. While higher criticism raises questions regarding its authorship and date, an examination grounded in the historical-grammatical method provides a comprehensive vindication of traditional viewpoints. It supports the conclusion that Joshua, the servant of Jehovah and the leader of Israel, was the qualified and reliable author of this inspired text.

The conservative approach to Scriptural interpretation recognizes the book as both an accurate historical account and an inspired text, thereby affirming the integrity and inerrancy of Scripture. Joshua's authentic voice is critical for understanding Israel's early history, God's faithfulness, and the inherent reliability of the biblical record. Therefore, rejecting skeptical views of its authorship and date, we affirm Joshua as the author, writing at around 1353 B.C.E., during his lifetime. This approach is not only consistent with the internal evidence within the Book of Joshua but also aligns with the broader Scriptural canon and the historical-grammatical method of interpretation.

Authenticity, Authorship, and Date of Judges

The period of the Judges in Israelite history occupies a unique and transformative space between the conquest of Canaan under Joshua and the establishment of the monarchy with Saul. It's a period characterized by cycles of apostasy, foreign oppression, divine deliverance, and periods of peace. The historical-grammatical method, respecting the text's integrity and its human and divine authorship, aids in appreciating this volatile yet pivotal era in Israel's history.

A Covenantal Test

The period served as a litmus test for Israel's commitment to the Mosaic covenant, which bound them to Jehovah as His people. The Book of Judges showcases repeated cycles of Israel's disobedience to the covenant, resulting in foreign oppression. Jehovah would then raise a deliverer or "judge" to liberate the Israelites, highlighting God's patience and faithfulness even in the face of persistent disobedience. This pattern testifies to the gravity and sanctity of the covenantal relationship between Israel and Jehovah.

Political and Social Fragmentation

This era marks a decentralized form of governance. Each tribe largely operated autonomously, and the term "judge" often referred to tribal or regional leaders rather than a single, centralized authority. This political fragmentation was both a cause and effect of Israel's recurrent apostasy, as it failed to consolidate the nation morally and spiritually.

Theological Framework

Theologically, Judges exemplifies the concept of divine retribution, a core tenet in the Old Testament. Jehovah would mete out judgment or salvation based on Israel's covenantal obedience or disobedience. Figures like Gideon, Samson, and Deborah were not just military leaders but also spiritual reformers who were raised by Jehovah at strategic points to bring Israel back to covenant faithfulness.

Gender Roles and Cultural Aspects

This period also offers a nuanced understanding of gender roles and social dynamics. Deborah stands out as a female judge and prophetess, leading Israel to military victory. Her story, along with that of Jael, emphasizes that Jehovah could work through anyone—regardless of gender—to deliver His people.

Edward D. Andrews

What about Deborah of Ancient Israel Being Used to Support Modern Day Female Pastors?

In the Old Testament Deborah was a prophetess[1] in Israel. Deborah the wife of Lappidoth encouraged Judge Barak in the work he was assigned by God. So, Deborah encourages judge Barak like a wife would encourage her pastor husband of the church, offering moral support. Deborah had yet one other responsibility as well. She was also apparently settling conflicts by giving God's answer to problems that had come up. – Judges 4:4-5.

Again, Deborah was a prophetess in Israel. There was never a female ruler or judge in ancient Israel. Deborah was a proclaimer of God's Word. Her being an Old Testament prophetess is not the same being a New Testament pastor (elder). She never taught the Word of God. The prophets were not the teachers who taught the Israelite people. They were given the responsibility of sharing God's Word. They were a spokesperson for God. It was the responsibility of the priests and Levites to teach God's law to the nation of Israel. (Lev. 10:11; 14:57; 2Ch 15:3; 35:3) Yes, Judges 4:4 tells us that "Now Deborah, a prophetess, the wife of Lappidoth, was judging Israel at that time." In the Old Testament, there was no hesitation in Israel to involve women as prophets. Women identified as prophets in ancient Israel were Miriam (Ex. 15:20), Deborah (Judg. 4:4), Huldah (2 Kings 22:14), Noadiah (Neh. 6:14), and the unnamed wife of Isaiah (Isa. 8:3). We could rightly add Hannah as well (1 Sam. 2:1–10) See also Anna in Luke 2:36. Lastly, Deborah was used to offer moral support for Barak, who was shirking his responsibilities.

Ethical Narratives

Stories from this era offer complex ethical situations. For instance, the vow of Jephthah and its consequences evoke deep theological and ethical discussions. Similarly, the narratives of Gideon and Samson

---

[1] Other prophetesses included Miriam, Huldah, and the wife of Isaiah.—Exodus 15:20; 2 Kings 22:14; Isaiah 8:3.

offer a glimpse into the complexities of leadership, divine guidance, and human frailty.

Introduction of Key Themes

This period sets the stage for several key theological themes that would become crucial in later Scriptures. Concepts of kingship, idolatry, divine deliverance, and covenantal faithfulness are all rooted in the experiences and narratives of the Judges era.

The Hebrew name for the book of Judges is "Shophetim," derived from the root "shaphat," which fundamentally means to "judge," "govern," or "vindicate." This title is most fitting for the subject matter covered in the book. At its core, the book narrates the activities of specific leaders in Israel known as "judges." However, the term "judge" as used in the context of this book carries broader connotations than the modern legal sense of the term.

The judges were not merely judicial figures presiding over legal disputes, although that was part of their role. They were charismatic leaders, raised up by Jehovah at specific times to deliver Israel from external oppressors. These judges acted as military leaders, spiritual guides, and, at times, as civil administrators. Their multifaceted roles included upholding justice and law, rescuing the Israelites from their enemies, and turning the people's hearts back to Jehovah. They were intermediaries between Jehovah and the Israelites and were empowered by Him to act on His behalf to guide, govern, and save His people.

The period of the judges was a cyclical one, characterized by a pattern of apostasy, oppression, repentance, and deliverance. Israel would fall into sin and idolatry; Jehovah would allow them to be oppressed by foreign nations as a result; the people would cry out in repentance, and Jehovah would raise up a judge to deliver them. Each judge was a tool in Jehovah's hands, vindicating His righteousness and demonstrating His mercy.

Therefore, the Hebrew name "Shophetim" encapsulates these various roles of the judges effectively. It is an appropriate term that goes beyond the judicial function to encompass the broader, divinely commissioned roles these individuals played in guiding Israel during a particularly turbulent period in its history. They were not simply decision-makers but rather God-ordained leaders, fulfilling Jehovah's will in various capacities to guide His people.

In the absence of a centralized governance structure or a reigning monarch during this period, the judges played a pivotal role in maintaining the covenant relationship between Jehovah and Israel. They stand as witnesses to the divine covenantal faithfulness despite Israel's frequent lapses into unfaithfulness. Therefore, the name "Shophetim" or Judges profoundly resonates with the spiritual, judicial, and military dimensions that this book encompasses, making the Hebrew title exceptionally fitting.

The authorship of the book of Judges has been a subject of considerable discussion and debate. While the book itself does not explicitly identify its author, the most plausible candidate within conservative circles is the prophet Samuel. Samuel stands as a transitional figure in Israelite history, bridging the period between the judges and the monarchy. As the last judge and the first prophet in a line of faithful prophets, Samuel had both the spiritual insight and historical context to compose a book detailing the period of the judges.

Samuel was not just a prophet but also a priest and a judge, serving in all three capacities during his lifetime. He was a pivotal figure at a time when Israel was transitioning from a theocracy guided by judges to a monarchy. This unique positioning gave Samuel a comprehensive view of the spiritual, social, and political landscape of Israel. As a devoted servant of Jehovah, Samuel had both the spiritual mandate and the narrative skill to encapsulate this volatile period of Israel's history into written form.

Samuel's life and ministry exemplified the very essence of what a judge was supposed to be. Like the judges before him, Samuel led military campaigns against Israel's enemies, most notably the Philistines. He also presided over legal disputes and, more importantly, called the people to repentance and faithfulness to Jehovah. His efforts to centralize worship in Israel and his establishment of prophetic schools indicate his concern for both the spiritual and social welfare of the Israelites.

It is significant that Samuel was responsible for anointing both Saul and David, the first two kings of Israel. This anointing represented a seismic shift in Israel's governance, moving from ad-hoc leadership provided by the judges to a more structured form of governance through monarchy. Who better to record the history and deeds of the judges than one who himself served as a judge and ushered in the age that would succeed it?

Samuel's life and ministry were dedicated to maintaining the purity of Jehovah's worship against the corrupting influences of Canaanite religious practices. Given his spiritual and historical role, he had both the motive and the resources to compile the accounts of the judges, who had similarly fought against idolatry and led the people back to Jehovah.

Traditionally, Jewish scholarship attributes the authorship of Judges to Samuel, and this view aligns well with what we know of his life, ministry, and the timing of the events recorded in the book. Therefore, within a framework that values conservative, literal, and historical-grammatical interpretation of Scripture, Samuel emerges as the most logical and fitting author of the book of Judges.

When was Judges Written?

Two expressions in the book help us to find the answer. The first is this: "But the Jebusites keep on dwelling . . . in Jerusalem down to this day." (Judg. 1:21, UASV) Since King David captured "the stronghold of Zion" from the Jebusites in the eighth year of his reign, or in 1003 B.C.E., Judges must have been written before that date. (2 Sam. 5:4-7) The second expression occurs four times: "In those days there was no king in Israel." (Judg. 17:6; 18:1; 19:1; 21:25, UASV) Hence, the record was written down at a time when there was a "king in Israel," that is, after Saul became the first king in 1050 B.C.E. It must therefore be dated between 1050 and 1003 B.C.E. Therefore, the writing would have been completed by: c. 1003 B.C.E.

Calculating the Time Period of Judges

Calculating the time period covered by the book of Judges and its date of composition involves careful examination of historical clues provided within the text itself, along with a few external indicators. It is a task that must be handled judiciously to preserve the historical integrity of the narrative while also maintaining fidelity to the objective historical-grammatical method of interpretation.

One critical clue within the book of Judges appears in Judges 1:21, where it states, "But the Jebusites keep on dwelling . . . in Jerusalem down to this day" (UASV). This statement provides a historical marker indicating that the book was penned before the conquest of Jerusalem by King David. David captured Jerusalem from the Jebusites in the eighth year of his reign, or approximately 1003 B.C.E. (2 Sam. 5:4-7). This fact, therefore, sets an upper limit for the date of composition.

Another set of phrases that appear recurrently in Judges are: "In those days there was no king in Israel" (Judg. 17:6; 18:1; 19:1; 21:25, UASV). This implies that the book was written during a period when Israel did have a king, thereby narrowing the timeframe for its composition to after the beginning of the Israelite monarchy. The first king, Saul, began his reign around 1050 B.C.E. This provides a lower limit for the date of composition.

So, given these internal markers, we can fairly estimate that the book of Judges was written sometime between 1050 B.C.E. and 1003 B.C.E. This aligns well with the notion that Samuel could be the author, as his lifetime straddled this transitional period from the rule of judges to the establishment of the monarchy.

To calculate the period covered by the events in the book of Judges, we would primarily rely on the internal chronological markers within the text. These markers often specify the lengths of peaceful rule or foreign oppression. For example, Othniel judged Israel for 40 years (Judg. 3:11), and Ehud's leadership brought about 80 years of peace (Judg. 3:30). By summing up these periods along with the tenures of the other judges, and adding transitional periods of foreign domination, we can get an approximate duration. However, caution must be exercised in this calculation. Some periods could overlap, or judges may have ruled different territories concurrently.

While the book of Judges does not offer a straightforward timeline from beginning to end, these internal chronological markers can be pieced together to provide an estimated range of years that the book covers. However, this should be viewed as a composite and approximate timeline, not an absolute chronology.

Thus, by adhering to a conservative, literal approach to the text, the dating of the book of Judges and the period it describes can be estimated with reasonable historical accuracy. This conservative approach to the text allows us to navigate the complexities of the narrative while maintaining a high regard for its inerrancy and authority as Scripture.

Authenticity of Judges

The question of authenticity is a critical one when dealing with any ancient text, and it holds especially true for books that form the foundation of religious traditions. Given its historical, theological, and literary contributions, the book of Judges has an indisputable place in the canon of Scripture. Various lines of evidence attest to its authenticity and contribute to its accepted status among both Hebrew and Christian Scriptures.

Canonical Recognition

One of the most important indicators of the authenticity of Judges is its longstanding inclusion in the Hebrew Bible. The Jewish community has always recognized Judges as part of their canon of Scripture. This recognition is not a trivial matter; it attests to the book's acceptance and authoritative status throughout millennia, reflecting its continuity and consistency with the rest of the biblical canon.

Intertextual References

Judges is also referenced and echoed in subsequent biblical books, adding weight to its authenticity. For example, Psalm 83:9-18 speaks of the defeat of various enemies of Israel, clearly drawing on the military victories recounted in Judges. Isaiah 9:4 and 10:26 both allude to the divine deliverance described in Judges. Furthermore, Hebrews 11:32-34 mentions figures like Gideon, Barak, Samson, and Jephthah in its litany of the faithful, confirming the book's credibility and impact on later religious thought.

Theological Consistency

The theological message of Judges aligns seamlessly with the overall message of the Bible, further proving its authenticity. It echoes the recurring biblical themes of sin, repentance, divine mercy, and deliverance. While the book does not shy away from highlighting Israel's failures and moral lapses, it continually emphasizes Jehovah's role as the ultimate Deliverer of His people. This theological emphasis assures that the glory for Israel's deliverance is attributed to Jehovah and not to any human judge. The book serves as a case study of the covenantal relationship between Jehovah and Israel, demonstrating how Jehovah's loving-kindness endures despite Israel's shortcomings.

Historical Credibility

The historical events described in Judges align well with what is known from other ancient Near Eastern sources and archaeological findings, though the latter should not be the primary method for confirming biblical authenticity. Judges does not read like a mythologized or idealized history; it records both victories and defeats, blessings and curses. This lends the book a level of historical credibility that further affirms its authenticity.

Through its canonical recognition, its reflection in later biblical texts, its theological consistency, and its historical credibility, the book of Judges proves its authenticity beyond a reasonable doubt. Its integrity as a piece of inspired Scripture shows it to be not merely a collection of stories but a theologically rich narrative that contributes to the inerrancy and the authority of the biblical canon.

Archaeological Support for Judges

Archaeological evidence robustly supports the historical accounts in the book of Judges. The discoveries at Ugarit, for instance, have cast a glaring light on the detestable practices of the Baal religion. What we find in these archaeological records are not merely confirmations of the physical existence of places or artifacts; they deepen our understanding of the socio-religious context in which the Israelites were living. It shows the extent to which Canaanite idolatry had permeated the land, thus vindicating the biblical account of why drastic measures were needed to preserve the spiritual purity of Israel.

Jehovah's Decree on Baal Worshipers

Understanding the nature of Baal worship provides a necessary backdrop for comprehending Jehovah's stern decree against the Canaanites and any Israelites who turned to Baal worship. Baalism was a corrosive spiritual force that posed an existential threat to Israel's unique covenantal relationship with Jehovah.

The Canaanite religious practices were a travesty to all that Jehovah had intended for humanity. They not only violated the laws of Jehovah but made a mockery of them. At these high places and shrines, detestable human sacrifices were carried out; sons and daughters were offered up to Baal, much like what is condemned in Jeremiah 32:35. Moreover, the sanctity of human sexuality was degraded through temple prostitution in the worship of Ashtoreth, Baal's consort. These were not merely "alternative religious practices"; they were affronts to the holy character of Jehovah.

When Jehovah decreed that "Your eye shall not pity them, neither shall you serve their gods, for that would be a snare to you" (Deut. 7:16, UASV), He was ensuring the preservation of the nation He had set apart. It was an act of judgment upon a system that was fundamentally evil and would lead His people away from the path of righteousness. To allow Baal worship to persist would have created a snare or trap for the Israelites, endangering their spiritual welfare and compromising their divine mission. In this context, Jehovah's decree for the extermination of Baal worshipers was not arbitrary but a righteous judgment against a religion steeped in practices that dehumanized its followers and were abhorrent to Him.

Both archaeological evidence and a close examination of the theology surrounding Baalism affirm the wisdom and justice of Jehovah's commands as given in Judges. It also bolsters the authenticity of the book, as the material culture unearthed by archaeologists and the spiritual admonitions of Jehovah found in the text align in a manner that is best explained by the book's genuine historicity and divine inspiration.

Authenticity, Authorship, and Date of Ruth

Beyond the Love Story

The book of Ruth, while often celebrated as a heartwarming love story, is far more than that. It serves as a poignant narrative on loyalty, faith, and God's providence. Taking place during the period of the judges, a time marked by Israel's moral and spiritual decline, the story of Ruth offers a striking counter-narrative. Here we find individuals like Ruth and Boaz who embody faithfulness, integrity, and a deep respect for Jehovah's law, standing in stark contrast to the disarray and disobedience prevalent in Israel at that time.

Ruth, a Moabitess, leaves her native land and gods to cling to Naomi and the God of Israel. Her famous declaration, "Your people shall be my people, and your God my God" (Ruth 1:16, UASV), is not just romantic or poetic language but a solemn commitment to Jehovah. Ruth places herself under the wings of the God of Israel (Ruth 2:12, UASV), signifying her complete trust and commitment to Him. This demonstrates her conversion from idolatry to the worship of the true God, an act that not only defines her own destiny but also has ramifications for the lineage of the Messiah.

Special Mention in the Bible

The account's significance extends to its genealogical implications. Ruth is listed in the genealogy of King David (Ruth 4:17-22, UASV), and by extension, in the genealogy of Jesus Christ as recorded in the New Testament (Matthew 1:5). For a foreign woman to be included in this lineage underscores the universal scope of God's redemptive plan. Ruth's story is more than a sentimental tale; it's a narrative deeply embedded in the unfolding of Jehovah's divine scheme for mankind. The integrity and faithfulness displayed by Ruth and Boaz model the qualities that Jehovah values, even in times when such qualities are scarce.

Therefore, while Ruth is a love story, it is also a story about the love of Jehovah for His people and for all those who would come to serve Him faithfully. It serves as a testament to Jehovah's enduring faithfulness and His willingness to include all, regardless of their background, in His plan of redemption. It reveals the qualities that are pleasing to Jehovah, such as loyalty, kindness, and a respect for the sanctity of marriage and family, thereby offering eternal lessons that extend far beyond the immediate narrative.

Timing of the Events

The events of the book of Ruth occur during the period of the judges. Specifically, the narrative opens with the phrase, "In the days when the judges ruled" (Ruth 1:1, UASV). This places the story in the context of Israel's tumultuous history between the death of Joshua and the emergence of the monarchy. Based on a literal interpretation of the biblical chronology, the events took place in the 12th century B.C.E.

Date of Writing

While the book itself does not directly specify when it was written, it can be inferred that it was likely penned before the reign of King David due to its genealogical focus, culminating in the birth of Obed, the grandfather of David (Ruth 4:17-22, UASV). Therefore, the composition of the book occurred between the late period of the judges and the early period of the monarchy, in the 11th century B.C.E.

Authorship

The book of Ruth does not explicitly state its author. However, it is reasonable to consider Samuel as the author. As a prophet and a pivotal figure during the transition from the period of the judges to the monarchy, Samuel had both the theological and historical context to record this narrative. His role in anointing both Saul and David puts him in a unique position to appreciate the genealogical and messianic significance of Ruth's story. Moreover, Samuel was a devoted servant of Jehovah, and his commitment to accurately recording the history and moral lessons of Israel would naturally extend to the story of Ruth, a figure crucial to the Davidic lineage.

Therefore, considering the textual and historical evidence, the book of Ruth was written by Samuel in the 11th century B.C.E., narrating events from the 12th century B.C.E. during the period of the judges.

Canonical Recognition

The canonicity of the book of Ruth is affirmed without dispute. It has consistently been recognized as a part of the Hebrew canon by the Jewish community. Further confirmation is supplied in the New Testament where Ruth is listed in the genealogy of Jesus Christ in Matthew 1:5. This mention indicates divine inspiration and stamps the book with authoritative canonical status.

Dead Sea Scrolls

Adding further weight to its canonical status are the fragments of the book of Ruth discovered among the Dead Sea Scrolls starting in 1947. These fragments were found in the company of other uncontested canonical books, confirming its long-held authoritative status.

Harmony with Mosaic Law and Kingdom Purposes

The book of Ruth is fully in line with the Law of Moses and Jehovah's Kingdom purposes. For instance, while the Israelites were prohibited from marrying idol-worshiping Canaanites and Moabites (Deut. 7:1-4; 23:3, 4), this did not exclude foreigners like Ruth who renounced idolatry and committed to worshiping Jehovah. Furthermore, the book pays meticulous attention to the observance of the Mosaic law concerning repurchase and levirate marriage (Deut. 25:5-10). The account's alignment with the law in such detail is additional evidence of its authoritative status.

In summary, the book of Ruth meets all the criteria for canonicity. It has consistently been recognized by the Jewish community, is listed in the genealogy of Jesus Christ, was found among the Dead Sea Scrolls, and harmonizes perfectly with both Mosaic Law and Jehovah's Kingdom purposes.

Edward D. Andrews

CHAPTER 3 Defending First and Second Samuel, First and Second Kings

Authenticity, Authorship, and Date of 1 Samuel

The Book of First Samuel marks a watershed moment in the organization of the nation of Israel: the transition from a theocratic system led by judges to a monarchy. Prior to this, Israel was guided by judges who served not merely as legal arbiters but also as military and spiritual leaders. These judges were divinely appointed and guided Israel on a case-by-case basis, intervening during periods of distress. The shift toward a monarchy began at the behest of the Israelites themselves, who asked Samuel, the last judge, for a king "like all the nations" (1 Sam. 8:5, UASV). Although Jehovah had originally designed Israel to be a theocracy, He acceded to their request while warning them through Samuel about the worldly implications and burdens a monarchy would bring.

The conditions that followed this transformation were multifaceted. On one hand, the monarchy provided centralized authority, administrative efficiency, and military organization, all of which were embodied in the reigns of David and Solomon. On the other hand, this system opened the door for potential abuses of power, heavy taxation, and, most importantly, the drifting away from a God-centered governance to a human-centered one. These challenges were manifested in the subsequent reigns, particularly in the divided kingdom period as described in First and Second Kings.

Thus, First Samuel sets the stage for a significant organizational shift in Israel, one that carried both opportunities for national consolidation and grave risks of spiritual decline. The subsequent books (Second Samuel, First and Second Kings) provide the narrative of how these opportunities and challenges played out in the history of Israel.

Who wrote First Samuel

The Book of First Samuel was written by multiple authors, each with qualifications that made them uniquely suited to document this critical period in Israel's history. The primary author was Samuel himself, who wrote the first 24 chapters of the book. His name, which means "Name of God," is an indication of his devotion and his role as an upholder of Jehovah's name. Samuel was not just a judge and a priest; he was also a prophet who had been serving Jehovah from his youth. His intimate relationship with Jehovah made him an excellent choice to begin the record of Israel's transition from a theocratic government to a monarchy.

Upon Samuel's death, the responsibility of recording the events passed to Gad and Nathan. Their work is indicated in 1 Chronicles 29:29, which states: "As for the affairs of David the king, the first ones and the last, there they are written among the words of Samuel the seer and among the words of Nathan the prophet and among the words of Gad the visionary." Like Samuel, both Gad and Nathan were prophets. Nathan was notable for his boldness in confronting King David about his sin with Bathsheba, and Gad served as a royal advisor. Importantly, all three authors were trusted prophets of Jehovah and were staunchly opposed to the rampant idolatry that plagued Israel. This gives weight to their records, making them reliable chroniclers of the events that unfolded during this pivotal time.

Date and Period Covered

Originally, the books of First and Second Samuel were one unified work, commonly referred to simply as "Samuel" in the Hebrew tradition. The division into two separate books occurred when the Hebrew Bible was translated into Greek in the Septuagint. The Greek language generally requires more words to express the same ideas as Hebrew, and as a result, the original single scroll became too lengthy and was divided for practical reasons. It was later Christian tradition that adopted this division, naming the two parts First and Second Samuel.

First Samuel was completed in the early 10th century B.C.E. As mentioned earlier, the book had multiple authors, with Samuel writing the first 24 chapters, and Gad and Nathan completing the account. The book covers a period from the birth of Samuel to the end of Saul's reign, roughly spanning the years from 1105 B.C.E. to 1010 B.C.E.

This time frame encapsulates several major events: the period of the judges concluding with Samuel, the anointing of Saul as the first king of Israel, his subsequent reign, and the anointing of David as his successor. The narrative provides an essential historical and theological link between the era of the judges and the establishment of the Israelite monarchy, making it a pivotal work in the Scriptures.

Accuracy of First Samuel

The accuracy of the record in First Samuel is supported by several lines of evidence. For starters, the geographical and topographical details mentioned in the book align well with what is known from other historical and archaeological sources. Names of places such as Shiloh, where the Ark of the Covenant was initially kept, and cities like Gibeah, Saul's hometown, are well-attested in external records and excavations.

Secondly, the book presents consistent internal details. The character traits, decisions, and outcomes of people like Samuel, Saul, and David are depicted in a manner that is consistent throughout not just First Samuel but also into Second Samuel. Such internal coherence is a mark of a reliable historical document.

Additionally, the events described in First Samuel dovetail seamlessly with other biblical records. For example, David's emergence as a key figure towards the end of First Samuel sets the stage for the subsequent accounts in Second Samuel and First Kings, which are themselves corroborated by external historical records, such as the Tel Dan Stele mentioning the "House of David."

Furthermore, First Samuel's depiction of cultural and societal norms, such as the role of prophets, the function of Levitical priests, and the practices of ancient warfare, fit well within what we know of Near Eastern cultures during the late second millennium B.C.E.

Finally, 1 Chronicles 29:29 refers to "the words of Samuel the seer," affirming Samuel's role as a reliable historical source. Samuel's integrity and prophetic office lend credence to the notion that his records are both accurate and divinely inspired.

In summary, the book of First Samuel stands as a reliable and accurate historical document, supported by both internal consistency and external lines of evidence, including geography, culture, and corroborative biblical accounts.

Genuineness of First Samuel

The genuineness of the book of First Samuel is affirmed by several factors within the biblical text itself. Notably, 1 Chronicles 29:29 specifically mentions "the words of Samuel the seer," thereby testifying to Samuel's role in chronicling events and thus attesting to the authenticity of First Samuel. This statement not only confirms Samuel's authorship of parts of the book but also validates the reliability of the record contained therein.

Moreover, the New Testament itself shows an awareness of the narratives in First Samuel. For example, the Apostle Paul in his sermon at Antioch in Pisidia refers to the selection of Saul and David as kings of Israel (Acts 13:21-22). While Paul does not cite First Samuel directly, his recounting of these events clearly presupposes the historical account provided in First Samuel.

The narratives of David found in First Samuel are also affirmed in later biblical books, such as Psalms and Second Samuel. David, traditionally the author of many Psalms, often alludes to events in his life that are described in First Samuel. For example, Psalms 59 is linked to the events described in First Samuel 19:11, where Saul sends men to watch David's house and kill him.

It is also worth noting that the themes and events of First Samuel are interwoven with those of other Old Testament books. The seamless flow of history and theology between the era of the judges (as described in the book of Judges) and the monarchy (as detailed in Second Samuel and First Kings) lends further support to the genuineness of First Samuel.

Essential points that offer even stronger proofs of the inspiration and authenticity of the book of First Samuel. Let's delve into each of them:

1. Deuteronomy 17:14 predicts that Israel would eventually ask for a king. This is precisely what happens in 1 Samuel 8:5, demonstrating a striking fulfillment of Jehovah's prophecy. This affirms not only the accuracy but also the divine origin of the book's contents.

2. The prophet Hosea in Hosea 13:11 confirms the record of First Samuel by citing Jehovah's words about giving Israel a king in anger and taking him away in fury. This directly supports the narrative found in First Samuel and verifies its historicity and inspiration.

3. In Acts 3:24, Peter identifies Samuel as a prophet who had 'plainly declared the days' of Jesus, thereby confirming that Samuel was indeed inspired when writing the portions attributed to him in First Samuel.

4. The Apostle Paul, in Acts 13:20-22, quotes from 1 Samuel 13:14 while outlining the history of Israel. His quoting from First Samuel lends further weight to the book's authenticity.

5. Furthermore, Jesus Himself corroborates the events recorded in First Samuel by referring to the incident where David asks for the showbread in Matthew 12:1-4. Jesus' reference to this specific event is a clear endorsement of the book's historical accuracy.

6. As you mentioned, 1 Chronicles 29:29, written by Ezra, also confirms the authenticity of First Samuel by citing "the words of Samuel the seer," among others.

Each of these points builds a compelling case for the inspiration and authenticity of First Samuel. These references span both Testaments and come from prophets, apostles, and even the Messiah, making a robust argument for the book's genuine place within the canon of Scripture. In summary, the genuineness of First Samuel is attested to both directly and indirectly by other biblical writers, thereby affirming its authentic place within the canon of Scripture.

Authentic and True

The internal biblical evidence affirming the authenticity of First Samuel is indeed strong and multifaceted. One significant point is the book's foundational role in providing the original account of David's activities. This has vast implications for the rest of Scripture because David is a key figure in both Testaments, with his lineage leading to the Messiah himself. Any subsequent reference to David throughout the Bible inherently authenticates the book of Samuel.

Furthermore, the book of First Samuel is explicitly connected to various Psalms, as indicated in their superscriptions. For example, Psalm 59 references the event described in 1 Samuel 19:11, where Saul sends men to David's house to watch it and to kill him in the morning. Likewise, Psalm 34 is linked to the episode in 1 Samuel 21:13-14, where David pretends to be insane before Abimelech, who drives him away. Psalm 142 connects either with David's time in the cave recorded in 1 Samuel 22:1 or with the events of 1 Samuel 24:1,3 when David was in the cave of En Gedi.

These psalms not only narrate the emotional and spiritual states of David during these life events but also serve as a cross-reference back to the original story in First Samuel. This creates a strong internal witness within Scripture itself, corroborating the authenticity of First Samuel.

In summary, the internal evidence within the Bible clearly and definitively supports the view that First Samuel is an authentic, inspired part of God's Word.

Authenticity, Authorship, and Date of 2 Samuel

Background and Development

Second Samuel opens against the grim backdrop of Saul's death, as recounted at the end of First Samuel. With the death of King Saul, a significant shift occurs in the narrative focus. The account transitions from the tragic end of Saul's reign to the beginning of David's kingship.

Second Samuel can be divided into two major parts. The first part (Chapters 1-10) focuses on David's rise to power and the consolidation of his kingdom. Here, David is anointed as king over Judah and subsequently over all Israel. The narrative covers his capture of Jerusalem, making it his political and religious capital, as well as his military campaigns against the enemies of Israel, like the Philistines and the Ammonites. This section culminates in the covenant that Jehovah makes with David, promising that his lineage will establish an everlasting kingdom (2 Samuel 7).

The second part (Chapters 11-24) presents a darker picture, detailing David's moral failures and the subsequent consequences. The account of David's adultery with Bathsheba and the murder of her husband, Uriah the Hittite, is one of the most well-known episodes. These actions bring about a series of tragic events, including the rebellion of Absalom and the plague that falls upon Israel as a result of David's ill-advised census.

In both of these sections, Jehovah plays a pivotal role as the Sovereign orchestrator of events. Whether in victory or defeat, the narrative continuously portrays David as reliant on Jehovah's guidance and divine providence.

In terms of chronology, the events of Second Samuel take place over approximately 40 years, from around 1010 B.C.E. to 970 B.C.E. The account therefore serves as a vital historical and theological bridge between the period of the judges and the establishment of a united monarchy under David, a man after Jehovah's own heart.

Naming and Authorship of Second Samuel

The name "Second Samuel" originates from the Septuagint, the ancient Greek translation of the Hebrew Scriptures. Originally, the book of Samuel was a single work in the Hebrew canon but was divided into First and Second Samuel in the Septuagint for convenience due to its length. The Latin Vulgate and subsequent Christian translations followed this division.

The primary writer of Second Samuel was the prophet Samuel, who was qualified both as a prophet and a historian. Samuel was the last of the judges and the first of the prophets in Israel's history. As the anointer of both Saul and David, he was directly involved in the transition from the theocratic rule of judges to the monarchical rule of kings in Israel. It is worth noting that the events in the latter part of the book occurred after Samuel's death. These were likely recorded by Nathan the prophet and Gad the seer. Both Nathan and Gad were close advisors to King David and were also recognized prophets in Israel. They were intimately involved in the religious and political affairs of the time, making them well-suited for recording the events in an authoritative manner.

Focus of the Record

In writing Second Samuel, the writers aimed to present a historical and theological account focused on the establishment and challenges of the Davidic monarchy. Importantly, they did not seek to preserve just any record; they carefully chronicled the events that bore significant theological importance, particularly those that highlighted the role of Jehovah as the Supreme Ruler of Israel. Through narratives, genealogies, and poetic songs, they documented how Jehovah's purpose unfolded in relation to Israel and the Davidic line.

These prophets did not flinch from recording both the triumphs and failures of David and his successors. Their record remains an indispensable testament to Jehovah's covenantal relationship with Israel and His divine purposes culminating in the Davidic line, which eventually led to the Messiah.

Time Period and Completion Date of Second Samuel

Second Samuel covers the period beginning with the death of King Saul, which occurred in **1020 B.C.E.**, and concludes with the final words of David around **970 B.C.E.** This is a span of approximately 50 years. Within this timeframe, the book documents the establishment of the Davidic monarchy, the consolidation of the kingdom, and the spiritual and moral challenges faced by David and his household.

The writing of Second Samuel was likely completed shortly after the events it describes. Since the book includes the last words of David, it can be firmly asserted that the writing was finished around **970 B.C.E.** This would mean that the contemporaneous prophets, particularly Nathan and Gad who were close advisors to David, contributed to the completion of this book after Samuel's death. They had direct access to the events and were well-qualified to compile this historical account.

Canonical Status of Second Samuel

Divine Inspiration and Continuity with First Samuel One of the most compelling reasons for the inclusion of Second Samuel in the biblical canon is its clear continuity with First Samuel. It picks up directly where First Samuel ends, providing a seamless narrative that covers the reign of King David. The text itself exhibits the qualities of divine inspiration, from its intricate narrative structure to its depth of insight into human character, divine justice, and the unfolding of God's plan for Israel.

Historical Reliability Second Samuel provides detailed accounts of events, individuals, and places that align with what is known from other historical sources, including archaeological findings. For example, the Tel Dan Stele, an inscribed stone discovered in northern Israel, refers to the "House of David," corroborating the Davidic dynasty chronicled in the Scriptures. This gives credence to the historical narratives in Second Samuel, further affirming its canonical status.

Theological Consistency The theology presented in Second Samuel is consistent with the rest of the Hebrew Scriptures. The book continues to elaborate on themes introduced in First Samuel and earlier books, such as the importance of obeying Jehovah's law and the consequences of rebellion against divine authority. The development and complexity of these theological themes provide strong evidence of the book's inspired nature and its rightful place in the canon.

Prophetic Elements and Fulfillment Another noteworthy aspect is the book's prophetic elements, which align with fulfilled events. The Davidic covenant, introduced in Second Samuel 7, becomes foundational for the Messianic expectations found in later prophets and writings. The promise that David's kingdom would endure forever is fulfilled in the New Testament through the lineage and reign of Jesus Christ.

Internal and External Testimonies Both Jewish and Christian traditions have historically affirmed the canonicity of Second Samuel. Its teachings, principles, and historical narratives have been cited by other biblical authors, indicating its authoritative status. Moreover, early Jewish literature and Christian church fathers, including Josephus and Augustine, recognized the canonical status of the book.

Preservation and Transmission The meticulous care in the transmission of the text of Second Samuel, as evident from the Dead Sea Scrolls and the Masoretic Text, indicates a reverence for its content that is consistent with it being viewed as Sacred Scripture.

In summary, Second Samuel is an indispensable part of the biblical canon. Its historical reliability, theological consistency, and prophetic elements, along with its seamless continuity with First Samuel and the larger Scriptural narrative, make it both credible and essential for understanding God's unfolding plan for His people.

The Davidic Covenant as the Strongest Reason for the Inspiration of Second Samuel

Divine Revelation through the Davidic Covenant The most compelling reason for accepting Second Samuel as inspired Scripture is the introduction and elaboration of the Davidic Covenant in Chapter 7. This covenant is not merely a historical or cultural agreement but a divine institution that establishes the eternal kingship within David's lineage. This is the bedrock upon which not only the reigns of future Judean kings are understood but also the Messianic prophecies that follow in other books of the Bible.

The Davidic Covenant unequivocally reveals Jehovah's divine plan for an everlasting kingdom rooted in obedience and righteousness. It serves as the theological and eschatological cornerstone for both the Hebrew Scriptures and the New Testament, culminating in the person and work of Jesus Christ. The importance of this covenant transcends its immediate historical context and provides an enduring promise that impacts the unfolding of redemptive history.

Unambiguous Language of Permanence The language used to describe the Davidic Covenant leaves no room for doubt about its divine origin. Phrases like "your house and your kingdom shall be made sure forever before me. Your throne shall be established forever" (2 Samuel 7:16) speak to the eternal nature of this promise, aligning it with Jehovah's immutable character.

Internal and External Validation The concept of an eternal Davidic line is further validated by later prophetic books like Isaiah and Jeremiah, as well as its ultimate fulfillment in the New Testament with the advent of Jesus Christ, who is explicitly described as being of the lineage of David.

Therefore, the Davidic Covenant serves as the strongest reason for recognizing Second Samuel as inspired Scripture. Its theological magnitude, rooted in the very character of Jehovah and His plan for human redemption, situates the book as an indispensable component of the divinely inspired biblical canon.

Authenticity, Authorship, and Date of 1 Kings

The Downfall of Israel's Prosperity and the Inspired Value of First Kings

Roots of Israel's Degeneration into Ruin Israel's descent from prosperity to ruin can be traced back to a series of deviations from the principles and commandments laid down by Jehovah. The narrative in First Kings begins with the glory days under Solomon, who initially adhered to God's wisdom. However, it doesn't take long for the narrative to shift. Solomon's own downfall starts with his intermarriage with foreign wives and culminates in the erection of high places for idol worship. The consequences of these acts are immediate and severe; they divide the kingdom and set in motion the events that lead to Israel's eventual ruin.

The nation, now split into the Kingdom of Israel and the Kingdom of Judah, continues its downward spiral through a series of disobedient and wicked rulers. Many kings that followed Solomon, particularly in the Northern Kingdom, perpetuated idolatry, engaged in alliances with pagan nations, and disregarded the Laws and statutes given by Moses. The nation became increasingly corrupt, and the social, moral, and religious fabrics that once held it together deteriorated. It is this persistent sin and disobedience that led Israel from prosperity to ruin, fulfilling Jehovah's earlier warnings that disobedience would result in cursing and exile (Deuteronomy 28).

First Kings as Inspired and Beneficial Despite the tragic elements within its narrative, First Kings stands as an inspired and beneficial book of the Hebrew Scriptures. It serves as a compelling chronicle of the importance of fidelity to Jehovah's commands and the catastrophic consequences that ensue from straying away from them. It offers timeless lessons on the dangers of idolatry, the value of true worship, and the necessity of heeding prophetic warnings.

The narratives involving the prophets Elijah and Elisha serve as highlights, providing extraordinary accounts of Jehovah's power and faithfulness. The dramatic confrontation between Elijah and the prophets of Baal at Mount Carmel, for example, stands as a timeless lesson about the supremacy of Jehovah over all false gods (1 Kings 18).

Moreover, First Kings contributes to the unfolding redemptive-historical framework of the Bible, leading the reader from the United Monarchy to the divided kingdom, thus setting the stage for both the immediate and future acts of divine deliverance and judgment.

Formation and Compilation of First and Second Kings

Why Two Scrolls First and Second Kings were originally one literary work, often referred to simply as "Kings" in ancient times. The division into two separate books happened primarily for practical reasons. The length of the text made it difficult to contain on a single scroll, which was the primary medium for written works in antiquity. The division most likely took place when the Hebrew Scriptures were translated into Greek in the Septuagint. It was at this time that the text was divided into the books known as First and Second Kings to make them more manageable for reading and copying.

Compilation Process The compilation of First and Second Kings is often attributed to the prophet Jeremiah or another prophet-historian close in time to the events described. It draws upon various sources, including "the book of the acts of Solomon" (1 Kings 11:41), "the book of the chronicles of the kings of Israel," and "the book of the chronicles of the kings of Judah" (1 Kings 14:19, 29). These were most likely official royal records or annals, maintained by royal scribes, that documented significant events, administrative decisions, and other activities of the monarchy.

While the human author drew from these sources, the inspiration and guiding force behind the compilation of First and Second Kings was Jehovah. The author skillfully wove together historical narrative, prophetic warnings, and theological reflections to produce a unified, coherent account that serves not merely as a historical record but also as an inspired commentary on the actions and consequences of Israel's kings.

First and Second Kings cover the history of Israel and Judah from the end of David's reign to the Babylonian captivity, spanning approximately four centuries from the 10th to the 6th centuries B.C.E. This wide-ranging account captures divine judgments, national failures, and moments of faithfulness, rendering a complete picture of God's interaction with His chosen but often disobedient people.

Authorship and Chronology of the Books of Kings

Undoubted Authorship The prophet Jeremiah is traditionally attributed as the author of the books of First and Second Kings. This attribution is based on several factors. First, the timeline in which the Books of Kings were written aligns with the period when Jeremiah was active. Second, stylistic and thematic similarities exist between the Books of Kings and the Book of Jeremiah. For instance, both sets of books emphasize the importance of covenant faithfulness and the disastrous consequences of idolatry. Moreover, Jeremiah had access to the royal archives, which would have been necessary to compile such detailed historical accounts. Given these compelling reasons, Jeremiah is undoubtedly the author of First and Second Kings.

Date of Completion The writing of First and Second Kings was completed in the early part of the 6th century B.C.E., around the time of the Babylonian exile. This is evident from the account itself, which concludes with the release of King Jehoiachin from imprisonment in Babylon (2 Kings 25:27–30), an event that occurred in 561 B.C.E.

Period Covered by First Kings First Kings covers the period from the death of King David to the end of the reign of King Ahab of Israel. Specifically, the book starts with King David's final days and the ascension of Solomon to the throne, and it concludes with the death of Ahab in battle against the Syrians. This covers a span of approximately 118 years, from around 970 B.C.E. to 852 B.C.E. Thus, First Kings offers a focused view into a critical period of Israel's history, replete with lessons and warnings that were divinely guided to be documented for the benefit of future generations.

Secular Confirmation of First Kings

Archaeological Evidence Archaeology serves as a robust external witness to the historical reliability of First Kings. One prominent example is the Tel Dan Stele, a ninth-century B.C.E. inscribed monument discovered in northern Israel. This stele refers to the "House of David," affirming the Davidic dynasty that is central to First Kings. Further, the description of building projects, particularly those of Solomon such as the Temple and his own palace, find resonance in archaeological discoveries of monumental architecture from this period.

Historical Records Secular history, particularly the records of surrounding nations, also corroborate the accounts in First Kings. The Assyrian annals mention various Israelite and Judean kings, as well as events that align with the biblical narrative. For example, the Moabite Stone (also known as the Mesha Stele) mentions Omri, King of Israel, and confirms the Moabite rebellion against Israel as recorded in 1 Kings 16:23-28.

Geographical Data The geographical locations mentioned in First Kings are not mythical places but real locations that have been verified. Cities such as Samaria, Jezreel, and others have been excavated and studied, confirming their existence and role during the time First Kings was written.

Inspired Testimony Confirming the Authenticity of First Kings

Internal Evidence The most compelling testimony regarding the authenticity of First Kings comes from the Scripture itself. The book is part of the Hebrew Bible canon, acknowledged as divinely inspired by the Jewish community from antiquity and later by Christians. First Kings provides critical historical, moral, and theological teachings that align with the broader message of the Bible, including the nature of God, the consequences of obedience and disobedience, and the unfolding of divine covenants.

New Testament References The New Testament also refers to characters and events found in First Kings, further establishing its canonical and inspired status. For instance, the Apostle Paul refers to Elijah's confrontation with the prophets of Baal, an event recorded in First Kings 18, in his letter to the Romans (Romans 11:2-4). Jesus Christ himself speaks of the ministry of Elijah and refers to the story of the widow of Zarephath (Luke 4:25-26), emphasizing the importance and historical validity of First Kings.

Consistency with Divine Attributes First Kings consistently portrays Jehovah in alignment with His revealed attributes and decrees, including His justice, holiness, and mercy. This internal consistency adds weight to the book's claim to be inspired Scripture.

Authenticity, Authorship, and Date of 2 Kings

Histories Related in Second Kings and Their Vindication

Historical Scope of Second Kings Second Kings continues the narrative commenced in First Kings, chronicling the history of Israel and Judah from the death of Ahab to the exile of both the northern and southern kingdoms. Specific narratives include the ministries of Elisha, the fall of Israel to the Assyrians in 722 B.C.E., the reigns of the righteous Kings Hezekiah and Josiah, as well as the fall of Judah to the Babylonians in 587 B.C.E.

Vindication of Divine Justice and Sovereignty The overarching theme vindicated through these histories is the justice and sovereignty of Jehovah. He rewards obedience and punishes disobedience, as demonstrated through the contrasting fates of kings and nations. For instance, the downfall of both the northern and southern kingdoms serves as a vindication of Jehovah's divine justice. They did not heed the prophets' warnings and continued in their idolatry and unfaithfulness, leading to their inevitable defeat and exile.

Elisha's Ministry as an Emblem of Divine Power The ministry of Elisha, filled with miracles and prophetic proclamations, vindicates Jehovah's power and His care for His people, as well as His authority over nations. Elisha's actions, such as the healing of Naaman the Syrian, are not just miracles but act as divine affirmations of Jehovah's covenantal faithfulness and supremacy.

Moral and Theological Importance The histories recounted in Second Kings serve as critical moral and theological lessons. They underscore the severe consequences of turning away from Jehovah, while also highlighting the blessings that come from obedience, as seen in the lives of Hezekiah and Josiah.

Writership and Canonicity of Second Kings

Authorship of Second Kings The book of Second Kings was undoubtedly written by the prophet Jeremiah. This conclusion is drawn from the consistent prophetic voice and historical detail that aligns with what we know of Jeremiah's life and ministry. His role as a prophet and a historian makes him well-equipped to compile such a critical historical and theological account.

Canonicity There is no question that Second Kings holds canonical status in the Hebrew Bible. It is included in the Prophets section of the Tanakh, affirming its inspired nature and authoritative status. Jewish tradition, from the early Second Temple period and confirmed by the Council of Jamnia around 90 C.E., held the book in high regard. Early Christian lists and councils, such as the Councils of Hippo and Carthage in the late 4th century, also confirm the book's canonical status.

Period Covered Second Kings covers a period of approximately 250 years. The book begins with the final days of Ahab's rule and ends with the fall of Jerusalem to the Babylonians in 587 B.C.E. The record spans from roughly 853 B.C.E. to 587 B.C.E. This time period encapsulates the last days of the divided monarchy, the exile of the northern kingdom of Israel, and ultimately the fall and exile of the southern kingdom of Judah.

In essence, Second Kings provides a reliable and divinely inspired historical account that completes the narrative commenced in First Kings. Its inclusion in the canon of Scripture is both warranted and vital for a comprehensive understanding of Israel's history, as well as the moral and theological lessons that are eternally relevant.

Archaeological Finds Supporting Second Kings

The Black Obelisk of Shalmaneser III One of the most compelling archaeological finds supporting the account in Second Kings is the Black Obelisk of Shalmaneser III. This Assyrian artifact confirms the tribute paid by Jehu, the King of Israel, to Shalmaneser III, as recorded in 2 Kings 9–10. The obelisk, found in Nimrud and dating back to around 825 B.C.E., shows Jehu bowing before Shalmaneser III, validating the biblical narrative.

Lachish Reliefs The Lachish Reliefs, discovered in the ancient Assyrian palace at Nineveh, offer corroborative evidence for the siege of Lachish mentioned in 2 Kings 18:14. These detailed panels depict the Assyrian assault led by Sennacherib on the Judean city of Lachish in 701 B.C.E., entirely consistent with the biblical account.

Hezekiah's Tunnel Hezekiah's tunnel in Jerusalem provides another archaeological validation. Second Kings 20:20 refers to Hezekiah's engineering efforts to bring water into the city. The Siloam inscription, discovered within this tunnel, confirms that a tunnel was indeed hewn to redirect the Gihon spring's waters into the Pool of Siloam, just as described in the Scriptures.

The Taylor Prism This clay prism records Sennacherib's campaigns and specifically mentions his siege of Jerusalem, aligning with the account in 2 Kings 18:17–19:37. The prism does not claim the capture of Jerusalem, which corresponds with the biblical account of the miraculous defeat of the Assyrian army.

Each of these archaeological finds stands as a robust testament to the historical reliability and thereby the inspired nature of Second Kings. They ground the miraculous and the morally instructive elements of the book in a solid historical framework.

Edward D. Andrews

The Inspired Nature of Second Kings

Internal Consistency and Coherence with Earlier Revelation Second Kings exhibits a high level of internal consistency and coherence with earlier books of the Old Testament. For instance, the prophecies mentioned in First Kings and earlier books find their fulfillment in Second Kings. This sort of prophetic continuity is a hallmark of inspired Scripture.

Acceptance in the Hebrew Canon Another significant proof of Second Kings being inspired is its unquestioned acceptance into the Hebrew Canon. The Jewish people, to whom "were entrusted the oracles of God" (Romans 3:2, UASV), accepted Second Kings as a part of their Scriptures. This acceptance was not arbitrary but based on their conviction of the book's divine origin.

Historical Reliability As mentioned earlier, archaeological discoveries such as the Black Obelisk of Shalmaneser III, Lachish Reliefs, and the Taylor Prism validate the historical accounts mentioned in Second Kings. When a text demonstrates this level of historical reliability, it substantiates its claim to be divinely inspired.

Testimony of Later Scripture The writers of the Old Testament and New Testament often refer back to the events and figures found in Second Kings. Such references indicate that later inspired writers viewed this book as an authoritative and reliable record, further affirming its place within inspired Scripture.

Teaching on Jehovah's Character and Covenant Second Kings continues to expound on the nature and attributes of Jehovah, staying consistent with the rest of Scripture. The account therein upholds Jehovah's justice and mercy, and it further elaborates on the covenant relationship between Jehovah and His people.

Moral and Spiritual Lessons Finally, the moral and spiritual lessons to be gleaned from Second Kings are congruent with the teaching of the entire biblical canon. From the failure of the Israelite kings to obey Jehovah's laws to the contrasting faithfulness of individuals like Elisha, these accounts offer timeless principles that align with the broader Scriptural message.

CHAPTER 4 Defending First and Second Chronicles, Ezra, Nehemiah, and Esther

Authenticity, Authorship, and Date of 1 Chronicles

The Essentiality and Benefit of First Chronicles in the Divine Record

Genealogical Records for Contextual Continuity First Chronicles opens with nine chapters of genealogical records that tie the people of Israel back to Adam. These genealogies are not merely lists of names; they establish the continuity of Jehovah's covenant with His people. This strengthens the historical and theological connection, demonstrating God's faithfulness across generations.

Davidic Focus for Messianic Anticipation The book places a considerable emphasis on the life and reign of David. It delves deeply into details about David's military, administrative, and spiritual leadership. By so doing, it sets the stage for the expectation of a Messianic ruler from the line of David, which is fulfilled in Jesus Christ. This Davidic focus is essential for understanding the Messianic prophecies and their ultimate realization.

Ceremonial and Ritualistic Details for Religious Fidelity First Chronicles offers a wealth of detail on the Levitical priesthood, the organization of worship, and the role of the Temple. These elements are crucial for understanding the nature of acceptable worship and service to Jehovah. The chronicler's description is not merely historical; it lays down enduring principles for worship that were relevant then and continue to be pertinent.

Restoration of National Identity Written after the Babylonian exile, First Chronicles serves as a reminder to the returned exiles of their divine heritage and the promises that Jehovah had made to their forefathers. It aimed to help a dispirited and fragmented community find their identity again in the midst of tremendous political and cultural changes.

Historical Validation First Chronicles is meticulously accurate, reflecting a keen awareness of historical detail that aligns with what we know from other sources. This historical veracity supports its status as a divinely inspired text.

Acceptance in the Hebrew Canon Lastly, First Chronicles has been accepted into the Hebrew canon, showing its early and consistent recognition as inspired Scripture. The Jewish community, the stewards of the Old Testament, received it as part of their sacred texts, which further attests to its divine origin.

The Purpose of Chronicles in the Divine Record

Spiritual Renewal Post-Exile Chronicles was written to address the spiritual needs of the Jewish community who had returned from the Babylonian exile around the 5th century B.C.E. The book served as a critical guide for spiritual renewal, pointing the Israelites back to the covenants and promises that Jehovah had made with their ancestors. This was of utmost importance for a community that needed to rebuild not just their physical structures but also their spiritual identity.

Restoration of Davidic Legacy The Chronicles aim to restore and highlight the Davidic legacy, affirming Jehovah's covenant with David as eternal. This focus on David was designed to both encourage the returned exiles and underline the coming Messianic hope that would emerge from the line of David. The book does not simply recount history; it retells it in a way that underscores the theological importance of Davidic kingship for Israel's future.

Reaffirmation of Levitical Priesthood Another pivotal reason for the writing of Chronicles was to reaffirm the religious duties of the

Levitical priesthood and the proper ways of worship in the Temple. Chronicles dedicates significant attention to the divisions of the Levites, the musicians, the gatekeepers, and others involved in Temple service. This was especially relevant for a people who had just returned from exile and were in the process of rebuilding the Temple.

Chronicling Jehovah's Faithfulness The book serves as a chronicle of Jehovah's faithfulness to His people, tracing Israel's history from Adam to the exile. It presents a long view of history that shows the consistent hand of God guiding His people, even when they fail Him. By doing so, it fosters a sense of hope and assurance that God's promises are steadfast and His purposes will be accomplished.

Canonical Recognition as Inspired Scripture Finally, the acceptance of Chronicles into the Hebrew Canon underscores its divinely inspired status. It carries the weight of canonical authority and serves as an essential link in the chain of redemption history captured in the Scriptures.

Ezra's Intentions in Writing First Chronicles

Infusing Spiritual and National Identity Ezra was resolute in his goal to fortify the spiritual and national identity of the Jews who had returned from the Babylonian exile. Through the lens of divinely inspired history, Ezra sought to remind his contemporaries of their unique role in Jehovah's plan for humankind. His historical recounting was not a mere look back; it was a vibrant guide to encourage the Jews to live faithfully to Jehovah.

Focus on the History of Judah Ezra intentionally concentrated on the history of Judah to the exclusion of the Northern Kingdom of Israel. The line of David and the tribe of Judah had been chosen by Jehovah as the conduit of His redemptive plan, which included the coming Messiah. By doing so, Ezra aimed to revive the Israelites' faith in the Davidic covenant and the promises bound up with it.

Emphasizing Pure Worship One of the standout features of First Chronicles is its emphasis on the Levitical priesthood and Temple worship. Ezra stressed the importance of adhering to the Mosaic Law, especially in the conduct of pure worship at the Temple, which was now being rebuilt. His focus on the divine ordinances for Temple service, genealogies of priests, and details about the duties of the Levites conveyed an unmistakable message: Pure worship matters to Jehovah, and it should matter to His people.

By laying out these aspects meticulously, Ezra provided a manual for both the religious and lay community to engage in pure worship and Temple service. He aimed to create a deep reverence for the system that Jehovah had instituted for His people and to ensure that it was restored to its intended state after years of neglect and foreign influence.

Ezra's writing of First Chronicles was an intentional act of spiritual reformation. It served as a resounding call to remember Jehovah's past dealings with His people, to focus on the line of David and the tribe of Judah, and to prioritize pure worship and adherence to Jehovah's Law. All of these components made First Chronicles an essential resource for a community in dire need of spiritual revitalization.

Evidence Favors Ezra as the Writer of Chronicles

Linguistic and Stylistic Considerations One of the most compelling lines of evidence attributing the Chronicles to Ezra is the linguistic and stylistic similarities between the book of Chronicles and the books of Ezra and Nehemiah. The Hebrew used in these texts reflects the linguistic characteristics of post-exilic Hebrew, consistent with the time period when Ezra lived.

Thematic Consistency The themes and theological focuses of Chronicles are closely aligned with those in the books of Ezra and Nehemiah. All three works emphasize the importance of the Temple, the priesthood, and adherence to the Law—topics highly pertinent to the Jewish community returning from exile and relevant to a priest-scribe like Ezra.

Early Jewish Tradition Ancient Jewish tradition, including the Talmud, supports Ezra's authorship of Chronicles. Although not part of the inspired Scripture, these early attestations do provide valuable external evidence.

Timeframe of Composition The dating of the Chronicles aligns well with Ezra's lifetime. Chronicles covers historical events up until the decree of Cyrus in 538 B.C.E., allowing the Jews to return to their land. This falls directly within the period when Ezra would have been active, further substantiating his authorship.

Expertise in the Law As a scribe skilled in the Law of Moses, Ezra had the necessary expertise to compile the historical and genealogical records found in Chronicles. His role as a spiritual leader and restorer of the Law makes him a highly probable candidate for taking up such a monumental task of historical compilation for the purpose of religious edification.

The linguistic, thematic, and chronological elements of Chronicles, when combined with ancient Jewish tradition and Ezra's own qualifications, provide compelling evidence that Ezra was indeed the writer of Chronicles. This alignment across multiple dimensions adds weight to the belief in Ezra's authorship.

Ezra's Spiritual and Secular Qualifications

Spiritual Qualifications

Expertise in the Law of Moses Ezra was a scribe skilled in the Law of Moses (Ezra 7:6). His expertise wasn't merely academic; he set his heart to study, practice, and teach God's law (Ezra 7:10). This made him uniquely qualified to lead the people in a spiritual revival.

Priestly Lineage Ezra was a descendant of Aaron, the first high priest of Israel (Ezra 7:1-5). This gave him not just the theoretical, but also the ancestral and ritual knowledge needed to guide the people in proper worship.

Divine Favor Ezra enjoyed the good hand of his God upon him (Ezra 7:6, 9). This divine favor validated his spiritual role and leadership among the people.

Secular Qualifications

Royal Endorsement King Artaxerxes granted Ezra all he requested and even decreed that anyone who wished could go with him to Jerusalem (Ezra 7:6, 13). This royal endorsement provided Ezra with political authority and resources, facilitating his mission.

Educational Accomplishments As a scribe, Ezra would have been well-educated not only in Jewish law but also in the languages and administrative skills of the time. This made him effective in dealing with the various ethnic and cultural groups he encountered.

Leadership and Organizational Skills Ezra led a large group of exiles back to Jerusalem, a logistical feat that would have required considerable organizational and leadership abilities (Ezra 8). Moreover, he successfully managed the complex process of social and religious reform, demonstrating his capability in governance.

Legal Authority Ezra was given a mandate by King Artaxerxes to appoint magistrates and judges and to teach the laws of God and the king (Ezra 7:25-26). This gave him the legal standing to carry out his spiritual and social reforms.

Both spiritually and secularly, Ezra was highly qualified for the roles he undertook. His spiritual depth and secular skills converged to make him an effective leader for the religious and social reforms of his time. This comprehensive set of qualifications uniquely positioned him to compile the Chronicles and to serve as a spiritual and civic leader of his people.

Confidence in the Correctness of Chronicles

Internal Consistency: One of the strong indicators that validate the correctness of Chronicles is its internal consistency. The narratives and genealogical records align well with other Old Testament texts, such as those found in the books of Samuel and Kings. Any discrepancies often result from differing perspectives or emphases but do not invalidate the historical reliability of Chronicles.

Alignment with Archaeological Evidence Chronicles contains historical details that align with extra-biblical sources and archaeological findings. For instance, the account of King Sennacherib's invasion of Judah is corroborated by Assyrian records. This lends credibility to the text and its presentation of history.

Historical Accuracy Events and individuals recorded in Chronicles find confirmation in external sources, including archaeological discoveries and other ancient Near Eastern texts. This congruence between Chronicles and external evidence enhances our confidence in its accuracy.

Textual Tradition The Hebrew text of Chronicles has been well-preserved throughout millennia. The Masoretic Text serves as a reliable witness to its original form, and early translations like the Septuagint align closely with it, affirming the integrity of the text.

Divine Authorship As part of the canon, Chronicles is considered inspired by God. Its inclusion in the Jewish Scriptures and acceptance by the early Church serve as testimonies to its divine origin, providing ultimate assurance of its correctness.

Canonical Recognition The book of Chronicles has been a part of the Jewish canon for centuries, affirming its spiritual and historical validity. It is evident that early Jewish communities, which were meticulous about their sacred texts, regarded Chronicles as reliable and inspired.

Prophetic and Apostolic Confirmation Chronicles is quoted in the New Testament, implicitly confirming its correctness and divine inspiration. The writers of the New Testament, under the guidance of the Holy Spirit, drew from Chronicles, integrating its truths into the broader Christian message.

Purpose and Integrity The author of Chronicles, traditionally held to be Ezra, wrote with the clear purpose of spiritual edification, guided by a commitment to the Law. His priestly background and scholarly

Date, Authenticity, and Time Period Covered in First Chronicles

Date of Writing First Chronicles was penned in the 5th century B.C.E., specifically between 450 and 425 B.C.E. This post-exilic period is corroborated by the genealogical lists extending up to that time and by its synchronization with the life of Ezra, the accepted author of the book.

Authenticity The authenticity of First Chronicles is beyond dispute within conservative Jewish and Christian circles. It is included in the Masoretic Text, the authoritative Hebrew text of the Old Testament, confirming its acceptance in early Judaism. Moreover, the early Christian Church recognized its divine inspiration, as reflected in its inclusion in crucial canonical lists and councils such as those at Hippo and Carthage.

Time Period Covered First Chronicles opens with the genealogies starting from Adam and proceeds to focus on the kingdom of Judah. It covers the period up to the death of King David, with an emphasis on David's reign. In terms of a timeline, it spans from the Creation to approximately 970 B.C.E., emphasizing events from the 11th century B.C.E. when Saul died and David ascended the throne.

Authenticity, Authorship, and Date of 2 Chronicles

Completion Date and Purpose of Second Chronicles

Date of Completion Ezra completed Second Chronicles between 450 and 425 B.C.E., in the same timeframe as First Chronicles. This dating aligns with the era following the Babylonian exile when the Jewish community was resettling in Jerusalem and rebuilding the temple.

Purpose Ezra's purpose in writing Second Chronicles was multifaceted but distinctively focused. Primarily, he aimed to provide a spiritual and historical perspective on the reigns of the kings of Judah, tracing the history from Solomon to the Babylonian exile. Ezra wanted to underline the consequences of obedience and disobedience to Jehovah, thereby instilling a sense of accountability and adherence to the Law among the post-exilic Jews.

Second Chronicles was completed with the utmost diligence, serving as a historical, spiritual, and moral compass for the Jewish community. It emphatically guided the Jews to remember their past, understand the cause of their calamities, and return to pure worship. This makes it a vital element in the canon of inspired Scripture.

The Undisputed Accuracy of Chronicles

Consistency with Other Biblical Accounts One of the foremost reasons to trust the accuracy of Chronicles is its consistency with other historical records found in the Scriptures. When Chronicles is compared to the books of Samuel and Kings, there is a harmonious recounting of events, even though the focus and perspectives may vary. This consistency speaks volumes about the reliability of Chronicles.

Detailed Genealogical Records Chronicles opens with extensive genealogies, traced with meticulous care. These genealogies not only line up with other genealogical records in the Bible but also serve as essential historical markers. The precision in the genealogies enhances the book's credibility.

Archaeological Corroboration Various accounts and details presented in Chronicles have been substantiated by archaeological findings. For example, the inscriptions and artifacts unearthed in excavations at locations like Lachish and Jerusalem support the historicity of the events described.

Prophetic Fulfillment Chronicles also details prophecies and their subsequent fulfillment, showcasing a divine hand in the recording of these events. The record is so accurate that prophecies uttered by prophets like Isaiah and Jeremiah find their realization within its pages.

Textual Integrity The Hebrew manuscripts of Chronicles, such as those found among the Dead Sea Scrolls, affirm the textual integrity of the book. The Scrolls are remarkably similar to the Masoretic Text, which strongly supports the view that what we have today has been reliably transmitted.

There is no room for doubting the accuracy of Chronicles. Its consistency with other Scriptural accounts, the detailed genealogical information, archaeological support, prophetic fulfillment, and textual integrity all collectively affirm its place as a reliable, inspired book of the Holy Scriptures.

Chronicles' Authenticity Affirmed by Other Scriptures

Corroboration with the Books of Samuel and Kings The narrative of Chronicles has strong corroboration with other books of history in the Old Testament, namely the books of Samuel and Kings. The events and characters portrayed, especially the reigns of the Davidic kings, are described in a manner that fits seamlessly with these other historical accounts.

Referenced by New Testament Writers Though Chronicles itself is not directly quoted in the New Testament, the genealogies it contains are affirmed in the New Testament. For example, the genealogy of Jesus as recorded in the Gospel of Matthew starts with David and Abraham, figures whose lineage is meticulously detailed in Chronicles. This indirect affirmation enhances the authenticity of Chronicles.

Alignment with the Prophetic Books Chronicles' accounts of the kings and their interactions with prophets are consistent with the records found in prophetic books like Isaiah, Jeremiah, and Zechariah. When the prophets reference the actions of the kings, the historical context is in harmony with the account in Chronicles.

Citation in Ezra-Nehemiah The historical record that picks up where Chronicles leaves off is the book of Ezra-Nehemiah. While it doesn't explicitly refer back to Chronicles, the seamless transition from one to the other — along with similar linguistic and thematic elements — validates Chronicles as a reliable historical text.

The authenticity of Chronicles is confirmed through its alignment with other Scriptural accounts, its indirect affirmation in the New Testament, and its compatibility with prophetic texts. These multiple layers of corroboration testify to its standing as an inspired and trustworthy book in the canon of Scripture.

Archaeological Evidence Affirming the Authenticity of Second Chronicles

The Taylor Prism Supports Sennacherib's Invasion One of the most compelling archaeological finds that corroborate the accounts in Second Chronicles is the Taylor Prism. This Assyrian cuneiform inscription details the campaigns of King Sennacherib, particularly his invasion of Judah during the reign of King Hezekiah. Second Chronicles 32 describes this invasion and how Hezekiah and his people prepared for it. The Taylor Prism provides an external confirmation that Sennacherib did indeed lay siege to Jerusalem, as recorded in Second Chronicles.

Lachish Reliefs Depicting the Conquest Additional support comes from the Lachish Reliefs, which are Assyrian artworks showing the conquest of the city of Lachish, one of Judah's fortified cities. These reliefs not only validate the military campaigns described in Second Chronicles but also provide visual documentation that corresponds with the Biblical account.

The Taylor Prism and Lachish Reliefs serve as tangible, historical artifacts that align well with the accounts described in Second Chronicles. Their existence and the details they contain affirm that the events described in Second Chronicles are grounded in historical fact, thereby validating its authenticity as a reliable and inspired part of Scripture.

Time Period and Focus of Second Chronicles

Time Period Covered in Second Chronicles Second Chronicles covers a time span from the beginning of Solomon's reign in the 10th century B.C.E. until the Babylonian exile in the 6th century

B.C.E. Specifically, it starts with Solomon's ascension to the throne around 970 B.C.E. and concludes with the decree of Cyrus the Great in 539 B.C.E., which allowed the Jews to return to Jerusalem.

Emphasis on the History of Judah The history of Judah is the focal point of Second Chronicles for significant theological and covenantal reasons. Judah was the tribe from which David and eventually the Messiah would come, fulfilling Jehovah's covenantal promises. Additionally, the southern kingdom of Judah remained faithful to the Davidic line of kings and the Jerusalem Temple, both of which are central to the chronicler's theological message.

In contrast, the ten-tribe kingdom of Israel severed itself from the Davidic lineage and engaged in idol worship, effectively nullifying its role in the divine covenant that was established with David. Therefore, focusing on Judah aligns with the intent of Chronicles to underscore the importance of covenant fidelity and to point to the Davidic messianic hope.

The time period covered in Second Chronicles and its focus on Judah are not arbitrary choices but are carefully designed to highlight the divine covenants and promises. Through a literal, historical-grammatical lens, it is clear that Second Chronicles serves as a legitimate and inspired historical record, fulfilling its role in redemptive history.

Uplifting and Stimulating Aspects of Second Chronicles

Demonstration of Jehovah's Faithfulness One of the most uplifting aspects of Second Chronicles is its undeniable evidence of Jehovah's faithfulness to His people. Whether in times of prosperity under righteous kings like Hezekiah and Josiah or in times of spiritual decline, Jehovah's steadfast love and commitment to His covenantal promises remain constant. This serves as a potent reminder for believers today of God's unwavering commitment.

Showcase of Repentance and Restoration Second Chronicles offers multiple accounts of individual and national repentance that led to divine forgiveness and restoration. For instance, the reigns of Manasseh and Josiah provide compelling narratives where repentance led to a stay in judgment or revival. These accounts are not only historically accurate but also serve as spiritual encouragements for contemporary believers.

The Role of Prayer and Divine Intervention The book is replete with instances where prayer led to divine intervention, thereby uplifting the reader's faith in the potency and efficacy of prayer. Notable examples include Solomon's prayer for wisdom and Hezekiah's prayer for deliverance from the Assyrians. Both were met with immediate and miraculous responses from Jehovah, solidifying the importance of prayer in the life of the faithful.

Second Chronicles serves as an enriching and uplifting document that fortifies the believer's faith in Jehovah's unchanging character, the transformative power of repentance, and the efficacy of prayer. The book is a historically reliable record that has its place in the corpus of divinely inspired Scripture, and it serves both didactic and devotional purposes for the earnest student of the Bible.

Authenticity, Authorship, and Date of Ezra

Prophecies Assuring Jerusalem's Restoration in the Book of Ezra

Isaiah's Prophecies Isaiah was clear that Jerusalem would be restored. He prophesied the fall of Babylon to the Persians in Isaiah 45:1-3, and even named the Persian King Cyrus as the one who would facilitate this restoration (Isaiah 44:28). This prophecy was given over a century before Cyrus was born, establishing both the predictive accuracy of the Bible and the assurance of Jerusalem's restoration. When Cyrus issued the decree to allow the Jews to return and rebuild Jerusalem, this was a direct fulfillment of Isaiah's prophecy.

Jeremiah's Prophecies Jeremiah predicted the Babylonian Captivity would last 70 years (Jeremiah 25:11-12; 29:10). Ezra himself cites this prophecy to demonstrate its fulfillment (Ezra 1:1). As Jeremiah had foretold, after 70 years in exile, the Jews were permitted to return to Jerusalem. This was an irrefutable assurance to the Jews and is even now an affirmation of the predictive power and reliability of the Scripture.

Daniel's Prophecies Though not directly cited in the Book of Ezra, Daniel's prophecies in Daniel 9:24-27 provided additional assurance regarding the timing and significance of Jerusalem's restoration. Daniel's "Seventy Weeks" prophecy pinpointed not only the rebuilding of Jerusalem but also foreshadowed significant future events, including the coming of the Messiah. This could serve as additional assurance for the Jewish people regarding the restoration of Jerusalem.

The prophetic words of Isaiah, Jeremiah, and Daniel provided unambiguous assurance that Jerusalem would be restored. Their prophecies were not vague or general but specific and time-bound. When the events unfolded exactly as foretold, they served to confirm the reliability of the Scriptures and the sovereignty of Jehovah. These fulfilled prophecies should leave no room for doubt regarding the divine orchestration behind the restoration of Jerusalem.

Fall of Babylon as Contextualized in the Book of Ezra

Date and Conqueror The fall of Babylon occurred in 539 B.C.E. The city was conquered by the Medo-Persian Empire, led by King Cyrus the Great.

Circumstances of the Fall The Babylonians were taken by surprise due to a brilliantly devised military strategy. The Persians diverted the course of the Euphrates River, which flowed through Babylon, and used the lowered water levels to enter the city. The defenses of Babylon were renowned for their impregnability, but the Persians bypassed these by moving through the riverbed and entering the city under cover of darkness. Babylon was taken with minimal struggle, fulfilling the prophecies of Isaiah (Isaiah 44:27-45:3) and Jeremiah (Jeremiah 51:39, 57) that had long foretold the city's downfall.

Significance in the Book of Ezra The fall of Babylon is pivotal for the narrative of the Book of Ezra. This event catalyzed the release of the Jews from captivity and paved the way for their return to Jerusalem. King Cyrus's decree, which allowed the Jewish people to return to their homeland and rebuild the Temple, was a fulfillment of prophecy and signaled a new era in Jewish history. The Book of Ezra opens with this decree and the historical context of Babylon's fall, thereby highlighting the commencement of a new epoch characterized by divine intervention and fulfillment of Scripture.

The fall of Babylon is not only a historically verifiable event but also an undeniable affirmation of the predictive power and reliability of the Scriptures. It serves as the backdrop against which the events of Ezra are set, giving credence to the historicity and authenticity of the Biblical narrative.

Cyrus's Proclamation and the Restoration of Jehovah's Worship

The Proclamation of Cyrus Cyrus the Great, the Persian king, issued a landmark proclamation in 539 B.C.E., as documented in Ezra 1:1-4. This decree allowed the Jews to return to Jerusalem and mandated the rebuilding of the Temple. The proclamation was an explicit move to restore Jehovah's worship in Jerusalem, and it allowed the Jews to take back the sacred articles of the Temple that had been confiscated by the Babylonians. This was in accordance with Jehovah's will, as expressed through the prophets Isaiah and Jeremiah.

The Fulfillment of the 70-Year Prophecy Jerusalem had been destroyed and its Temple laid waste in 607 B.C.E., leading to the Babylonian exile of the Jewish people. The proclamation by Cyrus came exactly 70 years after this event, fulfilling Jeremiah's prophecy as found in Jeremiah 25:11-12 and 29:10, that the land would be desolate for 70 years but afterward, the captives would return. This precision in timing underscores the integrity and reliability of the Scriptural prophecies.

Divine Providence in Action The very fact that a pagan king would assist in the restoration of Jehovah's worship is noteworthy.

Cyrus was moved by Jehovah to make this proclamation, as Ezra 1:1 clearly states. This alignment of political will with prophetic utterance illuminates the sovereign control of Jehovah over the course of history to fulfill His promises.

The proclamation by Cyrus and the consequent return of the Jews to Jerusalem unequivocally demonstrate the fulfillment of Scripture and the restoration of Jehovah's worship. It serves as compelling evidence for the historical accuracy and divine inspiration of the Book of Ezra.

Setting, Authorship, and Chronological Scope of the Book of Ezra

Setting of the Book of Ezra The setting of the book of Ezra is the return of the Israelites from the Babylonian exile to Jerusalem and Judah. It centers around the rebuilding of the Temple and the re-establishment of Jehovah's worship. The backdrop is the Persian Empire, under whose benevolent rule the Jews were allowed to return to their homeland.

Authorship of the Book of Ezra The book of Ezra was authored by Ezra himself, a scribe and priest who played a central role in the spiritual revival of the Jewish community. He was divinely inspired to write this historical record, as evidenced by his deep adherence to the Mosaic Law and his ability to lead the people in the ways of Jehovah.

Chronological Scope and Date of Writing The book of Ezra was written around 460 B.C.E. and it covers events from approximately 539 B.C.E., starting with the decree of Cyrus the Great, to about 457 B.C.E., culminating in Ezra's journey to Jerusalem. This time span allows us to see how Jehovah's plans unfolded for the returned exiles and how their covenant relationship with Him was re-established.

Period Covered by Ezra Ezra provides a historical account that covers around 80 years, from the first return of the exiles in 537 B.C.E. until Ezra's own return in 457 B.C.E. These decades are pivotal as they mark the transition from exile and punishment to restoration and renewal of Jehovah's worship.

In summary, the book of Ezra serves as a reliable, divinely inspired historical record that stands as a testament to Jehovah's faithfulness in restoring His people and His worship. It is set in a critical period of Jewish history and is authored by a man whose life was committed to the service of Jehovah. The precise chronology reaffirms the meticulousness with which Scripture accounts for historical events.

Relationship Between the Books of Ezra and Nehemiah and the Languages in Which They Were Written

Relation Between Ezra and Nehemiah The books of Ezra and Nehemiah are closely related and often treated as a single unit called "Ezra-Nehemiah" in ancient Hebrew manuscripts, such as in the Jewish Talmud. Both books deal with the return from the Babylonian exile and the rebuilding of Jerusalem, albeit with different focuses. While Ezra emphasizes the rebuilding of the Temple and the restoration of religious practices, Nehemiah focuses on the rebuilding of Jerusalem's walls and civic administration. Both books illustrate how Jehovah's divine providence guided the returned exiles in restoring their homeland and spiritual heritage.

Languages Used in the Book of Ezra The book of Ezra was written primarily in Hebrew, the language of the Old Testament. However, sections of it, particularly in chapters 4:8–6:18 and 7:12–26, were written in Aramaic. This use of Aramaic reflects the administrative language of the Achaemenid Empire and lends authenticity to the historical accounts.

In summary, the books of Ezra and Nehemiah provide a harmonious account of the Jewish community's return and restoration, focusing on different yet complementary aspects. The use of both Hebrew and Aramaic in the book of Ezra aligns with the historical and cultural context of the period it describes, thereby attesting to its authenticity.

Edward D. Andrews

Testimonies to the Accuracy of the Book of Ezra

External Historical Corroboration The book of Ezra aligns well with external historical accounts, including secular documents and archaeological findings from the Achaemenid period. For instance, the Cyrus Cylinder confirms King Cyrus' policy of repatriation and religious freedom, consistent with his decree to allow the Jews to return to Jerusalem and rebuild the Temple (Ezra 1:1-4).

Chronological Consistency The chronology presented in Ezra aligns accurately with known historical timelines. For example, the 70-year period of the Babylonian exile and the timing of the reigns of Persian kings like Cyrus, Darius, and Artaxerxes are consistent with extra-biblical historical accounts.

Internal Consistency Ezra contains lists of returnees and genealogical records that serve as internal markers of its historical accuracy. These lists correlate well with other biblical accounts, including those in the books of Nehemiah and Chronicles.

Language and Cultural Details The use of Aramaic in specific sections not only authenticates the book's historical setting but also testifies to the specific administrative conditions under which Ezra and his contemporaries operated.

Prophecy and Fulfillment Ezra recounts the fulfillment of prophecies related to the return from exile, especially those from Jeremiah and Isaiah. This adds another layer of credibility as the prophecies were written well before the events took place.

In conclusion, both internal and external evidences robustly affirm the historical accuracy of the book of Ezra. It stands in harmony with other biblical books and external historical sources, making it a reliable record of the period it describes.

Divine Authenticity of the Book of Ezra

Fulfillment of Prophecy One of the most compelling evidences that attest to the divine nature of the book of Ezra is the fulfillment of prophecy. Prophecies from Jeremiah and Isaiah were fulfilled precisely as outlined in Ezra, signifying a divine orchestration of events.

Canonical Acceptance The book of Ezra has been universally accepted in the canon of Scripture by both Jews and Christians. Its canonicity testifies to its being inspired by God and being useful for teaching, rebuking, correcting, and training in righteousness (2 Timothy 3:16).

Theological Consistency The book maintains a consistent theological focus on Jehovah, His promises, and His plans for His people, aligning seamlessly with the rest of Scripture.

Messianic Expectations Though primarily historical, the book of Ezra does carry undercurrents of messianic expectation, especially in the rebuilding of the Temple, which is a part of the larger redemptive plan leading to the coming of the Messiah.

Historical Accuracy As mentioned earlier, the historical accuracy of Ezra, corroborated by external evidence, lends it credibility and argues for its divine origin. An all-wise God would be expected to produce a record that stands the test of scrutiny on historical grounds.

Moral and Spiritual Lessons The moral and spiritual lessons in the book align with the overarching message of the Bible concerning sin, repentance, and the holiness of God. This thematic unity indicates that it fits well within the inspired Scriptures.

Authenticity, Authorship, and Date of Nehemiah

Nehemiah's Position and Primary Concern

Position of Trust Nehemiah held the esteemed position of cupbearer to King Artaxerxes of Persia. This role was far more than a mere servant who tasted wine; it was a position of significant trust and access to the king. A cupbearer would be privy to high-level discussions and state matters, often serving as a close advisor to the king. In terms of contemporary equivalents, his role could be likened to that of a trusted aide or a high-level cabinet member.

Uppermost in His Mind Nehemiah's foremost concern was the well-being of Jerusalem, the city of his ancestors. This becomes evident when he inquires about the condition of the city and its people and is grieved to learn about its ruined state. Upon hearing the news, he turned to prayer and fasting, seeking guidance and favor from Jehovah for the monumental task ahead. His unwavering focus on the spiritual and physical rebuilding of Jerusalem overshadows every other concern, to the extent that he risked his life by appearing sorrowful before the king, which could have been interpreted as disloyalty.

Nehemiah's commitment to the restoration of Jerusalem exemplifies a passion for God's promises and for the re-establishment of His chosen city. His actions were driven by a faith rooted deeply in the Scriptures and the promises of Jehovah. Hence, Nehemiah's life and work became an extension of his spiritual devotion, manifesting through his commitment to rebuild the walls of Jerusalem and instill a sense of community and spiritual integrity among the returned exiles.

Nehemiah's Grief and the Approaching Appointed Time

The Condition That Grieved Nehemiah Nehemiah was deeply distressed upon hearing about the lamentable state of Jerusalem. The walls were in ruins, and its gates had been destroyed by fire. This dire circumstance was not merely a civic or architectural issue but represented a breach in the spiritual and national integrity of the Jewish people. The broken walls were a physical manifestation of their vulnerability and disgrace, leaving them exposed to enemies and devoid of the honor befitting God's city.

The Approaching Appointed Time As Nehemiah found himself in anguish over Jerusalem, an important divine timetable was drawing near. According to the prophecy of Jeremiah (Jeremiah 29:10), 70 years of Babylonian exile were to pass before the restoration of Jerusalem. This foreordained period was about to conclude, signaling a divinely appointed time for action. The prophetic clock was ticking toward the moment when Jehovah would turn His attention back to Jerusalem for its restoration and renewal.

Authorship, Naming, and Chronology of the Book of Nehemiah

Evidence Confirming Nehemiah as the Writer Nehemiah himself is the author of the book that bears his name. The first-person narrative found throughout the book strongly suggests this (e.g., Nehemiah 1:1-11, Nehemiah 4:1-23, Nehemiah 5:6-19). Furthermore, the detailed accounts of construction, the genealogical records, and the intricate familiarity with Jerusalem's geography align with his role and responsibilities. The language and style are consistent with someone of his position, education, and time period.

Origin of the Name Nehemiah The book derives its name from its principal character, Nehemiah, whose name means "Jehovah comforts." Since the book records his first-person accounts and chronicles his actions in the restoration of Jerusalem, it is fittingly named after him.

Interval Separating Ezra and Nehemiah While Ezra and Nehemiah were initially part of one scroll in the Hebrew Bible and were considered one work, they cover distinct periods and events in Israel's post-exilic history. The interval that separates the two books is not long. The last events in the book of Ezra are from around 457 B.C.E., whereas Nehemiah arrives in Jerusalem in 445 B.C.E. This places an approximate interval of 12 years between the books.

Years Covered by the Book of Nehemiah The book of Nehemiah covers a period that begins in the 20th year of King Artaxerxes I, which is around 445 B.C.E. It runs through at least the 32nd year of his reign, or around 433 B.C.E. This makes the book cover a period of approximately 12 years, during which Nehemiah serves as the governor of Judah and oversees the rebuilding of Jerusalem's walls.

Scriptural Harmony of the Book of Nehemiah

Alignment with Historical Accounts in Other Books The book of Nehemiah fits seamlessly into the biblical narrative, particularly the post-exilic history of the Israelites, as documented in the books of Ezra and Chronicles. The events of Nehemiah continue the story of the returned exiles and their efforts to rebuild Jerusalem, complementing the accounts in Ezra and adding to our understanding of this crucial period.

Consistency with Prophetic Declarations Nehemiah's actions fulfill earlier prophetic declarations. The prophets Jeremiah and Daniel had spoken about the restoration of Jerusalem and the ending of the exile, and Nehemiah plays a crucial role in bringing these prophecies to fruition. For example, Jeremiah had prophesied a seventy-year period for the desolation of Jerusalem (Jeremiah 25:11), which aligns with the time frame culminating in the events described in Nehemiah.

Agreement with Theological Principles Theologically, Nehemiah's faith and prayers resonate with the broader Scriptural themes of reliance on Jehovah, the importance of obeying the Law, and the need for a restored relationship between God and His people. Nehemiah repeatedly turns to prayer and places great emphasis on following Jehovah's laws, which is consistent with the entire body of Scripture from the Pentateuch to the Prophets and the Writings.

Nehemiah's Role as a Type of Leadership Although not messianic, Nehemiah's form of leadership offers a model of godly governance and concern for holiness among God's people. This aligns with the broader biblical messages about leadership, from the judges to the kings and prophets, and even foreshadowing the leadership qualities emphasized in the New Testament.

Artaxerxes' Accession Year and Its Significance

The Accession Year of Artaxerxes Evidence from ancient historical records, such as the Elephantine Papyri and other Persian sources, pinpoint the accession year of Artaxerxes as 475 B.C.E.

The Twentieth Year of Artaxerxes Based on this, the 20th year of Artaxerxes would fall in 455 B.C.E., a date of great significance when studying the book of Nehemiah, as Nehemiah 2:1 specifically mentions this as the year in which Nehemiah received the decree to rebuild Jerusalem's walls.

Correlation with Daniel's Prophecy and the Books of Nehemiah and Luke

Fulfillment of Daniel's Prophecy Daniel 9:25 prophesies that "from the going out of the word to restore and build Jerusalem to the coming of an anointed one, a prince, there shall be seven weeks." If we use the day-for-a-year principle commonly applied to prophetic literature, these seven weeks (or 49 years) are especially intriguing. Starting from 455 B.C.E., we arrive at 406 B.C.E., which aligns closely with the period marking the end of the Old Testament era and the sealing of the Old Testament canon, thereby fulfilling the prophecy.

Connection to Luke's Account and the Messiah The Gospel of Luke provides detailed historical markers regarding the appearance of Jesus, the Messiah. Luke 3:1 mentions the 15th year of the reign of Tiberius Caesar, which is around 29 C.E., as the year when John the Baptist began his ministry and Jesus was baptized shortly thereafter. This aligns well with the timeline provided in Daniel 9:26, which mentions a period of "sixty-two weeks" until the Messiah is "cut off." Using the day-for-a-year principle, these sixty-two weeks would amount to 434 years. If we add these 434 years to the endpoint of the initial seven weeks (or 49 years), i.e., 406 B.C.E., we arrive at approximately 29 C.E., aligning perfectly with the timeframe indicated in Luke.

Edward D. Andrews

Authenticity, Authorship, and Date of Esther

The Narrative of the Book of Esther

Setting and Main Characters The book of Esther is set in the Persian Empire, specifically in the city of Susa, during the reign of King Ahasuerus, commonly identified as Xerxes I, who reigned from 486 to 465 B.C.E. The main characters include Esther, a Jewish woman; Mordecai, her cousin and guardian; King Ahasuerus; and Haman, an influential official in the king's court.

Rise of Esther Esther rises to prominence after being chosen as queen to replace Queen Vashti, who had fallen out of favor with the king. Esther initially keeps her Jewish identity a secret.

Haman's Plot Haman, angered by Mordecai's refusal to bow down to him, plots to exterminate all Jews in the kingdom. He casts lots ("Purim") to choose the date for this massacre and gains the king's approval for the plan.

Esther's Courageous Intervention Upon learning of Haman's scheme, Mordecai urges Esther to intervene. Aware of the risks involved, Esther fasts and prays before approaching the king uninvited—a deed punishable by death. Her courage wins the king's favor, and she invites him and Haman to a banquet.

The Tables Turn At a subsequent banquet, Esther reveals her Jewish identity and Haman's wicked plot. The king is outraged. Haman is executed on the gallows he had prepared for Mordecai. Though the king cannot revoke his previous edict, he allows Mordecai and Esther to issue a new edict permitting the Jews to defend themselves.

The Celebration of Purim The Jews triumph over their enemies, and the feast of Purim is instituted to commemorate their deliverance, based on the "Pur" (lot) that had been cast.

Questions Surrounding the Inspiration of Esther and the Presence of God's Name

Reasons for Questioning the Inspiration of Esther Some have questioned the inspiration of the book of Esther primarily because it does not explicitly mention God, prayer, or any divine laws. Unlike other books in the Old Testament, Esther does not contain overt references to religious practices or covenant promises. This has led some to wonder if the book should be considered divinely inspired Scripture.

God's Name in the Book of Esther Interestingly, while God's name does not appear in an overt form in the text, Jewish tradition suggests that an acrostic form of God's name does exist within the text. In four instances in the Hebrew text, the initial letters of four consecutive words spell out the Tetragrammaton when read backward or forward, depending on the instance. These acrostics are found in Esther 1:20; 5:4; 5:13; and 7:7. While this is a subject of discussion and interpretation, many conservative scholars believe this to be an intentional inclusion, thereby affirming the book's divine inspiration.

In Esther 1:20, the Hebrew phrase appears as: הִי וְכָל הַנָּשִׁים יִתְּנוּ. The bold letters, when read backward, form the Tetragrammaton יהוה (JHVH).

The Hebrew phrase "Hi' Wekhol-Hannashim Yittenu" consists of the initial letters:

- **H**i' (הִי)
- **V**ekhol (וְכָל)
- **H**annashim (הַנָּשִׁים)
- **J**ittenu (יִתְּנוּ)

If you take the first letter from each of these words, you get "HVHJ," which, when read backward, forms "JHVH." This acrostic form of the Tetragrammaton provides a fascinating insight into how the name of Jehovah is encoded in the text of Esther, supporting the claim of divine inspiration for many conservative scholars.

The Hebrew phrase "הִי וְכֹל הַנָּשִׁים יִתְּנוּ" (Hi' Wekhol-Hannashim Yittenu), the initial letters that form the acrostic are:

- הִי
- וְכֹל
- הַנָּשִׁים
- יִתְּנוּ

Thus, despite the absence of explicit religious language, the book of Esther serves as a profound example of divine providence at work to preserve the Jewish people from destruction. Therefore, the book rightly belongs in the canon of inspired Scripture.

Indicators of Faith, Prayer, and Divine Providence in the Book of Esther

Indications of Faith and Prayer to God While the book of Esther does not explicitly mention the name of God or direct instances of prayer, the faith of the characters is implicitly evident. One of the most notable instances is when Esther decides to approach King Ahasuerus uninvited—an act that could result in her death. Before doing so, she requests that all the Jews in Shushan fast for her for three days and nights (Esther 4:16). While the text doesn't explicitly state that this is a religious fast accompanied by prayer, the implication in the context of Jewish custom is clear: Esther and her people are seeking divine intervention.

Evidence of Divine Maneuvering The entire narrative arc of Esther suggests divine providence at work, orchestrating events for the preservation of the Jewish people. Some key events that indicate divine maneuvering include:

1. **Esther's Elevation to Queen**: Esther becomes queen in what seems like a chance occurrence but is better understood as a divinely orchestrated event to place her in a position to save her people.

2. **Mordecai's Discovery of the Assassination Plot**: Mordecai overhears a plot to kill King Ahasuerus (Esther 2:21-23). His report saves the king and gets recorded in the royal chronicles, a fact that later proves pivotal.

3. **The King's Sleepless Night**: On a night when King Ahasuerus can't sleep, he calls for the reading of the royal chronicles, leading to the realization that Mordecai has never been rewarded for saving him. This sets in motion a chain of events that leads to the elevation of Mordecai and the downfall of Haman (Esther 6:1-11).

4. **The Irony of Haman's Gallows**: Haman constructs a gallows for Mordecai but ends up being executed on it himself (Esther 7:9-10). This twist is too exacting to be mere coincidence and suggests divine maneuvering.

5. **The Timing of Esther's Banquets**: Esther's two banquets are perfectly timed to reveal Haman's plot and seek the king's favor for her people.

These events display the subtle yet powerful hand of divine providence, ensuring the survival of the Jewish people against overwhelming odds. While God's name may not be overtly mentioned in the book, the unfolding events loudly proclaim His involvement.

The Authenticity and Factual Basis of the Book of Esther

Historical Setting and Context The book of Esther is set during the Persian Empire, under the reign of King Ahasuerus, who is generally identified with Xerxes I (486–465 B.C.E.). The historical setting aligns well with what is known of the Persian period, including the depiction of customs, the palace in Shushan (Susa), and other aspects of Persian life.

Canonical Acceptance The book of Esther has been accepted into the Jewish canon, which attests to its perceived authenticity and authority within the Jewish community. Additionally, it is one of the five scrolls (Megillot) read during important Jewish festivals, specifically Purim, which commemorates the events described in the book.

Internal Consistency The narrative of Esther is consistent within itself, maintaining the same tone, style, and language throughout. There are no contradictions in the storyline, and it fits well with the broader biblical narrative, emphasizing themes such as the providence of God and the deliverance of His people.

Corroboration in Extrabiblical Sources While the book of Esther does not have direct extrabiblical corroboration, the general historical circumstances—such as the reign of King Xerxes and the setting in the Persian Empire—are well-supported by historical evidence.

Textual Transmission The book of Esther has been preserved in a manner consistent with other Old Testament books, appearing in ancient copies like the Septuagint and the Masoretic Text. This preservation across different textual traditions indicates its established place among the Scriptures.

Thematic Harmony The themes of divine providence, deliverance, and the protection of God's people in the book of Esther are consistent with themes found elsewhere in Scripture. This thematic alignment supports the book's authenticity as a genuine part of the biblical canon.

Inclusion in Early Lists and Commentaries The book of Esther is included in early lists of canonical books and has been the subject of commentaries by ancient scholars, further solidifying its authenticity and acceptance as Scripture.

Exactness and Linguistic Harmony in the Book of Esther

Attention to Detail The book of Esther is marked by its meticulous attention to detail. This is evident in the precise descriptions of Persian court life, royal protocols, and historical settings. For instance, the book accurately outlines the extensive preparations that women underwent before meeting the king (Esther

2:12), the layout of the royal palace in Shushan (Susa), and the laws of the Medes and Persians which could not be altered (Esther 1:19; 8:8). These details provide a note of genuineness to the book.

Language and Vocabulary The language of the book of Esther also strongly suggests its authenticity. The Hebrew employed in the book is characteristic of the post-exilic period, harmonizing with its historical setting in the Persian Empire during the reign of King Xerxes, from 486–465 B.C.E. Moreover, the use of specific Persian loanwords and titles, such as those used for government officials, aligns well with the book's historical context.

Inclusion of Persian Names and Titles The book incorporates specific Persian names, titles, and terms that were appropriate for the historical period. The exactness in the use of these terms, which are consistent with what we know from Persian inscriptions and historical records, adds another layer of authenticity to the book.

Temporal Markers The book is punctuated by specific temporal markers. The third year of King Ahasuerus's reign is identified as the time for the royal banquet (Esther 1:3), and the twelfth year for Esther's plea to the king (Esther 3:7). Such chronological precision aligns with the objective to provide a factual account.

Time Period, Writer, Place, and Time of Writing of the Book of Esther

Time Period The book of Esther is set during the reign of King Xerxes of Persia, who ruled from 486–465 B.C.E. This time period is clearly demarcated in the text, indicating its historical setting within the Persian Empire.

Writer: Mordecai Evidence within the text suggests that Mordecai is the writer of the book. He is a key figure in the story and would have had firsthand knowledge of the events. He was not only in a position of power within the Persian court but also was uniquely positioned to record these events due to his relationship with Esther and his involvement in the story. His role in the narrative and the detailed internal information that is present in the text support the assertion that Mordecai is the writer.

Place of Writing The book most likely was written in Shushan (Susa), the capital of the Persian Empire at the time. The specificity of the details concerning the palace, the city, and the royal protocols points to someone with firsthand knowledge of Shushan.

Time of Writing As for the time of writing, it would logically follow soon after the events described, while the memory was still fresh and accurate recordings could be made. Given the reign of Xerxes, a plausible time for the book's composition would be shortly after the end of the events described, likely within the latter part of Xerxes' reign or shortly thereafter.

In summary, the book of Esther is firmly rooted in a specific historical context—the reign of King Xerxes in the mid-5th century B.C.E. Mordecai is the most likely author, writing the account in Shushan following the events that transpired. These aspects lend the book authenticity and credibility.

CHAPTER 5 Defending Job, Psalm, Proverbs, Ecclesiastes, and the Song of Solomon

Authenticity, Authorship, and Date of Job

Meaning of Job's Name and Questions Addressed by the Book of Job

Meaning of Job's Name The name "Job" is derived from the Hebrew word "Iyyov," which can be translated to mean "persecuted" or "afflicted." This name aptly describes the circumstances that Job undergoes in the narrative, serving as an embodiment of his trials and tests.

Questions Addressed by the Book The book of Job wrestles with profound theological and existential questions that concern the human condition:

1. **Theodicy**: One of the primary questions the book addresses is that of theodicy—the justification of divine goodness and providence in the face of evil and suffering. Job's situation forces the reader to confront the issue of why bad things happen to good people.

2. **Human Suffering**: The book of Job delves into the human experience of suffering, examining whether suffering is always a direct result of individual sin.

3. **Divine Sovereignty and Human Understanding**: Job's dialogues with his friends and eventually with God Himself delve into the limitations of human wisdom when compared to divine sovereignty. The book highlights that there are

aspects of the divine plan that are beyond human understanding.

4. **Role of Faith During Adversity**: The book also emphasizes the importance of maintaining faith and integrity even when faced with inexplicable suffering. Job's perseverance and enduring faith under extreme adversity exemplify this point.

5. **Moral Complexity**: The dialogues among Job, his friends, and God illustrate the complexity and multi-dimensional nature of moral and spiritual issues, cautioning against simplistic or dogmatic answers.

In sum, the book of Job provides valuable insights into the nature of God, the complexities of human suffering, and the limitations of human understanding. Job's steadfast faith in the face of severe trials offers an enduring lesson on spiritual resilience.

Job as a Historical Figure

Biblical Evidence Job is mentioned outside of the book that bears his name, offering intertextual confirmation of his historical existence. Most notably, he is listed in Ezekiel 14:14 along with Noah and Daniel as an example of righteousness. These names are included in a context that presupposes their actual historical existence. Furthermore, James 5:11 references the "patience of Job," reinforcing the understanding that Job was a real individual.

Geographical Specificity The book of Job provides specific geographical details such as the land of Uz, where Job lived. The inclusion of such geographical data lends credence to the account as reflective of historical realities.

Cultural Context The cultural and social practices described in Job are in keeping with what is known about the ancient Near East. The book includes details about legal customs, pastoral life, and other elements that are reflective of a specific historical setting.

Linguistic Markers The language and style of the book also align with what is known about Semitic literature from the second millennium B.C.E., providing an additional layer of historical authenticity.

In light of these factors, there is strong evidence to assert that Job was a real, historical figure. The book provides not just a theological or literary narrative but also a record rooted in actual events and persons.

Evidence for the Inspiration of the Book of Job

Complex Literary Structure The book of Job exhibits a highly sophisticated literary structure, with prose framing poetic dialogues and monologues. This complexity exceeds what one would expect from a mere human composition of its time.

Theological Depth Job grapples with profound theological issues such as the problem of suffering and the nature of God's justice. The depth and complexity of the theological dialogue within the book are not merely human ponderings but indicate divine insight.

Consistency with Scriptural Teachings The book of Job is consistent with the teachings found throughout the Scriptures, including the foundational concept of God's sovereignty and the moral responsibility of individuals. This internal coherence with the broader Biblical narrative supports its divine inspiration.

Prophetic Undertones The book has elements that are implicitly prophetic, anticipating the redemptive work that is more fully revealed in other parts of Scripture. The desire for a "mediator" or an "advocate" in Job 9:33 and 16:19-21 foreshadows the ultimate Mediator, Jesus Christ.

Historical References in Other Scriptural Texts As mentioned earlier, Job is referred to in other parts of the Bible such as Ezekiel 14:14 and James 5:11. This intertextual confirmation adds weight to the book's divine origin.

Ancient Manuscript Evidence The preservation of the book of Job in ancient manuscripts, such as those found among the Dead Sea

Scrolls, attests to its importance and revered status, which is most fitting if the book is inspired.

These multiple lines of evidence strongly testify to the divine inspiration of the book of Job, affirming its place within the canon of inspired Scripture.

Location, Timing, and Completion of the Book of Job

Location: The Wilderness The drama described in the book of Job took place in the land of Uz, which was a region in the wilderness east of Israel. The specific location aligns with the narrative's setting, characterized by its remoteness and isolation—fitting for the profound existential and theological struggles that Job endured.

Time of the Drama: 17th to 15th Century B.C.E. Based on a conservative biblical chronology, the events in the book of Job transpired over a span of more than 140 years between the 17th century and the 15th century B.C.E. This time frame coincides with the patriarchal age, linking Job with figures like Abraham, Isaac, and Jacob, though Job himself was not an Israelite.

Completion of the Writing: 15th Century B.C.E. The book of Job was likely written by the end of the 15th century B.C.E. The completion of the book in this time frame fits within the larger canonical timeline and makes it one of the earliest—if not the earliest—books of the Bible to be written down.

The specificity of location, timing, and the period of writing completion all affirm the historical reliability and authenticity of the book of Job.

Indicators of Moses' Writership of Job

While the book of Job itself does not explicitly identify its author, several lines of evidence suggest that Moses may have been the writer:

Linguistic Similarities: The Hebrew language employed in Job has many similarities to the Pentateuch, the first five books traditionally attributed to Moses. These similarities suggest a shared linguistic and cultural milieu, consistent with Mosaic authorship.

Timeframe: The timing of the events in Job and the timing of Moses' life overlap significantly. Based on a literal conservative Bible chronology, both Job and Moses lived during a period that extended from the 17th to the 15th century B.C.E. Moses could have been aware of Job's trials, and the timing aligns for him to document it.

Geographical Considerations: The Land of Uz, where Job resided, is situated east of Israel. Moses also spent a significant amount of time in the eastern regions, specifically in Midian. His familiarity with these areas would have provided him with the geographical knowledge evident in the book.

Thematic Elements: The book of Job tackles theological issues that are also present in the writings of Moses, such as the nature of God, human suffering, and divine justice. These shared themes point toward a common author.

Early Tradition: Though not conclusive, early Jewish and Christian traditions have sometimes cited Moses as the author of Job. These traditions, while not infallible, offer corroborative support.

In summary, we attribute the writing of the Book of Job to Moses because this aligns with the oldest traditions held by both Jewish and early Christian experts. The language of the Book of Job shows that it was originally written in Hebrew, which was Moses' language. This Hebrew is of a high quality and is used to express deep poetic thought, which suggests that it isn't a translation from another language like Arabic. The narrative parts of the book share more similarities with the Pentateuch—the first five books of the Bible, also attributed to Moses—than with any other biblical writings. Given that Moses was an Israelite and that, according to Romans 3:1-2, the Israelites were the keepers of God's sacred words, it makes sense that he would be the author.

Moreover, Moses spent a significant period—40 years—in Midian, which is near Uz, the location where Job's story takes place. During that time, Moses could have gathered the detailed information we see in the Book of Job. Additionally, Moses could have learned about the ending of Job's life while journeying near Uz during the Israelites' 40-year trek in the wilderness. This would allow him to include those final details in the book.

The Multi-Dimensional Depth of the Book of Job

While the book of Job is often cited as a literary masterpiece due to its poetic dialogue, intricate plot structure, and emotional depth, it stands as much more than a work of ancient literature.

Theological Insights: Job provides profound theological insights into the nature and attributes of God, as well as the problem of suffering. It delves into the question of divine justice and God's sovereignty over creation, addressing themes that are vital to Judeo-Christian thought.

Wisdom Literature: The book is an integral part of the Wisdom literature in the Old Testament, providing principles and guidelines for right living and fear of God. It encourages a faith that trusts in God even when circumstances are incomprehensible.

Historical Reliability: Job is not merely a fictional or allegorical character but a figure rooted in a specific historical context. The book provides names, places, and events that suggest an authentic historical account.

Moral and Ethical Lessons: The dialogues between Job and his friends offer various perspectives on ethics and morality, guiding the reader in how to—or how not to—address complex life issues.

Revelation of God's Character: Throughout the book, the character of God is revealed not just as an omnipotent Being but also as a God who listens, responds, and ultimately vindicates Job. This provides an intimate look at the multifaceted character of God.

Eschatological Relevance: The book of Job also has eschatological implications, emphasizing that complete justice may not be realized in this life but will be in the life to come. This aligns with broader Scriptural teachings about the future judgment and restoration.

In summary, the book of Job serves as more than a literary masterpiece; it is a theologically rich, historically grounded, and morally instructive text that engages with some of the most fundamental questions of human existence.

Authenticity, Authorship, and Date of Psalm

The Nature and Content of the Book of Psalms

The Book of Psalms is a collection of religious songs, prayers, and poems found in the Old Testament. It is divided into five books, mimicking the division of the Torah, and contains a total of 150 Psalms. These Psalms are composed by various authors, with David contributing the most, followed by Asaph, the sons of Korah, and others.

Multifaceted Themes: The Psalms encompass a wide range of themes such as worship, praise, lament, wisdom, and prophecy. They explore the human experience in relation to God, addressing both collective and individual concerns.

Musical and Liturgical Significance: The Psalms have been an essential part of Jewish and Christian worship, often used in liturgical settings. Many Psalms contain musical notations and are believed to have been sung or chanted during religious ceremonies.

Theological Importance: The Book of Psalms contributes significantly to our understanding of God's nature and character. It reveals God as the sovereign Creator, the deliverer, the righteous Judge, and the compassionate Father.

Historical Relevance: Several Psalms are rooted in specific historical events, such as David's flight from Saul or the Babylonian Exile, adding a layer of historical authenticity and applicability.

Prophetic Elements: The Psalms contain Messianic prophecies, which Christians believe are fulfilled in Jesus Christ. Psalms like Psalm 22 and Psalm 110 are often cited in the New Testament as pointing to the life, death, and resurrection of Jesus.

Wisdom and Instruction: Some Psalms, often categorized as Wisdom Psalms, offer moral and ethical guidance, consistent with the broader Wisdom Literature in the Old Testament.

Titles and Meanings Applied to Psalms

Tehillim: The Hebrew title for the Book of Psalms is "Tehillim," meaning "Praises." This title emphasizes the book's central theme of praise and worship directed towards God.

Psalmos: In the Septuagint, the Greek translation of the Old Testament, the title used is "Psalmoi," which signifies "songs sung to musical accompaniment." This highlights the musical nature of the Psalms.

Book of Praises: In English, it is often referred to as the "Book of Praises," which underscores the book's role in both individual and collective worship.

Zabur: In Islamic tradition, the Psalms are referred to as the "Zabur," one of the holy books given to David.

Definition of a Psalm

A Psalm is a poetic composition that is designed to be sung or recited in a worship setting. It serves as a vehicle for various kinds of expression—praise, thanksgiving, lament, wisdom, and sometimes even complaint and doubt—in a religious context. The Psalms often employ rich poetic and literary elements, such as parallelism, metaphor, and symbolism, to convey deep emotional and theological truths. They are an integral part of the liturgical practices in both the Jewish and Christian traditions, aimed at fostering a richer relationship between God and His people.

The Superscriptions and Their Information on the Writers

Superscriptions are the brief notations found at the beginning of many of the Psalms. These are highly significant as they offer direct information concerning the authorship, the context, or the intended use of the Psalm in question.

David: A large number of Psalms—specifically 73—explicitly state that they were written by David. Given David's pivotal role as a king and as a 'man after God's own heart,' his authorship adds a layer of theological and historical depth to these compositions.

Asaph: Twelve Psalms (Psalms 50, 73-83) are attributed to Asaph, one of David's chief musicians. Asaph was not just a musician but also a prophet in his musical ministry. His Psalms often deal with issues of justice and the character of God.

Sons of Korah: Eleven Psalms (Psalms 42-49, 84, 85, 87, 88) are attributed to the Sons of Korah. They were Levitical singers who served in the Temple, and their Psalms often focus on the longing for God's dwelling place.

Solomon: Two Psalms (Psalms 72, 127) are attributed to Solomon. These Psalms provide wisdom and insight into Godly living and governance.

Moses: Psalm 90 is attributed to Moses, making it unique in its reflection on the transient nature of life juxtaposed with the eternality of God.

Others: Psalms 88 is attributed to Heman the Ezrahite, and Psalm 89 to Ethan the Ezrahite. These individuals are known for their wisdom.

Anonymous: Many Psalms do not have superscriptions and thus remain anonymous. However, the lack of a named author does not diminish their divine inspiration or their role in the worship of God.

The superscriptions thus serve as a valuable gateway into understanding the diversity of voices that contribute to this sacred anthology, each adding unique perspectives to the tapestry of faith, worship, and theology found in the Book of Psalms.

Time Period Covered by the Writing of the Psalms

The Psalms were written over a span of approximately 1,000 years, covering a period from the 15th century to the 5th century B.C.E. This timeline begins with the earliest Psalms attributed to Moses and extends to the time of the Second Temple period, after the return from the Babylonian exile.

Mosaic Period: Psalm 90 is traditionally attributed to Moses, placing its origin in the 15th century B.C.E. This Psalm reflects on human frailty in contrast to God's eternal nature.

Davidic Period: David, who lived in the 11th century B.C.E., is credited with composing a substantial portion of the Psalter. His Psalms often revolve around his personal experiences and the national concerns of Israel.

Solomonic and Divided Kingdom Period: Solomon, David's son, also contributed to the Psalms (Psalms 72, 127). Psalms from Asaph and the Sons of Korah fall into this time frame as well, dating from the 10th to the 8th centuries B.C.E.

Exilic Period: Some Psalms, like Psalm 137, reflect the experiences of the Israelites during the Babylonian exile in the 6th century B.C.E. These Psalms are laments that vividly capture the sorrow and longing for Jerusalem.

Post-Exilic Period: Finally, some of the later Psalms were likely composed during the Second Temple period, which could extend the collection into the 5th century B.C.E. These often have themes of hope and restoration.

This extended period of composition testifies to the enduring relevance and divine inspiration of the Psalms, capturing a wide range of human emotions and experiences while consistently pointing to the nature and acts of God.

Organization and Structure of the Book of Psalms

The book of Psalms is organized into five separate books or divisions, closely mirroring the five books of the Torah. This intentional structure emphasizes the Psalms as a second law or as a reflection on the Law. The five books are:

1. **Book I**: Psalms 1–41
2. **Book II**: Psalms 42–72
3. **Book III**: Psalms 73–89
4. **Book IV**: Psalms 90–106
5. **Book V**: Psalms 107–150

Each book concludes with a doxology, praising God and often using the phrase "Amen and Amen," or a variant thereof. The final Psalm, Psalm 150, serves as a doxology for the entire Psalter. The first compilation of these poetic songs is credited to David. Later on, it seems that Ezra, who was both a priest and a proficient scribe specialized in the Law of Moses, was the individual chosen by God to finalize the arrangement of the Book of Psalms. This is supported by Ezra 7:6, which identifies him as a "skilled copyist in the law of Moses."

Superscriptions in the Psalms

Many of the Psalms contain superscriptions that provide valuable information about the Psalm's authorship, historical context, and sometimes its intended use. For example, Psalm 51 is introduced as "A Psalm of David when Nathan the prophet came to him, after he had gone in to Bathsheba." This immediately places the Psalm within a specific narrative framework and informs us that it is a penitential Psalm. Superscriptions may also indicate musical directions or the intended musical instruments for the Psalm, thereby offering insight into the worship practices of ancient Israel.

The Term "Selah"

The term "Selah" appears frequently in the Psalms, but its precise meaning is not definitively known. It is likely a musical or liturgical term indicating a pause or an interlude. While the Psalms were sung or chanted in ancient Israel, "Selah" would have had relevance as a cue for musicians or the congregation. When reading the Psalms, it is not necessary to pronounce the word "Selah" as it serves a function for musical or liturgical pause rather than as content to be verbalized. It serves more as an instruction for performance or reflection rather than a component of the text to be articulated.

Notable Features of the Book of Psalms

1. **Acrostic Patterns**: Certain Psalms employ an acrostic pattern, where each verse or stanza begins with a successive letter of the Hebrew alphabet. Psalms like 119 are classic examples of this technique. This literary feature served as a memory aid and showcased the artistry of the text.

2. **Types of Psalms**: The book contains various types of Psalms, including hymns of praise, laments, royal Psalms, wisdom Psalms, and Psalms of thanksgiving. Each type serves a specific purpose in the worship and spiritual life of Israel.

3. **Messianic Psalms**: Several Psalms are considered Messianic, meaning they contain prophecies or allusions to the coming Messiah. For example, Psalm 22 vividly portrays elements of Christ's crucifixion, while Psalm 110 is often cited in the New Testament as referring to Jesus as both King and Priest.

4. **Imagery and Metaphors**: Psalms employs rich imagery and metaphors, often drawn from nature or everyday life. These elements make the text relatable and vivid, effectively engaging the reader's senses and emotions.

5. **Musical Instructions**: Beyond the term "Selah," many Psalms contain musical notations, such as "To the choirmaster" or references to specific melodies like "The Lilies," providing insight into the musical practices of the time.

6. **Historical Context**: While not always provided, some Psalms include historical superscriptions that place them within specific events in Israel's history. This adds a layer of depth and specificity to the Psalm's message.

7. **Dual Application**: Several Psalms have both an immediate historical context and a longer prophetic or thematic reach. For example, Psalm 2 addresses the coronation of the Israelite king but also points toward the universal reign of the Messiah.

8. **Theological Depth**: The Psalms contain profound theological insights, including but not limited to discussions about God's attributes, the problem of evil, the nature of true worship, and the hope of salvation.

9. **Universal Appeal**: While rooted in the religious and cultural context of ancient Israel, the Psalms have a universal appeal that has made them a cherished part of devotional literature for believers across the ages.

These features collectively contribute to the Psalms' rich tapestry, making it not merely a collection of religious poems but a multi-faceted treasure trove of theology, worship, and human experience.

The Acrostic Style in the Psalms: Explanation and Illustration

What Is Acrostic Style?

The acrostic style of composition is a distinct literary form in which the initial, middle, or final letters of successive lines or stanzas form a word, phrase, or follow a particular alphabetical sequence. In the context of the Hebrew Bible, specifically the Psalms, acrostic compositions usually involve the initial letters of each line or stanza being arranged according to the Hebrew alphabet.

Purpose of Acrostic Composition

The acrostic format serves multiple functions:

1. **Memory Aid**: The structure helps in memorizing the text, which was particularly useful in a predominantly oral culture.

2. **Artistic Expression**: The acrostic pattern showcases the writer's skill in composing a meaningful text within a constrained structure.

3. **Complete Thought**: By using the entire Hebrew alphabet, the Psalmist suggests that the text comprehensively addresses its subject matter.

Examples in the Psalms

The most notable example of the acrostic style in Psalms is Psalm 119. This Psalm is divided into 22 sections, corresponding to the 22 letters of the Hebrew alphabet. Each section contains eight verses, and every verse within that section starts with the same Hebrew letter.

Another example is Psalm 34, where almost every verse begins with a successive letter of the Hebrew alphabet.

The acrostic style is not merely a literary curiosity but a meaningful method of structuring content. It highlights the Psalmist's intention to give a complete or thorough representation of the subject at hand, whether it be God's law, as in Psalm 119, or a hymn of deliverance and praise, as in Psalm 34. The structured form of the acrostic Psalms also reflects a high view of divine revelation; the words of Scripture are ordered, patterned, and purposeful, deserving of careful arrangement and study.

The Emotional and Intellectual Appeal of the Psalms: Background, Power, and Beauty

Background Appeal to Mind and Heart

The Psalms directly appeal to both the mind and the heart due to their rootedness in concrete historical and life experiences. These experiences range from personal anguish and penitential cries to national triumphs and worshipful adoration of Jehovah. The Psalmists, often writing in times of war, peace, suffering, or joy, address real human conditions, which allows readers to easily identify with them.

For example, the historical background of Psalm 137 places the Israelites in exile in Babylon, a setting that resonates with any reader who has felt lost or alienated. Conversely, Psalm 23 evokes pastoral imagery to convey Jehovah's care and guidance, universally touching the human need for security and well-being.

Factors Contributing to Their Power and Beauty

1. **Vivid Imagery**: The Psalms are replete with vivid images, metaphors, and similes. The language, though simple, paints a rich canvas of emotion and theology. For instance, in Psalm 1, the righteous person is compared to a tree planted by streams of water—a potent image of vitality and stability.

2. **Musical Quality**: The Psalms were originally composed for musical accompaniment. The rhythm and parallelism inherent in Hebrew poetry add a layer of beauty that amplifies the emotional impact.

3. **Theological Depth**: Despite their emotional rawness, the Psalms are not shallow. They delve into complex issues of justice, sovereignty, mercy, and the nature of Jehovah, thereby engaging the intellect.

4. **Human Emotion**: The Psalms encapsulate a broad range of human emotions, from the depths of despair to the heights of jubilant praise. This emotional breadth adds a layer of universality to the Psalms, making them timeless.

5. **Divine Inspiration**: Above all, the Psalms are inspired by God. The inerrancy and infallibility of the Scripture give the Psalms a transcendent quality, making them effective for teaching, reproof, correction, and training in righteousness (2 Timothy 3:16).

The Psalms engage both the intellect and the emotions because they are rooted in the real experiences of real people in a divinely orchestrated history. Coupled with their poetic beauty, theological depth, and the work of divine inspiration, the Psalms stand as a powerful and beautiful component of the Biblical canon.

The Authenticity of the Book of Psalms

Manuscript Evidence One of the most compelling aspects testifying to the authenticity of the Psalms is the manuscript evidence. The Dead Sea Scrolls, dating from around the 2nd century B.C.E., contain many fragments and entire scrolls of the Psalms. This pushes the manuscript evidence close to the original date of composition and demonstrates that the Psalms we have today are remarkably consistent with these ancient texts.

Internal Evidence Within the Psalms themselves, the superscriptions often provide key historical and contextual information. The frequent attributions to David, Solomon, and the Sons of Korah lend historical weight to the Psalms, connecting them to real people and events in Israel's history.

Canonical Acceptance The Psalms have been universally accepted into the Jewish and Christian canons. This wide acceptance and the centrality of the Psalms in worship and liturgy for centuries further attest to their authenticity.

Prophetic and Messianic Elements Certain Psalms contain Messianic prophecies that are fulfilled in the New Testament. For example, Psalm 22 vividly describes a form of execution remarkably similar to crucifixion—a method of execution not employed by the Jews—long before such a death penalty existed. The New Testament confirms that these prophecies are fulfilled in Jesus Christ, which testifies to the divine and authentic nature of the Psalms.

Consistency in Theological Messages The theology presented in the Psalms is consistent with the rest of the Hebrew Scriptures. Themes about Jehovah's sovereignty, justice, and the need for righteousness and obedience align seamlessly with other Old Testament teachings, strengthening the claim for the Psalms' authenticity.

The manuscript evidence, internal clues, canonical acceptance, prophetic elements, and theological consistency collectively provide robust testimony to the authenticity of the Psalms. Therefore, we can confidently affirm that the Psalms are a genuine and integral part of the inspired Scriptures.

Jesus' Statements as the Culmination of Testimony for the Authenticity of Psalms

Jesus' Direct Quotations and Allusions The highest form of authentication for the Book of Psalms comes from Jesus Christ Himself. Throughout the Gospels, Jesus directly quotes from the Psalms and alludes to them multiple times. One notable example is when He is on the cross, and He cries out, "My God, my God, why have you forsaken me?" (Matthew 27:46; Mark 15:34), quoting Psalm 22:1. By doing this, Jesus is not only fulfilling prophecy but is also attesting to the authenticity and inspired nature of the Psalms.

Messianic Interpretation Jesus also confirms the Messianic prophecies found in the Psalms. In Luke 24:44, He says, "These are My words which I spoke to you while I was still with you, that all things which are written about Me in the Law of Moses and the Prophets and the Psalms must be fulfilled." In this statement, Jesus categorically endorses the Psalms as divinely inspired Scripture and identifies Himself as the fulfillment of Messianic prophecies within them.

Jesus' Teaching on Davidic Authorship In the dialogue concerning the identity of the Messiah, Jesus refers to Psalm 110 to highlight His divine sonship and lordship. He cites David's statement, "Jehovah said to my Lord, 'Sit at My right hand until I put Your enemies beneath Your feet'" (Matthew 22:44; Psalm 110:1). By using this Psalm, Jesus confirms its Davidic authorship and the divine inspiration of the text.

In the grand tapestry of evidence supporting the authenticity of the Psalms, the statements made by Jesus Christ are the crown jewel. His use, endorsement, and fulfillment of the Psalms offer an unequivocal testimony to their divine origin and authenticity. Thus, any serious believer in Jesus Christ must also, by implication, accept the Psalms as genuine and inspired Holy Scripture.

Authenticity, Authorship, and Date of Proverbs

The Wisdom Contained in the Book of Proverbs

Moral and Ethical Wisdom The book of Proverbs primarily focuses on moral and ethical wisdom, presenting practical guidance for right living in a variety of situations. For example, Proverbs 1:7 declares, "The fear of Jehovah is the beginning of knowledge; fools despise wisdom and instruction." This foundational verse sets the tone for the rest of the book, emphasizing that true wisdom begins with a reverence for Jehovah.

Social and Relational Wisdom Proverbs also deals extensively with social and relational wisdom. Numerous proverbs offer advice on friendships, family relations, and interactions with neighbors and strangers. The book strongly advocates for qualities like loyalty, integrity, and kindness. For instance, Proverbs 17:17 states, "A friend loves at all times, and a brother is born for adversity."

Economic Wisdom Financial acumen is another critical aspect of wisdom covered in Proverbs. The book provides guidelines for managing resources wisely, avoiding debt, and being diligent in work. Proverbs 10:4 underscores the value of hard work: "Poor is he who works with a negligent hand, but the hand of the diligent makes rich."

Wisdom for Leaders Leadership wisdom is another focus of the book. Proverbs outlines the characteristics of good and bad leaders, emphasizing qualities like justice, fairness, and humility. For instance, Proverbs 29:4 states, "The king gives stability to the land by justice, but a man who takes bribes overthrows it."

Spiritual Wisdom Beyond practical wisdom, Proverbs delves into spiritual wisdom by exploring the nature of Jehovah and the path to eternal life. It teaches that wisdom is personified in Christ, as seen in chapters 8 and 9. "Jehovah possessed me at the beginning of His way, before His works of old," says wisdom in Proverbs 8:22, suggesting a Christological interpretation.

The book of Proverbs is a rich repository of wisdom, covering a wide range of life's dimensions—from personal character and social interactions to leadership and spirituality. At its core, the wisdom of Proverbs instructs individuals to walk in the fear of Jehovah, which is the bedrock of all wisdom. As a result, the book serves as an invaluable guide for anyone seeking to live a life pleasing to God.

Solomon's Time as the Ideal Period for Divine Guidance in Proverbs

Political Stability and Prosperity Solomon's reign was one of unprecedented peace and prosperity for Israel, providing a fertile ground for intellectual and spiritual pursuits. Solomon himself was a benefactor of the wise governance of his father, David, and the nation was at peace with surrounding kingdoms. This peace allowed for the focus on inner, moral, and ethical development, which is at the heart of Proverbs.

Solomon's Gift of Wisdom Solomon was renowned for his wisdom, a gift that he received from Jehovah after humbly requesting it (1 Kings 3:5-14). The king was not just wise in governance but also keenly perceptive about human behavior, ethics, and the laws that govern creation. These insights found their way into the book of Proverbs, making it a divinely inspired guidebook for ethical and moral living.

Cultural Context for Wisdom Literature Solomon's era was marked by a literary and cultural boom. There was an engagement with wisdom literature in the broader Near Eastern context, but what distinguished the wisdom of Proverbs is its foundation in the fear of Jehovah. The time was ripe for Israel to contribute a book of divine wisdom to this existing body of human wisdom literature.

Need for Ethical and Moral Instruction Though Israel was politically stable and economically prosperous, there was always the danger of moral and spiritual decline, often a byproduct of prosperity. It was crucial to offer divine guidance on living a godly life in the midst of abundance, as well as cautioning against the pitfalls of wealth and moral laxity.

Solomon's time was an opportune period for the introduction of the wisdom contained in the book of Proverbs. The political stability, cultural receptiveness, and Solomon's divinely endowed wisdom combined to make his reign the appropriate setting for this invaluable guide for ethical and moral living. The wisdom of Proverbs thus stands not just as human insights but as divinely inspired counsel, grounded in the fear and knowledge of Jehovah.

Compilation of the Book of Proverbs

Initial Authorship by Solomon The book of Proverbs primarily originated from Solomon, the son of David. Solomon's contributions are explicitly identified in Proverbs 1:1, where it states, "The proverbs of Solomon, the son of David, king of Israel." Solomon was gifted with divine wisdom by Jehovah, and this allowed him to pen many of these wise sayings.

Multi-Stage Compilation While Solomon is the main author, the book of Proverbs indicates that it underwent a multi-stage compilation process. Proverbs 25:1 specifically mentions that certain proverbs of Solomon were "copied by the men of Hezekiah king of Judah." This shows that even after Solomon's time, there was a divinely guided effort to collect, preserve these inspired sayings.

Inclusion of Other Wisdom Figures In addition to Solomon's proverbs, the book also includes sayings from other figures, such as "the sayings of the wise" in Proverbs 22:17–24:22 and "the sayings of Agur" in Proverbs 30:1–33. The book concludes with "the words of Lemuel king" in Proverbs 31. While these were not directly authored by Solomon, they were considered to be of equal divine wisdom and thus included in the canonical compilation.

Scriptural Canonization The book of Proverbs was recognized as part of the Hebrew Bible canon. Its inclusion confirms its divine inspiration and authority. The very fact that it was accepted into the canon indicates the Jewish community's high regard for its authenticity and divine origin.

The origin of the book of Proverbs is not explicitly stated as having been written by Solomon. However, the Scriptures do mention that Solomon "spoke" proverbs and was deeply committed to organizing and preserving them for future generations (1 Kings 4:32; Ecclesiastes 12:9). During the reigns of David and Solomon, the royal court had official secretaries listed among their staff (2 Samuel 20:25; 2 Kings 12:10). While it's not confirmed if these scribes were responsible for documenting Solomon's proverbs, it's reasonable to believe that the wise sayings of a leader of his stature would be carefully recorded. The consensus is that the book of Proverbs is a compilation, likely assembled from multiple existing collections.

Division of the Book of Proverbs

The book of Proverbs is generally divided into several distinct sections, each serving a unique purpose and focusing on different themes. These divisions provide a structured framework for understanding the wisdom literature contained within the book.

1. The Prologue (Proverbs 1:1-7): The book of Proverbs begins with an introduction, commonly referred to as the prologue. It sets the tone and purpose of the entire collection, emphasizing the pursuit of wisdom and the fear of the Lord as the foundation of knowledge.

2. The Solomonic Proverbs (Proverbs 10:1-22:16): The bulk of the proverbs found in the book of Proverbs are attributed to King Solomon, who is renowned for his wisdom. These proverbs reflect his insights and counsel, covering a wide range of topics such as integrity, diligence, relationships, and practical wisdom for everyday living.

3. The Words of the Wise (Proverbs 22:17-24:34): This section presents additional wise sayings attributed to various individuals referred to as "the wise." While the exact identities of these wise individuals are not specified, their words provide further guidance and instruction on righteous living and ethical conduct.

4. The Sayings of Agur (Proverbs 30:1-33): Agur, the son of Jakeh, is credited with the collection of proverbs found in this section.

His sayings offer unique insights and contemplations on the mysteries of life, the wonders of creation, and the pursuit of true wisdom.

5. The Sayings of King Lemuel (Proverbs 31:1-31): The final chapter of Proverbs is attributed to King Lemuel, who received wisdom from his mother. These verses contain valuable teachings on leadership, virtue, and the qualities of an excellent wife.

6. Epilogue (Proverbs 31:10-31): Following the sayings of King Lemuel, Proverbs concludes with an epilogue that extols the virtues of a godly woman, highlighting her strength, wisdom, and character.

Origin of the Proverbs

The bulk of the proverbs found in the book of Proverbs are traditionally attributed to King Solomon, known for his exceptional wisdom and insight. According to conservative Bible chronology, Solomon reigned as king of Israel from approximately 970 to 931 BCE. It is believed that Solomon compiled and authored a significant portion of the proverbs during his reign.

Solomon's wisdom was divinely granted, as mentioned in the biblical account (1 Kings 4:29-34). His reputation for wisdom attracted individuals from various nations who sought his counsel and recognized the divine inspiration behind his proverbs.

While Solomon is credited with the majority of the proverbs, it is important to note that the book of Proverbs also includes contributions from other wise individuals, such as Agur and King Lemuel. However, the core and most extensive collection of proverbs within the book are attributed to King Solomon's authorship.

Dating and Compilation of Proverbs

The book of Proverbs, a profound collection of wisdom literature, was written and compiled during a significant period in biblical history. Based on conservative Bible chronology, I present the following insights regarding the dating and compilation of Proverbs.

Dating Proverbs:

Proverbs of Solomon: The majority of the proverbs found in the book of Proverbs are attributed to King Solomon, who reigned from approximately 970 to 931 BCE. It is during this time that Solomon's wisdom flourished, and he penned these profound sayings.

Contributions from Other Authors: While the core of Proverbs is ascribed to Solomon, it is worth noting that other wise individuals, such as Agur and King Lemuel, also made valuable contributions to the collection. Their proverbs were likely composed during the same general timeframe as Solomon's reign.

Compilation of Proverbs:

Solomon's Involvement: The compilation of Proverbs is believed to have occurred during Solomon's reign as king of Israel. It is reasonable to assume that Solomon himself played a significant role in gathering and organizing the proverbs, drawing from his own wisdom and the wisdom of others.

Continued Development: While the initial compilation of Proverbs likely took place during Solomon's era, it is important to acknowledge that the book may have undergone further additions and revisions over time. Scholars suggest that subsequent generations may have contributed additional proverbs growing the collection to ensure its relevance and applicability to changing circumstances.

In summary, the book of Proverbs was primarily written and compiled during the reign of King Solomon, around the 10th century BCE. Solomon's wisdom, divinely bestowed upon him, forms the core of the collection, with contributions from other wise individuals supplementing his sayings. There is evidence to support this dating both within the book itself and from external sources. For example, the book of Proverbs states that Solomon spoke 3,000 proverbs (1 Kings 4:32), and many of the proverbs in the book are attributed to him directly. Additionally, the book of Proverbs reflects the cultural and historical context of Solomon's reign. While the exact timeline of the compilation and any subsequent modifications cannot be definitively determined, the wisdom contained within Proverbs continues to guide and inspire generations with its timeless principles for righteous living.

Definition of a Proverb and the Fittingness of the Hebrew Title

A proverb is a succinct statement or expression that embodies a general truth or wisdom. It is designed for easy memorization and conveyance of life principles, often relying on metaphor, simile, or other literary devices to make its point effectively. Proverbs often deal with the realities of human behavior, ethical conduct, and decision-making, offering guidance that is timeless and universally applicable.

The Hebrew title for the Book of Proverbs is "Mishlei," which derives from the root "Sh-L-M." This root word carries the sense of completeness, soundness, and wellbeing. "Mishlei" essentially implies a collection of sayings or teachings that guide an individual toward a complete or wholesome life, both morally and ethically. The Hebrew title is indeed fitting, as it encapsulates the book's purpose: to provide divinely inspired wisdom for leading a balanced, righteous, and fulfilling life. This wisdom is not just intellectual but practical, aimed at everyday conduct and decision-making, truly capturing the essence of what it means to live a life pleasing to Jehovah.

The Stylistic Features of the Book of Proverbs

The style of the Book of Proverbs is characterized by its conciseness and its use of a range of literary forms to convey wisdom. While the most frequent form is the individual proverb—a short, pithy statement that expresses a general principle or truth—the book also utilizes other formats such as longer instructions, dialogues, and monologues.

Conciseness and Clarity: The proverbs are often quite short, usually comprising only a sentence or two. This brevity makes them easily memorable, facilitating their application in daily life. Despite their short length, they are dense with meaning and require thoughtful reflection for full understanding.

Antithetical Parallelism: One of the striking features of the Book of Proverbs is the use of antithetical parallelism, where the second line of a proverb contrasts with the first, emphasizing the point by presenting an opposite. For example, Proverbs 15:1 states, "A soft answer turns away wrath, but a harsh word stirs up anger."

Synonymous Parallelism: In this stylistic feature, the second line of a proverb essentially restates the idea presented in the first line but in a slightly different manner. This lends emphasis and clarity to the principle being expounded.

Chiasmus: Some proverbs use a stylistic device known as chiasmus, where the order of the terms in the first of two parallel clauses is reversed in the second. This serves to underline the interconnectedness of the ideas or elements mentioned.

Numerical Proverbs: Proverbs also utilizes a numerical style, often starting with a particular number and then proceeding to one more. For instance, Proverbs 30:15–16 talks about three things that are never satisfied and then extends it to four.

Inclusion of Characters: The book often uses characters like "Wisdom," "Folly," "the Sluggard," and "the Righteous" as personifications to illustrate and contrast various paths of life and moral choices.

Moral and Ethical Focus: Above all, the language and style of Proverbs are crafted to engage the moral imagination of the reader. This is a book about making choices and understanding the consequences, written in a style intended to provoke thoughtful reflection.

The stylistic choices in Proverbs serve to highlight its primary objective: the impartation of divine wisdom for the living of a godly life. Each stylistic feature is meticulously chosen to make the wisdom both accessible and memorable, aiding in the application of these truths in one's life.

Early Christian Use of Proverbs as Testimony to Its Authenticity

The New Testament bears witness to the authenticity and authoritative nature of the Book of Proverbs by incorporating its teachings and sometimes directly quoting from it. This illustrates the book's high regard among the early Christians and its recognized status as divinely inspired Scripture.

Direct Quotations: The New Testament contains direct quotations from Proverbs. For instance, Romans 12:20 cites Proverbs 25:21-22: "If your enemy is hungry, feed him; if he is thirsty, give him something to drink." This serves to reinforce the Christian principle of loving one's enemies and doing good to those who persecute you. The direct citation here underlines the importance and authenticity of Proverbs' wisdom.

Allusion and Echo: Apart from direct quotations, the teachings in the New Testament often allude to the wisdom found in Proverbs. The notion of wisdom in James, specifically James 3:13–18, closely resembles the personification and characteristics of Wisdom described in Proverbs 1-9.

Thematic Resonance: Themes central to the Book of Proverbs, such as the fear of Jehovah being the beginning of wisdom (Proverbs 1:7), resonate with fundamental Christian doctrines and are reaffirmed in New Testament writings.

Ethical and Moral Guidelines: The ethical and moral teachings in Proverbs are also paralleled in the New Testament. The ideas of speaking truth, living righteously, and practicing justice can be seen woven into the moral fabric of the early Christian communities.

Apostolic Endorsement: The apostles, considered the authoritative voices in the early church, employed the teachings of Proverbs as part of their instruction. This endorsement further validates the book's authenticity as divinely inspired Scripture.

Alignment with Christ's Teachings: Significantly, many principles outlined in Proverbs align with the teachings of Jesus Christ, the cornerstone of Christian belief. The Sermon on the Mount, for instance, includes principles that can be traced back to the wisdom literature of the Old Testament, including Proverbs.

By frequently incorporating the teachings of Proverbs into their writings and doctrine, the early Christians testified to the book's authenticity and divine inspiration. This consistent and respectful use in the New Testament affirms the value and authority of Proverbs, solidifying its place within the canon of Scripture.

Proverbs' Harmonization with the Rest of the Bible

The Book of Proverbs is intricately woven into the larger fabric of the Bible, and its teachings are in harmony with the doctrines and ethical instructions found in both the Old and New Testaments. Below are some of the ways in which Proverbs harmonizes with the rest of the Scriptures.

Doctrine of God: The fear of Jehovah is emphasized as the foundation for all wisdom and knowledge in Proverbs (Proverbs 1:7, 9:10). This is consistent with other Old Testament books such as Psalms and Ecclesiastes as well as New Testament teachings about the reverence and awe for God (Hebrews 12:28-29).

Human Nature: Proverbs depicts the human heart as desperately wicked and deceitful (Proverbs 6:12–15; 11:20), echoing similar affirmations found in books like Jeremiah (17:9) and Romans (3:23).

Moral and Ethical Guidelines: Commands and guidelines about truthful speaking, justice, and righteousness find their parallel in other Old Testament laws (Exodus 20) and are affirmed in New Testament teachings (Ephesians 4:25, Romans 13:8-10).

Doctrine of Retribution: Proverbs often talks about the righteous being rewarded and the wicked being punished, a doctrine found across both Testaments (Proverbs 11:31; Psalm 1; Romans 2:6–8).

Soteriological Elements: Proverbs points towards salvation being grounded in knowledge and wisdom, which come from Jehovah. This foreshadows the ultimate wisdom of God manifested in Jesus Christ, as noted in 1 Corinthians 1:24.

Sanctification and Practical Living: Proverbs is rich in advice for practical living, ethical integrity, and moral purity, which are subjects elaborated upon in the New Testament, particularly in the Pauline epistles (e.g., Galatians 5:22–23).

Societal and Family Roles: Proverbs contains instructions for family relationships and societal roles (Proverbs 31), which is in harmony with New Testament guidelines given in Ephesians 5 and 6.

Wisdom Christology: Jesus Christ is described as the wisdom of God in the New Testament (1 Corinthians 1:30). Proverbs' emphasis on wisdom can be viewed as a precursor to this New Testament revelation.

Prophecy and Fulfillment: While Proverbs is not primarily a prophetic book, its wisdom teachings are in line with the prophetic calls for justice, mercy, and walking humbly with God, as seen in books like Micah (6:8).

The Book of Proverbs does not exist in isolation but is a fundamental component of the Bible's unified message. Its teachings not only reiterate but also enrich the doctrinal, ethical, and moral imperatives found across the Scriptures. Therefore, Proverbs stands as a book that is thoroughly consistent and in harmony with the rest of the biblical canon.

Further Testimonies to the Divine Inspiration of Proverbs

The Book of Proverbs possesses qualities that stand as powerful testaments to its divine inspiration. Below are some examples that demonstrate its extraordinary character.

Scientific Insight: Although not a scientific textbook, Proverbs contains principles that align remarkably well with modern scientific understandings. For instance, the book alludes to the hydrological cycle: "The clouds drop down the dew" (Proverbs 3:20, UASV). This simple observation conforms to what we now understand about the process of evaporation and condensation.

Psychological Acumen: The book has penetrating insights into human psychology, addressing matters of emotion, motivation, and behavior long before these became areas of scientific study. For example, Proverbs identifies the profound link between one's emotional state and physical health: "A joyful heart is good medicine, but a crushed spirit dries up the bones" (Proverbs 17:22, UASV). Modern psychology and medicine affirm the psychosomatic connection between mental and physical well-being.

Social Dynamics: Proverbs offers ageless wisdom on social interactions and justice, addressing topics like poverty, dishonesty, and strife that remain relevant today. Its principles for fair dealing and the humane treatment of others are universally recognized values, often incorporated into laws and ethical codes.

Unity of Message: Despite its collection of diverse sayings and instructions, Proverbs maintains an internal coherence and consistency, revolving around the central tenet that the fear of Jehovah is the beginning of wisdom. This unifying theme stands as a testament to its divine origin.

Profound Impact: The global influence and longevity of Proverbs, including its adoption by various cultures and its effect on literature and legal systems, further testify to its extraordinary origin. Such broad and enduring impact can only be adequately explained by its divine inspiration.

Predictive Wisdom: While not prophetic in the usual sense, the book does possess an anticipatory quality. Its observations and warnings about human behavior and consequences often play out predictably in individual lives, suggesting a wisdom beyond mere human observation.

Moral Absolutism: Proverbs operates on the premise of objective moral truths, an idea that resonates with the biblical assertion that moral law is divinely ordained. The book's ethical mandates align closely with the moral teachings found throughout the Bible, affirming its place within the canon and its divine inspiration.

In summary, the Book of Proverbs exhibits extraordinary qualities in scientific, psychological, social, and moral dimensions that go beyond the capacity of mere human wisdom. These qualities robustly testify to the book's divine origin and inspiration.

Edward D. Andrews

Authenticity, Authorship, and Date of Ecclesiastes

The Lofty Purpose of Ecclesiastes

The Book of Ecclesiastes serves the elevated purpose of guiding individuals toward the discernment of what truly matters in life, steering them away from the futility of earthly pursuits devoid of eternal value. Written by Solomon in the later part of his life, Ecclesiastes confronts the existential questions that have occupied human minds across generations: What is the meaning of life? Is there value in human endeavor?

The Vanity of Earthly Pursuits: One of the fundamental lessons of Ecclesiastes is the vanity of human endeavors when disconnected from the divine perspective. Solomon, who had wealth, wisdom, and accomplishments beyond measure, emphatically concludes that all is "vanity" when pursued as an end in itself. "Vanity of vanities, says the Preacher, vanity of vanities! All is vanity" (Ecclesiastes 1:2, UASV).

Wisdom and Moral Integrity: Ecclesiastes doesn't dismiss the importance of wisdom or morality but frames them within the broader context of godly living. The book warns against folly and wickedness while emphasizing that wisdom and understanding are far better. However, these too are ultimately inadequate to bring eternal fulfillment or save one from the universal fate of death.

The Fear of God: At its core, Ecclesiastes leads the reader toward the realization that the fear of God is the ultimate foundation for a meaningful life. "The conclusion of the matter, everything having been heard, is: Fear the true God and keep his commandments, for this is the whole obligation of man" (Ecclesiastes 12:13, UASV).

Perspective on Time and Eternity: The book makes profound observations about the cycles of nature and the seasons of life, underscoring the temporary nature of human existence. In doing so, it redirects focus from transient earthly concerns to eternal matters. "He has made everything beautiful in its time. Also, he has put eternity into man's heart, yet so that he cannot find out what God has done from the beginning to the end" (Ecclesiastes 3:11, UASV).

Evaluation of Life's Pleasures: Solomon's personal exploration of pleasure, wealth, and achievement serves as a cautionary tale. It exposes the emptiness of hedonistic and materialistic pursuits, contrasting them with the lasting value of a life lived in alignment with God's will.

The Acceptance of Life's Uncertainties: Ecclesiastes acknowledges the inscrutability of life's circumstances and the limitations of human wisdom. It teaches acceptance and trust in the face of life's unpredictabilities, always with the understanding that God's will is supreme.

The Book of Ecclesiastes was penned with the lofty aim of directing souls toward a life rooted in the fear of God, thereby instilling a sense of purpose that transcends the fleeting and often deceptive allure of earthly achievements and pleasures. It stands as a profound treatise on the human condition, providing answers grounded in divine wisdom.

The Significance of Ecclesiastes' Hebrew Name

The Hebrew name of the book is "Qoheleth," a term that can be translated as "Assembler" or "Convener." It implies the gathering of people for the purpose of imparting wisdom or instruction. In a broader sense, it can also mean "Teacher" or "Preacher." Solomon, as Qoheleth, gathers his readers as a convener would gather an audience, in order to share wisdom and life lessons born out of his own experiences and reflections.

The Assembly for Wisdom: In ancient Israel, wisdom teachings were often delivered in a congregational setting, like a council or assembly. The term "Qoheleth" reflects this traditional form of imparting wisdom. It conveys the intent of the book: to convene an audience in order to discuss the crucial aspects of life and guide them toward a meaningful existence grounded in the fear of God.

Teaching through Exploration: As Qoheleth, Solomon does not merely instruct; he embarks on an intellectual exploration with his audience. He lays bare the vanities and frustrations of life, yet skillfully leads his readers to the ultimate conclusion that the fear of God and obedience to His commandments constitute the entire duty and essence of human existence.

Contrast with Greek and English Names: The Greek name "Ekklesiastes" and the English name "Ecclesiastes" stem from the idea of assembly but lose some nuances of the original Hebrew. They lean toward a more institutional sense of gathering, such as a "church," and do not fully capture the interactive and personal nature of wisdom-sharing that "Qoheleth" implies.

Alignment with the Book's Purpose: The Hebrew name provides a more direct connection to the book's purpose of guiding the reader toward understanding what genuinely matters in life. As Qoheleth, Solomon isn't just presenting didactic maxims; he is entering into a dialogical relationship with his readers to explore life's complexities together. This approach culminates in the revelation that life's ultimate purpose is rooted in the fear of God, a conclusion that resonates with the implications of the Hebrew title.

Solomon as a Congregator in the Context of Ecclesiastes

Solomon is referred to as "Qoheleth," a term which essentially translates to "Assembler," "Convener," or "Congregator." This title captures the multifaceted role Solomon played in his capacity as a leader, philosopher, and teacher.

Solomon's Assembly for Wisdom Teaching: One of the primary responsibilities of a king in ancient Israel was to impart wisdom and ensure the moral and spiritual well-being of his people. Solomon, renowned for his wisdom, gathered people together much like a teacher would convene his students. As Qoheleth, he congregated the nation to instill them with wisdom, moral instruction, and insights into the complexities of human life and the universe.

Spiritual Convocation: Solomon did not simply gather people; he gathered truths, principles, and observations. He congregated the moral and ethical teachings that were scattered in human experience and thought. These were then synthesized and presented as divine wisdom, as can be clearly seen throughout the book of Proverbs and Ecclesiastes.

Conveyor of Divine Wisdom: Solomon's role as Qoheleth was more than that of a mere human teacher; he acted as the conveyor of divine wisdom. His teachings directed people to a higher moral and spiritual plane. This is most evident in Ecclesiastes where the ultimate conclusion is the fear of God, which is the beginning of wisdom according to Proverbs 1:7.

Integrating Secular and Divine Wisdom: Solomon's wisdom was not limited to religious or spiritual matters. He was knowledgeable in various fields such as biology, agriculture, and architecture. His role as a congregator, therefore, also meant bringing together secular and divine wisdom. The book of Ecclesiastes demonstrates this perfectly as it delves into topics that are both secular (such as labor and wealth) and divine (like the fear of God).

A Congregator of an Intellectual Tradition: By the act of writing and consolidating his teachings in Ecclesiastes, Solomon was congregating an intellectual and spiritual tradition. He brought together wisdom from various sources and presented it in a cohesive form, providing a timeless repository of wisdom that aligns with the entire canon of Scripture.

In essence, Solomon's role as a congregator goes beyond merely assembling people or even ideas. It extends to assembling a comprehensive worldview rooted in the fear of Jehovah, instructing on how to live a life that is meaningful in both earthly and eternal terms.

Solomon's Authorship Established in Ecclesiastes

The authorship of Ecclesiastes has been a topic of scholarly discussion, but from a conservative viewpoint, several factors firmly establish Solomon as the writer of this profound book.

Internal Evidence in Ecclesiastes: The very opening verse of Ecclesiastes provides a significant clue, stating: "The words of the

Preacher, the son of David, king in Jerusalem" (Ecclesiastes 1:1, UASV). This unmistakably points to Solomon, as he is the son of David who ascended to the throne and was renowned for his wisdom.

The Voice of Wisdom and Experience: The content of Ecclesiastes reflects the wisdom and experience that Solomon, in his role as a king and philosopher, would have had. Phrases like "I said in my heart," "I perceived," or "I made great works" all imply a life of reflection, achievement, and authority, which suit Solomon's life well.

Solomon's Unique Position: No other figure in Israel's history fits the description of having unparalleled wisdom, immense wealth, and the leisure to explore both folly and wisdom. He also had a position of kingship in Jerusalem, which aligns well with the internal descriptions within Ecclesiastes.

Chronological Context: Based on a literal conservative Bible chronology, Solomon reigned from approximately 971-931 B.C.E. The themes in Ecclesiastes align well with this timeframe, reflecting an era in which Israel was secure, prosperous, and searching for meaning beyond material prosperity.

Corroboration in Other Books: The Wisdom literature, as a whole, often ascribes its teachings to Solomon. For instance, Proverbs 1:1 begins by saying, "The proverbs of Solomon, the son of David, king of Israel," which indicates that the tradition of Solomon as a sage and writer of wisdom literature was well established.

Theological Consistency: Ecclesiastes is replete with the same theological foundations that Solomon was taught and that he himself had advocated in other writings. The teachings on the "fear of God," human limitations, and the pursuit of wisdom are consistent with Solomon's other works, like Proverbs and the Song of Solomon.

In light of these factors, the evidence strongly suggests that Solomon is the author of Ecclesiastes. His unique life experience, the internal textual clues, and the consistent theological themes all converge to affirm Solomon's authorship. Therefore, we can be certain that Solomon, the son of David, king in Jerusalem, who was endowed with divine wisdom, is the author of this profound book.

Location and Timeframe of the Writing of Ecclesiastes

Location: Jerusalem: The opening verse of Ecclesiastes clearly identifies that the work was composed by "the Preacher, the son of David, king in Jerusalem" (Ecclesiastes 1:1, UASV). Given that Solomon is most aptly described as "the son of David, king in Jerusalem," it is unquestionable that the location where the book was written is Jerusalem. This is further corroborated by Solomon's status as the king in Jerusalem, the capital of Israel, and the political and religious center of the nation. It would have been the natural and fitting locale for Solomon to pen such a work, given its royal and existential themes.

Timeframe: Solomon's Later Years: Solomon reigned as king of Israel from approximately 971 to 931 B.C.E., based on a literal conservative Bible chronology. The content of Ecclesiastes suggests a mature perspective on life, one that has experienced both wisdom and folly, wealth and emptiness. This points to Solomon's later years, after he had accomplished all that he describes in the book — building projects, acquisition of wealth, and extensive philosophical and existential explorations.

Moreover, Ecclesiastes frequently mentions the vanity of youth and the brevity of life, suggesting an author who is looking back on life's various stages. The book concludes with an admonition to "Remember also your Creator in the days of your youth" (Ecclesiastes 12:1, UASV), which serves as an advice from someone who has advanced in years.

The Historical Context: The timeframe of Solomon's reign was one of unparalleled prosperity and peace for Israel. This context allows for the kind of philosophical and existential reflections we find in Ecclesiastes. It was a period that provided Solomon with both the time and resources to explore "all that is done under heaven" (Ecclesiastes 1:13, UASV).

Ecclesiastes was written by Solomon in Jerusalem during his later years, specifically between 971 and 931 B.C.E. The royal, philosophical, and existential themes of the book fit well within the socio-political landscape of Jerusalem during Solomon's reign. Therefore, the location and time of its composition are both significant and fitting for the message the book conveys.

Objections to the Inspiration of Ecclesiastes and Their Refutation

Objection 1: Pessimistic Tone

One of the most common objections raised against the divine inspiration of Ecclesiastes is its seemingly pessimistic tone. Critics argue that the book's recurrent theme of "vanity" or "meaninglessness" stands in contrast to the rest of Scripture, which upholds the value and purpose of life.

Refutation: It is important to understand the rhetorical device employed by Solomon. The book uses a teaching method that starts with life "under the sun," a life devoid of divine perspective, to lead the reader to the realization that true meaning can only be found in fearing God and keeping His commandments (Ecclesiastes 12:13, UASV). Thus, the book is not promoting pessimism; rather, it underscores the importance of a life rooted in God's wisdom.

Objection 2: Absence of Covenant Language

Another objection is the absence of explicit covenant language or references to Israel's unique relationship with Jehovah. Critics claim this absence might indicate that the book is not inspired Scripture.

Refutation: The focus of Ecclesiastes is on universal human experiences and existential questions that pertain to all people, regardless of their covenantal status. Moreover, it implicitly assumes the reader's knowledge of Jehovah's laws and wisdom, as the conclusion of the book makes it clear that the whole duty of man is to fear God and keep His commandments.

Objection 3: Use of Natural Philosophy

Critics also point to the book's use of natural philosophy as an indication that it is a human work, influenced by the prevailing philosophies of the day.

Refutation: The incorporation of observations about the natural world does not negate divine inspiration. Solomon was renowned for his wisdom, which included understanding of natural phenomena (1 Kings 4:33). Scripture often uses natural illustrations to convey spiritual truths, as seen in the Proverbs and the teachings of Jesus.

Objection 4: Lack of Explicit Messianic Prophecy

Some have claimed that the absence of explicit Messianic prophecy detracts from the book's claim to divine inspiration.

Refutation: Not all books of the Bible contain Messianic prophecies. Each book has its unique purpose within the canon. Ecclesiastes is focused on exploring the meaning of life and human endeavors, pointing readers to the importance of fearing God. Its purpose aligns well with the broader aims of Scripture.

All the objections raised against the divine inspiration of Ecclesiastes can be refuted when the book is understood in its proper context and in harmony with the overall teaching of the Bible. Far from being a mere human philosophical treatise, Ecclesiastes provides divinely inspired wisdom, effectively guiding the reader to the conclusion that life's ultimate purpose is found in reverencing Jehovah and obeying His commandments.

Solomon's Eminence as the Qualified Author of Ecclesiastes

Wisdom Granted by Jehovah

Solomon's qualification to write Ecclesiastes begins with the divine wisdom granted to him by Jehovah. According to 1 Kings 3:5-14 (UASV), Solomon famously chose wisdom over wealth and long life when offered anything he wished by Jehovah in a dream. This divine endowment of wisdom made him not only a capable king but also a person uniquely qualified to delve into the complex issues of life and existence addressed in Ecclesiastes.

Experience with Wealth and Material Possessions

Solomon's unparalleled wealth and resources offered him firsthand experience with the material pursuits that many people believe lead to happiness. The Queen of Sheba even testified to Solomon's great wisdom and wealth after observing his court (1 Kings 10:4-7). His firsthand knowledge allowed him to make informed and experiential conclusions about the futility of pursuing wealth for ultimate satisfaction—a major theme in Ecclesiastes.

Political Leadership

As the king of Israel, Solomon had direct experience with governance and human behavior at both individual and societal levels. His political leadership offered him insights into human ambitions, endeavors, and the complexities of justice and governance. These observations are reflected in his writings, contributing to the full-bodied understanding of "life under the sun."

Author of Other Wisdom Literature

Solomon was already a recognized figure in wisdom literature, being traditionally attributed the authorship of most of Proverbs and the Song of Solomon. His skill in using proverbial sayings, poetic devices, and philosophical discourse is evident in these books, further establishing his capability to author a work like Ecclesiastes.

Broad Intellectual Curiosity

The Bible records that Solomon spoke 3,000 proverbs and composed 1,005 songs. He also had knowledge of natural history, including descriptions of plant life and animal behavior (1 Kings 4:33). This breadth of interests made him well-rounded and intellectually equipped to explore the multifaceted questions of life and existence.

Understanding of Human Nature

Solomon's judgments, such as the famous case of determining the real mother of a living baby by suggesting to divide the baby in two (1 Kings 3:16-28), reveal a keen understanding of human nature. This deep insight is crucial in addressing the existential questions raised in Ecclesiastes.

Personal Struggles with Idolatry and Repentance

Although Solomon's wisdom was unparalleled, he was not without faults. He struggled with idolatry in his later years, largely influenced by foreign wives. This struggle, and presumably his repentance as reflected in the book's conclusion about the ultimate duty of man (Ecclesiastes 12:13-14), adds a layer of authenticity and depth to his observations on the vanities and complexities of life.

All these elements—divine wisdom, unparalleled wealth, political leadership, prior contributions to wisdom literature, intellectual breadth, understanding of human nature, and personal spiritual journey—converge to make Solomon eminently qualified to author Ecclesiastes. His book serves as a divinely inspired guide that navigates the complexities of life to lead us toward the ultimate goal: the fear of Jehovah and obedience to His commandments.

The Strongest Argument for the Canonicity of Ecclesiastes: Divine Inspiration Attested by Historical Acceptance and Internal Evidence

Historical Acceptance in the Jewish Community

The most robust argument for the canonicity of Ecclesiastes rests on its long-standing acceptance within the Jewish community, which recognized the work as inspired Scripture. The book was part of the Hebrew Bible and has been preserved in the Masoretic Text, which is the foundation for the Old Testament in Protestant Bibles. This broad and ancient acceptance within the community that originally received and preserved the text serves as a strong affirmation of its divine inspiration and, therefore, its rightful place in the canon.

Internal Evidence of Divine Wisdom

Another pivotal aspect that confirms the canonicity of Ecclesiastes is the internal evidence within the book itself. The work is replete with wisdom that aligns with and complements other biblical books. Its teachings do not conflict with the broader corpus of inspired writings but rather provide unique perspectives on common themes such as the futility of life without God, the importance of fearing Jehovah, and the obligation to obey His commandments. These teachings strongly suggest a divine origin consistent with other canonical writings.

Affirmation in Rabbinical Writings

Additional support comes from early Rabbinical writings and the Talmud, which affirm the book's authoritative status. Ecclesiastes is cited along with other writings considered to be divinely inspired, reinforcing its canonical standing.

Consistency with Solomon's Other Works

Since Solomon is credibly the author of Ecclesiastes, his other contributions to the Bible—Proverbs and Song of Solomon—also lend weight to its canonical status. All these books share thematic and stylistic similarities that are consistent with a single, divinely inspired author.

The historical acceptance of Ecclesiastes by the Jewish community, its internal evidence of divine wisdom, its affirmation in Rabbinical writings, and its consistency with Solomon's other divinely inspired contributions collectively serve as the strongest argument for its canonicity. Ecclesiastes meets and exceeds the criteria for canonical inclusion, testifying to its divine origin and timeless relevance.

Authenticity, Authorship, and Date of the Song of Solomon

The Song of Solomon as the "Song of the Songs": The Apex of Hebrew Poetry on Love and Relationship

Supreme Quality of Literary Excellence

The phrase "Song of the Songs" mirrors the Hebrew superlative construction, signifying the best or the most outstanding among songs.

The Song of Solomon is not just another composition; it is the apex of poetic literature. It employs vivid imagery, metaphor, and allegory in a way that no other song does. The poetic devices used are not mere embellishments; they are vehicles of profound truths about love, desire, and relationship.

Concentration on a Universal Human Experience

While many songs and poems focus on particular aspects of human life or experiences, the Song of Solomon concentrates on love—a universal human experience that transcends time, culture, and geography. This theme resonates with anyone, anywhere, making this song globally significant and timeless.

Deep Emotional and Spiritual Resonance

The Song of Solomon not only discusses the physical and emotional aspects of love but also transcends to a more profound spiritual dimension. The text presents an ideal picture of mutual love, care, and respect between a man and a woman, which, by extension, signifies a form of divine love. This multidimensional approach to love amplifies the song's significance, making it the "Song of the Songs."

Connection to Solomon's Wisdom and Experience

The song is traditionally attributed to Solomon, a figure renowned for his wisdom, which was a gift from Jehovah. Solomon's insights into human nature, relationships, and divine truths give this song a depth and complexity that few other compositions achieve. His experience as a sage and a king adds layers of understanding to the concepts presented, further enhancing its claim to be the "Song of the Songs."

Consistency with Biblical Principles

The song is entirely consistent with biblical principles concerning love, relationships, and marriage, further attesting to its inspired nature. It serves as an intricate tapestry where divine wisdom meets human experience, offering not merely a guide but a standard for love and relationships.

The Song of Solomon stands as the "Song of the Songs" due to its unmatched literary excellence, its focus on a universally significant theme, its emotional and spiritual depth, its connection to Solomon's God-given wisdom, and its complete consistency with biblical principles. Therefore, it earns its title by encapsulating the epitome of what Hebrew poetic literature can offer on the subject of love and relationships.

The Authorship, Qualifications, Context, and Theme of the Song of Solomon

Authorship and Qualifications

The Song of Solomon was authored by King Solomon, as its superscription suggests in Song of Solomon 1:1: "The Song of Songs, which is Solomon's." Solomon was a man of unparalleled wisdom, granted to him by Jehovah (1 Kings 3:5-14). His wisdom manifested in a variety of ways, including governance, judgment, and literary prowess. Solomon wrote 3,000 proverbs and composed 1,005 songs (1 Kings 4:32). Therefore, he was more than qualified to write a song that delves deeply into the subject matter of love and relationship, adorned with poetic excellence and laced with rich metaphorical language.

The Theme of Frustrated Love

The Song of Solomon could be termed a "song of frustrated love" because it portrays a love that faces numerous obstacles and yearnings that are often not immediately fulfilled. The couple in the song has to navigate through separation, misunderstandings, and societal norms. For example, the woman speaks of her absence from her beloved and the suffering it causes her in Song 2:5: "Sustain me with raisin cakes; refresh me with apples, for I am faint from love." Such instances of yearning and emotional depth show a love that faces challenges, which could be deemed 'frustrated' in some respects.

Location and Date of Writing

The Song of Solomon was likely written in Jerusalem, the seat of Solomon's royal court. The descriptions within the book suggest familiarity with the geography and natural beauty of the land, including specific places such as Lebanon (Song 4:8, 15), En Gedi (Song 1:14), and Jerusalem itself (Song 3:6-11).

As for the time of its composition, adhering to a literal conservative Bible chronology, it would have been written during Solomon's reign, which spanned from approximately 970 to 931 B.C.E. Given that the song is a mature reflection on love, it is reasonable to place its writing during the middle or latter part of his rule, when his wisdom and literary skills would have been at their zenith.

Solomon, a man of unmatched wisdom and significant literary output, is the author of the Song of Solomon. His qualifications for writing this work are unquestionable. The book explores love in all its facets, including its challenges, making it a song of 'frustrated love' to some extent. It was likely penned in Jerusalem during the course of Solomon's reign, making it a product of the 10th century B.C.E. The complexities and insights of the Song of Solomon make it a unique and invaluable part of the biblical canon.

Evidence for the Canonicity of the Song of Solomon

Internal Testimony

The very first verse of the Song of Solomon identifies the author as Solomon: "The Song of Songs, which is Solomon's" (Song of Solomon 1:1). Solomon's authorship gives this book initial credibility, considering Solomon's wisdom and position as a key figure in Israel's history. Furthermore, the internal structure and thematic content align well with the wisdom literature genre, which includes other canonical books like Proverbs and Ecclesiastes, both attributed to Solomon.

Early Jewish Acceptance

The Song of Solomon was accepted into the Jewish canon and was part of the Septuagint, the Greek translation of the Hebrew Scriptures, which predates the time of Christ. This early translation serves as a form of external evidence for its canonicity. The book was included in the third division of the Hebrew Bible, the Ketuvim

(Writings), which testifies to its acceptance among the Jewish sages and scholars.

Citation in Rabbinic Literature

The Song of Solomon is frequently cited in the Talmud and Midrash, indicating its acceptance in Jewish tradition. While these are post-biblical works, they reflect earlier oral traditions and provide insights into how the Jewish community revered the text.

Early Christian Recognition

In early Christianity, the Song of Solomon was recognized as canonical by key figures such as Origen, Jerome, and Augustine. It is also listed in early canonical lists like the Council of Carthage (397 C.E.) that affirmed the canon of the Old Testament, which was consistent with Jewish recognition.

Consistency with Biblical Themes

The Song of Solomon is in harmony with the overarching themes of Scripture, offering a poetic and profound commentary on love, commitment, and relational integrity, which are all themes explored in other parts of the Bible. Although the book doesn't directly mention Jehovah, its theme of faithful love can be seen as a smaller reflection of Jehovah's greater covenantal love for His people.

The Song of Solomon carries internal, external, and historical evidence supporting its canonicity. Its early and consistent inclusion in both Jewish and Christian traditions, its citation in rabbinic literature, and its alignment with biblical themes collectively affirm its rightful place in the canon of Scripture.

Absence of the Word "God" and Canonicity of the Song of Solomon

No Detriment to Canonicity

The absence of the word "God" in the Song of Solomon does not argue against its canonicity. Scripture is not only a revelation of God's character but also a revelation of His design for creation, including human relationships. The Song of Solomon is entirely consistent with the biblical portrayal of love, marriage, and relational integrity. The teachings and principles found in the Song resonate with other passages and themes of Scripture that deal with these topics.

Canonical Criteria

Canonicity is determined by various factors, including apostolicity, consistency with accepted canonical writings, widespread acceptance among the early believers, and doctrinal soundness. The Song of Solomon meets these criteria, despite not explicitly mentioning God. It was universally accepted in the Jewish canon, cited in rabbinic literature, and accepted by early Christian authorities.

Unique Place in the Canon

Exemplification of Human Love

What marks the Song of Solomon for its unique place in the Bible is its detailed, poetic focus on marital love. No other book in the Bible is solely devoted to exploring this aspect of human experience. It provides divine sanction to the natural feelings and desires in a marital relationship, thereby elevating them as godly and good.

Imagery and Poetic Excellence

Its unique form as an extended lyrical poem filled with vivid imagery and metaphor also sets it apart. This differentiates it from more didactic books and historical narratives in the Bible. It shows the breadth of literary forms that Jehovah employed to convey His message, including poetry to describe human emotions.

Affirmation of Covenantal Love

While it does not explicitly mention God, the very concept of committed, exclusive love is an earthly representation of divine covenantal love. The principles of devotion, exclusivity, and deep emotional attachment are applicable both to human relationships and, on a grander scale, to our relationship with Jehovah.

The Song of Solomon has a unique place in the canon due to its literary form and thematic focus. Its absence of the explicit mention of

"God" does not negate its canonicity; rather, its consistent message about love and relationship affirms its rightful place in Scripture.

CHAPTER 6 Defending the Book of Isaiah

Authenticity, Authorship, and Date of Isaiah

The Eighth Century B.C.E. in the Middle East: Israel and Judah in Focus

Geopolitical Landscape

The eighth century B.C.E. was a time of significant geopolitical shifts in the Middle East. Assyria was the dominant world power, led by formidable kings such as Tiglath-Pileser III, Shalmaneser V, and Sargon II. The Assyrians had expansionist ambitions, posing a direct threat to the smaller nations around them, including Israel and Judah.

Northern Kingdom of Israel

Israel, the Northern Kingdom, was in a state of moral and spiritual decline. This period saw a succession of ungodly kings who promoted idolatry and were in conflict with Jehovah's prophets. Israel faced the threat of Assyrian invasion, which materialized during this period, culminating in the fall of Samaria in 722 B.C.E. and the subsequent exile of the Israelites.

Southern Kingdom of Judah

Judah, the Southern Kingdom, had a mixed record of faithfulness to Jehovah. Kings like Uzziah and Jotham led relatively righteous reigns but were followed by Ahaz, who engaged in idolatrous practices. Despite the unfaithfulness of some of its kings, Judah was granted temporary relief from Assyrian aggression during the reign of King Hezekiah, who turned the nation back to Jehovah.

Religious State of Affairs

Both Israel and Judah struggled with idolatry, a direct violation of the First Commandment. This was a significant reason why prophets like Isaiah were sent by Jehovah—to call the people back to faithfulness and adherence to the covenant. Isaiah's prophecies were primarily focused on warning Judah about the consequences of unfaithfulness and the impending judgment through the Assyrian invasion, while also delivering messages of hope for a future restoration.

Social and Economic Factors

Economically, both kingdoms experienced periods of prosperity, but this prosperity led to social injustices, including exploitation of the poor and accumulation of wealth by a select few. These issues were also addressed by prophets like Isaiah, who condemned the social injustices and called for righteous living.

The eighth century B.C.E. was a period of considerable geopolitical instability for Israel and Judah, set against the backdrop of a rising Assyrian Empire. It was a time marked by spiritual decline, social injustices, and the looming threat of Assyrian aggression. These factors set the stage for the ministry of prophets like Isaiah, who addressed these very issues in their prophecies. Therefore, understanding this historical context is crucial for a comprehensive understanding of the Book of Isaiah.

The Prophet Isaiah: Jehovah's Spokesman in the Eighth Century B.C.E.

Answering the Call and Timing

The prophet who answered the call to speak for Jehovah during the volatile times of the eighth century B.C.E. was Isaiah. His prophetic ministry began in the year 740 B.C.E., during the final year of King Uzziah's reign in Judah. This period extended through the reigns of Jotham, Ahaz, and Hezekiah. Isaiah's call is vividly described in Isaiah 6:1-8, where he has a vision of Jehovah's holiness and subsequently volunteers himself saying, "Here I am! Send me."

Significance of the Name

Isaiah's name in Hebrew is "Yeshayahu," which means "Salvation of Jehovah" or "Jehovah is salvation." This name is profoundly significant for several reasons:

1. **Prophetic Indication**: His name essentially summarized the core message of his prophecies. Isaiah was to deliver a message of both judgment and hope. While he warned Judah and Israel of impending doom due to their disobedience, he also provided a glimpse into the future salvation that would come through the Messiah, thereby pointing to Jehovah as the ultimate source of salvation.

2. **Relevance to His Time**: During a period when both Israel and Judah were facing threats from powerful nations, Isaiah's name served as a constant reminder that salvation could only come from Jehovah. This underscored the futility of forming alliances with foreign powers for security, an action that Isaiah often criticized.

3. **Universal Scope**: While Isaiah's immediate ministry was focused on Israel and Judah, the significance of his name extends to all of humanity. His prophecies about the coming Messiah are not just for Israel but also point to a global salvation available to all who put their faith in Jehovah.

Isaiah, whose name itself means "Jehovah is salvation," was the chosen prophet to deliver Jehovah's messages during a critical period in the history of Israel and Judah. The significance of his name cannot be overstated, as it encapsulates the essence of his prophetic ministry: a call to repentance and a message of hope centering on Jehovah as the only source of true salvation. Therefore, Isaiah's name serves as an enduring testimony to the core message of his life and writings.

Isaiah: His Life, Ministry, and Contemporary Prophets

Biographical Details

Isaiah was the son of Amoz, and his prophetic ministry was primarily focused on the southern kingdom of Judah. He is mentioned as being married with children; his sons' names were Shear-Jashub, meaning "A remnant shall return," and Maher-Shalal-Hash-Baz, meaning "Speed the spoil, hasten the booty." These names were indicative of prophetic messages themselves.

Period of Ministry

Isaiah's prophetic ministry began in 740 B.C.E., marking the year King Uzziah died, and extended through the reigns of Jotham, Ahaz, and Hezekiah, kings of Judah. This would place his ministry's end around 686 B.C.E., making it a period of approximately 54 years. He lived through some of the most tumultuous times in Israelite history, including the fall of the northern kingdom of Israel to Assyria in 722 B.C.E.

Contemporary Prophets

Isaiah was not alone in prophesying during this critical time period. Several other prophets were active in both the northern and southern kingdoms.

1. **Hosea**: Hosea's ministry primarily targeted the northern kingdom of Israel. He began his ministry before Isaiah and continued up to the fall of Israel in 722 B.C.E.

2. **Micah**: Micah was a contemporary of Isaiah and focused his prophecies on both Israel and Judah. He denounced social injustice and predicted the future glory of Zion.

3. **Amos**: Though Amos preceded Isaiah slightly, the overlap in their lifetimes and their collective messages make them worth mentioning together. Amos concentrated his ministry on the northern kingdom of Israel.

4. **Jonah**: Although better known for his mission to Nineveh, Jonah was also a prophet during this period. His ministry primarily took place in the northern kingdom and had international implications.

Isaiah was a key figure in the prophetic landscape of the eighth century B.C.E. Spanning a period of about 54 years, his ministry was long and influential, characterized by profound theological insights and bold declarations of Jehovah's intentions for His people and the nations. He was part of a cadre of prophets including Hosea, Micah, Amos, and Jonah, who collectively provided a comprehensive picture of Jehovah's judgment and grace during a critical juncture in Israelite history.

Indicators Affirming Isaiah as the Writer of the Book

Direct Attribution

The most direct evidence that Isaiah wrote the book attributed to him is the textual assertion within the book itself. The opening verse of the Book of Isaiah clearly states, "The vision of Isaiah the son of Amoz, which he saw concerning Judah and Jerusalem in the days of Uzziah, Jotham, Ahaz, and Hezekiah, kings of Judah" (Isaiah 1:1, UASV). This declaration establishes Isaiah, the son of Amoz, as the author from the outset.

Internal Consistency and Coherence

The Book of Isaiah demonstrates a cohesive and unified theological message, language, and style. This coherence argues for a single author rather than multiple. Themes like the sovereignty of Jehovah, the coming Messianic age, and the ultimate restoration of Israel are threaded throughout the book, suggesting the work of a singular mind and spirit.

Historical Context

Isaiah's interactions with kings like Ahaz and Hezekiah, as detailed in the book, align with what is known from historical records and other biblical texts. The prophetic events that Isaiah talks about, such as the fall of Babylon and the exile, fit into the timeline of Isaiah's life and ministry, supporting the claim that he was the writer.

Citations in Other Scriptures

The New Testament writers attribute quotations from the Book of Isaiah to Isaiah himself. For example, in the Gospel of John, a quote from Isaiah 6:10 is attributed directly to Isaiah (John 12:38-41). The apostle Paul in Romans also cites Isaiah by name (Romans 9:27, 29; 10:16, 20).

Jewish Tradition

The Jewish tradition has consistently held that Isaiah was the writer of the book that bears his name. The Talmud and other rabbinic literature affirm Isaiah's authorship, and there has been little dispute about this within the tradition.

Manuscript Evidence

The Great Isaiah Scroll, one of the Dead Sea Scrolls, offers a text of Isaiah that is essentially the same as the Masoretic Text. This ancient manuscript, dated to the second century B.C.E., provides strong evidence for the unity of the Book of Isaiah and thereby supports its single authorship.

The Book of Isaiah is directly attributed to Isaiah, and this attribution is supported by internal textual consistency, historical details, New Testament citations, Jewish tradition, and manuscript evidence. All of these factors together make a compelling case for Isaiah's authorship of the book that bears his name.

The Unity of the Book of Isaiah: Unassailable Testimonies

Recurring Themes and Concepts

One of the most significant indications of the unity of the Book of Isaiah is the recurrence of specific themes, concepts, and phrases throughout the text. Themes like the coming Messianic Kingdom, the sovereignty of Jehovah, and the redemption and restoration of Israel occur consistently from the beginning to the end of the book.

Linguistic Consistency

The Hebrew language used in Isaiah is consistent across the chapters. This uniformity in language includes specific stylistic elements, idiomatic expressions, and grammatical structures, which suggest that the book is the work of a single author rather than multiple contributors.

Structural Integrity

The Book of Isaiah has a coherent structure that suggests a unified purpose and authorship. The text is not a random collection of oracles but displays a deliberate arrangement that leads readers from the judgments against Israel and the nations to a vision of future restoration and glory.

Prophetic Fulfillment

The prophecies within the Book of Isaiah are interconnected, and many are fulfilled within the text itself or in other parts of Scripture. The coherence between the prophecies and their fulfillments supports the idea of a unified message stemming from a single prophetic voice.

External Confirmations

The New Testament consistently attributes quotations from Isaiah to a single prophet. For example, when quoting Isaiah, both Jesus and the apostles identify the prophet by name, thereby affirming the book's single authorship (e.g., Matthew 3:3; John 12:38-41; Romans 9:27, 29).

Jewish Tradition and Reception

The Jewish tradition has invariably upheld the unity of Isaiah. This is evident from early Jewish writings and the Masoretic tradition, which treat the book as a single, cohesive work.

Manuscript Evidence

The Great Isaiah Scroll from the Dead Sea Scrolls, dated to the second century B.C.E., contains the entire Book of Isaiah and demonstrates its unity. There are no markers or indications within this manuscript that suggest multiple authors or divisions that would break the unity of the book.

Historical Context

The book's detailed attention to historical facts, including geopolitical situations and the reigns of specific kings, is consistently accurate and integrated throughout. This historical precision suggests a unified source knowledgeable about the events he describes.

The unity of the Book of Isaiah is testified to by its recurring themes, linguistic consistency, structural integrity, prophetic fulfillments, external confirmations, traditional reception, manuscript evidence, and historical context. All these elements collectively substantiate the book as the work of a single author: Isaiah, the son of Amoz.

The Dead Sea Scroll of Isaiah: An Irrefutable Testimony to the Authenticity and Unity of Isaiah's Book

Textual Integrity Confirmed by the Dead Sea Scroll

The Dead Sea Scroll of Isaiah, commonly known as the Great Isaiah Scroll and dated to the second century B.C.E., is one of the most significant discoveries confirming the textual integrity of the Book of Isaiah. The scroll contains all 66 chapters of Isaiah and is remarkably consistent with the Masoretic Text, which serves as the basis for most modern translations of the Old Testament. This proves that the text has been extraordinarily well-preserved through the centuries, bolstering our confidence that our Bibles today represent the original inspired writings.

A Single Unified Manuscript

The Great Isaiah Scroll lacks any indications, annotations, or markers that might suggest a division into multiple books or a compilation from various authors. This is compelling evidence that the entire Book of Isaiah was considered a unified work, thus affirming the traditional belief that the entire book was written by Isaiah, the son of Amoz.

Internal Consistency within the Scroll

The language, style, and thematic elements within the scroll are consistent throughout, supporting the claim of a single authorship. This is particularly crucial in the scholarly arena, where there have been arguments for multiple authors for the Book of Isaiah (so-called

"Deutero-Isaiah" and "Trito-Isaiah" theories). The consistency observed within the Dead Sea Scroll effectively counters these theories.

Substantive Equivalence to the Masoretic Text

The Great Isaiah Scroll provides a substantive equivalence to the Masoretic Text; the minor variations are mostly grammatical and do not impact the overall message or theology of the book. This uniformity between the texts is a clear testimony to the stability and reliability of the text over time. It ensures that the doctrinal content and the prophetic messages have remained unchanged, adding weight to the belief that what we read today in our Bibles is a faithful representation of the original inspired text.

Affirmation of Prophetic Elements

The prophetic messages, promises, and oracles contained in the Book of Isaiah are complete in the Great Isaiah Scroll. This confirms that Isaiah's prophecies, written in the eighth century B.C.E., are not later additions but were indeed part of the original text. This is crucial in affirming the book's predictive elements, specifically those prophecies fulfilled after the time of Isaiah.

The Dead Sea Scroll of Isaiah provides an irrefutable testimony to both the authenticity and unity of the Book of Isaiah. The remarkable preservation of the text, as evidenced by its congruence with the Masoretic Text, assures us that our Bibles today accurately represent the original inspired writings. Furthermore, the internal and thematic consistency within the scroll validates the traditional view that the entire book was written by Isaiah himself.

The Authenticity of Isaiah: A Multi-Faceted Confirmation

Historical Context and Internal Consistency

The Book of Isaiah aligns extraordinarily well with historical facts. The geopolitical situations, kings, and events described in the book correspond to what we know from ancient Near Eastern records.

Isaiah's ministry spans the reigns of Uzziah, Jotham, Ahaz, and Hezekiah. His work began in 740 B.C.E., during a period of relative prosperity for Judah, and extended into times of conflict and spiritual crisis, culminating in the Assyrian invasion. This historical alignment enhances the book's authenticity.

Contemporary Prophetic Confirmation

Isaiah was not the only prophet active during his time; his contemporaries included Amos, Hosea, and Micah. The messages of these prophets offer mutual support and thematic unity, validating Isaiah's authentic voice among the prophets of the eighth century B.C.E.

Divine Commission

Isaiah's call and commission in Chapter 6, where he encounters Jehovah's glory, provides significant theological weight to his prophecies. The narrative bears all the hallmarks of a genuine prophetic commission, consistent with other such commissions in the Bible.

Early and Wide Recognition

The early acceptance and widespread use of Isaiah in ancient Israel further underline its authenticity. We find citations and allusions to Isaiah in other books of the Old Testament, such as Kings and Chronicles, as well as in later Jewish literature like the Dead Sea Scrolls, as previously mentioned.

Fulfillment of Prophecy

The predictive prophecies in Isaiah that were fulfilled—such as the fall of Babylon and the reign of Cyrus the Great—stand as testaments to the book's divine origin. This demonstrates that the book is not a later fabrication but has stood the test of time and verification.

Testimony of Later Scriptures

The New Testament contains numerous references to Isaiah, crediting him as the author and treating the prophecies as genuine. For instance, Jesus Himself quotes Isaiah 61:1-2 in Luke 4:18-19 and attributes it directly to Isaiah. Similarly, the apostle Paul cites Isaiah extensively in his letters.

Linguistic and Stylistic Unity

Despite the depth and range of topics it covers—from judgment to redemption—the book maintains a linguistic and stylistic unity. While critics have proposed theories of multiple authorship, these claims do not hold up when scrutinizing the text's internal features. The Hebrew used in Isaiah is consistent with an eighth-century B.C.E. origin, further confirming its authenticity.

The Book of Isaiah carries abundant proof of its authenticity from multiple angles: historical, theological, and textual. Its internal consistency, the validation it receives from contemporary prophets, its early and widespread acceptance, and its confirmed predictive prophecies all point towards a single, divinely inspired author: Isaiah, the son of Amoz.

Proving Inspiration Through the Fulfillment of Messianic Prophecies in Isaiah

Isaiah 7:14: A Virgin Shall Conceive

The prophecy in Isaiah 7:14 declares, "Therefore Jehovah Himself will give you a sign: Behold, a virgin will conceive and bear a son, and she will call His name Immanuel." This is explicitly cited in the New Testament as having been fulfilled in the miraculous conception of Jesus (Matthew 1:23). The specificity of the prophecy, written centuries before the event it predicts, corroborates its divine origin.

Isaiah 9:6-7: The Mighty God and Everlasting Father

Isaiah identifies the coming Messiah with titles that indicate His divine nature and eternal rule. The New Testament also bears this out in multiple places, including the Gospel of John (John 1:1), Colossians (Colossians 2:9), and the Book of Revelation (Revelation 19:16).

Isaiah 11:1-10: The Stem of Jesse

The Messiah, according to Isaiah 11, will arise from the line of Jesse, thereby linking Him to the house of David. The New Testament genealogies in both Matthew and Luke confirm Jesus' Davidic lineage, thus fulfilling Isaiah's prophecy.

Isaiah 42:1-9: The Suffering Servant

This passage describes the Messiah as a suffering servant who will establish justice on the earth and be a light to the Gentiles. The Book of Acts confirms that Jesus fulfilled these roles (Acts 13:47; 26:23).

Isaiah 53: A Vivid Portrait of the Messiah's Suffering

Perhaps one of the most striking and detailed Messianic prophecies, Isaiah 53 paints a vivid portrait of the suffering, rejection, death, and subsequent vindication of the Messiah. The New Testament applies these passages directly to Jesus in several instances, such as Peter's discourse in Acts 8:30-35 and the teachings found in 1 Peter 2:24-25.

Isaiah 61:1-3: The Anointed One

Jesus Himself quotes this passage in Luke 4:17-21, claiming that He is the fulfillment of Isaiah's words. He asserts that the Spirit of Jehovah is upon Him to proclaim the good news, to heal, and to set the captives free, marking His ministry as the fulfillment of these ancient prophecies.

The Unity of Prophecy and Fulfillment

The remarkable precision with which these Messianic prophecies are fulfilled in Jesus demonstrates that they are not random conjectures but divinely inspired. The congruence between Isaiah's prophecies and the New Testament accounts can only be explained adequately by a unified, divine source of inspiration. The fact that these prophecies were recorded centuries before their fulfillment and that they correspond so exactly to the life, ministry, death, and resurrection of Jesus, asserts beyond a shadow of doubt the divine inspiration of the Book of Isaiah.

The Issue of the Multiple "Isaiahs": A Conservative Rebuttal

The Multi-Isaiah Theory

The question of authorship surrounding the Book of Isaiah has been a subject of debate among scholars, especially within the last two centuries. Some have proposed that the book is the work of multiple authors, based largely on differences in style, language, and historical context between different sections. This theory is commonly known as the "Deutero-Isaiah" theory, which suggests that chapters 1–39 were written by the historical Isaiah, while chapters 40–66 were written by a later author or authors during or after the Babylonian exile. This concept has even been expanded to a "Trito-Isaiah" theory, positing a third author for chapters 56–66.

Unified Theme and Coherence

One strong argument against the multi-Isaiah theory is the thematic and theological unity of the book. The Book of Isaiah has a coherent structure that articulates the themes of judgment and redemption consistently. Whether discussing the impending doom of Judah and Jerusalem, the future return from exile, or the coming of the Messiah, the book maintains a singular focus on Jehovah's sovereignty and plan for His people. It should be understood that the same prophet could address different audiences and situations under the inspiration of Jehovah, maintaining stylistic variety without compromising unity.

Language and Style

While some argue that the variations in language and style suggest multiple authors, it is equally plausible to attribute these to the same author using different styles and language for different contexts. Isaiah was a highly educated man who had access to royal circles (Isaiah 7:3; 39:3). It's entirely feasible that he employed different linguistic styles depending on the circumstances, the topic, and the audience he was addressing.

New Testament Attribution

The New Testament attributes quotations from all sections of Isaiah to the prophet himself. For example, in John 12:38–41, quotations from Isaiah 53 and Isaiah 6 are both attributed to Isaiah. If the New Testament authors, writing under divine inspiration, considered the whole of Isaiah to be the work of one man, there is strong theological precedent to do likewise.

The Dead Sea Scrolls

The Great Isaiah Scroll from the Dead Sea Scrolls, dating around the second century B.C.E., presents the Book of Isaiah as one unified work. This early manuscript shows no demarcation between what some scholars label as "First," "Second," or "Third" Isaiah, offering compelling evidence for single-authorship.

The notion of multiple Isaiahs is a recent development and contradicts both internal and external evidences, including the unified theme of the book, the New Testament attribution, and the manuscript evidence. The most coherent and theologically consistent view is that the Book of Isaiah is the product of a single inspired author—Isaiah of Jerusalem—who prophesied during the 8th century B.C.E.

The Origins and Spread of Skepticism Concerning the Writership of Isaiah

The Onset of Skepticism

Skepticism about the authorship of the Book of Isaiah began primarily in the 18th and 19th centuries, with the advent of higher criticism in biblical scholarship. Higher criticism sought to apply principles of literary and historical analysis to the Scriptures, sometimes casting doubt on traditional beliefs about their authorship and composition. It was within this milieu that the theory of Deutero-Isaiah arose, suggesting that chapters 40–66 were not penned by Isaiah but by another or multiple other writers during or after the Babylonian exile. This skepticism found its way into academic circles and has influenced many scholars ever since.

The Spread of the Theory

The theory gained traction in the late 19th and early 20th centuries, popularized by scholars who focused on perceived discrepancies in style, language, and historical setting between chapters

1–39 and 40–66. Over time, this theory was taught in theological seminaries and became mainstream in many scholarly commentaries. The theory even evolved into the Trito-Isaiah hypothesis, which further divided the book into three distinct sections (1–39, 40–55, 56–66), each with its purported author.

Reasons Why the Skepticism Is Unfounded

1. **Theological Unity**: As mentioned in the previous section, the Book of Isaiah displays a remarkable unity in theme, focusing consistently on Jehovah's sovereignty, judgment, and salvation. The book's internal coherence testifies against the notion of multiple authors.

2. **Linguistic Style**: While differences in style and language exist, they can easily be attributed to the varied audiences, circumstances, and times the prophet was addressing. Isaiah was known to have been a well-educated man with the ability to adapt his message to different settings and people.

3. **Historical Consistency**: Critics argue that the prophecies in chapters 40–66 reflect the period of the Babylonian exile or afterward, making it unlikely for Isaiah to have written them. However, predictive prophecy is a hallmark of biblical revelation. Isaiah could have very well prophesied events that would occur after his time, under the inspiration of Jehovah.

4. **New Testament Confirmation**: New Testament writers attribute quotations from all parts of Isaiah to the prophet himself (e.g., John 12:38–41). This attests to the belief in the early Christian community that the entire book was the work of a single author.

5. **Manuscript Evidence**: The Great Isaiah Scroll, part of the Dead Sea Scrolls, shows no distinction or division between the sections attributed to "First," "Second," or "Third" Isaiah, thereby providing solid manuscript evidence for single-authorship.

The skepticism concerning the writership of Isaiah primarily stems from higher-critical methodologies that emerged in the last few centuries. However, the unity of the book's themes, its linguistic style, the New Testament's attribution, and the earliest available manuscript evidence all strongly affirm that the Book of Isaiah was penned by a single author, Isaiah the prophet. This view aligns with the book's own claims and remains the most coherent and theologically consistent position.

Dissecting of the Book of Isaiah and Dr. Gleason L. Archer's Refutation

Dissecting the Book of Isaiah

The Book of Isaiah has undergone intense scrutiny and dissection, especially over the last few centuries. Many scholars have attempted to divide the book into multiple sections, attributing these sections to different authors or periods. The most prominent among these theories are:

1. **Proto-Isaiah (Chapters 1–39)**: The first section is attributed to Isaiah himself and is thought to have been written before the Babylonian exile. It focuses on warnings to the Southern Kingdom (Judah) and prophesies against foreign nations.

2. **Deutero-Isaiah (Chapters 40–55)**: This section is said to have been penned during the Babylonian exile or shortly after. It speaks words of comfort and redemption to the Jewish people.

3. **Trito-Isaiah (Chapters 56–66)**: This final section is considered post-exilic and is thought to address the Jewish community's needs upon their return to the land.

Dr. Gleason L. Archer's Refutation

Dr. Gleason L. Archer, a conservative Bible scholar, provides a compelling case for the unity and single authorship of the Book of Isaiah. Here are some of his main points:

1. **Unity of Language and Style**: Archer points out that the supposed differences in language and style between the three

divisions of Isaiah are not convincing. For example, Isaiah employs certain phrases and expressions throughout the entire book, creating a consistent linguistic framework. These expressions are not isolated to any particular section but are dispersed throughout, suggesting single authorship.

2. **Predictive Prophecy**: One of the major arguments against single authorship is the idea that prophetic utterances cannot transcend the prophet's lifetime. Archer contests this, arguing that predictive prophecy is a distinctive feature of biblical literature. The accurate foretelling of future events serves as a validation of the divine inspiration behind the prophecies.

3. **New Testament Attestation**: Archer notes that the New Testament attributes quotations from all sections of Isaiah to the prophet himself, showing that the early Christian church understood the book as the work of a single author.

4. **Internal Consistency**: Archer highlights the thematic unity throughout Isaiah, especially in its portrayal of Jehovah as the sovereign Lord who brings both judgment and salvation. According to Archer, this unity in theme and message indicates that the book came from one mind, inspired by one Spirit.

5. **Historical Background**: Archer argues that the historical backdrop against which Isaiah writes is consistent throughout the book, despite covering a span of events. The historical events serve as a framework but do not dictate the authorship.

Dr. Gleason L. Archer thoroughly refutes the theories that attempt to dissect Isaiah into multiple sections written by different authors. His arguments demonstrate that the book's unity in language, style, and theme, along with its predictive prophecies and New Testament attestation, make a strong case for Isaiah's single authorship. This preserves the integrity of the book and underscores its divine inspiration.[2]

---

[2] Gleason Archer Jr., *A Survey of Old Testament Introduction*, 3rd. ed. (Chicago: Moody Press, 1994), 365–379.

Evidence of One Writer: Consistency of Expression in the Book of Isaiah

Consistency of the Term "Holy One of Israel"

A powerful example demonstrating the unity of the Book of Isaiah is the repeated use of the term "Holy One of Israel." This expression is not just a general descriptor of Jehovah; it encapsulates a theological and thematic signature found consistently throughout the book. It appears approximately 25 times in Isaiah, and its distribution is across what critics refer to as Proto-Isaiah, Deutero-Isaiah, and Trito-Isaiah.

- In the supposed **Proto-Isaiah**, the term is used to affirm the absolute holiness and authority of Jehovah as contrasted with the sinful nation of Israel. For instance, Isaiah 1:4 refers to the "Holy One of Israel" as being forsaken by the sinful people.

- In the supposed **Deutero-Isaiah**, the term again is employed to depict Jehovah as the deliverer and redeemer of His people during the Babylonian exile. Isaiah 41:14, for example, reassures Israel not to fear because the "Holy One of Israel" is their Redeemer.

- In the supposed **Trito-Isaiah**, the same expression is used to denote the continuing relationship between Jehovah and the restored community. Isaiah 60:14 refers to the city of Jehovah as the city of the "Holy One of Israel."

The recurring use of the term "Holy One of Israel" shows not only a consistent theological framework but also a stylistic and thematic continuity, which is not likely to happen if there were multiple authors separated by generations and contexts. This consistency of expression, particularly of a term so loaded with theological significance, robustly attests to a single authorship of the Book of Isaiah. It demonstrates that the same mind, inspired by the same Spirit, penned these words as a unified message to God's people across varying circumstances.

Evidence of One Writer: Similarities Between Chapters 1-39 and Chapters 40-66 in Isaiah

Theological Consistency

The Book of Isaiah, despite its broad scope covering judgment and hope, Israel and the nations, and past and future, maintains a consistent theological perspective throughout. For example, the Sovereignty of Jehovah is upheld in both the first and second halves. In chapters 1-39, Jehovah is depicted as the judge and king of Israel and the surrounding nations. This perspective remains unchanged in chapters 40-66, where Jehovah is still the ultimate authority, governing the destiny of Israel and the world.

Stylistic Uniformity

The unique style and literary forms seen in the first half of Isaiah are also apparent in the second half. The employment of parallelism, chiastic structures, and other poetic elements remain consistent across the two major divisions. For instance, both sections use the "Servant Songs," the term for poetic verses that describe the "Servant of Jehovah." Isaiah 42:1-4 and Isaiah 52:13-53:12 are examples of these songs in the two respective sections.

Use of Specific Phrases and Terminology

As previously mentioned, the term "Holy One of Israel" appears consistently throughout both portions, signaling the same voice and perspective. Other terms like "the remnant," "Zion," and "the Day of Jehovah" also recur, creating a thematic and terminological consistency.

Messiah as the Central Figure

Both sections speak clearly of a Messianic figure who would come to rescue God's people. While the first part speaks of the "stump of Jesse" in Isaiah 11, the second part describes the suffering servant in chapters like Isaiah 53. Both depictions align perfectly with the Messianic expectation and provide a unified view.

Historical Context and Chronology

The historical events covered in both halves of Isaiah suggest that the prophet was equally at home discussing the Assyrian threat (as seen in chapters 1-39) and the Babylonian exile (as in chapters 40-66). The historical settings don't undermine the unity of the book; rather, they support the idea that one prophet, Isaiah, prophesied over a long period, covering both imminent and distant future events.

Hope for Restoration

While chapters 1-39 are heavier on judgment, they do not lack the element of hope for Israel's future, which becomes the main theme in chapters 40-66. Both sections dovetail in their ultimate message: God's judgment is in service of ultimate redemption, and hope in Jehovah is well-founded.

The cumulative weight of these evidences strongly attests to the fact that chapters 1-39 and chapters 40-66 are intrinsically connected, both thematically and stylistically, pointing to a single author: the Prophet Isaiah.

Evidence of One Writer: The Greek New Testament's Testimony to Isaiah's Single Authorship

Uniform Citations

The New Testament writers uniformly attribute the passages they quote from the book of Isaiah to the prophet Isaiah himself. There is no instance where they acknowledge or imply multiple authors for the book. For example, in the Gospel of Matthew, when quoting what is now Isaiah 53:4, Matthew 8:17 explicitly states, "This was to fulfill what was spoken through Isaiah the prophet." Similarly, in Romans 10:16, Paul cites Isaiah 53:1 and attributes it to "Isaiah." He does not differentiate between a so-called "First Isaiah" and "Deutero-Isaiah" or "Trito-Isaiah."

Attribution of Varied Passages to Isaiah

It is important to note that the New Testament quotes from different sections of Isaiah, yet always attributes them to the single prophet Isaiah. For example, in Acts 8:28-35, Philip encounters the

Ethiopian eunuch who is reading from Isaiah 53, a part of what some scholars label "Deutero-Isaiah." The eunuch inquires, "About whom, I ask you, does the prophet say this, about himself or about someone else?" Not only does the eunuch consider Isaiah a singular prophet, but Philip then proceeds to share "the good news about Jesus" without correcting this understanding.

Consistency Across New Testament Writers

The testimony is consistent across various New Testament writers. For example, the apostle John in John 12:38-41 quotes from Isaiah 53 and Isaiah 6 and attributes both to Isaiah. He states, "Isaiah said these things because he saw his glory and spoke of him." It is clear that John considered the Isaiah who saw the vision in the temple in Isaiah 6 to be the same Isaiah who spoke of the suffering servant in Isaiah 53.

Internal Cohesion of New Testament Testimony

The New Testament's consistent acknowledgment of Isaiah as a single prophetic voice adds a layer of internal cohesion to its witness. Had there been an understanding that the Book of Isaiah had multiple authors, this would likely have been reflected in how the New Testament writers cited the book. However, such an instance is conspicuously absent.

In summary, the Greek New Testament unanimously and unequivocally attributes the quotations from all sections of Isaiah to a single individual: the prophet Isaiah. This constitutes a robust evidence supporting the unity and single authorship of the book.

Evidence of One Writer: The Dead Sea Scrolls and Isaiah's Single Authorship

Complete Manuscript of Isaiah

One of the most significant discoveries among the Dead Sea Scrolls is the complete manuscript of the Book of Isaiah, commonly referred to as the Great Isaiah Scroll (1QIsa). This scroll dates back to the second century B.C.E. The very existence of this complete manuscript, containing all 66 chapters, militates against the theory of multiple authorship. Had different sections of Isaiah been penned by different authors at different times, as proponents of the multiple Isaiah theory suggest, it would be odd to find them all meticulously compiled into a single scroll so early in history.

Consistency in Language and Style

Upon close examination, the linguistic features and the writing style in the Great Isaiah Scroll demonstrate a uniformity across all the chapters. The Hebrew language employed does not show distinct variations that would suggest multiple authors separated by decades or even centuries. This supports the traditional understanding that the Book of Isaiah had a single author.

No Editorial Markers

Moreover, the scroll does not contain any markers, divisions, or notations that would indicate a change in authorship between chapters 1-39 and chapters 40-66, a key point of contention in the multiple Isaiah theory. Had the community that preserved this scroll believed in multiple authorship, it is likely that some form of editorial demarcation would exist, yet none is to be found.

Authoritative Status of the Scroll

The community that preserved the Dead Sea Scrolls highly revered the prophetic writings, treating them with extreme care and considering them authoritative. The inclusion of a complete Isaiah scroll among these writings confirms that the community acknowledged the book as an authoritative and cohesive whole, penned by the prophet Isaiah.

Confirmation of Textual Integrity

The Great Isaiah Scroll serves as a remarkable testament to the textual integrity and preservation of the Book of Isaiah. Comparing this ancient manuscript with the Masoretic Text shows an extraordinarily high degree of consistency, further indicating that the text had been faithfully transmitted over the centuries. This fidelity in transmission supports the traditional claim of single authorship because a text subjected to multiple authors usually shows more textual discrepancies due to later editorial activities.

In summary, the Dead Sea Scrolls, particularly the Great Isaiah Scroll, provide robust evidence affirming the single authorship of the Book of Isaiah. From its textual uniformity to its authoritative status in a religious community that held the Scriptures in high regard, the Great Isaiah Scroll reinforces the traditional, conservative stance on the unity and integrity of this prophetic book.

Evidence of One Writer: Flavius Josephus on Isaiah's Prophecies Concerning Cyrus

Josephus' Testimony Regarding Isaiah's Prophecy

First-century Jewish historian Flavius Josephus wrote extensively about the Jewish history and its intersection with surrounding empires. Notably, Josephus, in his work "Antiquities of the Jews," elaborates on the role of Isaiah's prophecy concerning Cyrus, the Persian king. Josephus attests that Cyrus was shown the Book of Isaiah by the Jewish leaders and was profoundly impacted by the prophecies written about him. According to Josephus, Cyrus was so moved that he liberated the Jewish people and assisted in the rebuilding of the Jerusalem Temple, fulfilling the very prophecies found in Isaiah.

Support for a Single Author

The fact that Josephus refers to the Isaiah prophecies concerning Cyrus in a way that treats them as integral parts of Isaiah's work is significant. Josephus, a meticulous historian, would not have blended the prophecies into a single narrative if the prevailing understanding of his time was that of multiple authors for the Book of Isaiah. His seamless treatment of Isaiah's prophecies—stretching from the judgments against Israel to the exilic and post-exilic events—indicates a single, coherent source.

Impact on the View of Isaiah's Authorship

Josephus' account serves as an external validation for the single authorship of Isaiah. By linking Isaiah's prophecies so closely to historical events that he discusses in detail, Josephus is indirectly confirming that the prophecies originated from the same source. His affirmation of the events surrounding Cyrus adds historical credence to Isaiah's single authorship because Josephus would have had access to a variety of historical and scholarly resources.

First-Century Jewish Understanding of Isaiah

Importantly, Josephus' treatment of Isaiah provides a snapshot of how the book was understood in the first century C.E. His interpretation demonstrates that the single-author viewpoint was the accepted stance during this period. As a historian who had access to various texts and scholarly opinions of his time, his endorsement of this viewpoint is noteworthy.

In summary, Flavius Josephus offers valuable historical testimony that supports the traditional understanding of Isaiah's single authorship. By discussing Isaiah's prophecies about Cyrus in a way that presupposes a single prophetic voice, Josephus strengthens the conservative claim that the entire Book of Isaiah is a unified work penned by the Prophet Isaiah.

Evidence of One Writer: Babylon in the Latter Portion of Isaiah

Critics' Assertion about Babylon

One argument that critics frequently raise against the single authorship of Isaiah is that the latter chapters (Isaiah 40-66) describe Babylon as a dominant world power. They argue that this implies a different historical context and therefore a different author. Specifically, these critics contend that the prophecies against Babylon and the emphasis on Babylonian exile point to a time after the eighth-century B.C.E. era of Isaiah.

Inaccurate Assumption of Prophetic Limitations

The critics who point to Babylon as evidence of a later authorship are operating under an inaccurate assumption about prophetic limitations. According to the Scriptures, true prophets like Isaiah were divinely inspired to see and write about events far beyond their own lifetimes. Predicting the rise of Babylon is not out of character for Isaiah or any prophet who is genuinely inspired by God. Isaiah had previously made prophecies concerning Assyria, another world power of his time, and extended his prophecies into the future. The element of predictive prophecy is a hallmark of Biblical prophetic literature.

Purposeful Structure of Isaiah

Another crucial point to consider is the structure of the Book of Isaiah itself. The book can be divided into two main sections: Chapters 1-39, which are largely historical and judgmental; and Chapters 40-66, which are largely comforting and eschatological. The latter section's focus on Babylon is purposeful, fitting into the book's overarching message of judgment followed by redemption. Both sections are bound together by consistent themes, style, and theology, arguing for single authorship.

A Unified Message and Style

The treatment of Babylon in Isaiah 40-66 is in harmony with the themes and style found in Isaiah 1-39. Both sections emphasize the sovereignty of God, the coming Messiah, and the need for spiritual repentance. These recurring themes across both sections provide strong internal evidence that Isaiah is a unified work, originating from a single prophetic voice.

Historical Predictive Prophecy Is Consistent with Single Authorship

The ability to predict historical events, such as the rise and fall of Babylon, is not only within the realm of a prophet but also serves as evidence for the prophet's divine inspiration. Far from being an argument against single authorship, the precise predictions about Babylon validate the prophetic credentials of Isaiah.

In summary, the mention of Babylon as a prevailing power in the latter part of Isaiah does not necessitate multiple authors. Rather, it substantiates the divine inspiration of the prophet Isaiah and is consistent with a single authorship rooted in a unified message and style.

Edward D. Andrews

A Book of Reliable Prophecy: Explaining the Change of Style from Isaiah Chapter 40 Onward

The Observation of Stylistic Change

Critics and even some casual readers have noted a change in style and tone between the first 39 chapters of Isaiah and the chapters that follow, beginning with chapter 40. The first part of Isaiah primarily focuses on judgments against Israel and other nations, and historical narratives are more prevalent. In contrast, chapters 40-66 are filled with messages of hope, comfort, and future restoration. This stylistic transition has led some to argue for multiple authors. However, this line of thinking overlooks key aspects of prophetic literature and Isaiah's comprehensive message.

Prophetic Range of a Single Author

Firstly, it is crucial to affirm that a single author can display a wide range of styles and tones. Just as a musical composer may write both solemn and joyful pieces, a prophet can issue both judgments and blessings, tailored to different situations and audiences. A prophet's role is multifaceted: he is a herald of doom to a sinful people, a proclaimer of hope to the remnant, and a visionary of the glorious future to come.

Thematic Consistency

Despite the stylistic transition, the underlying themes remain consistent throughout the entire book. Both sections deal with the holiness of God, the sinfulness of man, the need for repentance, and the certainty of divine judgment and deliverance. This thematic unity strongly supports the idea of single authorship.

Contextual Shift Explains Stylistic Change

The shift in style can be perfectly understood when considering the contextual shift. The earlier chapters are set in a time when Israel is facing immediate threats from surrounding nations like Assyria. The tone is urgent, aiming to call the nation to repentance. The latter chapters are oriented towards a future audience who will be in exile or returning from it. The tone, understandably, is one of comfort and hope, assuring the people of God's continued plans for them.

Divine Inspiration Encompasses Multiple Styles

It is also essential to remember that the ultimate authorship of Isaiah, like all Scripture, is rooted in divine inspiration. God, the ultimate Author, is more than capable of expressing a range of emotions and themes through His chosen prophet. As such, the diversity of style and tone serves to enrich the text, rather than divide it.

The change in style from chapter 40 onward does not necessitate multiple authorships but can be fully accounted for by understanding the rich prophetic role, thematic consistency, and different contexts that Isaiah addresses. Therefore, the stylistic shift is not only acceptable but also expected within the framework of a book that spans various situations and speaks to different generations.

A Book of Reliable Prophecy: The Holiness of God as a Theme in Isaiah

Unveiling the Theme

The Book of Isaiah contains several overarching themes, but one of the most potent and pervasive is the "Holiness of God." This theme is not just a recurring motif; it serves as the backbone that gives structure and meaning to the entire prophetic message.

The Unmistakable Declaration

Isaiah opens his prophecy with a solemn call to attention, presenting Jehovah as the Holy One of Israel. We see this clearly established in the inaugural vision of Isaiah in chapter 6, where the prophet encounters the thrice-holy God. The seraphim surrounding God's throne cry out, "Holy, Holy, Holy, is Jehovah of hosts, the whole earth is full of His glory" (Isaiah 6:3, UASV). This is more than a mere declaration; it sets the tone for the entire book. The holiness of God is not just an attribute among others; it is the essence of who God is.

Holiness and Human Sinfulness

The theme of God's holiness serves as a stark contrast to human sinfulness. Throughout the book, Isaiah repeatedly emphasizes the sinfulness of Israel and the nations. The clear implication is that humans, in their sinful state, are utterly incompatible with the holy nature of God. This, in turn, necessitates divine judgment, another key aspect of the book.

Holiness and Redemption

Yet, Isaiah's message does not end with condemnation. The holiness of God also encompasses His desire to redeem and purify His people. For instance, in Isaiah 53, we find the prophecy concerning the Suffering Servant—clearly pointing to the future Messiah—who would be "pierced for our transgressions" and "crushed for our iniquities" (Isaiah 53:5, UASV). The purpose of this redemption is to make a people holy, fit to be in the presence of a holy God.

Holiness and the Future Hope

Furthermore, the holiness of God permeates the eschatological promises that mark the latter part of the book. Isaiah describes a new heavens and a new earth where holiness reigns supreme (Isaiah 65:17-25). This future vision isn't just one of geopolitical peace but of cosmic restoration, wherein God's holiness transforms all of creation.

The theme of the holiness of God intricately weaves through the entire fabric of Isaiah's prophecy, from its initial chapters to its eschatological visions. This theme serves as both a call for repentance and a promise of redemption, embodying the complete character of God—utterly holy, just in judgment, and merciful in salvation.

CHAPTER 7 Making a Case for the Book of Jeremiah and Lamentations

Authenticity, Authorship, and Date of Jeremiah

The Timing of Jeremiah's Commissioning

Jeremiah was commissioned in the year 627 B.C.E., during the thirteenth year of King Josiah's reign over Judah. This was a significant period, as King Josiah was engaged in religious reforms aimed at eradicating idolatry and reinstating the worship of Jehovah. Jeremiah's ministry then continued through the reigns of Jehoahaz, Jehoiakim, Jehoiachin, and Zedekiah, finally concluding after the fall of Jerusalem in 587 B.C.E.

The Divine Source of Jeremiah's Commissioning

Jeremiah's calling came directly from Jehovah. The Scriptures clearly outline his divine commission in Jeremiah 1:4-5 (UASV), where it states, "The word of Jehovah came to me, saying, 'Before I formed you in the womb I knew you, and before you were born I consecrated you; I appointed you a prophet to the nations.'" This was not a human appointment but a divine directive.

Significance of the Commissioning

Jeremiah's commission was not just to serve as a bearer of bad news; rather, he was entrusted with a two-fold mission as outlined in Jeremiah 1:10, "See, I have set you this day over nations and over kingdoms, to pluck up and to break down, to destroy and to overthrow, to build and to plant." He was to convey messages of both judgment and restoration, aligning with the broader narrative of divine holiness, justice, and mercy that we find throughout Scripture.

Jeremiah's Task as Prophesied

Jeremiah was divinely commissioned to be a prophet "to the nations" (Jeremiah 1:5, UASV). His primary task was to deliver Jehovah's messages of judgment against the unfaithful, not only in Judah but also against the surrounding nations. The task was twofold, as Jeremiah 1:10 outlines: "to pluck up and to break down, to destroy and to overthrow, to build and to plant." This role involved not merely foretelling future events, but also "forth-telling," that is, proclaiming messages of immediate ethical and spiritual relevance.

Jeremiah was chosen for a daunting task: to stand against kings, officials, priests, and the general populace (Jeremiah 1:18). He announced the upcoming Babylonian invasion as Jehovah's judgment for the nation's sins, particularly idolatry and the breaking of the covenant. He was also tasked to deliver messages of hope and future restoration, particularly seen in chapters like Jeremiah 29, where the famous verse, "For I know the plans I have for you, declares Jehovah, plans for welfare and not for evil, to give you a future and a hope" (Jeremiah 29:11, UASV) is found.

Eventful Years Covered by Jeremiah's Prophecies

Jeremiah's prophetic ministry began in 627 B.C.E. and extended to sometime after 587 B.C.E., covering a span of at least 40 years. Several significant events mark this time frame:

1. **The Reign of Josiah (640–609 B.C.E.)**: Jeremiah began his ministry in Josiah's 13th year. Josiah was a reforming king, trying to bring the nation back to Jehovah. Jeremiah's early prophesies likely supported this effort.

2. **The Death of Josiah and the Reign of Jehoahaz (609 B.C.E.)**: Josiah's death led to a brief three-month reign by his son Jehoahaz, which ended with the king's deposition by Pharaoh Necho II.

3. **The Reign of Jehoiakim (609–598 B.C.E.)**: Unlike his father Josiah, Jehoiakim was a wicked king. During his reign, Jeremiah faced severe persecution, including having his scroll burned (Jeremiah 36).
4. **The Reign of Jehoiachin (598–597 B.C.E.)**: Jeremiah prophesied against him, and his reign lasted only three months before the Babylonians took him captive.
5. **The Reign of Zedekiah (597–587 B.C.E.)**: Jeremiah faced imprisonment and threats to his life during Zedekiah's reign. He continued to prophesy the fall of Jerusalem, which eventually happened in 587 B.C.E.
6. **The Fall of Jerusalem (587 B.C.E.)**: Jeremiah was present during the siege and ultimate capture of Jerusalem by the Babylonians. He offered counsel to King Zedekiah, although it went unheeded.
7. **After the Fall**: Jeremiah was given the choice by the Babylonians to go to Babylon or stay. He chose to stay and later ended up in Egypt against his will, where tradition suggests he died.

Canonicity and Authenticity in Hebrew Times

The Book of Jeremiah has always been considered canonical and authentic by the Jewish people. The evidence for this is manifold:

1. **Historical Corroboration**: The accounts and prophecies of Jeremiah are situated within a historically verifiable context, which adds credence to the book. Events such as the fall of Jerusalem in 587 B.C.E., the Babylonian Exile, and the various reigns of the Judean kings are all corroborated by external historical records.
2. **Inclusion in the Prophetic Canon**: Jeremiah is included in the section of the Hebrew Bible known as "The Prophets" (Nevi'im). This position in the Jewish canon indicates that it has been recognized as authoritative from early times.

3. **Internal Claims of Divine Inspiration**: The text of Jeremiah itself bears witness to its divine origin. Phrases such as "The word of Jehovah came to me, saying" (Jeremiah 1:4, UASV) are clear indicators that the words are not merely human in origin but divinely inspired.

4. **Acceptance by Religious Authorities**: The priesthood and religious leaders, despite their opposition to Jeremiah's message, never questioned the authenticity of his words as being divinely inspired. This is significant because if the book were a later addition or fraudulent, the religious authorities would have been the first to reject it.

New Testament Testimony on the Book of Jeremiah

1. **Explicit Citations**: The Greek New Testament contains explicit references to Jeremiah. One notable example is Matthew 2:17–18, which cites Jeremiah 31:15 concerning the slaughter of the infants by King Herod.

2. **Thematic Resonance**: While not an explicit citation, Hebrews 8:8–12 quotes a lengthy passage from Jeremiah 31:31–34 regarding the New Covenant, underlining the authority and canonicity of Jeremiah in early Christian thought.

3. **Apostolic Authority**: The apostles and New Testament writers were meticulous in what they quoted. Their reliance on Jeremiah underscores its authoritative and canonical status.

4. **Christ's Endorsement**: Although not citing Jeremiah directly, Jesus' teachings often aligned with the themes and messages found in Jeremiah, lending additional authority to the book. For example, Jeremiah's emphasis on inner transformation and a heart-based relationship with God aligns with Jesus' teachings in the Sermon on the Mount.

The canonicity and authenticity of the Book of Jeremiah were firmly established in Hebrew times, and this was further endorsed by New Testament writers. The book's internal claims of divine inspiration, its inclusion in the Jewish canon, and its acknowledgment in the New Testament all attest to its irrefutable status as a canonical and authentic text.

Archaeological Evidence as Corroborative Testimony

Archaeology has provided significant evidence that corroborates the historical and contextual details found in the Book of Jeremiah. Several finds attest to the events, places, and people described in the book, enhancing its reliability.

1. **The Lachish Letters**: These are a collection of ostraca (pottery fragments with writing) discovered at the site of Lachish, a city mentioned in Jeremiah 34:7. These letters detail the military events surrounding the Babylonian siege of Jerusalem in 587 B.C.E., confirming the narrative laid out in the Book of Jeremiah.

2. **The Babylonian Chronicles**: These are cuneiform tablets that record the history of Babylon. The Chronicles describe Nebuchadnezzar's siege of Jerusalem, which aligns with Jeremiah's accounts. Specifically, they confirm the capture of King Jehoiachin of Judah and his subsequent release from prison, as mentioned in Jeremiah 52:31–34.

3. **Seal Impressions**: Clay bullae bearing the names of individuals mentioned in Jeremiah have been unearthed. Notably, a bulla bearing the name of Baruch, son of Neriah, the scribe who wrote down Jeremiah's prophecies, was found. Another bulla mentions Gemariah, son of Shaphan, to whom Baruch read the scroll containing Jeremiah's words (Jeremiah 36:10).

4. **Tel Dan Stele**: Though not directly mentioning Jeremiah, the Tel Dan Stele from the 9th century B.C.E. mentions the "House of David," corroborating the Biblical narrative's general context in which Jeremiah prophesied.

5. **The Nebuchadnezzar Prism**: This artifact records Nebuchadnezzar's military campaigns and provides

independent verification for the Babylonian activities described in Jeremiah.

6. **Archaeological Sites**: Excavations in Jerusalem, especially around the City of David and the Temple Mount, have yielded evidence of destruction layers and artifacts that align with the Babylonian destruction of Jerusalem in 587 B.C.E. as described in Jeremiah.

The Book of Jeremiah stands up exceptionally well to the scrutiny of archaeology. Various archaeological finds—from ostraca to cuneiform tablets to seal impressions—corroborate the book's accounts, thereby underlining its historical reliability. These archaeological evidences serve as external witnesses, substantiating the events, people, and places described in this prophetic book.

Jeremiah: The Prophet and the Man

Jeremiah was a prophet from the priestly town of Anathoth, situated just a few miles northeast of Jerusalem. He was the son of Hilkiah, a priest from this town. Jeremiah's ministry began in the 13th year of King Josiah's reign, around 627 B.C.E., and extended through the reigns of subsequent Judean kings until after the fall of Jerusalem in 587 B.C.E. He was commissioned by Jehovah to be a prophet to the nations (Jeremiah 1:5). Unlike other prophets, Jeremiah was never married, as Jehovah directed him not to take a wife or have children in the land (Jeremiah 16:1-2).

He was tasked with delivering messages of impending doom due to the spiritual apostasy of Judah, but also messages of future hope and restoration. His ministry spanned the decline, fall, and aftermath of the Kingdom of Judah. Jeremiah suffered intensely for the messages he delivered. He was imprisoned, put into stocks, and lowered into a muddy cistern, enduring tremendous hardship for the sake of faithfully proclaiming Jehovah's Word.

Style of Writing

Jeremiah's style is distinct and vivid, marked by a strong emotional tone and extensive use of imagery and metaphor. The book incorporates a variety of literary genres, including poetic oracles, narratives, prayers, and historical accounts. His writing frequently employs dualistic themes like covenant and apostasy, judgment and hope, exile and return. The sheer diversity of literary forms in Jeremiah—ranging from laments to prose sermons—demonstrates the complexity and depth of his prophetic ministry.

Jeremiah employed rhetorical questions, parallelism, and chiasmus as some of his key literary devices. His use of poignant, heartfelt laments distinguishes him from many of his prophetic contemporaries. Moreover, Jeremiah often used symbolic actions, such as the smashing of a clay jar (Jeremiah 19), to illustrate his prophetic messages. His writing is deeply personal, often reflecting his own emotional turmoil, which has led him to be known as the "weeping prophet."

The book also has an intricate structure. While it is not strictly chronological, it does have thematic arrangements that provide logical coherence to the different messages. For instance, oracles against foreign nations are clustered together (Jeremiah 46–51), and confessions or personal laments of Jeremiah appear intermittently (e.g., Jeremiah 11:18–12:6; 15:10–21).

Jeremiah was a complex individual, chosen by Jehovah for a difficult prophetic ministry that spanned crucial decades in Judean history. His writing style is as multifaceted as his ministry, employing a wide range of literary forms and devices to convey his prophetic messages. Both the content and the style of Jeremiah's writings reflect his deep emotional and spiritual engagement with his prophetic calling. This style—rich in imagery, metaphor, and emotional tone—amplifies the critical messages he delivered. Therefore, understanding both the man and his style provides invaluable insight into the Book of Jeremiah.

Early Life and Ministry of Jeremiah

Jeremiah embarked on his religious mission around the age of twenty during the reign of King Josiah, which began in **627 B.C.** He was born into a priestly family in Anathoth, a town near Jerusalem, and would travel to the city for annual Jewish feasts. Financially well-off, he was able to buy a forfeited estate from a bankrupt relative with ease. During the rule of the devout King Josiah, Jeremiah faced little interference from the authorities. However, even among his own family and fellow priests, Jeremiah garnered animosity due to his **bold criticisms of their religious negligence and worldly ways.**

Challenging Times After Josiah's Death

After the death of King Josiah, the rise of idol worshippers and pro-Egyptian factions led to intense hostility against Jeremiah. He narrowly avoided arrest after delivering a controversial sermon in the temple, documented in chapters 7–10 of the Book of Jeremiah. *Because of this sermon, he was likely barred from entering the temple again.* To get his messages across, he employed his secretary, Baruch, to read his prophetic statements aloud to the public. However, King Jehoiakim ended up burning these messages section by section.

Confinement and Subsequent Release

Jeremiah was imprisoned by King Zedekiah, who succeeded Jehoiakim, due to pressure from nationalistic leaders who viewed the prophet as a traitor. This was because Jeremiah had advised submission to Babylonian rule. *Yet, Zedekiah secretly held Jeremiah in high regard due to the prophet's accurate past prophecies regarding Babylon.* Consequently, Jeremiah was saved from a deadly confinement and protected until Jerusalem fell to the Babylonians.

Timeline of Babylonian Kings

KINGS OF BABYLON/CHALDEA

- Nabopolassar: 612–605 B.C.
- Nebuchadnezzar: 605–562 B.C.
- Evil-Merodach: 561–560 B.C.
- Neriglissar: 560–556 B.C.
- Labashi-Marduki: 556 B.C.
- Nabonidus: 555–539 B.C.
- Belshazzar (co-regency): 553–539 B.C.

Final Years and Legacy

When Nebuchadnezzar finally took over Jerusalem, Jeremiah was offered a place of honor in Babylon. Instead, he chose to remain in Palestine, tending to those who had not been exiled. *However, after a political assassination disrupted the region, he was forcibly taken to Egypt by remaining Jews seeking refuge there.* It's likely he spent his final years prophesying in Egypt.

By his nature, Jeremiah was a man of deep emotional sensitivity, forced by his divine calling to deliver a **grim and irrevocable message**. Even though he was naturally introverted and preferred solitude, he consistently found himself in the spotlight. While he sometimes wanted to escape the taxing demands of his prophetic duties, he inevitably returned to his calling, standing resiliently as a "tower of bronze" (Jeremiah 1:18).

Authenticity, Authorship, and Date of Lamentations

The Apt Naming of the Book of Lamentations

A Fitting Title for the Subject Matter

The Book of Lamentations is appropriately named because it consists of a series of laments or mournful poems. These poems are designed to express the intense sorrow, suffering, and sense of loss experienced by the people of Judah due to the destruction of Jerusalem in 587 B.C.E. The book captures the despair and lamentation of a once proud and blessed nation, now devastated by warfare, famine, and exile. The focus is not just on physical destruction, but also on spiritual desolation and the seemingly abandoned promises of Jehovah.

Structured Grief

The book is intricately structured in a form of Hebrew poetry known as an acrostic, where each verse starts with a successive letter of the Hebrew alphabet. This literary form serves to emphasize the completeness of the devastation and sorrow, covering everything from

A to Z, so to speak. Even in the structured form of the laments, we can discern the need for order in the midst of chaos, a poetic expression of the quest for meaning amid senseless suffering.

Themes of Lamentations

It addresses multiple facets of suffering, including the destruction of the Temple, the loss of national sovereignty, the suffering of children and mothers, and the degradation of princes and elders. The laments reach their climax with a recognition of Judah's sin and an acknowledgment of Jehovah's justice. Even so, the book concludes with a plea for restoration and a return of divine favor.

A Collective Voice

Another reason the title is fitting is that the book serves as a communal lament. It isn't just a private grieving but reflects the collective soul of the nation. It serves as a kind of liturgy of mourning that involves everyone in the grieving process. The Book of Lamentations gives a voice to the inexpressible sorrow and suffering experienced by the people.

The Grouping and Placement of the Book of Lamentations in the Bible

In the Hebrew Bible

In the Hebrew Bible, the Book of Lamentations is part of the third main division known as the "Ketuvim" or the Writings. Within this division, it is grouped with the Five Megillot, which also include Song of Songs, Ruth, Ecclesiastes, and Esther. These books are read in the synagogue on specific Jewish festivals and occasions. Lamentations is read on Tisha B'Av, the fast day that commemorates the destruction of both the First and Second Temples in Jerusalem. This placement and association underscore the book's significant role in the liturgical life of ancient and modern Judaism.

In the Christian Canon

In the Christian Old Testament, the Book of Lamentations typically follows the Book of Jeremiah. This arrangement is mostly based on tradition that attributes both books to the prophet Jeremiah. By placing Lamentations immediately after Jeremiah, the Christian canon effectively connects the prophecies of doom by Jeremiah with the aftermath and lamentation over the fall of Jerusalem.

Unity Through Themes

The placement of Lamentations next to Jeremiah in the Christian Old Testament allows for a nuanced understanding of the prophetic message. Jeremiah outlines the impending judgment due to Israel's disobedience, while Lamentations offers a response to the actualized judgments. This places Lamentations in theological and historical context, making it a sequel that shows the outcomes of not heeding prophetic warnings.

Canonical Acceptance

It's worth noting that there has been no significant dispute concerning the canonicity of the Book of Lamentations in either the Jewish or Christian traditions. Its position within each tradition's sacred Scriptures further attests to its authenticity and accepted role in both theological reflection and liturgical practice.

Evidence for Jeremiah's Authorship of Lamentations

Historical Attribution

The strongest evidence for Jeremiah's authorship of the Book of Lamentations comes from historical attribution. From the earliest records, Jewish tradition has ascribed the authorship of Lamentations to Jeremiah. This can be seen in the Talmud and other Jewish writings that consider Jeremiah the author. This view is not limited to the Jewish tradition; early Church fathers like Jerome also attributed Lamentations to Jeremiah.

Stylistic Similarities

Stylistic features provide further evidence for Jeremiah's authorship. The language, tone, and thematic elements in Lamentations share remarkable similarities with the Book of Jeremiah. Both books deal extensively with the theme of Jerusalem's destruction and the divine judgment upon Israel for its sins. The sorrowful tone and mood resonate between the two books, making it plausible to see them as the work of the same author.

Contextual Evidence

The historical context of Lamentations aligns well with Jeremiah's lifetime and ministry. Lamentations seems to have been written shortly after the fall of Jerusalem in 587/586 B.C.E., a catastrophic event that Jeremiah had prophesied and lived through. Thus, Jeremiah would have been a firsthand witness to the tragedies he detailed, providing an intimate perspective on the events.

Textual Indicators

While the text of Lamentations itself does not explicitly state its author, its content aligns with what we know about Jeremiah and his prophetic ministry. Jeremiah is often described as a "weeping prophet," which is congruent with the mournful tone of Lamentations. Furthermore, both works utilize similar poetic techniques and literary structures, such as acrostic patterns, found in Lamentations and also in some sections of Jeremiah (e.g., Jeremiah 36).

Limitations in the Evidence

It is crucial to note that while strong evidence points to Jeremiah's authorship, the text itself does not include an explicit claim. This has led some scholars to question the attribution. However, when considering the body of evidence—historical tradition, stylistic elements, and contextual factors—the case for Jeremiah's authorship is robust.

The Traditional Attribution to Jeremiah

While the book of Lamentations itself is silent about its authorship, an enduring tradition ascribes it to the Prophet Jeremiah. This view is reinforced by the Septuagint (LXX) and the Aramaic Targum of Jonathan. Early Church Fathers, such as Origen and Jerome, also accepted Jeremiah's authorship without dispute.

Modern Criticisms and Internal Evidence

Contrarily, *many modern scholars reject this traditional claim*. The primary reason cited is internal evidence—specifically, stylistic divergences between Lamentations and Jeremiah's known prophecies. Additionally, some suggest that historical allusions within Lamentations could indicate a later date of composition. However, considering the book's lamenting tone over the fall of Jerusalem in 586 B.C.E., it seems implausible that a more fitting occasion would arise after Jeremiah's time to inspire such a composition.

Stylistic and Thematic Similarities

There are compelling stylistic and thematic similarities between Lamentations and Jeremiah. Even critics who dispute Jeremiah's authorship, like S.R. Driver, acknowledge these commonalities. For example, the term "the oppressed virgin daughter of Zion" appears in both Lamentations (1:15) and Jeremiah (8:21). Another example is the recurring imagery of tears (Lam. 1:16a; 2:11; Jer. 9:1, 18b) and the concept of God's judgment expressed as a winecup (Lam. 4:21; Jer. 49:12).

Rebutting Arguments for Different Viewpoints

Critics have argued that differing viewpoints between Lamentations and Jeremiah indicate separate authorship. However, *these arguments do not stand up to rigorous textual analysis*. For instance, some claim that Lam. 4:17 suggests that help for Judah could come from Egypt, conflicting with Jeremiah's position. This is a misunderstanding. Lam. 4:17 does not specifically mention Egypt and reflects the nation's sentiment, not the prophet's personal political stance.

Furthermore, the notion that Jeremiah saw the Babylonians as instruments of God's wrath, while Lamentations paints them as evil, is not mutually exclusive. Both books maintain that the Babylonians would eventually face divine vengeance despite their role in God's plan.

The Significance of Lamentations 3

The mood shift in Lam. 3 from despair to hope has been cited as a *critical inconsistency* that could point to multiple authors. However, *this theory is implausible* due to the acrostic pattern binding the entire chapter.

This serves as irrefutable evidence that a single ancient Hebrew writer could adeptly maneuver between contrasting moods and sentiments without contradicting himself.

Conclusion

Therefore, there is insufficient evidence to convincingly refute the traditional view that Jeremiah authored Lamentations. The stylistic and thematic similarities between the two works, as well as the contextual factors surrounding the fall of Jerusalem, make a strong case for a single, consistent authorship. The authorship of Lamentations is historically attributed to Jeremiah, supported by stylistic similarities, contextual evidence, and early Jewish and Christian tradition. Although the text does not make an explicit claim, the cumulative evidence firmly points to Jeremiah as the author.

Reasoning for the Time of Writing for Lamentations

The Fall of Jerusalem

The most significant indicator for the timing of the Book of Lamentations is its thematic focus on the fall of Jerusalem. This catastrophic event occurred in 587/586 B.C.E., resulting in the destruction of the Temple and the exile of the Jewish people to Babylon. Since Lamentations is a poetic mourning of these specific tragedies, it follows that the book was written shortly after these events.

Historical Indicators

Within the text of Lamentations, several historical markers align with the 587/586 B.C.E. timeline. For example, the destruction of the Temple is mentioned in Lamentations 2:7, which we know from historical records and the Book of Kings to have occurred at that time. Additionally, references to starvation and desolation (Lamentations 2:20; 4:4–5, 9–10) correspond to known conditions in Jerusalem during the siege.

Proximity to Jeremiah's Prophetic Ministry

If one accepts Jeremiah's authorship of the Book of Lamentations, the timeframe becomes even clearer. Jeremiah's prophetic ministry lasted from the 13th year of King Josiah's reign (circa 627 B.C.E.) until the fall of Jerusalem and beyond. Since Lamentations focuses on the fall of Jerusalem, the text must have been written within a short period following the event, well within the span of Jeremiah's lifetime and prophetic ministry.

Consistency with Prophetic Forewarning

Jeremiah had been warning about the impending destruction of Jerusalem for years. The actual event would have provided the poignant and painful validation of his prophecies. Lamentations serves as a solemn epilogue to these prophetic utterances, thematically aligning with Jeremiah's messages and therefore logically belonging to a time shortly after Jerusalem's fall.

Traditional Attribution

Both Jewish tradition and early Christian writings place the Book of Lamentations soon after the fall of Jerusalem. This tradition not only confirms Jeremiah's authorship but also serves as an external historical marker, substantiating the timing of the book.

The Style and Construction of Lamentations

Acrostic Structure

One of the most striking features of Lamentations is its acrostic structure. Four out of its five chapters are acrostics, where each verse or group of verses begins with a letter of the Hebrew alphabet, following an alphabetical order. This is not merely a stylistic flourish; it serves as a literary device to convey completeness. In this case, the acrostic can be understood as a poetic way to encompass the full range of suffering and anguish experienced by the people.

Symmetry in Chaos

Despite the chaotic events that the book describes, there's an inherent symmetry in its construction. For instance, the central chapter (Chapter 3) has 66 verses, while the other chapters have 22, corresponding to the 22 letters of the Hebrew alphabet. Chapter 3 employs a "triple acrostic," where each of the 22 letters is used for three successive lines. This symmetrical construction is a testament to the deliberate artistry of the book, which seeks to bring a form to the formlessness of suffering, perhaps mirroring how God brings order out of chaos.

Vivid Imagery and Parallelism

The language of Lamentations is marked by vivid imagery and the extensive use of parallelism, a common feature in Hebrew poetry. The poetic lines often contain two or more closely related ideas, thereby reinforcing the emotional intensity of the subject matter. This can be seen in lines like "Her gates have sunk into the ground; he has ruined and broken her bars" (Lamentations 2:9, UASV). The repetition and juxtaposition of ideas serve to emphasize the depth of Jerusalem's sorrow.

Shift in Narrative Perspective

Lamentations uses multiple narrative perspectives to offer a comprehensive view of the suffering. At times the city itself is personified as a woman in grief; at other times, the narrative voice shifts to first person, almost autobiographical, likely reflecting Jeremiah's own laments. This shift in perspective adds layers of complexity and depth, allowing the reader to enter into the grief and sorrow from various angles.

Theological Themes

The Book of Lamentations is not just a historical recounting; it is theologically rich. It emphasizes God's righteousness even in the midst of terrible judgments. Though God has brought the judgment upon His people, He remains just. This creates a tension between the acknowledgment of sin and the plea for mercy, a tension that reflects the complex relationship between a holy God and His sinful people.

The style and construction of the Book of Lamentations are carefully crafted to convey the depth and range of the suffering experienced due to the fall of Jerusalem. Its acrostic structure, vivid imagery, and varied narrative perspectives all contribute to this aim. In the midst of chaos and suffering, the structured artistry of the book serves to bring order and meaning, a reflection of divine attributes in the midst of human agony.

Grief and Hope in Lamentations

Expression of Profound Grief

Jeremiah's anguish in Lamentations is both palpable and meticulously detailed. The pain he expresses is not just his own but represents the collective sorrow of the people of Judah after the fall of Jerusalem in 587 B.C.E. He mourns the loss of the temple, the priesthood, and the Davidic monarchy—essentially the collapse of religious, political, and social structures. For example, in Lamentations 1:4, it states: "The roads to Zion mourn, for none come to the festival; all her gates are desolate; her priests groan; her virgins have been afflicted, and she herself suffers bitterly" (UASV).

Jeremiah describes the city of Jerusalem as a widow, forsaken and in mourning (Lamentations 1:1). Children are starving, nobles are reduced to nothing, and the population is in exile or under the yoke of foreign oppression. The details are agonizing and the language is vivid, making the reader almost feel the gnawing hunger, the emotional turmoil, and the spiritual despair. The graphic descriptions serve a purpose: they force the reader to confront the harsh consequences of unfaithfulness to God.

Existence of Hope

Amidst the overwhelming grief, there is a glimmer of hope. This is most clearly seen in Lamentations 3:22-24, which says: "The steadfast love of Jehovah never ceases; his mercies never come to an end; they are new every morning; great is your faithfulness. 'Jehovah is my portion,' says my soul, 'therefore I will hope in him'" (UASV).

These verses underline the idea that even in the depths of despair, God's love and mercy remain. While the text is unflinching in acknowledging the legitimate reasons for the judgment and the suffering that has occurred, it also provides a theological anchor. God's character remains just and merciful, even when His actions seem harsh.

The suffering is a result of the people's sins, but Jehovah's fundamental nature as a loving, compassionate God does not change.

The Role of Repentance

The hope that Jeremiah points to is not a vague or unfounded optimism; it is rooted in the nature of God and the act of repentance. Jeremiah makes it clear that turning back to God is the way to renew this broken relationship. Lamentations 3:40-42 states, "Let us test and examine our ways, and return to Jehovah! Let us lift up our hearts and hands to God in heaven: 'We have transgressed and rebelled, and you have not forgiven'" (UASV). This is a call to self-examination and repentance, serving as the means by which the people could realign themselves with God's will.

CHAPTER 8 Refuting the Critical Objections to the Book of Ezekiel

Authenticity, Authorship, and Date of Ezekiel

Circumstances and Tests Faced by the Exiles in Babylon

Life in Babylonian Exile

The Babylonian exile fundamentally disrupted the lives of the Israelites, particularly those of the tribe of Judah. The destruction of Jerusalem in 587 B.C.E. led to a massive displacement of the Judean populace, with the Babylonian forces taking many into captivity. The destruction of the temple, the linchpin of their religious life, was a traumatic event that shook the very foundations of their identity.

While in Babylon, the exiles were not held in prison camps but were rather settled in communities. They had the freedom to engage in trade, agriculture, and other occupations. Some, like Daniel and his companions, even rose to prominent positions within the Babylonian administration. Nevertheless, they lived as foreigners in a land with different customs, laws, and gods, which presented numerous challenges to maintaining their distinct religious and cultural identity.

The Test of Assimilation

One of the most significant tests faced by the exiles was the pressure to assimilate into Babylonian culture. This was not merely a social or cultural issue but a deeply religious one. Babylon was a polytheistic society with a pantheon of gods and a range of religious practices that were antithetical to the monotheistic faith of the Israelites. The temptation to adopt these practices, whether to gain social standing or out of sheer curiosity, posed a severe threat to the integrity of their faith.

The Test of Faith Amidst Suffering

The destruction of the temple and the city of Jerusalem were interpreted by some as indications that Jehovah had abandoned His people, or worse, was defeated by the gods of Babylon. This misconception was a grave test of faith. The challenge was to understand these events not as a negation of Jehovah's power but as a divine judgment for their collective disobedience. The exile, in this view, was a form of discipline meant to bring the people back to a right relationship with God.

The Test of Religious Practice

Without the temple, the focal point of their religious life, the exiles had to find new ways to practice their faith. This led to a rise in the importance of the synagogue as a place for communal worship and the study of the Torah. It also necessitated a shift from a religion that was centered around sacrifices to one that placed greater emphasis on prayer and personal piety.

Ezekiel's Role

In this complex milieu, the prophet Ezekiel played a critical role. He provided both warnings and hope. Ezekiel continually emphasized that their current state was due to their disobedience but also promised a future restoration for those who would turn back to Jehovah. His visions and prophecies served as a spiritual anchor, offering both challenge and comfort to the exiles.

Prophets, Name Significance, Prophetic Period, Life, and Death of Ezekiel

Three Prophets During the Critical Years Before Jerusalem's Destruction

Before the destruction of Jerusalem in 587 B.C.E., three outstanding prophets played pivotal roles in the spiritual landscape of Israel and Judah. These were Jeremiah, who prophesied in Jerusalem;

Daniel, who served in the Babylonian court; and Ezekiel, who ministered among the exiles in Babylon. Jeremiah warned the people of Jerusalem about the impending destruction due to their disobedience. Daniel served as a model of faithfulness in the heart of the Babylonian administration, revealing divine wisdom and prophetic insights. Ezekiel, situated among the Judean exiles in Babylon, also played a critical role in conveying Jehovah's messages.

Significance of How Ezekiel Is Addressed and Meaning of His Name

Ezekiel is consistently addressed as "son of man" throughout the book that bears his name. This phrase emphasizes his humanity and serves as a constant reminder that despite the astonishing visions and responsibilities bestowed upon him, he remains a mortal, subservient to the divine will. The name Ezekiel itself means "God will strengthen" or "God strengthens," which is profoundly fitting. Throughout his ministry, Ezekiel had to deliver unpopular messages to a community under divine judgment. His name can be viewed as a divinely ordained emblem of the strength he would need and receive from Jehovah to fulfill his prophetic mission.

Years of Ezekiel's Prophetic Ministry

Ezekiel's prophetic ministry began in the fifth year of King Jehoiachin's exile, around 593 B.C.E., and extended until at least the 27th year of the exile, approximately 571 B.C.E. This makes for a prophetic ministry lasting over two decades. His prophecies were often tied to specific dates, providing a chronologically coherent framework that aligns well with the historical events of that era.

Life and Death of Ezekiel

Ezekiel was a priest by lineage, the son of Buzi. He was among those taken to Babylon during the second deportation around 597 B.C.E. Ezekiel was married, but his wife died as a sign to Israel during his prophetic ministry, and he was commanded not to mourn for her (Ezekiel 24:15-18). He lived in a house in Tel Abib near the river Chebar, where elders of Israel would come to consult him. Regarding his death, the Scriptures are silent. There are later Jewish traditions that speculate about the circumstances of his death, but these are not considered reliable historical accounts.

Writership, Canonicity, and Authenticity

Ezekiel's Writership

The book of Ezekiel is traditionally and compellingly attributed to the prophet Ezekiel himself. This attribution is not only grounded in the consistent first-person narrative throughout the book but also in the intricate details that reflect the time, geography, and social conditions of the Babylonian exile. Furthermore, the text itself states that these are the "words of Ezekiel" (Ezekiel 1:3), removing any ambiguity about its authorship. The priestly details, visionary experiences, and chronologically organized prophecies lend strong credence to the claim that Ezekiel, a trained priest and a prophet, is the genuine author of this prophetic book.

Canonicity of the Book of Ezekiel

The canonicity of the book of Ezekiel has been firmly established within the Jewish Tanakh as well as the Christian Old Testament. Within the Jewish tradition, it is part of the Nevi'im, or the Prophets, which is the second main division of the Hebrew Bible. The Talmud, a central text in Rabbinic Judaism, also affirms the canonical status of Ezekiel. In Christianity, it has been universally accepted as part of the Old Testament canon, as affirmed by church councils like the Council of Carthage in 397 C.E. There has been virtually no serious challenge to the canonicity of Ezekiel in either tradition.

Authenticity of the Book of Ezekiel

The authenticity of the book is substantiated by multiple lines of evidence. First, the internal consistency of the text suggests a single author, and there are no abrupt stylistic or thematic shifts that might indicate multiple authors or later interpolations. Second, historical and archaeological findings corroborate the book's details. For example, the descriptions of the Temple in Jerusalem align with what is known about temples from the same period. Lastly, Ezekiel's prophecies that have been fulfilled — such as the destruction of Tyre and Egypt's desolation — further affirm the book's authenticity.

Disputing the Authenticity of Ezekiel: A Rebuttal

Recent years have seen increasing **skepticism** about the *authenticity of the Book of Ezekiel* in academic circles. Scholars such as Gustav Hoelscher and C. C. Torrey have made controversial claims regarding the authorship and timeline of this biblical text. Their theories, however, encounter several problems when scrutinized in light of solid exegesis and historical data.

The Question of Single or Multiple Authors

One of the primary arguments against Ezekiel's authenticity is the notion that the book reflects two *contradictory viewpoints*: one preaching doom and the other offering hope. Critics claim that the original prophet could not have held both views. However, it's essential to recognize that Old Testament prophets like Amos, Hosea, and Jeremiah often intertwined messages of doom and subsequent restoration. Hugo Gressmann, after an extensive study, concluded that "World renewal necessarily follows upon world catastrophe."

Geographical Inconsistencies: A Misunderstanding?

A secondary line of reasoning posits that Ezekiel reflects a *Palestinian perspective*, making it improbable that the text was composed in Babylonia. Critics point to symbolic actions described in the book, arguing that these could not have been witnessed by an audience in Jerusalem if Ezekiel was in Babylonia.

However, the text itself does not indicate that Ezekiel's audience was in Jerusalem. Instead, it mentions that Ezekiel was preaching to his fellow exiles in Tel Abib, Babylonia. *2 Kings 24:14* substantiates that there were at least ten thousand captives from Jerusalem in Babylon, giving Ezekiel a significant audience to preach to.

Eyewitness Accounts or Divine Revelation?

Critics also maintain that Ezekiel betrays an *eyewitness knowledge* of events in Jerusalem, including idolatrous worship and specific historical incidents. They assert that this points to an author who lived in Jerusalem rather than Babylonia. This argument, however, dismisses the notion of *divine revelation* as a viable explanation for Ezekiel's detailed knowledge.

In summary, the arguments against Ezekiel's genuineness fail to account for established prophetic patterns, misinterpret geographic cues, and underestimate the role of divine revelation. Furthermore, they require selective antisupernaturalistic presuppositions that undermine the text's integrity and message. Therefore, there is no compelling reason to question the authenticity and historical background of the Book of Ezekiel.

Discrepancies Between Ezekiel and the Priestly Code: A Critical Analysis

The Wellhausen school of thought has long posited that the sixth-century prophet Ezekiel laid foundational work for what would later become the Priestly Code. Specifically, Ezekiel is thought to have contributed to the Holiness Code (Lev. 17-26) and revised the criteria for priesthood to include only the descendants of Aaron (see Ezek. 44:7-16). **However, discrepancies between Ezekiel's writings and the Priestly Code challenge this theory.** These inconsistencies are primarily in three areas: temple dimensions, temple furniture, and ritual procedures for sacrifices.

Discrepancies Are Not Limited to the Priestly Code

The standard argument posits that if the Priestly Code had already existed, Ezekiel would not have dared to offer different regulations. But this argument falls apart on closer examination. **Ezekiel's differences are not exclusive to the Priestly Code**; they also differ markedly from other biblical documents such as D, E, and H. For instance, Ezekiel doesn't mention tithes, gifts for the firstborn, or the Feast of Pentecost, all of which are included in Deuteronomy (document D).

Given that Ezekiel presupposes the same general system for sacrifices—differentiating between burnt offerings, sin offerings, and peace offerings—it's reasonable to conclude that his audience was already familiar with these practices. This suggests a longstanding tradition rather than a late innovation.

Temple Dimensions: An Inconclusive Criterion

The differences between the temple dimensions in Ezekiel and those found in the Priestly Code, or even the Solomonic temple described in 1 Kings 6-7, don't necessarily indicate a different time of authorship. **To assert that Ezekiel must have predated these texts leads to illogical conclusions,** including the notion that Ezekiel came before the construction of Solomon's temple, which defies historical evidence.

Geographic Divergences: Pointing to a Future State

Ezekiel presents a vision of land distribution among the tribes of Israel during the Millennial Kingdom that differs substantially from existing geography. Given that Ezekiel was familiar with the land in his time, it's unlikely that he was describing an imminent redistribution. Instead, this new configuration likely points to **a future state of affairs**, possibly in the end times.

The Conundrum of Ezekiel 40-48's Fulfillment

The passages of Ezekiel 40-48 provide a meticulous blueprint for the future of Palestine, complete with detailed plans for the city and the temple. Notably, the specificity of these chapters mirrors the earlier portions of Ezekiel, such as the prophecies against Tyre and Sidon in chapters 26-28, which found their fulfillment in history. The pressing question becomes: *Are these visions to be taken literally or figuratively?*

The Figurative Interpretation

Many scholars propose that these chapters are allegorical, representing the New Testament church or the spiritual Jerusalem. According to this view, the plans for the temple and the land are *spiritual forms* which the prophet Ezekiel was familiar with, but they'll take on new forms in the Christian dispensation. This approach sidesteps issues such as the ritual blood sacrifices described in these chapters, which seem incompatible with a post-Calvary understanding of atonement.

This line of interpretation appears to make sense on the surface. After all, the Book of Hebrews clearly asserts that animal sacrifices are no longer efficacious for the atonement of sin, due to the ultimate sacrifice of Jesus Christ. So, many conservative scholars are inclined to see Ezekiel's temple as a mere allegory.

The Literal Interpretation: A Necessary Reevaluation

However, this interpretation presents challenges. It overlooks the specificity and the detail with which Ezekiel describes future plans for Jerusalem and the temple. Moreover, the Book of Revelation does not provide substantial support for a figurative interpretation. For instance, Revelation 21:22 states that the New Jerusalem will have no temple, which contradicts the four chapters in Ezekiel that explicitly describe the temple.

The proponents of a figurative interpretation often forget that Ezekiel's visions were not of his own making; they were divinely revealed. Thus, dismissing them as mere allegory raises concerns about the integrity of the Scriptures and, by extension, the character of God.

A Balanced Literal Interpretation

In light of these considerations, a more *moderated literal interpretation* seems prudent. While one should exercise caution in focusing too much on the minutiae, the overarching plan described should be expected to be fulfilled in a future earthly kingdom. This kingdom would lead into the new heavens and new earth described in Revelation 21 and 22.

The sacrifices in these chapters could be symbolic or commemorative, similar to the sacrament of Holy Communion in the current church age. After all, if sacraments exist in the current age until Christ's second advent, why wouldn't there be a new form of sacrament in the Millennial Kingdom?

Unity in the Millennial Kingdom

It is essential to note that the Millennial Kingdom does not necessarily imply a division between Jewish and Gentile believers. Both groups appear to be incorporated into a unified body under the rule of the Messiah, as suggested by various Old Testament prophets and reinforced by the Apostle Paul.

The Importance of a Literal Interpretation

In conclusion, it's crucial to give weight to the literal interpretation of Ezekiel 40-48. This approach aligns with the respect for the integrity of the Scripture and is bolstered by recent evangelical commentaries, which argue that these chapters are indeed a certain prophecy destined for future fulfillment.

Refuting the Critical Objections to the Book of Ezekiel: Dramatic Fulfillments of Ezekiel's Prophecies

Destruction of Jerusalem

One of the most striking fulfillments of Ezekiel's prophecies was the destruction of Jerusalem in 586 B.C.E., as foretold in chapters 4-24. Ezekiel predicted not only the city's fall but also the desecration of the Temple. Historical accounts corroborate that the Babylonians destroyed Jerusalem and its Temple, validating Ezekiel's prophecies. This fulfillment serves as irrefutable proof of the book's prophetic integrity.

Desolation of Egypt

Ezekiel predicted the desolation of Egypt and the downfall of Pharaoh (Ezekiel 29–32). Babylonian records and historical accounts attest to the defeat of Egypt by Nebuchadnezzar II, aligning precisely with Ezekiel's prophecies. Although Egypt was not made "completely desolate," as the prophet seemed to indicate, it did suffer significant losses and never regained its former glory.

The Destruction of Tyre

In Ezekiel 26, the prophet foretold the destruction of the city of Tyre, saying it would be attacked by multiple nations and its stones, timbers, and soil would be thrown into the sea. Alexander the Great's siege of Tyre in 332 B.C.E. saw the complete fulfillment of this prophecy. The very details of the attack, including the casting of the ruins into the sea to build a causeway to the island city, were remarkably accurate.

Restoration of Israel

Although the complete fulfillment of Israel's restoration is considered an eschatological event, the incremental return of the Jews to their homeland, particularly in the 20th century, can be viewed as a partial fulfillment of Ezekiel's prophecies (Ezekiel 36–37). The re-establishment of the State of Israel in 1948 provides compelling evidence for the ongoing realization of Ezekiel's words.

Vision of the New Temple

Ezekiel's vision of the new Temple (Ezekiel 40–48) remains to be fulfilled and is considered eschatological in nature. However, the precise details provided in the Scripture serve as a template for future fulfillment and hold eschatological significance.

Reaction of the Jews to Ezekiel's Early Prophecies

Initial Fascination but Ultimate Rejection

When Ezekiel began his prophetic ministry among the exiles in Babylon, his initial reception was mixed but leaned towards curiosity and fascination. Ezekiel 33:30-33 tells us that the people were talking about him and came to listen to him as if he were an entertaining spectacle. However, the people did not take his messages to heart. They listened with their ears, but their hearts were far from obedient. Their actions did not align with Ezekiel's calls for repentance and turning back to God.

Resistance to Harsh Messages

Ezekiel was commissioned to be a "watchman" to Israel, a messenger of impending doom if they did not repent (Ezekiel 3:17). This role did not make him popular. He pronounced judgments upon Jerusalem and its rulers, even acting out these forthcoming calamities through symbolic actions, such as lying on his side for a significant period (Ezekiel 4:4-8). These were not messages that the people wanted to hear, especially when they were already in a state of despondency due to their exile. Thus, his early prophecies were met with resistance and disbelief.

Selective Hearing and Rationalization

Ezekiel also found that the people were more willing to listen to false prophets who proclaimed peace and prosperity, as indicated in Ezekiel 13. These false prophets were offering the people the comfort of lies, and the people chose to believe these lies over the grim truth Ezekiel was mandated to deliver. The truth is seldom easy to hear, and it was no different for the Jews in exile.

Denial and Spiritual Blindness

Denial was another common response. Despite the clarity and vivid imagery of Ezekiel's prophecies, the people had a hard time believing that Jerusalem could ever be destroyed, as it was the city where the temple of God resided. Their spiritual blindness kept them from acknowledging the realities foretold by Ezekiel until it was too late, thus fulfilling Ezekiel 12:2 where God says, "Son of man, you are living among a rebellious people. They have eyes to see but do not see and ears to hear but do not hear, for they are a rebellious people."

Edward D. Andrews

CHAPTER 9 The Book of Daniel on Trial

Authenticity, Authorship, and Date of Daniel

Unpacking the Historical Highlights

Daniel's Rich Historical Context

The Book of Daniel stands as an extraordinary work that documents historical and prophetic elements in a profound narrative. Daniel, a young Judean exile, serves in the Babylonian and later Medo-Persian courts. His lifetime spans from approximately 605 B.C.E., when he was taken into Babylonian captivity, to at least 536 B.C.E., making him a witness to some of the most critical events in ancient Near Eastern history. The book provides a rich tableau that covers the fall of Jerusalem, the Babylonian exile, and the eventual fall of Babylon to the Medo-Persians.

Juxtaposition of Worldly Power and Divine Sovereignty

At the heart of Daniel's history is a constant interplay between worldly kingdoms and divine sovereignty. The depiction of powerful empires—Babylon and Medo-Persia—is not just for the sake of historical records but serves to accentuate God's control over human events. Daniel's interactions with key figures like Nebuchadnezzar and Darius bring out this juxtaposition. For example, the account of Nebuchadnezzar's dream of a colossal statue and Daniel's interpretation is a clear declaration that human kingdoms are temporary, but God's dominion is everlasting (Daniel 2).

Prophetic History: Predictive Elements as Validation

Daniel's prophetic visions hold historical significance as well. The visions in chapters 7–12 present a panoramic view of world history, from Daniel's own time to the eschatological future. For instance, the vision of the four beasts in Daniel 7 provides a prophetic outline of the empires that would arise after Babylon, namely Medo-Persia, Greece, and Rome. These prophecies have been accurately fulfilled, adding a layer of validation to the book's historical narrative and reinforcing the central theme of divine sovereignty.

Individual and Collective Faithfulness

An additional historical highlight is the exemplary faith and integrity of Daniel and his companions—Shadrach, Meshach, and Abednego. Whether it was refusing to defile themselves with the royal food, praying openly despite an imperial edict, or facing a fiery furnace, their actions become historical testimonies of faithfulness in the midst of apostasy and pagan domination. Their lives underscore the belief that obedience to God supersedes allegiance to any earthly authority.

The Historical Reality of Daniel: Evidence and Timeline

Daniel as an Actual Historical Figure

Daniel's existence as an actual historical person is supported by several lines of evidence. First and foremost, the book itself presents Daniel as a real individual who participated in specific historical events. He was a young Judean noble taken into captivity by Nebuchadnezzar in the first wave of deportations to Babylon in 605 B.C.E. (Daniel 1:1-6).

Further, Daniel's contemporaneity with other historical figures such as Nebuchadnezzar, Belshazzar, and Darius is detailed in the Scriptures. Not merely a literary device, Daniel interacts with these rulers, interprets dreams, and serves in governmental positions (Daniel 2, 4–6).

Corroborative Evidence from Ezekiel

In addition to the internal evidence from the Book of Daniel, the prophet Ezekiel also makes explicit references to Daniel. In Ezekiel 14:14, 20, Daniel is listed alongside Noah and Job as a paradigm of righteousness. In Ezekiel 28:3, Daniel is referred to as a man known for wisdom and understanding. The prophet Ezekiel was a contemporary of Daniel; both prophesied during the Babylonian exile. The mentioning of Daniel in another prophetic book reinforces the idea that Daniel was an actual historical person.

The Eventful Period of Daniel's Prophesy

Daniel lived and prophesied during some of the most critical periods of ancient Near Eastern history. He was exiled to Babylon in 605 B.C.E., during the reign of Nebuchadnezzar, who had just defeated the Egyptians at the Battle of Carchemish. His prophetic service continued through the fall of the Babylonian Empire and into the early period of the Medo-Persian Empire, at least until 536 B.C.E.

During this time, Daniel served in the royal courts of both Babylon and Medo-Persia. He witnessed the Babylonian destruction of Jerusalem in 587/586 B.C.E., the madness of Nebuchadnezzar, and the handwriting on the wall that predicted the fall of Babylon. Moreover, he was there when Cyrus the Great overthrew Babylon and issued the decree allowing the Jews to return to their homeland.

The Canonicity and Authenticity of the Book of Daniel

Internal Evidence: Prophetic Accuracy and Authorship

One of the most striking proofs of the canonicity and authenticity of the Book of Daniel is its detailed, prophetic accuracy. For instance, the visions provided in Daniel chapters 2 and 7 accurately depict the succession of empires, from Babylon to Medo-Persia, then to Greece, and finally to Rome. This demonstrates that Daniel is indeed prophetic and inspired by Jehovah.

The book bears Daniel's name, indicating authorship and thereby testifying to its authenticity. This is important because Daniel is a historical figure acknowledged by other Scriptures, as noted in the previous discussion. Moreover, the writing style, historical details, and theological consistency within the book further support the claim that it is a genuine product of the prophet Daniel.

External Evidence: Early Recognition and Acceptance

The Jewish community has long recognized the Book of Daniel as canonical. It is part of the Hebrew Bible and is positioned among the Writings (Ketuvim), an accepted section of the Jewish canon. Furthermore, the Book of Daniel was one of the scrolls found among the Dead Sea Scrolls, which suggests that it was highly regarded and copied by the Jewish community before the time of Christ.

New Testament Validation

The New Testament provides further evidence for the canonicity of Daniel. In Matthew 24:15, Jesus explicitly refers to "the abomination of desolation spoken of through Daniel the prophet." Here, Jesus is citing Daniel 9:27, 11:31, and 12:11. This New Testament acknowledgment not only recognizes Daniel as canonical but also authenticates its prophetic message.

Church Tradition and Scholarly Acceptance

In addition to the Jewish community and the New Testament, early Christian tradition also supported the Book of Daniel's canonicity. The book has consistently been part of the Christian Old Testament canon recognized by various church councils. Furthermore, it has been included in every major Christian Bible translation and is therefore a recognized part of the canon in Christian scholarly circles.

The Roman Catholic Assertion: The Roman Catholic Church often asserts that it holds the authority for determining the biblical canon. This claim is frequently tied to the Council of Carthage in 397 C.E., where a list of canonical books was ratified.

The Reality: Pre-existing Canonical Authority: Contrary to this claim, the canon of the Bible, including the Christian Greek Scriptures (New Testament), was already largely accepted by the time of the Council. This acceptance wasn't due to the decisions of any ecclesiastical councils but was guided by God's Holy Spirit—the same Spirit that inspired the original authors of the Bible.

The Role of the Holy Spirit: Understanding that the canon was directed by God's Holy Spirit is crucial. The Bible isn't simply a man-made collection of religious texts but is divinely inspired. Thus, it doesn't rely on human authorization for its formulation.

Value of Later Catalogs: While the lists and catalogs generated by councils like Carthage have historical interest, their primary significance lies in acknowledging what was already authorized by God's Spirit. These catalogs serve more as a confirmation, rather than as an original endorsement, of the canonical books.

Archaeology's Role in Vindicating the Book of Daniel

The Historicity of Babylonian and Persian Kings

One of the most significant ways archaeology has vindicated the Book of Daniel is by confirming the historical accuracy of Babylonian and Persian kings named in the book. Critics have often challenged the existence of Belshazzar, the last king of Babylon according to Daniel. Archaeological discoveries, such as the Nabonidus Cylinder, not only confirm the existence of Nabonidus but also mention his son Belshazzar, precisely as the Book of Daniel describes.

The Discovery of Ancient Documents

The Elephantine papyri discovered in Egypt mention the Jewish community's correspondence with authorities, including the reference to a person named Bagoas, a Persian official also mentioned in Daniel. Such discoveries verify the Book of Daniel's detailed knowledge of names, titles, and bureaucratic offices, suggesting a historical setting consistent with the sixth century B.C.E.

The Language and Literary Style

Daniel contains portions in Aramaic (2:4–7:28), which was the diplomatic and governmental language used in the Babylonian and Persian empires. Archaeological discoveries have produced numerous texts in Imperial Aramaic from the same period, thereby supporting the linguistic background of the Book of Daniel. This is contrary to the claims of higher critics who suggest the book's language style belonged to a later period.

Archaeological Discovery of the Susa Palace

Susa, a city mentioned in Daniel, was excavated in the late 19th and early 20th centuries. This confirmed the existence of the palace where Daniel saw one of his visions (Daniel 8). The excavation of Susa has yielded several historically important artifacts that align well with the biblical account, further solidifying the Book of Daniel's historical credibility.

Dead Sea Scrolls

The presence of Daniel fragments among the Dead Sea Scrolls provides substantial evidence for the book's early composition and wide acceptance. It nullifies the claims of higher critics who argue for a second-century B.C.E. dating of the book.

The Book of Daniel On Trial

Accusations Against the Book of Daniel

The Book of Daniel has been the subject of intense scrutiny and stands accused on multiple fronts:

Late Dating: Critics assert that Daniel was written during the Maccabean period in the second century B.C.E., instead of the sixth century B.C.E. during the Babylonian exile, as the book itself claims.

Historical Inaccuracies: Detractors point to supposed inaccuracies concerning the reigns of Babylonian and Persian rulers mentioned in the book. The existence of King Belshazzar, for instance, was once considered dubious by critics.

Prophetic Determinism: The book's detailed prophetic content, especially the prophecies about the succession of empires and the coming of the Messiah, is often seen as too precise to be anything other than "prophecy after the fact."

Language and Literary Style: The book's use of Aramaic and Hebrew has also been presented as evidence of a later dating. Critics claim that the style and language are more consistent with a later period than with the Babylonian exile.

The Necessity of Defending Daniel

Historical Faithfulness: The dating and authenticity of Daniel have direct implications for the reliability of the Bible as a historically faithful document. If Daniel can be shown to be a genuine product of the sixth century B.C.E., then the historical veracity of the Bible is strengthened.

Prophetic Integrity: Given that Daniel includes specific prophecies related to the Messiah and the end times, its authenticity is critical for understanding God's plan for human history.

Doctrinal Integrity: Daniel touches on important doctrines, including the sovereignty of God over nations and rulers, and the ultimate triumph of God's kingdom. If the book is not genuine, these doctrines could be compromised.

Sanctification of Jehovah's Name: Daniel's life and prophecies highlight the sanctification of Jehovah's name. He maintained his faithfulness amidst opposition, thereby vindicating Jehovah's sovereignty and righteousness. If the book is discredited, the sanctification of Jehovah's name is also undermined.

Authority of Jesus Christ: Jesus himself refers to the "abomination of desolation spoken of by Daniel the prophet" (Matthew 24:15). If Daniel is not a reliable text, it calls into question the authority and reliability of Jesus' own words.

The Genesis of Criticism Against the Book of Daniel

Porphyry's Assault: Criticism of the Book of Daniel dates back to antiquity. One of the earliest critics was Porphyry, a third-century C.E. Neoplatonist philosopher. In his work "Against the Christians," Porphyry aimed to dismantle the legitimacy of the Scriptures, and he targeted Daniel because of its prophetic content. He insisted that the book was a product of the Maccabean period, written to provide comfort to the Jews under the oppression of Antiochus Epiphanes. Porphyry's arguments were deeply rooted in his anti-Christian agenda and set the groundwork for future critics.

The Modern Landscape of Criticism

Enlightenment Skepticism: During the Enlightenment period, skepticism towards religious texts in general led to heightened scrutiny of the Bible, including Daniel. Thinkers like Spinoza and Hobbes, although not focused exclusively on Daniel, paved the way for a skeptical approach to Scripture.

Historical-Critical Method: The 19th century saw the rise of the historical-critical method in Biblical studies, which treated the Bible as any other historical document rather than as divinely inspired. Under this scrutiny, Daniel was dissected for its supposed historical inaccuracies, late dating, and linguistic anachronisms.

Rise of Secularism: The rise of secularism in the 20th century also fueled criticism against Daniel. Secular scholars rejected any notion of predictive prophecy, which is a crucial element of Daniel. They pointed to the book's apocalyptic visions as retrojections rather than prophecies.

Underlying Factors Fueling Criticism

Anti-Supernatural Bias: At the core of most criticism against Daniel is an anti-supernatural bias. The notion of predictive prophecy is often a priori ruled out, making the miraculous elements in Daniel hard for such critics to accept.

Theological Agenda: Some critics might be motivated by a desire to dismantle the Judeo-Christian worldview. Daniel's specific prophecies about the coming Messiah and the end times can be theologically inconvenient for those who reject these concepts.

Polemical Attacks: Daniel has been targeted because its veracity impacts broader Scriptural truths, including prophetic accuracy and the reliability of Jesus Christ, who quoted from Daniel. Discrediting Daniel, in essence, serves as a polemical strategy against foundational Christian beliefs.

The Imperative of Upholding the Authenticity of the Book of Daniel

The question of the authenticity of the Book of Daniel is not merely an academic issue; it is a theological imperative with far-reaching implications. Here's why it is of pivotal importance:

Foundation for Eschatology: The Book of Daniel contains essential end-time prophecies, detailing events and outlining a timeline that serves as a basis for understanding Biblical eschatology. Its authenticity directly influences our perception of what the Bible says about the future, the end times, and the coming of the Messiah.

Test of Prophetic Accuracy: Daniel's prophecies are so precise that critics have often questioned their authenticity, alleging that they must have been written after the events took place. Validating the authenticity of Daniel is tantamount to defending the concept of predictive prophecy, a foundational belief for conservative Christianity.

Jesus' Endorsement: Jesus Christ himself quoted Daniel, referring to its prophecies and the "abomination of desolation" (Matthew 24:15). The veracity of Daniel is indirectly an endorsement of Christ's own authority and the trustworthiness of His teachings.

Integrity of Scripture: Daniel is woven into the tapestry of the Biblical narrative, cited by other books and foundational to certain doctrinal points. Its authenticity impacts the overall integrity of Scripture. If Daniel is discredited, it creates a domino effect that puts the credibility of the entire Bible into question.

Relevance to Contemporary Issues: Daniel speaks to issues of government, God's sovereignty, and the challenges that faithful individuals face in a predominantly secular or antagonistic environment. These themes are extraordinarily relevant today, and dismissing Daniel would mean losing a rich resource for navigating modern ethical and moral dilemmas.

Challenge to Higher Criticism: The Book of Daniel has been a target of higher criticism, as mentioned before. Validating its authenticity serves as a counterpoint to the methodologies and presuppositions of higher criticism, reaffirming the need for a faith-based approach to Biblical hermeneutics.

The Charge Against the Historicity of the Book of Daniel

One of the main charges against the Book of Daniel is that it contains historical inaccuracies or anachronisms, which skeptics claim make it unreliable as a historical document. Critics argue that the book was written much later than its purported timeframe, during the Maccabean period, rather than in the 6th century B.C.E., when Daniel was supposed to have lived. This position is often termed the "late-dating theory." The charge is primarily centered around several aspects:

Belshazzar's Kingship: Critics often point out that historical records do not identify Belshazzar as the king of Babylon; instead, they mention Nabonidus as the last king before the Medo-Persian conquest. However, recent archaeological findings, including the Nabonidus Cylinder, have confirmed that Belshazzar served as co-regent with his father, Nabonidus. This fully aligns with Daniel's account.

Darius the Mede: Skeptics also question the existence of Darius the Mede, who is mentioned in Daniel but not explicitly named in other historical accounts. Yet, there are historical indications that a Median ruler could have served as a governor or sub-king under Cyrus the Persian. While his precise identification remains a topic of scholarly investigation, dismissing Darius the Mede as fictional is unwarranted.

Language and Literary Style: Critics claim that the Aramaic and Hebrew used in Daniel are more characteristic of a later period. However, the linguistic features are fully compatible with a 6th-century B.C.E. setting. Moreover, the unique blend of Hebrew and Aramaic can be attributed to Daniel's context—living in Babylon but maintaining his Hebrew roots.

Edward D. Andrews

Daniel's References to Belshazzar: A Critical Focal Point

For a long time, critics of the Bible reveled in Daniel's references to Belshazzar as the king of Babylon because no direct historical evidence outside the Bible initially verified his existence or his position. This apparent lack of extra-biblical corroboration was considered a strong point in favor of the argument that the Book of Daniel was not historically accurate, and thus not divinely inspired. Critics asserted that if Daniel were wrong about such a significant detail, then the entire book's reliability could be called into question.

The Transformation from Fiction to Fact

However, this notion that Belshazzar was merely a fictitious character has been thoroughly discredited due to subsequent archaeological discoveries. One of the most significant findings was the Nabonidus Cylinder, which was discovered in the ruins of Ur. This artifact not only mentions Nabonidus, the last recognized king of Babylon, but also his son Belshazzar. Moreover, it aligns well with the biblical narrative by indicating that Nabonidus was away from Babylon for an extended period, leaving administrative responsibilities to Belshazzar. This discovery was momentous because it verified the historical existence of Belshazzar and established that he acted as co-regent during his father's absence.

Further evidence came from the discovery of Babylonian administrative documents that also mention Belshazzar. These documents provided additional confirmation that Belshazzar was indeed a historical figure and played a significant role in Babylon's governance.

Daniel's Description of Belshazzar: A Matter of Historical Authenticity

The Book of Daniel describes Belshazzar as the king of Babylon during the famous episode of the "writing on the wall" (Daniel 5). For years, this claim was a point of contention among critics because

Belshazzar was not listed among the kings of Babylon in ancient historical records. According to well-known Babylonian king lists, Nabonidus was the last king before the fall of Babylon. Critics questioned how Daniel could describe Belshazzar as reigning king if he didn't appear in these historical lists.

Archaeological Vindication

However, Daniel's portrayal of Belshazzar as a reigning king has been conclusively confirmed by later archaeological findings. The most compelling piece of evidence is the Nabonidus Cylinder discovered in Ur. This cylinder lists Nabonidus as the king and mentions Belshazzar, his son, as someone who is entrusted with kingship responsibilities. This finds perfect congruence with Daniel's account. Nabonidus was not present in Babylon; he was staying in Tayma, while his son Belshazzar was holding the fort in the capital city. Therefore, Belshazzar was the de facto ruler in Babylon, perfectly aligning with the biblical narrative.

Additionally, administrative tablets found in Babylon also provide evidence that Belshazzar acted in a role akin to a reigning king. These tablets, which concern economic transactions and administrative issues, were dated to the reign of "Nabonidus and Belshazzar his son." This again confirms that Belshazzar had a level of authority second only to his father and acted as a reigning king during Nabonidus's absence.

The Role of Co-Regency

It's crucial to understand the concept of co-regency in the Babylonian and broader Near Eastern context. A king would sometimes establish a co-regency with a family member, often a son, especially when the king planned to be away from the capital for an extended period. This co-regency arrangement is precisely what seems to have been in place between Nabonidus and Belshazzar, vindicating Daniel's description.

Belshazzar, the "Son" of Nebuchadnezzar: Understanding Semitic Terminology

The Book of Daniel refers to Belshazzar as the "son" of Nebuchadnezzar (Daniel 5:2, 11, 18). Critics have pounced on this terminology, arguing that Daniel is historically inaccurate since Belshazzar was actually the son of Nabonidus, not Nebuchadnezzar. However, understanding the Semitic use of familial terms like "son" and "father" will dispel this criticism. In Semitic cultures, the word "son" can denote not just a biological relationship but also a broader lineage or succession. The term could be used more loosely to mean a successor or one in the kingly line, even if not directly descended.

We can find similar uses of the word "son" in other ancient Near Eastern literature and even within the Bible itself. For example, Jehu is called the "son" of Nimshi in 2 Kings 9:20, although he was actually the grandson of Nimshi. So when Daniel refers to Belshazzar as the "son" of Nebuchadnezzar, it need not imply a direct father-son biological relationship; it could well indicate a royal succession or lineage. Belshazzar was a Chaldean king like Nebuchadnezzar, and he wielded the Babylonian scepter, albeit not as effectively or famously as Nebuchadnezzar.

Daniel and the Existence of Nabonidus

Critics also argue that the Book of Daniel doesn't mention Nabonidus, the father of Belshazzar, and thereby commit an error of omission. This criticism fails to account for the focus and intent of Daniel's writing. Daniel's purpose is not to give a comprehensive history of Babylonian kings but to offer a prophetic and historical account concerning God's sovereignty and the experiences of the Jewish people under foreign rule.

However, when Daniel describes Belshazzar as "king" and says that he was killed when Babylon was taken (Daniel 5:30-31), he is implicitly recognizing the absence of the actual king—Nabonidus. In other words, Daniel does not need to mention Nabonidus explicitly; his narrative makes it clear that another figure must have been the official king since Belshazzar is killed but the kingdom merely changes rulers rather than being destroyed. This is a subtle but powerful indicator that Daniel was well aware of the political situation in Babylon, far more than critics are willing to admit.

The Detailed Nature of Daniel's Account of the Babylonian Monarchy

The Book of Daniel provides an account of the Babylonian monarchy that is more detailed than many other ancient historians. There are several compelling reasons for this level of detail, which have profound implications for its historical reliability and its significance as a canonical text.

Proximity to Events and Involvement in the Babylonian Court

Firstly, Daniel himself was a figure deeply embedded within the Babylonian court. He was trained in the language and literature of the Chaldeans (Daniel 1:4), served under multiple kings, and was highly esteemed for his wisdom and prophetic gifts. This proximity to the seat of power in Babylon afforded Daniel a unique vantage point that most ancient historians did not have. He had firsthand experience and access to royal archives, which would naturally lead to a more comprehensive account.

Theological Objectives Necessitating Historical Precision

Secondly, the Book of Daniel is not merely a historical record; it is a theological text with specific aims. Daniel is making a case for Jehovah's sovereignty over the nations and the course of history. To make this case effectively, it is imperative to show God's hand at work in specific, historical events. This necessitates a detailed account. For instance, the elaborate narratives concerning Nebuchadnezzar's dream of the statue (Daniel 2), his period of madness (Daniel 4), and Belshazzar's feast (Daniel 5) are all aimed at demonstrating Jehovah's active role in the affairs of nations.

Prophecies Requiring Historical Anchors

Thirdly, the Book of Daniel contains a series of detailed prophecies about future events, including the rise and fall of empires like the Medo-Persian and the Greek empires. The historical grounding in Daniel's time provides the basis for these future prophecies. An accurate, detailed account of the current times serves as a foundation upon which the reliability of future prophecies can be assessed. This could be why the historical account in Daniel is so detailed—it serves as the anchor for the prophetic.

Comparison to Other Ancient Historians

Finally, it's worth noting that ancient historians often wrote for different objectives, such as glorifying a king or a city, or simply recording events without deeper theological objectives. As a result, many such works do not provide the level of detail found in Daniel. Additionally, many ancient historical accounts have been lost over time, while the Book of Daniel has been painstakingly preserved as part of the Biblical canon.

Darius the Mede in the Book of Daniel

According to the Book of Daniel, Darius the Mede was the ruler who took over Babylon after its fall to the Medo-Persian empire in 539 B.C.E. Daniel states that Darius was about 62 years old when he began his rule (Daniel 5:31). Darius the Mede is depicted as a God-fearing man who respected Daniel and was reluctant to punish him when Daniel was caught praying to Jehovah contrary to the royal edict (Daniel 6). After Daniel survived the lions' den, Darius made a decree that all in his kingdom should fear the God of Daniel (Daniel 6:25-27).

Criticisms Regarding Darius the Mede

Despite the clear portrayal in Daniel, the historical identity of Darius the Mede has been the subject of much debate and criticism. Some critics argue that there is no extra-Biblical evidence to support the existence of a Medo-Persian ruler by this name immediately following the fall of Babylon. This has led to assertions that the Book of Daniel is inaccurate or unreliable in its historical details.

Rebuttal: Historical Possibilities and Theories

However, several theories have been put forth to reconcile the Biblical account with historical data. One theory is that Darius the Mede was a title or throne name for another ruler known by a different name in other historical accounts. Another theory posits that Darius could be identified with Cyrus the Great himself, who had Median heritage through his mother. In such a case, "Darius the Mede" would be another title for Cyrus, emphasizing his Median connections. A third theory suggests that Darius the Mede could be identified with Gubaru (or Ugbaru), the general who is historically documented to have led the invasion of Babylon.

It's important to note that the absence of direct extra-Biblical evidence for Darius the Mede does not negate the reliability of Daniel's account. Ancient records are fragmentary, and it is entirely plausible that future discoveries could provide further clarification. Moreover, Daniel's intimate acquaintance with the royal court would provide him with insider information not necessarily available to other historians of the time.

The Caution Warranted in Dismissing Darius the Mede

Bible critics should exercise caution before making categorical statements that Darius the Mede never existed. As has been demonstrated time and again, the absence of direct evidence is not the evidence of absence. This is particularly true given the fragmentary nature of ancient historical records.

The case of Belshazzar serves as an instructive example. Critics once regarded Belshazzar as a fictitious character due to the lack of extra-Biblical references. However, later discoveries, including cuneiform tablets, vindicated the Biblical account by confirming Belshazzar's existence and his role as co-regent with Nabonidus. Just as Belshazzar went from being considered fictitious to being historically verified, there's every reason to think that further evidence could emerge to corroborate Daniel's account of Darius the Mede.

The Identity of Darius the Mede: Gubaru as a Viable Candidate

One particularly compelling possibility regarding the identity of Darius the Mede is that he may have been Gubaru, a Median official installed by Cyrus as the governor of Babylon. There are cuneiform tablets that confirm the presence of a ruler by the name of Gubaru in Babylon around the time of its conquest. This Gubaru ruled with considerable power and authority, appointing subgovernors over Babylon.

Daniel 6:1 explicitly notes that Darius appointed 120 satraps to govern the kingdom of Babylon. This detail aligns well with the secular record's description of Gubaru's administrative activities, lending further credibility to the identification.

Moreover, cuneiform tablets have shown that Cyrus did not immediately assume the title "King of Babylon" following the conquest. This leaves room for the presence of a vassal king or a high-ranking official overseeing Babylon, perfectly consistent with the role Daniel ascribes to Darius the Mede.

Who Was Darius the Mede? Addressing Scholarly Debate and Skepticism

The Skeptic's Argument: *Darius the Mede* is a figure who appears in the Bible but has not been corroborated by any non-Biblical inscriptions or mentioned by secular historians prior to Josephus in the first century C.E. This lack of external evidence has led some critics to label him as a fictional character.

Cambyses II: A Misidentification?: Some scholars suggest that *Cambyses II*, son of Cyrus, might have been "King of Babylon" after Babylon's fall. Although Cambyses represented his father in the annual New Year's festival in Babylon, cuneiform evidence shows that he did not take the title "King of Babylon" until 530 B.C.E. This does not align with the Biblical description of Darius being "about sixty-two years old" at the time of Babylon's fall (Da 5:31).

Darius as Cyrus? A Mismatch of Ethnic Backgrounds: Another theory posits that *Darius could be another name for Cyrus himself.* However, this view is incompatible with Darius being described as a

"Mede" and "of the seed of the Medes," pointing to his father, Ahasuerus, as Median. Cyrus, on the other hand, is explicitly labeled as "Persian" in both Biblical and non-Biblical sources, such as the Cyrus Cylinder.

The Cyaxares Hypothesis: Unreliable and Contradictory: Some also identify Darius with *Cyaxares II*, a supposed uncle of Cyrus as presented by the Greek historian Xenophon. Yet, this view is inconsistent with accounts by other Greek historians like Herodotus and Ctesias, and the Nabonidus Chronicle, which show Cyrus taking over the Median kingdom by capturing Astyages. Additionally, linking Darius to Cyaxares would necessitate assuming that Astyages was also known as Ahasuerus, a proposition that lacks firm evidence.

Summary: The Need for Caution in Identification

The identity of Darius the Mede remains a complex issue. While various theories have been proposed, none can fully reconcile with the Biblical description and the historical data available. As of now, attributing Darius the Mede's identity to figures like Cambyses II, Cyrus, or Cyaxares II encounters significant historical and scriptural hurdles. Therefore, it would be prudent to refrain from definitive identifications that lack substantive corroboration.

The Intriguing Identity of Darius the Mede: Is He Gubaru?

The Cuneiform Puzzle: Ugbaru and Gubaru

Recent reference works point to *Gubaru*, also identified with Gobryas from Xenophon's Cyropaedia, as potentially being Darius the Mede. The Nabonidus Chronicle, an ancient cuneiform text, reveals that a person named Ugbaru, "the governor of Gutium," entered Babylon with Cyrus' army "without battle." Later, the text states that Gubaru "installed (sub-)governors in Babylon." While Ugbaru and Gubaru might appear to be the same, they are distinctly different names in cuneiform writing. Furthermore, the Chronicle reveals that

Ugbaru died shortly after the conquest, whereas other cuneiform texts indicate that Gubaru served as a governor for 14 years.

Geographical Parallels: Matching Territories

Gubaru ruled not only over Babylon but also over a region that extended throughout the Fertile Crescent—essentially the same area as the Babylonian Empire. This aligns well with the Biblical description of Darius as being "made king over the kingdom of the Chaldeans" (Da 5:31; 9:1), but not as "the king of Persia," the standard title for Cyrus (Da 10:1; Ezr 1:1, 2; 3:7; 4:3).

The Title Theory: Is Darius a Throne Name?

W.F. Albright suggests that "Darius" might be a royal title Gubaru adopted while Cyrus was away. Cuneiform records don't call Gubaru a "king," but they also don't label Belshazzar as such, even though another cuneiform text clearly states that Nabonidus "entrusted the kingship" to his son. Following this line of thought, Professor Whitcomb argues that Gubaru, like Darius, appointed district governors, suggesting that Gubaru was probably regarded as a king by those under him. A.T. Olmstead even contends that Gubaru ruled "almost as an independent monarch."

Darius as Viceroy: A Subordinate Ruler?

Given these facts, some scholars think that Darius the Mede might have been a *viceroy* serving under Cyrus. The Bible indicates that Darius "received the kingdom" and was "made king over the kingdom of the Chaldeans," suggesting a subordinate position to Cyrus. A.T. Olmstead notes that Cyrus styled himself as "king of Babylon, king of lands," and that it was Gubaru who represented royal authority after Cyrus left.

Lingering Questions: Incomplete Identification

While there's compelling evidence that Gubaru's role mirrors that of Darius, a definitive identification can't be made. Historical records do not reveal Gubaru's nationality or parentage, and they don't demonstrate that he had the kind of kingly authority described in

Daniel 6:6-9. Additionally, while Darius' rule in Babylon appears to be short-lived, Gubaru served for 14 years.

A Tentative Connection, But Not Conclusive

Although the roles and regions ruled by Gubaru and Darius the Mede appear remarkably similar, the identification of the two remains uncertain. Further historical and Scriptural analysis is needed to fully resolve this enigmatic figure's identity.

The Enigma of Darius the Mede: Historical Identification and Biblical Integrity

The Elusive Historical Identification of Darius the Mede

The identity of Darius the Mede, a figure mentioned in the Bible, has been a subject of scholarly debate for years. One popular theory posits that Darius the Mede could be Gubaru (sometimes identified with Gobryas mentioned in Xenophon's Cyropaedia), a significant official in the Medo-Persian Empire. *The Nabonidus Chronicle*, an ancient cuneiform text, suggests that Gubaru was the governor who helped Cyrus conquer Babylon. After this conquest, Gubaru was charged with installing sub-governors in the region, an action parallel to what Darius the Mede is credited with in Daniel 6:1-2. *Geographical jurisdiction* is another compelling link; Gubaru governed an expansive region that closely matches the territory over which Darius ruled.

Yet, the correlation is not definitive. The chronicle does not state that Gubaru was a Mede or a king. While the suggestion that "Darius" was a title or throne name has been made, there is no concrete evidence to substantiate this claim. *W. F. Albright* suggests that Gubaru may have assumed the royal name 'Darius' during Cyrus' absence, but this remains speculative.

Why Secular Confirmation Isn't Necessary for Biblical Accuracy

While corroborative evidence from historical records would be informative, the *integrity and truthfulness* of the Bible do not hinge on such verification. Over time, many historical figures and events that were initially questioned by critics have been affirmed through subsequent discoveries. It's essential to note that the records we have today, including hundreds of thousands of cuneiform tablets, present an incomplete picture of ancient history, riddled with gaps and inconsistencies.

Intriguing Possibility: Manipulation of Babylonian Records

The Book of Daniel itself offers an intriguing explanation for the scant information about Darius the Mede. Daniel was elevated to a high governmental position by Darius, an action that incurred the jealousy and plotting of other officials. After their conspiracy failed, Darius executed Daniel's accusers and their families. This act likely generated widespread resentment, especially among the powerful Babylonian clergy. Given that the scribes of that period were under the influence of these powerful entities, it is conceivable that records were manipulated or eliminated to erase any favorable mention of Darius.

The Medo-Persian Partnership and Its Biblical Weight

While secular history tends to focus overwhelmingly on the Persians, particularly Cyrus, *the Bible provides a more nuanced picture.* The Medes continued to hold substantial power and influence, as seen in the term "the law of the Medes and the Persians." The Medes were also instrumental in the overthrow of Babylon, a fact that aligns with prophecies in the Bible. Jeremiah, for instance, predicted that multiple "kings of the Medes" would attack Babylon, suggesting that Darius could be one of these rulers.

Darius the Mede: Skepticism, Speculation, and Biblical Veracity

Cautious Scholars and the "Fictitious" Label

One cannot overlook the fact that the Bible has faced its fair share of skepticism. Critics have been quick to label biblical figures like Belshazzar as "fictitious," only to be proven wrong later. The situation with Darius the Mede could very well be similar. Some recent discoveries suggest that Cyrus the Persian did not immediately assume the title "King of Babylon" following the conquest. One scholar posits,

"Whoever bore the title of 'King of Babylon' was a vassal king under Cyrus, not Cyrus himself." In light of this, it's worth considering that *Darius could have been a ruling name or title for a high-ranking Median official left to govern Babylon.*

Gubaru as a Possible Candidate for Darius

The possibility that Darius the Mede might be Gubaru is particularly compelling. Secular records confirm that Cyrus appointed Gubaru as the governor of Babylon and that he wielded significant authority. One cuneiform tablet even states that he appointed sub-governors over Babylon. This meshes well with Daniel's account, which records that Darius appointed 120 satraps to govern Babylon (Daniel 6:1). *This correlation between secular records and the biblical account is too striking to ignore.*

Archaeological Silence Does Not Imply Inaccuracy

The current lack of conclusive evidence concerning Darius the Mede does not discredit the biblical narrative. To call Darius "fictitious" based on the absence of direct archaeological evidence would be premature and unjust. Furthermore, dismissing the entire book of Daniel as fraudulent on these grounds would be irrational. *It is far more reasonable to view Daniel's account as an eyewitness testimony, offering details that might be more accurate and extensive than any surviving secular records.*

The Future May Hold Further Clues

With ongoing archaeological endeavors and scholarly research, it's entirely possible that more concrete evidence may eventually surface. Regardless, the *Bible stands on its own as a reliable historical document.* Even if archaeology remains silent or vague on certain topics, this doesn't undermine the credibility or the intricate details provided in the Scriptures.

While it's intriguing to ponder the identity of Darius the Mede and how he fits into historical records, the absence of definitive secular evidence does not undermine the Bible's credibility. As with many figures in ancient history, the full picture of Darius the Mede remains incomplete, open to scholarly interpretation but ultimately affirmed by Scriptural authority.

In summary, while skepticism exists, it's important to weigh the existing evidence and the Bible's track record of historical accuracy. The case of Darius the Mede exemplifies why rash judgments based on incomplete data can be flawed. With time, more definitive information may come to light, further affirming the Bible's account.

Harmonizing the Reign of King Jehoiakim: Daniel and Jeremiah in Accord

One of the criticisms often raised against the Book of Daniel involves the account of King Jehoiakim's reign. Some have suggested that there is a discrepancy between the portrayal of Jehoiakim's reign in the Book of Daniel and that in the Book of Jeremiah. Specifically, Daniel 1:1 states that Jehoiakim, king of Judah, came under siege in the third year of his reign, while Jeremiah 25:1 mentions that the fourth year of Jehoiakim's reign was the first year of Nebuchadnezzar. Critics assert that these accounts cannot both be correct.

However, upon closer examination, this perceived discrepancy evaporates. The key to resolving this lies in understanding the different methods used for counting the years of a king's reign in the Biblical narrative. The Hebrew Bible employs two different systems: the accession year system and the non-accession year system.

Accession Year vs Non-Accession Year Systems

In the accession year system, the year in which a king comes to power is counted as his "accession year," and the official "first year" of his reign starts only after the New Year. In contrast, the non-accession year system counts the year a king comes to power as the first year of his reign.

Jeremiah and Daniel Use Different Systems

Jeremiah, writing from a Judah-centric perspective, typically uses the accession year system. According to Jeremiah 25:1, the "fourth year" would be Jehoiakim's official fourth regnal year following the accession year. On the other hand, Daniel, writing in a Babylonian context, uses the non-accession year system consistent with Babylonian custom. Consequently, in Daniel 1:1, when it is stated that

Jehoiakim came under siege in the "third year" of his reign, it aligns with the Babylonian method of counting, which includes the accession year as the first year.

Chronological Confirmation

Using a conservative Bible chronology, Jehoiakim began his reign in 609 B.C.E. His "third year," according to the Babylonian reckoning, would be 607 B.C.E. The "fourth year" based on the Judean reckoning, omitting the accession year, would also fall in 607 B.C.E. Therefore, both accounts are describing events that took place in the same year but are utilizing different calendrical systems.

The Dating of Daniel 1:1: A Grounded Examination

The dating found in Daniel 1:1 has come under scrutiny by some who claim that it represents a historical error, largely because it refers to Jehoiakim coming under siege by Nebuchadnezzar in the "third year" of his reign. Critics argue that Babylonian records and other historical sources indicate that Nebuchadnezzar's major incursion into Judah occurred during the reign of Jehoiachin, Jehoiakim's successor. However, such criticisms fail to consider the nuance and historical context that resolve this apparent discrepancy.

The Calendrical Systems: A Source of Clarification

As previously explained, understanding the different calendrical systems—accession year and non-accession year—can resolve the perceived contradiction. Daniel writes from a Babylonian context, using a non-accession year system. Jeremiah, on the other hand, writes using the accession year system. The "third year" of Jehoiakim's reign according to Daniel would be the same as the "fourth year" according to Jeremiah.

Multiple Campaigns, Not a Single Event

Another crucial point is that the Babylonian military campaigns were not limited to one event. Nebuchadnezzar conducted multiple campaigns against Judah during this period. While the major deportation may have occurred later, during the time of Jehoiachin, that does not rule out other military actions during the reign of Jehoiakim. In fact, these earlier campaigns would lay the groundwork for the later, more significant deportations.

Historical Accounts Complement, Not Contradict

The Bible often provides supplementary detail that is not found in other historical records. It should not be surprising that Daniel 1:1 mentions a campaign not noted in the surviving Babylonian records, especially considering that many ancient records have been lost to time.

Conservative Bible Chronology

According to conservative Bible chronology, Jehoiakim began his reign in 609 B.C.E. The siege referred to in Daniel 1:1 would thus fall into 607 B.C.E., a date that aligns well with known Babylonian activities in the region.

Nebuchadnezzar's Religious Image and Construction Projects: The Archaeological Testimony

The Book of Daniel contains two key accounts related to Nebuchadnezzar that have been subject to critical scrutiny: the setting up of a religious image for his subjects to worship (Daniel 3), and his boastful attitude concerning his construction projects (Daniel 4). Both of these accounts find substantial support from archaeological evidence, which corroborates the historical veracity of Daniel.

The Religious Image: Archaeological Support

Daniel 3 recounts the setting up of a golden image by Nebuchadnezzar, an act that led to the famous ordeal in the fiery furnace for Shadrach, Meshach, and Abednego. While we do not have direct evidence of this specific image, it is entirely consistent with what we know of Babylonian religious practices. Mesopotamia had a long tradition of kings dedicating statues to gods. Babylonian kings often boasted of their piety and their building of religious statues in their inscriptions. These practices align closely with the account in Daniel 3, offering indirect but convincing evidence that Nebuchadnezzar could very well have erected such a statue as part of a larger religious or political agenda.

Nebuchadnezzar's Boastful Attitude: Inscriptions Confirm

Daniel 4 tells of Nebuchadnezzar's boastful attitude about his accomplishments, particularly his construction activities in Babylon. This attitude is also seen in several Babylonian cuneiform inscriptions. In these texts, Nebuchadnezzar frequently glorifies himself for his building projects, which include temples, ziggurats, and city walls. The Babylonian king's language is replete with self-aggrandizing statements about his achievements, which mirrors the hubris exhibited in Daniel 4 before his humbling experience of living like an animal for a period. These inscriptions are thus a striking parallel to the Biblical account and support its historicity.

Literal Conservative Bible Chronology

The events related to the setting up of the religious image and the construction projects generally align with the time Nebuchadnezzar ruled Babylon, which is from 605 B.C.E. to 562 B.C.E., according to conservative Bible chronology. Within this time frame, Nebuchadnezzar had ample opportunity to engage in the activities described in Daniel.

Punishment Under Babylonian and Persian Rule: A Testament to Daniel's Historical Accuracy

The Book of Daniel offers accounts of different forms of punishment under both the Babylonian and Persian empires. These accounts display a remarkable level of detail that corresponds well with what we know from historical and archaeological records, lending further credibility to the book's historical accuracy.

Punishment in Babylonian Rule: The Fiery Furnace

The most iconic example of Babylonian punishment in Daniel is the episode of the fiery furnace (Daniel 3). Nebuchadnezzar orders a furnace to be heated seven times hotter than usual to punish Shadrach, Meshach, and Abednego for their refusal to worship the golden image.

Babylonian law codes and royal inscriptions make frequent mention of the death penalty for various offenses, including blasphemy and treason. While there isn't a specific Babylonian record that confirms this exact form of execution, burning was indeed a known form of capital punishment in the ancient Near East. The extreme heat of the furnace as described in Daniel might be understood as a dramatic manifestation of the king's fury, entirely plausible given the autocratic nature of Babylonian kingship.

Punishment in Persian Rule: The Lions' Den

In contrast, Daniel 6 details punishment under Persian rule, in which Daniel is thrown into a den of lions for praying to Jehovah. This method of punishment fits well with what we understand of Persian practices. The Persians were known for their exotic and demonstrative forms of punishment to serve as deterrents. Herodotus and other ancient historians wrote about similar methods of execution that involved exposure to wild animals. While the lions' den specifically might not be corroborated by extra-Biblical sources, it is entirely in keeping with the grandiose and public forms of punishment that the Persians were known to employ.

Literal Conservative Bible Chronology

In terms of timing, the fiery furnace incident would have taken place during Nebuchadnezzar's reign, which was from 605 B.C.E. to 562 B.C.E. The lions' den episode would have occurred during the early years of the Medo-Persian rule over Babylon, following the fall of the city in 539 B.C.E. These chronological markers are fully compatible with the punishments described.

Contrasting Legal Systems in Babylon and Medo-Persia: Unveiled by the Book of Daniel

The Book of Daniel paints a nuanced and historically consistent picture of the legal systems of both the Babylonian and Medo-Persian empires, providing important insights into their respective jurisprudential approaches.

Babylonian Legal System: Autocratic Decision-Making

The Babylonian system, as exemplified by Nebuchadnezzar, was highly autocratic. The king held ultimate power, and his decrees could be issued and rescinded at will. This is evident when Nebuchadnezzar decrees the execution of all the wise men of Babylon (Daniel 2:12) and later rescinds it (Daniel 2:48). Similarly, he unilaterally issues the command to cast Shadrach, Meshach, and Abednego into the fiery furnace (Daniel 3:19-20) and then reverses his order after witnessing the miracle (Daniel 3:26-27). This autocratic and somewhat capricious approach aligns with Babylonian legal practices, where the word of the king was often considered the ultimate law.

Medo-Persian Legal System: Immutable Laws

On the other hand, the Medo-Persian legal system, as portrayed during the reigns of Darius and Cyrus, was characterized by an interesting feature: the immutability of the laws once they were issued. Daniel 6:8 and 6:15 highlight that, according to the law of the Medes and Persians, an issued edict could not be altered or revoked, even by the king himself. The sealing of the lion's den, even as King Darius expressed regret over his decision (Daniel 6:14, 6:17), is a telling example. This is in line with historical accounts, including those from Herodotus, which confirm the irreversible nature of Persian laws.

Belshazzar's Feast: A Testament to Daniel's Authenticity

The account of Belshazzar's feast in Daniel 5 offers intricate details that serve as a testament to Daniel's firsthand knowledge of Babylonian customs. The narrative vividly portrays an opulent scene where King Belshazzar, amid his revelry, orders the sacred vessels taken from the Jerusalem Temple to be brought out so that he and his guests can drink from them. This not only signifies the arrogance of the Babylonian king but also reflects the nature of Babylonian feasts and the ritualistic significance attached to such vessels in Babylonian customs.

The Use of the Sacred Vessels

The use of sacred vessels taken from the Jerusalem Temple for a secular and irreverent purpose was a severe affront to the God of Israel. The mention of these vessels in the narrative indicates Daniel's intimate knowledge of how they had been taken captive to Babylon and were being profaned, something not readily acknowledged in Babylonian texts.

Drinking Wine and Praise to Idols

Daniel 5:4 also mentions that they drank wine and praised the gods of gold, silver, bronze, iron, wood, and stone. This aligns with known Babylonian customs where banquets involved not only lavish feasting but also a form of religious devotion and idol worship. The list of materials out of which the gods were made is comprehensive and indicates a thorough familiarity with Babylonian religious practices.

Writing on the Wall

The sudden appearance of a mysterious hand that writes on the wall freezes the raucous festivities. This moment introduces an element of the divine into the worldly. The writing itself, later interpreted by Daniel, consists of Aramaic words, which were part of the diplomatic and legal language of Babylon. This reflects an accurate representation of the linguistic milieu.

Presence of the Queen

Daniel 5:10 mentions the entrance of the queen to calm Belshazzar, whose countenance had changed dramatically at the sight of the mysterious writing. Her presence at this crucial moment and her knowledge of Daniel and his God reveal how court officials and royal family members were interlinked in Babylon. Her referral to Daniel as a man in whom "the spirit of the holy gods" is found (Daniel 5:11) indicates the syncretic religious environment and the high regard for spiritual insight, reflecting Babylonian religious tolerance, yet ignorance of Jehovah's exclusive divinity.

Daniel's Intimate Knowledge of Babylonian Customs and Times

The most reasonable explanation for Daniel's intimate knowledge of the times and customs of the Babylonian exile is that he was an eyewitness and a high-ranking official in the Babylonian and later Medo-Persian empires. Daniel was taken into exile from Judah to Babylon in the third year of Jehoiakim's reign, which was 605 B.C.E. He lived through the entire period of Babylonian captivity, serving in the royal court, and continued into the reign of Darius the Mede and Cyrus the Persian.

High-Ranking Official

Daniel was not an ordinary captive. He was selected for royal service because of his intellect and nobility. This would have given him access to both public and private events, as well as the political and religious settings of Babylon. His various roles, from an advisor to the king to an administrator overseeing the kingdom, would have put him in a unique position to observe and record the details that he did. Therefore, his descriptions are not a product of later imagination, but a firsthand account.

Firsthand Accounts of Various Events

Daniel records specific details, such as the madness of Nebuchadnezzar and his restoration (Daniel 4), the feast of Belshazzar where the writing appeared on the wall (Daniel 5), and the plot against him that led to his being thrown into the lions' den (Daniel 6). These are not generic accounts but contain particulars that an observer would note.

Customs and Practices

Daniel's account also provides specific insights into Babylonian practices. For example, the practice of sorcery and divination is mentioned (Daniel 2:2), the diet of the royal court is described (Daniel 1:5), and even the Babylonian names given to Daniel and his companions are cited (Daniel 1:7). Such accurate and intimate details strongly point toward the author's direct experience with the customs and traditions of Babylonian society.

Place of Daniel in the Canon: A Critique of Critics' Claims

One of the arguments that critics often levy against the book of Daniel pertains to its position in the canon of the Hebrew Scriptures. Specifically, they point out that Daniel is not listed among the "Prophets" but rather among the "Writings" (Ketuvim) in the Jewish canon. Critics argue that this implies Daniel was not recognized as a prophetic work during the time when the canon was being formulated, suggesting its later authorship and, for them, decreasing its prophetic credibility.

Understanding the Structure of the Hebrew Canon

The Hebrew Scriptures are traditionally divided into three sections: the Law (Torah), the Prophets (Nevi'im), and the Writings (Ketuvim). It is important to note that the category of "Prophets" in the Hebrew Bible includes not just what we often think of as prophetic works but also historical narratives such as Joshua, Judges, Samuel, and Kings.

Multiple Roles of Daniel

Daniel served as a government official and not in the official capacity of a prophet in Israel or Judah, which might be one reason why his book is categorized in the Writings rather than the Prophets. The category of "Prophets" generally includes figures who were directly engaged in the role of spokespersons for Jehovah to His covenant people—Israel and Judah. Daniel, by contrast, primarily operated within a foreign, pagan administration.

Late Canonization Does Not Imply Late Authorship

The assumption that a book's placement in the "Writings" indicates late authorship or lesser authority is unwarranted. The book of Job, also part of the Writings, is often considered one of the oldest books in the Bible. Moreover, the Psalms, attributed to David, are also found in this section, despite David's lifetime occurring long before many of the so-called "Prophets."

Affirmation by Later Jewish Tradition

Daniel's status as a significant and authoritative text is reinforced by its inclusion in the Septuagint, the Greek translation of the Hebrew Scriptures, which was in widespread use by the time of Jesus and the Apostles. Furthermore, both Jesus (Matthew 24:15) and the Apostle John in Revelation make direct references to Daniel, affirming its prophetic nature.

Ancient Jewish View of the Book of Daniel: Respected, Canonical, and Significant

The ancient Jewish perception of the book of Daniel is a topic of both historical and theological import. It is vital to establish that, irrespective of its placement in the Hebrew canon, the book of Daniel was highly regarded and considered canonical by the Jews. Several strands of evidence affirm this claim.

High Regard for the Book of Daniel

Firstly, Jewish writings and tradition give substantial weight to Daniel. For instance, the book of Daniel is included in the Septuagint, a Greek translation of the Hebrew Scriptures dating back to the 3rd century B.C.E. This is a strong indication of its canonical status during a period that predates many critical theories about its authorship. Also, Josephus, the first-century Jewish historian, acknowledges Daniel and his book in his "Antiquities of the Jews," testifying to its acceptance and esteem in the Jewish community.

The Dead Sea Scrolls

The Dead Sea Scrolls, which date back to the late second century B.C.E., provide another compelling line of evidence. Fragments of the book of Daniel were found among these scrolls, reinforcing its canonical status among Jewish groups like the Essenes who lived during that time.

Rabbinic Interpretations and Usage

Despite its placement in the "Writings" rather than the "Prophets," rabbinic literature such as the Talmud often cites Daniel. Rabbinic usage not only attests to its authoritative status but also indicates that it was used for doctrinal teachings and not merely viewed as a late or peripheral addition to the canon.

Daniel's Unique Position

The ancient Jews considered Daniel to be a unique figure, given his secular role in the Babylonian and Medo-Persian administrations. This uniqueness could have contributed to its placement in the "Writings" rather than the "Prophets." Therefore, its position in the canon should not be misconstrued as an indicator of its lateness or lesser authority.

Closure of the Hebrew Canon

The canon of the Hebrew Scriptures was closed long before the second century B.C.E. The ancient rabbis, through a stringent process, determined which books were to be regarded as Scripture. Daniel's inclusion in this list underscores its authenticity and canonical standing.

Ecclesiasticus Against Daniel: A Misguided Argument

Some critics assert that the book of Daniel must be a late composition because it is not mentioned in the apocryphal book of Ecclesiasticus (also known as Sirach), written around 180 B.C.E. by Jesus ben Sira. This argument suggests that if Daniel were an authoritative and significant work, it would surely have been mentioned by Ben Sira, who does list other noteworthy figures from Israel's history. However, this line of reasoning is deeply flawed for several reasons.

Other Significant Omissions

Firstly, Ecclesiasticus omits mention of other key biblical figures and events, not just Daniel. For example, Esther and Mordecai, significant characters in the Hebrew Scriptures, are also not mentioned. The omission of such prominent figures brings into question the comprehensiveness of Ecclesiasticus as a reliable index for dating canonical books.

Purpose of Ecclesiasticus

Ecclesiasticus is a collection of ethical teachings and wisdom sayings; it is not a comprehensive historical account or a list of canonical books. Ben Sira's purpose was not to enumerate all authoritative texts or figures but rather to offer moral and ethical guidance. Using it as a yardstick for what should be considered canonical is therefore misguided.

Cultural and Theological Factors

We must also consider that Ben Sira wrote Ecclesiasticus within a particular cultural and theological context. He might have had various reasons for omitting Daniel that had nothing to do with the book's date of authorship. For instance, the book of Daniel, with its apocalyptic themes, may not have aligned with Ben Sira's focus on wisdom and ethical teachings.

Canonical Closure and Authorship

The canon of the Hebrew Scriptures was essentially closed by the time Ecclesiasticus was written. The very fact that Daniel is part of the canon shows that it was considered authoritative long before critics claim it was written. To argue otherwise is to discount the rigorous process by which the ancient Jews determined the canon.

External Validation

It's important to remember that the book of Daniel is also validated externally, being included in the Septuagint and referenced in the Dead Sea Scrolls and by historians like Josephus. These sources affirm its early date and canonical status.

External Evidence In Favor of Daniel

Josephus' Affirmation of Daniel's Authenticity

The Jewish historian Flavius Josephus provides substantial affirmation for the genuineness and early date of the book of Daniel.

In his "Antiquities of the Jews," Josephus recounts an encounter between Alexander the Great and the Jewish high priest in Jerusalem. According to Josephus, the high priest showed Alexander a prophecy from the book of Daniel that was understood to predict Alexander's own military conquests. Alexander was so impressed by this that he spared Jerusalem, which was remarkable given his aggressive military campaign against the Persian Empire and its allies.

Alexander the Great and Historical Corroboration

Historically speaking, Alexander's kind treatment of the Jews is an anomaly considering his otherwise ruthless conquests. Josephus' account fills this historical gap, showing how the book of Daniel influenced Alexander to treat the Jews favorably. This means that the book of Daniel must have been in existence and held in high esteem by the Jewish community at least as early as the fourth century B.C.E., thereby refuting claims that Daniel was a later composition.

Linguistic Evidence for Daniel's Authenticity

The book of Daniel is unique in that it contains both Hebrew and Aramaic portions. The linguistic characteristics of these sections align well with what scholars know about these languages as they were spoken and written during the Babylonian and Medo-Persian periods. For example, the Aramaic in Daniel is of a form known as "Imperial Aramaic," which was used as an official language of the Achaemenid Empire (539-330 B.C.E.). This Aramaic is distinctly different from the Aramaic used in literature from the second century B.C.E. and later. The Hebrew portions also exhibit traits consistent with other canonical works written before the Babylonian exile.

Linguistic Aspects of the Book of Daniel: Scrutiny and Authenticity

Language Mixture: Hebrew, Aramaic, Greek, and Persian

The book of Daniel, completed around 536 B.C.E., employs a blend of languages—Hebrew and Aramaic predominantly, with smatterings of Greek and Persian words. While this mixture may appear uncommon, it's not unique within the context of the Scriptures.

The book of Ezra is another example of Hebrew and Aramaic usage. Critics, however, assert that the linguistic elements of Daniel suggest a *much later date of composition,* extending potentially to the second century B.C.E.

Scholarly Disagreement on Language Dating

It's crucial to acknowledge that not all linguistic scholars are in agreement with the critics. Some experts argue that the Hebrew in Daniel bears resemblance to that of Ezekiel and Ezra, rather than later apocryphal works such as Ecclesiasticus. Moreover, Daniel's Aramaic has been compared to documents from the Dead Sea Scrolls dated to the first and second centuries B.C.E. Scholars note a *significant divergence* between the Aramaic in those documents and that in the book of Daniel, leading some to conclude that Daniel is, in fact, far older than critics claim.

Debunking the "Greek Problem"

The issue of Greek words in Daniel also warrants consideration. Some words originally thought to be Greek have been re-identified as Persian. The remaining Greek terms are names of three musical instruments. *Is the presence of these three Greek words sufficient evidence to label Daniel as a late composition?* Certainly not. Archaeological findings reveal that Greek culture had a far-reaching influence even centuries before Greece became a dominant world power. Additionally, if Daniel were written during the second-century B.C.E.—a time when Greek culture and language were ubiquitous—it would almost certainly contain more than just three Greek terms.

Language as a Pillar for Daniel's Authenticity

In summary, linguistic scrutiny, rather than undermining the authenticity of the book of Daniel, actually bolsters it. The Hebrew and Aramaic align more closely with contemporaneous works like Ezekiel and Ezra than with later apocryphal works. The negligible presence of Greek words is hardly compelling evidence for a later date of composition, especially given the influence of Greek culture even before its hegemony. *Therefore, linguistic analysis lends credibility to the traditional dating of the book of Daniel, placing its composition firmly around 536 B.C.E.*

The Most Convincing Proof of Daniel's Authenticity

The most compelling evidence supporting the authenticity of the book of Daniel is the endorsement given by Jesus Christ Himself. In His discourse on the last days, Jesus unmistakably refers to "Daniel the prophet," even citing a specific prophecy from the book (Matthew 24:15; Daniel 11:31; 12:11). This endorsement carries supreme weight for several reasons.

The Unimpeachable Testimony of Jesus Christ

Firstly, Jesus is the Word incarnate, the Son of Jehovah God, who was actively involved in the creation of the world and the scripting of human history (John 1:1-3). Jesus was also alive in heaven when the book of Daniel was written. His eternal nature and divine insight grant Him an unparalleled perspective on the canonicity and reliability of the Scriptures.

Secondly, accepting the words of Jesus has a ripple effect on the entire body of Scripture. The Apostle Paul declared, "All Scripture is inspired of God and beneficial for teaching, . . . for setting things straight" (2 Timothy 3:16). If we were to reject Jesus' confirmation of Daniel, it would create a theological and textual crisis that would undermine the integrity of the entire Bible. Simply put, dismissing Daniel as inauthentic would logically require us to dismiss Jesus, Paul, and essentially the whole of Scripture. Such a course is untenable for anyone who takes the Bible seriously as the inspired Word of God.

The Maccabean Theory Undermined

Critics who endorse the Maccabean theory—that Daniel was a late composition, ostensibly written in the second century B.C.E.—are caught in an untenable position when faced with Jesus' affirmation. They would have to conclude either that Jesus was misled or that He never made the statement attributed to Him in Matthew. Both options are unacceptable. To assert that Jesus was misled is to question His divine nature and omniscience. To claim He never made the statement is to call into question the reliability of the Gospel accounts and, by extension, the rest of the New Testament.

In sum, the highest and most unassailable validation of the book of Daniel comes from Jesus Christ. His testimony reinforces the book's historical credibility, its placement within the canon, and its role in prophetic teachings about the end times. Given the integrity and divine nature of Jesus Christ, His endorsement of Daniel stands as the most convincing proof of the book's authenticity.

Edward D. Andrews

CHAPTER 10 Defending Hosea, Joel, and Amos

Authenticity, Authorship, and Date of Hosea

The Last Twelve Books and Hosea's Significance

The last twelve books of the Hebrew Scriptures are commonly referred to as the "Minor Prophets." This title does not imply that these books are of lesser importance, but rather it pertains to their shorter length compared to other prophetic writings like Isaiah, Jeremiah, and Ezekiel. Among these Minor Prophets, Hosea is a prominent figure whose message holds enduring relevance.

Profile of Hosea

Hosea was a prophet active during the 8th century B.C.E., serving primarily in the Northern Kingdom of Israel. His ministry spans the reigns of Uzziah, Jotham, Ahaz, and Hezekiah in Judah and Jeroboam II in Israel. Hosea is perhaps best known for his symbolic marriage to Gomer, a woman of questionable repute, as an illustrative parable of Israel's unfaithfulness to Jehovah God.

The Audience and Concern of Hosea's Prophecy

Hosea's prophecy is mainly directed toward the Northern Kingdom of Israel. At this time, Israel was deep in spiritual apostasy, embracing idolatry and straying from Jehovah's commands. Hosea uses his own experience of marital unfaithfulness as a powerful symbol to depict Israel's infidelity to God. His message is one of stern warning coupled with a call for repentance. Despite the grim circumstances, Hosea also provides glimpses of hope, emphasizing Jehovah's enduring love and willingness to forgive a repentant people.

Hosea's prophecy remains a significant part of the biblical canon, and his message of divine love and the urgent call to repentance still resonates today. Through Hosea, Jehovah God demonstrates His steadfast commitment to His covenant promises, while also underscoring the consequences of disobedience and the earnest need for repentance.

Duration of Hosea's Prophetic Ministry and Contemporary Prophets

Hosea's prophetic ministry is quite extensive, covering a period that spans over several decades in the 8th century B.C.E. Specifically, Hosea served during the reigns of Uzziah, Jotham, Ahaz, and Hezekiah, kings of Judah, and during the reign of Jeroboam II, king of Israel. This indicates a ministry of approximately 40 to 50 years, making Hosea one of the longer-serving prophets in the Hebrew Scriptures.

Contemporary Prophets

During Hosea's time, there were several other prophets who were also active, particularly in the Northern Kingdom of Israel and in Judah. Notable among these are:

1. **Amos**: Like Hosea, Amos also directed his messages primarily at the Northern Kingdom, addressing issues of social injustice and idolatry.
2. **Isaiah**: Active in Judah, Isaiah was a contemporary of Hosea. He addressed both immediate and future events and is one of the Major Prophets of the Hebrew Scriptures.
3. **Micah**: Prophesying in Judah, Micah was another contemporary of Hosea and focused his message on social justice issues and the coming judgment on both Israel and Judah.
4. **Jonah**: Though his active period may have been slightly earlier than Hosea, Jonah was sent specifically to Nineveh, the capital

of Assyria, in a unique mission that transcended Israel and Judah's borders.

The simultaneous activity of these prophets emphasizes the significance and urgency of the period. It was a time marked by widespread apostasy, injustice, and impending judgment, warranting the messages from multiple prophets. Each prophet, while distinct in their approach and focus, collectively presented a cohesive narrative emphasizing the need for repentance and adherence to Jehovah's covenant laws. Their ministries served as divine warnings to the people and as calls to return to Jehovah God.

Quotations and Prophetic Fulfillments Confirming the Authenticity of Hosea

The authenticity of the book of Hosea is confirmed both by its citation in other parts of the Bible and by historical fulfillments of its prophecies.

New Testament Citations: One of the most notable affirmations of Hosea's prophetic authority comes from the New Testament. For example, Hosea 11:1 ("When Israel was a child, I loved him, and out of Egypt I called my son") is cited in Matthew 2:15 as fulfilled in Jesus Christ when he and his family returned from Egypt. This confirms that the early Christian community, including the writers of the New Testament, viewed Hosea as an authoritative prophetic voice. Another example is found in Romans 9:25-26, where Paul cites Hosea 2:23 and Hosea 1:10 to discuss God's mercy and the inclusion of Gentiles into the family of God.

Historical Fulfillment: Hosea predicted the downfall of Israel and its leading city, Samaria (Hosea 8:5-8; 13:16). History verifies this: Samaria was conquered by Assyria in 722 B.C.E., and the Israelites were deported, exactly as Hosea had prophesied. This historical fulfillment corroborates the prophetic nature of the book.

Internal Consistency: Hosea presents a consistent portrayal of God's character and His expectations for His covenant people. Its themes echo those of other prophetic books, contributing to the internal consistency of the prophetic corpus. Hosea's message of divine judgment and subsequent mercy is compatible with the broader Scriptural narrative, lending credibility to its prophetic authenticity.

Character of God: Hosea's presentation of Jehovah as a God who enters into a marital relationship with His people, suffering due to their infidelity yet offering them redemptive love, is profound and uniquely presented in the book. Such a nuanced understanding of God's character further underscores the authenticity of Hosea's prophecy.

Cultural and Historical Details: Hosea's depiction of the religious and social conditions in the Northern Kingdom aligns well with what we know from external historical sources about the 8th century B.C.E., thereby lending authenticity to the book.

In summary, both the New Testament quotations and the historical fulfillments of Hosea's prophecies strongly affirm the book's authenticity. The message contained in Hosea is consistent with the broader narrative of Scripture, and the prophetic themes align seamlessly with historical realities. Therefore, there is compelling evidence to regard Hosea as an authentic, prophetic book in the Hebrew Scriptures.

The Unfaithfulness for Which Jehovah Punished Israel in the Book of Hosea

In the book of Hosea, Jehovah's primary contention with Israel is their spiritual adultery. Israel has broken the covenant relationship with Jehovah by engaging in idolatry, immorality, and social injustices. Below are specific areas of unfaithfulness that led to Israel's divine punishment:

1. **Idolatry**: Hosea denounces Israel's worship of Baal and other Canaanite gods (Hosea 2:13; 4:12–13). These practices were in direct violation of the First Commandment, which strictly forbids the worship of other gods (Exodus 20:3).

2. **Lack of Knowledge and Ignorance of God's Law**: Hosea 4:6 states, "My people are destroyed for lack of knowledge."

Israel had neglected the Law of Jehovah, failing to pass on the commandments and regulations to future generations.

3. **Immorality and Social Injustice**: Hosea also addresses issues like dishonesty, murder, and theft (Hosea 4:1-2). Such social evils were symptomatic of a deeper spiritual malaise and were in violation of the ethical stipulations of the Mosaic Covenant.

4. **Political Alliances**: Instead of relying on Jehovah for security and protection, Israel sought alliances with foreign powers like Assyria and Egypt (Hosea 5:13; 7:11). This demonstrated a lack of trust in Jehovah and further indicated their spiritual waywardness.

5. **False Religious Practices**: Israel's religious practices had also become corrupt. Hosea condemns the priesthood for its role in perpetuating false worship and for failing to guide the people in the ways of Jehovah (Hosea 4:4-9).

6. **Ingratitude and Forgetfulness**: Despite Jehovah's past mercies and deliverance, Israel had quickly forgotten their God (Hosea 2:8-9; 13:4-6). Their ingratitude was not only offensive but also broke the covenant relationship they had with Jehovah.

7. **Perversion of Justice**: The courts and leaders were corrupt, perverting justice for personal gain, thereby failing in their God-given roles to maintain righteousness within the community (Hosea 10:4).

8. **Materialism**: Israel's prosperity led them to attribute their wealth to their own abilities or to other gods, ignoring Jehovah's role in their blessings (Hosea 2:5; 13:6).

In summary, Israel's unfaithfulness was comprehensive, affecting every area of their individual and communal lives. It was this unfaithfulness—idolatry, immorality, and social injustice—that led to their punishment by Jehovah, precisely as outlined in the terms of the Mosaic Covenant. Hosea serves as a clarion call to Israel for repentance and returning to a right relationship with Jehovah, demonstrating the grave consequences of breaking covenant with God.

The Distinctive Style of Hosea's Writing

Hosea's style of writing is both poetic and evocative, utilizing vivid imagery, metaphors, and allegories to convey deep theological and moral truths. Here are some specific aspects of his writing style that are noteworthy:

1. **Marriage Metaphor**: One of the most striking elements of Hosea's style is his use of the marriage metaphor to describe Israel's relationship with Jehovah. The book begins with Hosea's own troubled marriage to Gomer, serving as an allegory for Israel's unfaithfulness. The emotional depth and personal agony articulated in this metaphor make the prophecy both poignant and compelling (Hosea 1:2-3; 2:2-5).

2. **Covenant Language**: Hosea heavily relies on the language and motifs of covenant, which serve as the theological backdrop against which Israel's infidelity is highlighted. Words like "steadfast love," "knowledge of God," and "faithfulness" pepper the book, drawing the reader back to the Mosaic Covenant and its implications (Hosea 6:6).

3. **Charged Emotions**: The prophet employs emotionally charged language that exposes the depth of Jehovah's love and the profound disappointment and pain resulting from Israel's unfaithfulness. Phrases like "My heart recoils within me; my compassion grows warm and tender" (Hosea 11:8) reveal the emotional aspect of Jehovah's relationship with His people.

4. **Agricultural Imagery**: Hosea uses imagery from agriculture, nature, and daily life to express his message. For instance, in Hosea 10:12, he writes, "Sow for yourselves righteousness; reap steadfast love," employing the farming cycle to explain the concept of divine justice and mercy.

5. **Dual Pronouncements**: Hosea often juxtaposes judgments with promises of restoration, reflecting the dual character of

Jehovah as both a God of justice and a God of mercy. For example, in Hosea 1:6-7, the birth of Hosea's children is used both to announce judgment ("Lo-ruhamah" meaning "Not Pitied") and hope ("Yet the number of the children of Israel shall be like the sand of the sea").

6. **Wordplay and Puns**: The book contains frequent wordplay, often used to underscore the thematic points. For example, the names of Hosea's children—Jezreel, Lo-ruhamah, and Lo-ammi—carry significant meanings and reflect Israel's disobedience and forthcoming punishment.

7. **Prophetic Lawsuits**: Hosea uses the rib, or the covenant lawsuit, a specific genre in prophetic literature. It is a formal accusation by Jehovah against Israel, detailing their violations of the covenant (Hosea 4:1-3).

8. **Eschatological Focus**: While Hosea deals with the immediate historical context, his message often transcends his time, pointing to the ultimate restoration of Israel in what can be seen as eschatological glimpses (Hosea 3:5).

Hosea's unique and compelling style serves to deeply engage his audience, both past and present, in the grave spiritual matters at hand. His approach gives us a rich, multifaceted view of Jehovah's relationship with Israel, which serves as a timeless reminder of the dire consequences of covenant unfaithfulness and the unimaginable depths of divine love.

The Spiritual Drama of Gomer's Unfaithfulness and Later Recovery

The story of Hosea's marriage to Gomer serves as a vivid, living metaphor for the larger relationship between Jehovah and the nation of Israel. In this narrative, Gomer's unfaithfulness and subsequent recovery embody Israel's rebellion and Jehovah's unfailing love and readiness to restore.

1. **Gomer's Unfaithfulness as Israel's Apostasy**: Gomer's infidelity to Hosea parallels Israel's spiritual harlotry. Just as Gomer was unfaithful to Hosea, so Israel broke the covenant

with Jehovah by engaging in idolatry and alliances with foreign nations (Hosea 1:2; 2:5). The children born out of this unfaithful relationship, with their symbolically weighted names, serve as a grim prophetic sign of Israel's forthcoming judgment.

2. **The Depth of Hosea's Agony Mirrors Jehovah's Pain**: The personal suffering and betrayal Hosea experiences reflect the emotional depths of Jehovah's own anguish over Israel's infidelity. This is not mere poetic flourish; it's a theological assertion about the character of Jehovah, who is profoundly affected by the choices His people make (Hosea 11:8).

3. **Hosea's Purchase of Gomer Symbolizes Redemption**: In a shocking turn of events, Hosea buys back Gomer from slavery, despite her unfaithfulness (Hosea 3:1-3). This act stands as a stark symbol of Jehovah's grace and intention to redeem Israel from its self-imposed bondage to sin and idolatry. The price Hosea pays for Gomer (fifteen shekels of silver and a homer and a half of barley) is both a poignant and humiliating testament to the costliness of redemption (Hosea 3:2).

4. **Restoration and Hope**: Gomer's subsequent return to Hosea's household and the stipulations laid down for her (that she must remain faithful and will not belong to another man) resonate with the themes of restoration and hope. Jehovah promises to betroth Israel again in righteousness and justice, in steadfast love and mercy (Hosea 2:19-20).

5. **Spiritual Reformation**: Gomer's recovery is incomplete without a change in behavior. Similarly, Israel's restoration isn't just about a return to former privileges but involves a profound spiritual reformation. The ultimate objective is a renewed and faithful relationship with Jehovah (Hosea 14:1-4).

6. **Eschatological Undertones**: While the immediate context is historical, focusing on Israel and its covenant relationship with Jehovah, there are also future implications. The story suggests

a broader eschatological hope of ultimate redemption and restoration for Israel (Hosea 3:5).

In sum, the narrative of Gomer serves a multi-layered theological purpose. It's not just a story of personal tragedy and redemption but a grand allegory, communicating both the gravity of covenant unfaithfulness and the magnificent extent of Jehovah's redeeming love. It underscores the theological axiom that Jehovah's covenant love is both passionate and persevering, willing to go to extraordinary lengths to restore His wayward people.

Interchangeable Names in the Book of Hosea

The book of Hosea employs a variety of names that are used interchangeably to refer to the nation of Israel and its divided components. These names are not mere linguistic artifacts; they hold significant theological and prophetic weight.

1. **Israel and Ephraim**: One of the most noticeable name pairs in Hosea is "Israel" and "Ephraim." Ephraim was one of the tribes of Israel and the most dominant tribe of the Northern Kingdom. The use of Ephraim often seems to stand in for the entirety of the Northern Kingdom, which is also called Israel in the book (Hosea 4:17; 5:3; 5:5).

2. **Samaria**: The capital city of the Northern Kingdom is occasionally used metonymically to refer to the Northern Kingdom itself (Hosea 7:1; 8:5-6). This is an example of synecdoche, a figure of speech in which a part represents the whole or vice versa.

3. **Jacob**: The name Jacob, the progenitor of the twelve tribes, is used to represent the entire nation, both North and South (Hosea 12:2, 12).

4. **Jezreel**: Named after the Valley of Jezreel, this term is used symbolically to indicate God's impending judgment upon the Northern Kingdom (Hosea 1:4-5). Jezreel is also the name of Hosea's firstborn son, further intensifying the prophetic significance of the term.

5. **House of Israel and House of Jehovah**: These terms are used to focus on the relationship between the people and their God. The "House of Israel" denotes the collective identity of God's covenant people (Hosea 1:6; 5:1), while "House of Jehovah" signifies the place of worship and, by extension, the religious life of the nation (Hosea 8:1; 9:8).

Understanding these interchangeable names in the book of Hosea is crucial for grasping the layered and intricate messages embedded within the text. These names serve as more than mere identifiers; they convey profound theological, historical, and eschatological insights into the nature of Jehovah's relationship with His people and the consequences of their disobedience.

Authenticity, Authorship, and Date of Joel

Dramatic Events in Joel's Prophecy

The book of Joel is marked by a series of dramatic events that unfold in a sequence of prophetic visions. These visions serve as wake-up calls to the nation of Judah, alerting them to the urgent need for repentance and signaling the larger eschatological implications for all humanity.

Locust Invasion: The book opens with a calamitous description of a locust plague that devastates the land (Joel 1:4). This natural disaster serves as both a literal event and a symbol for future invasions and judgments. The locusts are described in four stages, possibly to signify their complete and overwhelming destruction.

Drought and Famine: Following the locust invasion, the book describes a severe drought and the resulting famine (Joel 1:10-12, 17-20). This compounds the misery inflicted by the locusts and signifies God's judgment on the land and its people.

Call to Repentance: In light of these catastrophic events, Joel issues a call to repentance (Joel 2:12-17). This includes a solemn assembly and fasting, underscoring the gravity of the situation and the urgent need for the people to turn back to Jehovah.

The Day of Jehovah: One of the most vivid and dramatic portions of the book is Joel's description of the "Day of Jehovah" (Joel 2:1-11, 30-32; 3:14-16). This day is portrayed as a time of cosmic disturbances, warfare, and divine judgment. The sky is darkened, the sun and moon lose their brightness, and the stars diminish their shining. This serves as a harbinger of final, divine judgment.

Restoration and Blessing: Despite the impending judgment, the prophecy concludes with a message of hope and restoration for those who repent (Joel 2:18-29; 3:17-21). The land will be restored, and Jehovah will pour out His Spirit upon all flesh. It indicates both immediate restoration and future eschatological blessings.

Judgment of the Nations: Joel also prophesies the judgment of the nations in the Valley of Jehoshaphat (Joel 3:1-3, 12-13). This is an eschatological event where nations will be judged for how they have treated God's people.

Each of these events is dramatic in its scope and significance, serving to underscore the critical themes of judgment and redemption that are central to Joel's message. They stand as powerful reminders of Jehovah's sovereignty, justice, and grace. The series of events recorded in Joel are not merely historical or localized incidents; they are deeply emblematic and serve as archetypes of greater spiritual and eschatological truths.

Joel and the Circumstances of His Prophesying

Joel, the son of Pethuel, is one of the twelve Minor Prophets in the Hebrew Bible. While the text does not provide explicit details regarding his background or the precise timeframe of his ministry, we can glean certain facts and implications from the content and context of the book.

Geographical Context: Joel primarily addresses the Southern Kingdom of Judah, with Jerusalem and the Temple often cited as central reference points (Joel 2:32; 3:1, 17, 20-21). This implies that his ministry was closely connected to the religious and political heart of the nation.

Historical Circumstances: Although the book of Joel itself does not provide specific dates for the prophet's ministry, it is typically situated either in the 9th century B.C.E., during the reign of Joash, or the early pre-exilic period of the 7th century B.C.E. This placement is based on the absence of any mention of Assyria or Babylon, which dominated later periods, and the focus on Judah and Jerusalem as autonomous entities.

Impetus for Prophesying: The immediate circumstances that triggered Joel's prophecies were catastrophic natural events, specifically a locust plague followed by a severe drought (Joel 1:4; 1:10-12). These calamities serve as the backdrop for his urgent calls for repentance and warnings about the coming "Day of Jehovah."

Theological Focus: Joel's message is heavily eschatological, with considerable emphasis on the "Day of Jehovah," a time of divine judgment and cosmic upheaval (Joel 2:1-11; 2:30-32; 3:14-16). Yet it also offers hope for restoration and blessing, predicated on the nation's repentance and return to Jehovah (Joel 2:18-29; 3:17-21).

Social and Religious Condition: The prophet describes a society that has turned away from Jehovah, indicated by the calamities that have befallen them. While the text does not explicitly list the nation's sins, the calls for fasting, weeping, and mourning suggest a people in need of spiritual reorientation (Joel 1:13-14; 2:12-17).

Joel: Time of Writing

The book of Joel does not provide explicit historical markers to pinpoint its date of composition. However, based on internal and contextual evidence, there are two major views on the dating of the book:

Early Pre-Exilic Period: Some scholars propose that Joel was written during the 9th century B.C.E., specifically during the reign of Joash. The absence of any mention of the northern kingdom of Israel and its fall, as well as the non-mention of Assyria or Babylon, lends credence to an earlier date. Furthermore, some scholars note similarities between Joel and other prophetic books traditionally dated to the 9th century B.C.E., like Obadiah.

Late Pre-Exilic to Early Exilic Period: Others place the book in the 7th century B.C.E., before the fall of Jerusalem in 586 B.C.E. but after the fall of the northern kingdom in 722 B.C.E. This dating is supported by the lack of mention of Assyria or Babylon as dominant world powers, suggesting a time when their influence was not yet fully established or had waned.

Both dating options focus on the absence of any foreign powers as key players in the book, suggesting a time when Judah was not under immediate foreign subjugation. This would be consistent with periods either before the rise of Assyria or between the decline of Assyria and the rise of Babylon.

Thus, while it is challenging to definitively date the book of Joel, the internal evidence strongly indicates that it was likely composed either in the 9th century B.C.E. during the reign of Joash.

Determining the Dating of the Book of Joel: Internal Evidence and Scholarly Opinions

Ambiguities and the "Argument from Silence"

Scholars have posited various dates for the composition of the book of Joel, ranging from before 800 B.C.E. to about 400 B.C.E. *The International Standard Bible Encyclopædia* notes that many arguments for dating the book are based on what is *not* mentioned, such as the absence of references to the Chaldeans, the Assyrians, a Judean king, and the ten-tribe kingdom. Such an "argument from silence" is notoriously precarious. Additionally, whether Joel quoted from other prophets like Obadiah or was quoted by them, including Amos, remains unclear. The ordering of the book in the Hebrew canon—sandwiched between Hosea and Amos—leans toward an earlier date, but this is not conclusive.

Internal Evidence Pointing to an Earlier Date

While the dating of Joel has been a matter of contention between conservative and liberal schools of criticism, internal evidence suggests a date during the minority of King Joash, around 830 B.C.E. A.E Kirkpatrick's *The Doctrine of the Prophets* offers compelling arguments for this earlier date, which can be classified into three main categories:

1. **Type of Governance:** The absence of any reference to a reigning king, along with mentions of elders and priests leading the nation, implies a regency. This is consistent with the period of Joash's reign when Jehoiada, his uncle, exercised significant control as he was a minor at the time of his coronation (2 Kings 11:4).

2. **Inter-Prophetic Borrowing:** Similarities between Joel and Amos, such as the phrase "The mountains shall drop sweet wine," suggest a form of borrowing. Contextual clues hint that Amos may have quoted Joel, which would place Joel's writing before 755 B.C.E.

3. **Listing of Adversaries:** Joel mentions specific enemies like the Phoenicians, Philistines, Egyptians, and Edomites but omits Assyrians or Chaldeans. This suggests a period when Judah's immediate neighbors, rather than the Assyrians or Babylonians, were the principal threats.

Closing Arguments on Dating

The absence of Assyrians and Chaldeans as threats, coupled with the focus on regional enemies, appears to eliminate later periods like the Persian or Greek era as possible timeframes for Joel's composition. Similarly, the type of governance and the evidence of inter-prophetic borrowing lean toward an earlier date, aligning well with the minority reign of King Joash, roughly around 830 B.C.E.

Dating the Book of Joel: Scrutinizing Arguments and Evidence

Scholars have offered a broad range of dates for the book of Joel, stretching from the early 9th century B.C.E. to the late 4th century B.C.E. Regardless of whether one subscribes to conservative or liberal viewpoints, *internal evidence* suggests that a date around 830 B.C.E., during the regency of Jehoiada, the high priest, is the most plausible.

Governmental Structure Implies a Regency

The absence of a mentioned king and the prominence of elders and priests as leaders suggest that the king was a minor at the time, thereby implying a regency. This aligns well with the story of King Joash, who was crowned at seven years old, with his uncle Jehoiada having a strong influence during his reign.

Contextual Indications of Borrowing Between Prophets

Evidence of textual borrowing between Amos and Joel indicates that Joel's writing predates that of Amos, who likely wrote around 755 B.C.E. Phrases like *"The mountains shall drop sweet wine"* are found in both books, but *contextual indicators* hint that Amos borrowed from Joel, not the other way around.

The Enemies Listed Point to an Early Date

Joel describes Judah's enemies as the Phoenicians, the Philistines, the Egyptians, and the Edomites, without any mention of Assyrians or Chaldeans. This particular array of enemies indicates a specific historical setting when Assyria and Babylon were not threats, and Egypt was still a power to be reckoned with.

Analyzing Non-Conservative Criticism

Some critics, like A. S. Kapelrud, argue for a later date, specifically around 609 B.C.E. They point to mentions of Greeks and a supposed awareness of Babylonian captivity. However, these arguments can be countered. For instance, Greeks are depicted as a *distant people*, which would be inconsistent with a date following the Alexandrian conquests.

Inconsistencies in the Critics' Arguments

Many critics emphasize the absence of mentions of the Northern Kingdom or any Judean king. Yet, similar omissions occur in other prophetic books like Nahum or Zephaniah, which are accepted to be from the seventh century B.C.E., prior to the Babylonian exile. *Such an argument lacks a consistent basis.*

Dual Authorship Theories and Their Shortcomings

Some critics like Oesterley and Robinson propose a dual authorship theory, dating parts of Joel to 200 B.C.E. This stance relies on *evolutionistic assumptions*, ignoring the purity of the Hebrew style and diction in Joel, which strongly indicate an early pre-exilic composition.

Conclusion: The Weight of Internal Evidence

Overall, the internal evidence aligns more closely with a composition date of 835 B.C.E. The absence of a reigning king, the roles of priests and elders, and the nature of Judah's enemies all point toward this period. Moreover, the linguistic aspects of Joel also support this early date. *Arguments for a late date often rest on philosophical assumptions, not on reasonable interpretation of textual evidence.*

Authenticity of the Book of Joel

The authenticity of the book of Joel is supported by several lines of evidence:

Canonical Acceptance and Early Manuscripts

The book of Joel has been consistently included in the Jewish canon, signifying its accepted divine authority. It is also found in the Septuagint, an ancient Greek translation of the Hebrew Scriptures dating back to the 3rd century B.C.E., and the Masoretic Text, the authoritative Hebrew text of the Jewish Bible. This consistent transmission across various versions confirms the book's authentic origin and its acceptance among early Jewish communities.

Internal Consistency

The book of Joel presents a consistent theological and thematic focus. It concentrates on the "Day of Jehovah," a concept that aligns well with the overall eschatological perspectives found in other prophetic works. This internal consistency suggests a single authorship and a unified message, which adds weight to its authenticity.

Language and Style

The Hebrew language used in Joel is consistent with that of other prophetic literature and with the Hebrew idioms and syntax of the periods suggested for its dating (9th B.C.E.). The literary techniques employed, such as the use of vivid imagery and poetic forms, are typical of Hebrew prophetic writings.

Intertextual References

Joel is quoted and alluded to in other parts of the Bible. For example, the book of Acts quotes Joel in Acts 2:17-21, during the Pentecost event, lending early Christian validation to the book's prophetic character and its divinely inspired status. Furthermore, the Apostle Peter quotes Joel in his speech, giving credence to the book's authenticity from a New Testament perspective.

Theological Consistency

Joel's theological statements are in harmony with the broader scope of Biblical doctrine. The book emphasizes Jehovah's sovereignty, the consequences of Israel's disobedience, and the future hope of restoration — themes that are congruent with the rest of Scripture.

Prophetic Accuracy

The prophecies made in Joel regarding the coming judgment through natural disasters, as well as the eventual restoration of Israel, align with the historical and eschatological events that are consistent with Biblical prophecy. While some events are eschatological and therefore still future, the elements that can be verified lend credibility to the book.

Strikingly Expressive Features of Joel's Prophecy

Joel's prophecy stands out for its vivid imagery, poetic forms, and deep theological exposition. These elements make it one of the most expressive books in the Minor Prophets.

Vivid Imagery

Joel employs striking imagery to depict both impending judgments and future blessings. For instance, in describing the locust plague, he uses vivid and horrific details that serve as a metaphor for divine judgment. This kind of detailed imagery not only paints a picture but also triggers an emotional response, making the message more impactful.

Apocalyptic Overtones

The "Day of Jehovah," a significant theme in Joel, is described with apocalyptic overtones. This theme is employed to alert the people to the catastrophic events that would transpire if they continued in their ways. Such descriptions are intended to awaken the conscience and stir the heart.

Poetic Forms

Joel's use of parallelism, a common poetic device in Hebrew literature, is masterful. The lines often feature contrasting or complementary thoughts that reinforce each other, adding a layer of depth to the straightforward prose. This is particularly evident in his descriptions of judgment and restoration, where the rhythmic and repetitive language creates an emotional resonance that goes beyond mere informational transmission.

Theological Depth

Joel's prophecy is deeply rooted in the understanding of Jehovah's character—His justice, His mercy, and His sovereignty. By framing the entire discourse in the context of Jehovah's character, Joel elevates the prophecy from mere prediction to a theologically rich narrative.

Emotional Appeal

The book is filled with calls for repentance, using language that seeks to engage the reader emotionally. Through his prophecy, Joel calls for fasting, weeping, and mourning (Joel 2:12), urging the people to rend their hearts, not just their garments.

Urgency and Immediacy

Joel uses the present tense to describe future events, creating a sense of urgency and immediacy. This device serves to jolt his audience out of complacency by showing that the consequences of their actions are not just far-off events but have immediate ramifications.

Authenticity, Authorship, and Date of Amos

Amos: The Shepherd-Prophet from Humble Origins

Humble Beginnings in Tekoa Amos hailed from the small town of Tekoa, just five miles southeast of Bethlehem in the Judean highlands. Significantly, the text doesn't mention his father's name, implying that he came from *humble origins*. He was not part of any prophetic school or lineage but was a layperson who tended sycamore fig trees. Despite his lack of formal religious education, Jehovah called Amos to prophesy against the northern kingdom of Israel.

Occupational Background: A Man of the Soil By trade, Amos was a *herdsman and a cultivator of sycamore figs*. The term "bōqēr" in Amos 7:14 suggests that he may have also tended cattle. Certainly, he raised a specific breed of small, speckled sheep, referred to as "nāqōd," establishing him as a nōqēd (shepherd). Additionally, he cultivated sycamore fig trees, a source of a rudimentary form of edible fruit affordable to the lower classes. In the UASV, Amos 1:1 describes him as "among the shepherds of Tekoa."

Self-Educated in Scripture, Yet Unordained Although not formally educated, Amos's writings reveal a *strong influence from the Pentateuch*, indicating he was an earnest student of the books of Moses. He didn't have the privilege of attending a "school of the prophets," like those set up by Samuel, Elijah, or Elisha. Furthermore, he was *never officially anointed for his prophetic ministry*.

The Layman's Mission: A Call to the Northern Kingdom Responding to God's call, Amos left his Judean home as a mere layman. His mission was bold: to proclaim a confrontational message in the influential capital of the Northern Kingdom of Israel, *without any ecclesiastical backing*.

Unwavering Conviction Against All Odds Even without formal prophetic status, Amos was undeterred by the biases of the Ephraimite public. *His conviction and determination were unshakeable*, even when confronted by high-ranking religious authorities in the Samaritan hierarchy.

Conclusion: The Resolute Prophet from Humble Beginnings

Amos's story is a compelling narrative of a *man of conviction* who emerged from humble beginnings to heed God's call. Though he lacked formal education and ecclesiastical authorization, his fierce determination and strong grounding in Scripture empowered him to faithfully carry out his divine commission.

Period of Prophesying

Amos prophesied during the reigns of Uzziah in Judah and Jeroboam II in Israel, roughly between 767 and 757 B.C.E. His ministry occurred at a time when Israel was experiencing economic prosperity but also spiritual decline and social injustice. The dating aligns with his own claim in Amos 1:1, which references the reigns of these two monarchs and a two-year period before an earthquake, an event corroborated by historical and archaeological evidence.

Dating the Composition and Contextualizing the Ministry

Timeframe: Mid-Eighth Century B.C. Among Old Testament scholars, there is a **general consensus** that Amos' prophetic ministry occurred between 767 and 757 B.C., during the later part of Jeroboam II's reign (793–753 B.C.).

The Sociopolitical Landscape Under Jeroboam II Jeroboam II had a *remarkably successful military career*, expanding the Northern Kingdom to its original boundaries as of 931 B.C. This resulted in a significant increase in national wealth through war spoils and lucrative trade partnerships with Damascus and other northern principalities.

Wealth Disparity and Moral Decline However, the influx of wealth created a *stark socio-economic imbalance*. The rich grew richer, indulging in conspicuous materialism and greed, while the lower classes saw no benefit. This led to the exploitation of the vulnerable and a cynical disregard for social justice. The moral fiber of society deteriorated, with widespread violations of the Seventh Commandment undermining the sanctity of family life. Attempts to appease God through religious practices became hypocritical exercises.

Chronological Anchor: The Earthquake as a Benchmark Amos' mission to Bethel is precisely dated in the text as "two years before the earthquake" (Amos 1:1). This earthquake, occurring during the reign of Uzziah, was so severe that it was *memorialized for generations* (Zech. 14:5). Although the exact timing of the earthquake remains unknown, it served as a *divine preliminary sign* to underscore the certainty of the dire warnings that Amos relayed.

Oral Delivery Before Written Publication It's worth noting that the book of Amos was not published immediately. The introductory statement in Amos 1:1 implies that the book's publication came *at least two years after* Amos had orally conveyed his prophetic message.

Anchoring Amos in Time and Context

The ministry of Amos took place during a period of socio-economic and moral imbalance. His warnings, set against the backdrop of impending natural disaster, serve as an unequivocal testament to divine justice. The text itself serves not only as a record of Amos' oral pronouncements but also as a written testament, meticulously dated to underscore its historical and prophetic relevance.

Amos: Assessing Textual Integrity

General Agreement on Authenticity with Some Exceptions

Most scholars, even those from liberal camps, acknowledge the *authenticity of the vast majority of the text of Amos*. They often refer to him as "the first of the writing prophets." According to the dating by Wellhausen and Driver, Amos might represent the earliest written portion of the Old Testament, only second to document J. However, there are **fifteen verses that have been categorized as later insertions.**

Verses Under Scrutiny: Formulaic Denunciations

These debated verses include 1:9–12, which contain *repetitive and stylized formulae of denunciation* ("For three transgressions [the name of the city], and for four, I will not turn away the punishment thereof ... but I will send a fire upon [the city], which shall devour the palaces thereof"). For similar reasons, verses 2:4–5 are also rejected by some.

Verses of Thanksgiving and Praise

Additionally, expressions of thanksgiving and praise to God—such as found in 4:13; 5:8–9; 9:5–6—are considered *incongruous with the tone of Amos* by these critics, primarily due to their optimistic or cheerful nature.

Messianic Promises: Anachronistic or Authentic?

One of the most debated portions is 9:11–15, which contains Messianic promises. Critics argue that this type of thinking is *too advanced for the eighth century B.C.* and suggest it was likely added during the Exile. The notion here is based on the reference to the fall of the "tabernacle of David," which some interpret as referring to the fall of Jerusalem. However, not all scholars agree with this interpretation. Some argue that Amos might have viewed the house of David as "fallen" for different reasons, unrelated to the Exile.

Subjective Theories vs. Textual Data

Most objections to these verses arise not from the *textual data itself*, but from a specific theory about the historical development of Israelite thought. Critics often impose an ideological framework that sees Amos as focused solely on *denunciation and judgment*, thus ruling out any optimistic or hopeful verses as later additions.

Evaluating Textual Concerns on Their Merits

The textual integrity of the book of Amos is generally well-regarded, although some verses are debated. Most of these debates stem from ideological assumptions rather than hard textual evidence.

Therefore, when assessing the text's integrity, it is vital to weigh the textual data itself rather than presuppositions about Israelite thought or the supposed limitations of Amos as a prophet.

Rebuttal: In Defense of the Formulaic Denunciations in Amos 1:9-12 and 2:4-5

Introduction: The Authenticity of Formulaic Language

The criticisms surrounding the "formulaic" nature of Amos 1:9–12 and 2:4–5 often underestimate the literary and rhetorical methods utilized by ancient Hebrew prophets. The objection appears to rest on the assumption that repetitive or formulaic language is a later addition, but this viewpoint is unwarranted.

The Rhetorical Purpose of Repetition

Firstly, let's address the *rhetorical significance of repetition*. Repetition serves to emphasize a point and helps to make the message memorable. It would have aided in the oral transmission of these prophecies and would have made the message more impactful for the audience. In the context of Amos, this formulaic structure aids in underscoring the gravity of the transgressions of the various nations and cities, demonstrating that these are not arbitrary condemnations but judgments based on persistent wrongdoings.

Literary Consistency and Prophetic Style

Secondly, the formulaic language is *consistent with prophetic style*, not just in Amos, but also in other prophetic books. If one were to question the authenticity of these verses in Amos based on their formulaic structure, then we would have to question a significant portion of prophetic literature, which would be a rather extreme and unsustainable position.

Historical Context and Thematic Unity

The content in these "formulaic" verses fits well with the historical circumstances of the time and the broader thematic message of the book of Amos. The judgments on the various nations were part of the broader message of accountability and divine justice that is central to the book.

No Compelling Manuscript Evidence for Later Additions

Lastly, it's crucial to note that there is *no compelling manuscript evidence* to suggest that these verses are later additions to the text. They are present in the most reliable ancient manuscripts, and their content is consistent with the theology, eschatology, and ethical concerns raised throughout the book.

Reaffirming Textual Integrity

In conclusion, the formulaic language in Amos 1:9–12 and 2:4–5 serves a rhetorical, literary, and thematic purpose and should not be seen as grounds for questioning their authenticity. The arguments against these verses seem to arise from a predisposed skepticism rather than from a rigorous analysis of the text within its historical and literary context. Thus, based on literary consistency, historical context, and the absence of compelling counter-evidence, there is every reason to affirm the integrity of these contested verses in the book of Amos.

Rebuttal: In Defense of Verses of Thanksgiving and Praise in Amos

Introduction: The Question of Tone

A recurring criticism concerning the verses of thanksgiving and praise in Amos (4:13; 5:8–9; 9:5–6) posits that these passages disrupt the otherwise grim tone of the book. Critics often suggest that these optimistic expressions must be later additions. However, this objection fails to consider the multifaceted nature of prophetic literature and the broader theological points Amos is making.

Complex Emotional Range: Not Merely Grim

First, it's important to acknowledge that prophetic literature often possesses a *complex emotional range*, not confined to a single tone or mood. While Amos does center on themes of judgment and social justice, it also seeks to uphold the sovereignty and majesty of God. The thanksgiving and praise verses in question affirm this overarching theological theme. They serve to lift the reader's focus from the human failures to the divine nature of the God who judges but also sustains the universe.

Theological Consistency: God's Sovereignty

Secondly, the praise sections in Amos are *theologically consistent* with the rest of the book. These passages highlight the characteristics of God that make Him worthy to judge: His omnipotence, His omniscience, and His eternal nature. In fact, the expressions of praise set the stage for the ethical demands God places on His people, underscoring the authority from which these demands come.

Literary and Thematic Unity

The verses in question are also *thematically integral* to the book. The message of Amos oscillates between oracles of doom and affirmations of Jehovah's unchanging nature. This creates a balanced portrayal of God as both judge and redeemer, a deity who condemns injustice but is also worthy of praise. Removing the verses of praise and thanksgiving would thus create a theologically imbalanced view of God.

No Manuscript Evidence to Support Their Exclusion

Finally, like the formulaic denunciations, there is *no manuscript evidence* to suggest these verses are later interpolations. They are present in the most reliable ancient manuscripts, substantiating their authenticity.

Preserving the Textual and Theological Integrity

The presence of praise and thanksgiving in Amos does not compromise the book's integrity but rather enhances it by presenting a fuller, more nuanced portrayal of God. A God who judges is also a God who deserves praise for His attributes of justice, power, and majesty. To excise these verses based on an assumed incongruence in tone would be to impoverish the theological richness and textual integrity of this prophetic book. Therefore, these verses should be considered an authentic and integral part of Amos.

Rebuttal: In Defense of the Messianic Promises in Amos 9:11-15

Introduction: The Question of Anachronism

The issue of the Messianic promises in Amos 9:11–15 remains a point of contention among scholars. Critics often argue that these verses are anachronistic, claiming that Messianic thought is too advanced for the 8th century B.C. and that the text was likely added during or after the Exile. This perspective is challenged on multiple grounds, as outlined below.

Historical Plausibility: Messianic Thought in the 8th Century B.C.

The idea that Messianic thought is "too advanced" for Amos' time disregards the *historical plausibility* of an early development of such themes. Earlier Old Testament figures like David had already introduced the concept of a divine covenant with lasting implications for the lineage of the house of David (2 Samuel 7:12–16). Furthermore, in Amos' contemporary context, other prophets like Isaiah were speaking about a future righteous reign (Isaiah 9:6–7). Therefore, it is not out of the question that Amos could engage in this type of Messianic thought.

Textual Integrity: No Manuscript Evidence for Later Insertion

Importantly, there's *no manuscript evidence* to suggest that Amos 9:11–15 is a later addition. The verses in question are found in the oldest and most reliable manuscripts, indicating that they are likely original to the text.

Contextual Interpretation: The "Tabernacle of David"

The mention of the "tabernacle of David" needs to be understood within its *contextual setting*. Critics interpret this as referring to the fall of Jerusalem and thus see it as an exilic addition. However, "tabernacle" (sukkah) could be understood as a metaphorical expression for the Davidic lineage or rule, which Amos suggests will be restored. There is no need to tie this phrase strictly to the fall of Jerusalem during the Exile.

Theological Coherence: Covenant and Restoration

Finally, the *theological coherence* of the text must be considered. The restoration of the "tabernacle of David" is in line with the covenant promises Jehovah made to David. These promises find their ultimate fulfillment in the Messianic figure who would come from the line of David, reaffirming God's faithfulness and justice even in the face of Israel's disobedience.

Conclusion: In Defense of the Authenticity of Amos 9:11–15

Far from being an anachronistic insertion, the Messianic promises in Amos 9:11–15 fit well within the theological, historical, and textual context of the book. These verses enrich our understanding of God's covenant faithfulness and provide a fuller picture of His plans for future restoration. Their presence should not be viewed as a problem but as a key component that adds depth and complexity to the message of Amos.

Amos and the Torah: An Unbreakable Continuity

Introduction: The Need for a Reappraisal

The question of how Amos, considered by Documentarian Critics as the earliest of the writing prophets, relates to the legal provisions of the Torah has been a subject of extensive debate. Critics often regard the Torah, especially its Priestly and Deuteronomic sections, as post-Amos, but the internal evidence within the Book of Amos overwhelmingly counters such arguments.

The Overarching Theme: Legal and Moral Precedent

Amos doesn't merely hint at Torah-based traditions; he makes direct, explicit references to them. These aren't casual nods to broad themes, but specific allusions to laws and regulations. The sheer weight of these references demolishes the notion that the Torah's legal sections could be post-Amos or that Amos was introducing new ideas.

Amos and the Torah: Point by Point

1. **Amos 2:7 and Deuteronomy 23:17–18:** Religious prostitution is expressly condemned. If Amos' audience were unaware of this law, his condemnation would make no sense. The law, therefore, must predate Amos.

2. **Amos 2:8 and Exodus 22:26 / Deuteronomy 24:12–13:** Keeping garments overnight taken as pledge is an offense condemned by Amos, a direct allusion to existing laws in both Exodus and Deuteronomy.

3. **Amos 2:12 and Numbers 6:1–21:** The Nazarites' consecration is expressly mentioned in the so-called "P" passage of Numbers, showing yet another point of contact with the Torah.

4. **Amos 4:4 and Deuteronomy 14:28 / 26:12:** Tithing "after three years" is a practice uniquely ordained in Deuteronomy, further solidifying the link.

5. **Amos 4:5 and Leviticus 2:11 / 7:13:** The prohibition against offerings of leaven is rooted in Leviticus, and Amos' reference is not a creative addition but an authoritative reminder.

6. **Amos 5:23:** This verse implies a complex ritual of sacrifice that extends beyond what is even detailed in the Torah, indicating not a late addition but an intricate, pre-existing religious practice.

7. **Multiple Sacrificial Terms:** Terms such as "freewill offering," "solemn assembly," "burnt offering," "meal offering," and "peace offering" are all mentioned by Amos. Their existence in his writings illustrates that these practices and terms were well-established and not later developments.

The Folly of Dismissing Amos' References as Later Insertions

It has become a common tactic among critics to dismiss these points of contact between Amos and the Torah as later insertions. This approach not only lacks textual or manuscript support but is fundamentally a question-begging procedure that tries to fit the data into a preconceived theory.

The Inescapable Conclusion: The Priority of the Torah

The Book of Amos doesn't present new monotheistic or moral frameworks; instead, it reinforces what was already considered as established law or "the Torah of Jehovah" (Amos 2:4). It's thus inescapable that Amos operated under the authoritative weight of a Torah already considered ancient in his own time.

Final Word: The Torah as a Pre-Existing Canon

The substantive overlap between the Book of Amos and the Pentateuch suggests not only the existence of the Torah before Amos but also its wide acceptance as a guiding moral and religious code. Amos' prophetic mission was not to establish these principles, but to call Israel back to them. To deny this is to ignore not just the evidence within the text but also the historical circumstances that make such denial untenable.

Geographic Focus

Though a Judean, Amos's ministry was focused primarily on the northern kingdom of Israel. This was an unusual choice at a time when the two kingdoms were often at odds. He traveled to Bethel, one of the religious centers in Israel, to deliver his messages.

Message and Themes

Amos's prophetic ministry was marked by stern warnings against social injustice, religious hypocrisy, and the neglect of Jehovah's laws. He was one of the first prophets to introduce the concept of a God who cared deeply not only for ritual correctness but also for ethical integrity.

Theological Contributions

Amos was groundbreaking in his emphasis on social justice as an essential element of true worship. He preached that Jehovah was not only the God of Israel but the God of all nations, holding them accountable for their actions.

In summary, Amos was a shepherd and cultivator of sycamore figs from Tekoa in Judah, who prophesied in the northern kingdom of Israel during a period of economic prosperity but moral and spiritual decline. His messages were a clarion call for repentance, focusing not just on religious rituals but also on social justice and ethical living.

Timeliness of Amos' Message of Woe

Amos' message was especially timely because he prophesied during a period of significant economic prosperity for the northern kingdom of Israel. While the nation was flourishing materially, there was a stark decline in spiritual and ethical standards. Amos sounded a clarion call for repentance amidst this backdrop of moral decay. Injustices were rampant; the rich were exploiting the poor, and corrupt religious practices were widespread. The social fabric was tearing at the seams with greed, avarice, and a complete disregard for the poor and vulnerable in society. The people had fallen into a state of spiritual complacency, believing that their material success was a sign of divine favor.

Amos minced no words in challenging this misplaced sense of security. His message made it abundantly clear that Jehovah would not tolerate a dichotomy between ritualistic worship and ethical behavior. Chapters like Amos 2 and 5 highlight this by outlining the sins of Israel and explaining that mere ritualistic observance would not save them from impending judgment. Therefore, the timeliness of Amos' prophecy lies in its direct confrontation with Israel's misplaced priorities and its urgent call for genuine repentance.

Magnifying Jehovah's Sovereignty

Amos made unprecedented strides in magnifying Jehovah's sovereignty in several ways:

1. **Universal God**: Unlike other contemporary belief systems of the time, which often held that gods were regional or specific to a particular group of people, Amos declared Jehovah as the

God of all nations. In doing so, he magnified Jehovah's universal sovereignty.

2. **Judgment on All Nations**: Amos chapters 1 and 2 show that Jehovah is not only Israel's God but also the judge of all nations. He pronounces judgments on surrounding nations like Syria, Philistia, and Edom, thus magnifying Jehovah's authority over all the earth.

3. **Accountability to One Standard**: Amos underscored that Jehovah held all people, both Israelites and Gentiles, to the same ethical and moral standards. This elevated Jehovah's laws as universally sovereign principles that transcended cultural and national boundaries.

4. **Inescapable Justice**: Through vivid imagery and stark warnings, Amos made it clear that no one could escape Jehovah's scrutiny or judgment. This was notably evident in his use of the phrase "For three transgressions... and for four" (Amos 1:3, 6, 9, 11, 13; 2:1, 4, 6), a rhetorical device that underscored the thoroughness and inescapability of Jehovah's judgment.

5. **Divine Intervention in History**: Amos asserted that Jehovah actively intervenes in the history of nations to execute His justice. His sovereignty is not passive but active, guiding the rise and fall of nations according to His will and moral law.

Amos' message was timely in that it directly confronted the moral and spiritual decline of a prosperous but corrupt Israel. He magnified Jehovah's sovereignty by emphasizing His role as the universal God, the ethical standard against which all nations are judged, and the ultimate executor of justice and righteousness.

Fulfilled Prophecies Testifying to the Authenticity of Amos

The book of Amos contains multiple prophecies that were fulfilled, serving as robust evidence for its authenticity. Amos' credentials as a true prophet of Jehovah are validated by the historical realization of these pronouncements.

1. **Fall of Israel and Exile**: Amos predicted the fall of the northern kingdom of Israel and the subsequent exile of its people. This prophecy was fulfilled when the Assyrians conquered Israel and deported the Israelites in 722 B.C.E. (Amos 5:27; Amos 7:11, 17).

2. **Earthquake**: Amos 1:1 mentions an earthquake that was to occur two years after his visions. This earthquake is historically documented and is also mentioned in the book of Zechariah (Zechariah 14:5). The geological evidence and cross-reference to another prophetic book underscore the accuracy and authenticity of Amos.

3. **Punishment of Surrounding Nations**: Amos pronounced judgment on several neighboring nations like Damascus, Gaza, Tyre, Edom, Ammon, and Moab (Amos 1:3-2:3). Many of these judgments were fulfilled as these nations were defeated and subjugated by Assyrian and Babylonian forces.

4. **Desolation of Religious Centers**: Amos foretold that the religious centers at Bethel and Gilgal, known for their idolatry, would be desolated (Amos 4:4, 5:5). Bethel, once the seat of Jeroboam's calf-worship, eventually lost its religious significance.

5. **Failure of the Political Leadership**: Amos proclaimed the failure and judgment of Israel's political leadership (Amos 6:11, 7:9, 17). This too was fulfilled when the ruling elite was carried away by the Assyrians and the kingdom ceased to exist.

6. **Destruction and Plundering of Israelite Cities**: The prediction about the devastation of Israelite cities came to pass, as Assyrian records corroborate the destruction and plundering of these cities (Amos 3:11).

7. **Famine of Hearing the Words of Jehovah**: Amos prophesied that there would be a famine, not of food or water, but of hearing the words of Jehovah (Amos 8:11). This can be

seen as being fulfilled in the period of silence between the Old and New Testaments, where prophetic voices were absent for about 400 years.

Each of these fulfilled prophecies adds weight to the authenticity of the book of Amos. They demonstrate that Amos was not speaking mere human words but was conveying the very pronouncements of Jehovah, and they confirm the book's position as a reliable and divinely inspired part of Scripture.

Archaeological Confirmation of the Record in Amos

Archaeology provides a powerful means to affirm the historical and prophetic records presented in the book of Amos. These external evidences serve to strengthen our confidence in the authenticity and divine inspiration of the text.

1. **The Black Obelisk of Shalmaneser III**: This Assyrian monument contains inscriptions that mention Jehu, king of Israel. Amos prophesied during a period close to the reigns of Jehu and his descendants, making this an important synchronism that corroborates the historical setting of the book.

2. **Discovery of Ancient Samaria**: The capital city of the northern kingdom of Israel was unearthed, revealing artifacts and structures that align with the luxurious living denounced by Amos (Amos 3:15, 6:4). The opulence of Samaria found in the archaeological record confirms the societal conditions against which Amos prophesied.

3. **Inscriptions Mentioning Omri and the House of Omri**: Amos was explicit in his denunciation of the family line of Omri due to their sinful conduct (Amos 6:1). Inscriptions like the Mesha Stele refer to Omri and validate the historical significance of this dynasty, supporting the context in which Amos prophesied.

4. **Assyrian Annals Confirming Conquests**: Assyrian records corroborate the military campaigns against Israel and

surrounding nations, precisely aligning with Amos' prophecies of judgments against Israel and its neighbors.

5. **Earthquake Evidence**: Amos 1:1 mentions a significant earthquake. Geological layers in the region compatible with a seismic event have been dated to around the time Amos would have prophesied, providing physical evidence for the Biblical account.

6. **Cuneiform Tablets on Socio-Economic Conditions**: Tablets have been found that provide details on the social and economic conditions of the time, aligning well with Amos' criticism of social injustice and economic exploitation (Amos 2:6-8; 5:11).

7. **Discovery of Ancient Bethel and Gilgal**: These were key religious centers mentioned by Amos (Amos 4:4; 5:5). Excavations have revealed altars and religious paraphernalia that match the Biblical description, confirming the idolatrous practices that Amos condemned.

8. **Artifacts Reflecting Religious Practices**: Idols, altars, and other religious items have been found that resonate with the false worship practices that Amos criticized, thereby adding another layer of historical verification to the text.

Through each of these archaeological discoveries, we see a consistent affirmation of the historical and social context as described by Amos. This cumulative evidence serves to further solidify the book of Amos as a trustworthy and divinely inspired component of Scripture.

What Clinches the Authenticity of Amos

The book of Amos stands as an authentic component of the Biblical canon, and this is unequivocally attested by New Testament citations. Two decisive affirmations of the book's authority come from Stephen and James in the Acts of the Apostles.

Stephen's Paraphrase in Acts 7:42, 43: Stephen, in his defense before the Sanhedrin, paraphrases Amos 5:25-27. Here, Stephen refers to the worship of Moloch and Rephan, practices that Amos also sharply criticizes. Stephen's use of this passage is crucial. Not only does it affirm that the book of Amos was recognized as authoritative Scripture by the early Christians, but it also shows that its messages were understood to have ongoing relevance for the people of God. By drawing on Amos, Stephen makes an implicit but strong argument for the book's authenticity and divine inspiration.

James' Quotation in Acts 15:15-18: In the Jerusalem Council, where the apostles and elders were discussing whether Gentile Christians should be required to follow Jewish customs, James quotes Amos 9:11, 12 to support his argument. James points out that Amos had prophesied the rebuilding of "the fallen tent of David" and the inclusion of the Gentiles in God's plan. By using this citation to resolve a doctrinal issue of high import, James unequivocally affirms the authenticity and authority of the book of Amos. His quote serves as an apostolic endorsement that this prophetic work is not only genuine but also carries divine authority in matters of doctrine and practice.

The inclusion of these passages in Acts signifies that early Christians, including the apostles, viewed the book of Amos as a legitimate and authoritative part of Scripture. These New Testament affirmations clinch the authenticity of the book of Amos, leaving no room for doubt concerning its rightful place in the canon of Scripture.

CHAPTER 11 Defending Obadiah, Jonah, and Micah

Authenticity, Authorship, and Date of Obadiah

The Primacy of the Message in the Book of Obadiah

In the book of Obadiah, the focus is unquestionably on the message, not the messenger. Obadiah himself is one of the least described prophets in the Scriptures. Very little is said about him, his lineage, or his personal life. The absence of these biographical details, which are often included for other prophets, underscores that the focus is intended to be squarely on the message he delivers.

1. **Lack of Biographical Details**: Unlike Jeremiah or Isaiah, whose familial lineage and historical context are detailed, Obadiah is introduced without such descriptors. This deliberate omission indicates that the importance lies in what is being said, rather than who is saying it.

2. **The Message's Universal and Timeless Application**: The prophetic word against Edom is profound in its ethical and moral implications, extending beyond any specific historical or cultural context. The condemnation of Edom serves as a timeless warning against pride, complacency, and hostility against God's people.

3. **Emphasis on Divine Pronouncements**: The book is filled with "Thus says the Lord Jehovah" declarations, emphasizing that the warnings and judgments are directly from Jehovah. The frequent use of these phrases centers attention on the divine origin of the message rather than on Obadiah as an individual.

4. **Immediate Engagement with the Message**: From the first verse, Obadiah plunges into the vision that Jehovah has shown him, without detours or preambles that involve his personal circumstances. This directness serves to keep the reader's attention on the prophecy itself.

5. **The Message's Inclusion in the Canon**: The very inclusion of Obadiah in the canon of Scripture—despite its brevity and lack of biographical detail—testifies to the significant weight and divine origin of its message. It has been preserved and esteemed not because of who Obadiah was, but because of the God-given revelation he conveyed.

In summary, the structure, content, and presentation of the book of Obadiah all direct attention away from the prophet himself and toward the divinely inspired message he carried. This makes it clear that the message, rather than the messenger, is of paramount importance.

Focus of Obadiah's Prophecy and the Security of Edom

The prophecy of Obadiah is focused squarely on the nation of Edom. Edom was a country southeast of Israel and was inhabited by the descendants of Esau, Jacob's brother. It's essential to grasp the relationship between Edom and Israel to appreciate fully the weight of the prophecy. These were kindred nations; however, Edom exhibited consistent animosity toward Israel, which made the prophecy especially poignant.

Sources of Edom's Sense of Security

1. **Geographical Advantage**: One of the foremost factors that contributed to Edom's sense of security was its geographical location. Edom was known for its mountainous terrain, notably the rock city of Petra, which was easily defensible. This rugged landscape gave the Edomites the impression of being untouchable. Obadiah 1:3-4 makes it clear that they dwelt in

the "clefts of the rock" and set their dwelling "on high," thinking that they were beyond reach.

2. **Pride and Arrogance**: The Edomites' sense of security was also deeply rooted in pride and arrogance. This is evident from the words in Obadiah 1:3, "The pride of your heart has deceived you." They took great confidence in their wisdom, military capabilities, and alliances with other nations.

3. **Economic Prosperity**: Edom was a prosperous nation, benefiting from trade routes that passed through its territory. This economic stability added another layer to their false sense of security.

4. **Perceived Indifference of Divine Retribution**: The Edomites were not only secure in their human capacities but also harbored a misguided notion that they were beyond divine judgment. They considered themselves invulnerable, even to divine forces.

Obadiah's prophecy is a scathing indictment against Edom's pride, misplaced confidence, and hostility towards Israel. The prophecy pulls no punches in declaring that Jehovah would bring them low for their arrogance and animosity against His people. In essence, Obadiah's prophecy serves as a divine confrontation against the false securities that Edom relied upon. It magnifies Jehovah's sovereignty and justice, showing that no nation, no matter how secure it feels, is beyond the reach of His judgment.

Edomites' Relationship with Israel: A Breach of Brotherhood

The Edomites had not acted as brothers to Israel, despite their shared lineage traced back to Isaac. Edom descended from Esau, and Israel from Jacob, making them technically brothers by ancestry. Yet, their relationship was anything but fraternal, marked by a longstanding tension and hostility.

Documented Instances of Edom's Animosity

1. **Initial Refusal of Passage**: In Numbers 20:14-21, when the Israelites were journeying to the Promised Land, Edom refused them passage through their territory. Not only did they deny this basic courtesy, but they also came out against Israel with a formidable army, thereby heightening the tension between the two nations.

2. **Taking Advantage During Israel's Vulnerability**: During times of Israel's vulnerability, Edom exploited the situation instead of offering help. For example, when the Babylonians attacked Jerusalem, Edom is remembered for their cruelty in standing by and even taking part in the looting (Obadiah 1:11-14).

3. **Prolonged Hostility**: Books like 1 Samuel and 1 Kings record continuous warfare and animosity between Edom and Israel. King David had to subdue Edom (2 Samuel 8:13-14), which indicated a relationship strained far from the ideals of brotherhood.

4. **Culmination in Obadiah's Prophecy**: Obadiah's prophecy itself serves as a divine indictment against Edom for their sustained animosity against Israel. Verses like Obadiah 1:10 state clearly, "Because of the violence done to your brother Jacob, shame shall cover you, and you shall be cut off forever."

Betrayal of Covenant Relationship

The relationship between Edom and Israel was not just social or political; it was covenantal because of their shared ancestry. By acting in ways that displayed clear aggression and neglect towards Israel, Edom had effectively broken this covenant of brotherhood. The intensity of their betrayal is one reason why Jehovah through Obadiah spoke judgment against them.

In summary, Edom had long abandoned the responsibilities and ethical obligations that come with being a brother to Israel. Their actions over centuries had proven this, and Obadiah's prophecy was a divine denunciation of their betrayal, confirming that they had not acted as brothers to Israel.

Obadiah: Time of Writing

let's delve into the scholarly argument for the dating and background of the Book of Obadiah, particularly addressing the claims made in the paragraphs you've presented.

1. **Date and Context of Obadiah's Denunciation**: The basis of Obadiah's denunciation against Edom lies in their treacherous behavior when Jerusalem was desolated by the Babylonians. Edom, not content with being passive spectators, participated in the looting and even handed over fleeing Judeans to the enemy. Given the visceral detail of these acts in the book of Obadiah, it is highly probable that the text was written when these events were fresh in collective memory. The suggested date of 588 B.C.E. aligns well with these details and is consistent with a literal, historical-grammatical interpretation of Scripture.

2. **Contradictory Dating Theories**

    - **Ahaz's Reign**: The claim that the book dates to the reign of Ahaz faces a significant issue. There is no record of Jerusalem being captured and despoiled during Ahaz's time, as Obadiah 11 would imply.

    - **Jehoram's Time**: While Edom did rebel against Judah during Jehoram's reign, the extent of the conflict as described in Obadiah does not fit with the historical accounts available for Jehoram's period.

3. **Jeremiah's Influence**: The evidence suggests that Jeremiah adapted content from Obadiah, not vice versa, giving weight to an earlier date for Obadiah. Obadiah's writing is more terse, suggesting Jeremiah expanded upon it, rather than Obadiah condensing Jeremiah's content.

4. **Obadiah 20 and 'Captivity'**: The word 'captivity' in Obadiah 20 doesn't necessarily mean a large-scale deportation. It can refer to a smaller group or even individuals. Thus, this doesn't demand a post-exilic date for the book.

5. **Source Division Theories**: The various attempts to divide Obadiah into multiple sources are largely speculative and derive from a methodological skepticism toward predictive prophecy. These theories do not fit well with an objective historical-grammatical interpretation and should be viewed critically.

6. **Theological Perspective**: The Edomites serve as a typological representation of those who oppose God's people. Obadiah's message of divine judgment against them has both a historical and eschatological dimension.

7. **Fulfillment and the Fate of Edom**: By the time of Malachi in the 5th century B.C.E., the Edomites had already lost their ancestral territories to the Nabateans, which can be considered a partial fulfillment of Obadiah's prophecies.

Therefore, the evidence overwhelmingly supports the dating of Obadiah to approximately 588 B.C.E., after the fall of Jerusalem. This date is in harmony with the historical-grammatical method of interpretation, taking into account the literal context, the linguistic details, and the historical setting. It best explains the intensity of the denunciations against Edom and fits well with the data available from other books of Scripture and external sources.

Let's break down the Book of Obadiah and how it fits with the date of 588-587 B.C.E.

Verse 1

"The vision of Obadiah. Thus says Jehovah God concerning Edom..." Obadiah has a vision concerning Edom, which is descended from Esau, Jacob's brother. Edom's animosity towards Israel can be traced back to their ancestral roots. The time of 588 B.C.E. corresponds well to the period just before the fall of Jerusalem in 587 B.C.E., during which Edom acted against Israel.

Verses 2-4

"Behold, I will make you small among the nations..." Edom, though small, had a sense of invincibility due to its geographical location, built into mountains and cliffs. However, Jehovah declares their coming downfall.

Verses 5-6

"**If thieves came to you, if robbers came by night...**" Edom would suffer a total loss, unlike a common thief who takes only what he needs. The metaphor here signifies the totality of their forthcoming destruction.

Verses 7-9

"**All your allies have driven you to the border...**" Edom's supposed allies would betray them. This could have been particularly relevant when geopolitical alliances were shifting rapidly during the period of 588-587 B.C.E.

Verses 10-14

"**Because of the violence done to your brother Jacob...**" Here, the text condemns Edom for taking advantage of Israel's misfortune, particularly relevant if it was during the siege and fall of Jerusalem in 587 B.C.E. Edom not only failed to assist but actively participated in the plunder.

Verse 15

"**For the day of Jehovah is near upon all the nations...**" This predicts a coming judgment not just for Edom but all nations, fitting the climate of judgment and upheaval of the time.

Verses 16-18

"**For as you have drunk on my holy mountain...**" The metaphor of drinking seems to refer to the participating in the looting and perhaps the desecration of the Temple in Jerusalem. Edom would face a similar desecration and loss.

Verses 19-21

"**Those of the Negev shall possess Mount Esau...**" The concluding section paints a picture of restoration for Israel, while Edom remains desolate. The geographical areas mentioned here would come under control of the returning Israelites, post-exile, reaffirming that Jehovah's plan for Israel was not thwarted.

Summary

The themes and circumstances described in Obadiah match well with what is known about the geopolitical situation around 588-587 B.C.E., especially with the fall of Jerusalem and Edom's role during that period.

Authenticity of the Record of Obadiah

The book of Obadiah holds a unique place as the shortest book in the Old Testament, yet its brevity does not in any way diminish its authenticity or impact. Multiple aspects affirm the genuineness and credibility of Obadiah's record, anchoring it firmly within the canon of Scripture.

Internal Consistency

The book maintains a level of internal consistency in theme, style, and message, focused primarily on the divine judgment against Edom and the eventual restoration of Israel. There's an evident cohesiveness in the theological expressions used, underscoring the work of a single, inspired author.

Historical-Cultural Context

Obadiah fits well within the historical and cultural contexts of the prophetic literature. The book's focus on Edom as the subject of God's judgment is consistent with the geopolitics of the period. Edom was historically hostile to Israel, a tension that dates back to their ancestors, Jacob and Esau. During the period around 588-587 B.C.E., Edom participated in the plundering of Jerusalem, aligning closely with the judgment themes in Obadiah.

Canonical Acceptance

The Jewish community included Obadiah in the Twelve Minor Prophets, a single scroll in Hebrew tradition, affirming its canonical status. Its inclusion in the Septuagint and the subsequent Christian canon evidences the recognition of its authenticity across diverse religious traditions.

Theological Consistency

The theological principles set forth in Obadiah are consistent with other biblical texts. The themes of divine judgment and retribution against the unrighteous, as well as the promise of restoration for Israel, parallel the major tenets of other prophetic books.

Intertextual Confirmations

The New Testament does not directly quote Obadiah, but the themes and eschatological aspects of the book are consistent with the New Testament teaching about God's judgment and the restoration of His people.

Fulfillment of Prophetic Requirements

The litmus test for a true prophet, as outlined in Deuteronomy 18:21-22, involves the accurate fulfillment of predictions. Obadiah's focus is not so much on specific near-term events but rather on the inevitable divine judgment against Edom and the restoration of Israel. The Edomites gradually lost prominence and were eventually lost to history. Meanwhile, Israel experienced both judgment and restoration, in line with the prophecies of Obadiah.

Secondly, a true prophet speaks in alignment with previous revelation (Deuteronomy 13:1-5). Obadiah passes this test by affirming the covenantal promises made to Israel while also echoing the judgments uttered by earlier prophets like Amos against Edom.

Appropriateness of the Name

The name "Obadiah" is deeply appropriate for the book's content and its author's vocation. Derived from the Hebrew, the name means "Servant of Jehovah." Obadiah serves as Jehovah's mouthpiece, proclaiming the divine message of judgment and hope. In an era marked by political unrest and spiritual decay, Obadiah's name signifies his role as an emissary of divine will. He is the servant of Jehovah, declaring God's judgment against a proud and haughty Edom while promising restoration for Israel.

In sum, the book of Obadiah is robust in its authenticity and truthfulness. It satisfies the tests for prophetic utterance and exists in harmony with the broader canonical and theological landscape of Scripture. Moreover, the name Obadiah encapsulates the essence of who he was—a servant of Jehovah, faithful in delivering a message that was both timely and timeless. Therefore, Obadiah's contribution to the canon should not be underestimated; though brief, it remains an indelible component of divine revelation.

Authenticity, Authorship, and Date of Jonah

Key Questions Answered in the Book of Jonah

The book of Jonah delves into several profound theological and moral questions, including:

1. **Can Anyone Escape Jehovah's Presence and Will?** Jonah's futile attempt to flee from Jehovah's directive to go to Nineveh illustrates that one cannot escape the omnipresence of Jehovah or thwart His divine plan (Jonah 1:3-10).

2. **Is Jehovah Concerned Only with Israel?** The book makes it evident that Jehovah's compassion and judgment are not restricted to Israel but extend to Gentile nations as well. Nineveh, an Assyrian city, was the focus of Jehovah's concern, proving that His mercy is universal (Jonah 3:10).

3. **Is Repentance Possible for the Wicked?** The Ninevites, who were known for their wickedness, repented at Jonah's message, and Jehovah relented from the disaster He had planned. This signifies that even those entrenched in sin have the opportunity for repentance and divine forgiveness (Jonah 3:5-10).

4. **Can Human Prejudice Limit Divine Compassion?** Jonah's anger over Nineveh's repentance and Jehovah's mercy toward them reveals that human prejudice does not influence Jehovah's compassionate nature (Jonah 4:1-3).

Jehovah's Mercy as Depicted in Jonah

1. **Unconditional Mercy**: Jehovah's decision to spare Nineveh after their repentance highlights His merciful character. There were no strings attached; the people repented, and Jehovah responded with mercy (Jonah 3:10).

2. **Patience with His Prophets**: Despite Jonah's initial disobedience and later bitterness, Jehovah showed patience and still used him for His purposes. This reveals Jehovah's merciful treatment even of those who should know better (Jonah 4:4-11).

3. **Educational Mercy**: Jehovah not only shows mercy but teaches it. The book concludes with Jehovah educating Jonah on the value of compassion and mercy, again demonstrating His merciful nature not just in actions but also in patient instruction (Jonah 4:9-11).

4. **Mercy Beyond Israel**: Jehovah's mercy to a foreign city stresses the point that His compassion is not limited by geography, ethnicity, or even the wicked past of those who stand before Him. His is a universal mercy available to all who repent and turn to Him (Jonah 1:2; 3:10).

In summary, the book of Jonah vividly portrays the mercy of Jehovah as unconditional, patient, instructive, and universal. It serves as a powerful reminder that Jehovah's mercy extends to all individuals and nations willing to repent and seek His face.

Jonah: Time of Composition

Authorship and Dating

The book of Jonah doesn't clearly state its author, but it's reasonable to think Jonah himself wrote it, reflecting on a critical moment in his ministry. The use of the past tense, "הָיְתָה" (hāyetâ), when talking about Nineveh (3:3) suggests that it was written some time after the events. A probable timeframe for its writing would be around 793-760 B.C. The use of third person is not out of the ordinary; even Moses, in the Torah, speaks of himself that way, as do historical figures like Xenophon and Julius Caesar in their works.

Liberal Criticism and Late Dating

Some critics argue that Jonah was written much later, around 430 B.C., as a sort of *allegory or fiction* intended to oppose the "narrow nationalism" of Jewish leaders like Ezra and Nehemiah. According to this view, the book aims to challenge policies that excluded Samaritans from worship and led to divorces from foreign wives. This perspective mainly rests on a theory about the evolution of religious ideas in Israel.

Allegorical Interpretations

These critics often suggest an allegorical reading: Jonah symbolizes *disobedient Israel*, the sea stands for the Gentiles, the whale represents Babylon, and the three days Jonah spent inside the whale signify the Babylonian captivity. In this reading, the book of Jonah becomes a call to the Jews of the fifth-century B.C. to break free from an insular mindset and share their faith more widely.

Problems with the Allegorical View

However, when you closely examine the text, this *allegorical interpretation doesn't hold up well.* For instance, if the whale symbolizes Babylon, what does Nineveh represent? And what about the ship departing from Joppa? Also, why would three days symbolize seventy years of captivity? No solid evidence supports the notion that such universalistic views were prevalent among the Jews of the fifth-century B.C. The argument becomes circular when critics cite Jonah and Ruth as evidence for a stage of Jewish thought, claiming that these books must have been written at that time because they fit this supposed ideological stage.

In summary, the most straightforward reading—anchored in the text and in keeping with a *literal translation philosophy* and *Historical-Grammatical method* of interpretation—supports an earlier date of composition and views the book as a real account of historical events.

Jonah: Assessing the Historical Authenticity

The book of Jonah has often come under scrutiny for its historical accuracy. Critics propose several points to argue against its literal historicity. Let's delve into these objections one by one and scrutinize their validity.

1. The Title "King of Nineveh"

Critics argue that it is historically incorrect for Jonah to refer to the Assyrian king as merely the "king of Nineveh." They say that this suggests the book was written at a much later date when Assyria was no longer a world power. However, this objection is easily dispelled when we consider that ancient writers, regardless of their language or origin, were well aware that Nineveh was the capital of Assyria. Moreover, Hebrew historical texts often use the capital city to refer to the ruler of the entire realm. For example, Ahab, while being the king of Israel, is referred to as the "king of Samaria" in 1 Kings 21:1.

2. Use of the Past Tense in Describing Nineveh

The second objection is that Jonah refers to Nineveh in the past tense, as if it no longer existed when the text was written. Critics argue that this implies that the book was written after Nineveh's decline. However, the text is likely emphasizing that Nineveh *had already become* a significant city at the time of Jonah's visit, which would be around 793-760 B.C. The Hebrew perfect tense, *hāyetâ*, can carry this nuance.

3. The Size of Nineveh

Some scholars find the enormous size attributed to Nineveh implausible. The text states that it took three days for Jonah to walk through the city. Critics say this is an exaggeration. However, this neglects the fact that Jonah was not merely walking but stopping to preach at various locations. Moreover, estimates based on the text suggest a very large population that would require such a time frame for Jonah's mission. Comparatively, a hike from Dan to Shiloh, a distance of 60 miles, would also take about three days.

4. The Repentance of Nineveh

The rapid and widespread repentance of Nineveh is deemed inconceivable by critics. They say it's unlikely that an entire city would so swiftly turn to God upon hearing the preaching of a foreign prophet. However, the text makes it clear that God was directing the events and rendering the preaching effective. It's worth noting that during the time Jonah could have visited—likely under the reign of Adad-Nirari III or Assurdan III—there were significant reasons for the Ninevites to be receptive to such a message. Whether due to religious shifts towards monolatry under Adad-Nirari III or catastrophic events like plagues and eclipses under Assurdan III, the stage was set for the Ninevites to heed Jonah's warning.

In summary, each objection raised against the historical authenticity of Jonah can be adequately addressed, reinforcing the credibility of this biblical narrative.

Linguistic Arguments for Dating Jonah

Aramaisms in the Text of Jonah

Scholars who argue for a post-exilic date for the book of Jonah often point to various words and phrases that seem to be influenced by Aramaic language. However, closer inspection shows that these linguistic features do not necessarily imply a late date.

1. **The Term "Sephînâ"**: Jonah 1:5 uses the word Sephînâ, meaning "ship," as an alternative to the more common Hebrew word ʾoniyyâ. Although this term is frequent in Aramaic, it originates from the Hebrew root sāphan, which translates to "to cover." This root is also common in Phoenician inscriptions, indicating that this term might have been borrowed from Canaanite language rather than Aramaic.

2. **The Verb ʾašat in Jonah 1:6**: This verb, which means "to remember," appears in the hithpael stem in the text. While it is

found in early Aramaic texts like the Elephantine Papyri, its usage in Jonah does not correlate with its Aramaic or Syriac forms. Moreover, the term exists in other Hebrew texts, such as Song of Solomon and Job, albeit with different meanings ("artifact" and "thought, opinion" respectively).

3. **Relative Pronoun šê**: This term appears in its simple form in Jonah 4:10 and in compounds in 1:7 and 1:12. Contrary to the idea that this is an Aramaism, šê is not an Aramaic word. In fact, this term also appears in early Hebrew writings like the Song of Deborah. It is also prevalent in Phoenician inscriptions, implying that its usage could be native to the Canaanite or Phoenician sailors onboard Jonah's ship.

Several other alleged Aramaisms are also cited, but these generally lack robust supporting evidence. Words like hēṭîl (to throw) and qerî'ah ("preaching") are common to both Hebrew and Aramaic. The term ṭa'am, meaning "edict," might have been a nod to the Assyrian term ṭēmu, fitting the narrative context.

The Authority of Jesus on the Historicity of Jonah

Jesus' Affirmation of Jonah's Historicity: In light of criticisms against the historical authenticity of Jonah, it is crucial to consider the New Testament. In Matthew 12:40-41, Jesus explicitly refers to the events in the book of Jonah as historical facts. If Jonah's story were merely allegorical, then by extension, the death and resurrection of Jesus, to which he compares Jonah's experience, would also be allegorical. This would contradict the entire premise of Christian faith.

Judgment by Nineveh's Repentance: Further, in Matthew 12:41, Jesus highlights the repentance of the people of Nineveh as a basis for judgment against his own generation's unbelief. If the Ninevites had not actually repented, Jesus' reproach would be baseless. It is therefore vital to acknowledge the historicity of the book of Jonah to maintain the authority and teachings of Jesus.

In conclusion, the linguistic arguments for a late date for Jonah are not convincing. Moreover, the statements by Jesus in the New

Testament firmly establish the historicity of the events in Jonah, which ought not to be disregarded.

Jonah: Assessing Textual Integrity

Addressing the Composition Debate

Liberal scholars often assert that the book of Jonah is pieced together from different sources. They focus particularly on Jonah's psalm of thanksgiving in Jonah 2:2-9. Critics like Wellhausen argue that this psalm feels out of place for two main reasons:

1. **Discrepancy in Prayer Type**: Jonah 2:1 says that Jonah "prayed," using the Hebrew verb *hitpallēl*. Critics note that the following psalm doesn't contain petitions to God but rather offers thanks.

2. **Timing of Thanksgiving**: They also point out that Jonah expresses his gratitude before he is safely on dry land, which supposedly makes his thankfulness premature.

Countering the Critics

However, these arguments overlook key aspects of Hebrew spirituality and the specific context of Jonah's situation.

1. **Versatility of Prayer**: Firstly, within Hebrew tradition, thanksgiving is considered an integral part of prayer. This is evident in various Psalms and passages like 2 Samuel 7:27, where praise and adoration toward Jehovah are framed as forms of prayer. Therefore, using *hitpallēl* in 2:1 doesn't contradict the nature of the following psalm.

2. **Contextualizing Thanksgiving**: Secondly, as Young aptly notes, the psalm is not about being thankful for escaping the whale but for being saved from drowning *by* the whale. When seen from this angle, there is no inconsistency between Jonah's psalm and the narrative it is set within.

Moreover, Wilhelm Moeller has observed that Jonah's psalm bears notable similarities to the psalms of David, offering further integrity to the text.

Unpacking Rationalist Claims

Liberal scholars like Eissfeldt dissect Jonah into two separate legends: chapters 1-3, focusing on Jonah's disobedience, and chapter 4, which discusses Jonah's dispute with God over extending grace to non-Israelites. They suggest that the story of Jonah being swallowed by a fish, common to other ancient literatures, must therefore be a legend.

Questioning the Skepticism

In response, it's crucial to assert that just because a story is found in legends does not mean it cannot be factual. Essentially, Eissfeldt's argument rests on an a priori assumption that miracles cannot happen. Conclusions based on such premises are as dubious as the premises themselves.

When viewed through the lens of unbiased literary analysis, there is no compelling reason to believe that the book of Jonah is a composite text. Thus, the text maintains its integrity both thematically and contextually.

The Authenticity of the Book of Jonah: An Unassailable Examination

As a preeminent Hebrew Old Testament scholar, it is my informed conviction that the book of Jonah is an authentic text that should not be dismissed as mere legend or folklore. This position is substantiated through rigorous textual analysis, historical considerations, and literary coherence. Below, I will delve into multiple aspects that testify to the authenticity of the book of Jonah.

Textual Consistency: The Role of Hebrew Linguistics

Let's first address the linguistic integrity of the text. The book of Jonah is composed in Classical Biblical Hebrew, consistent with the time period it claims to narrate. The use of specific verbs like *hitpallēl* (to pray) links the text to broader Hebrew tradition and spirituality, thus strengthening its authenticity. Words and phrases used are in harmony with the rest of the Hebrew Bible, making it unlikely to be a later or composite addition.

Historical Context

The book of Jonah sets the prophet's mission against the backdrop of the Assyrian city of Nineveh, which was a prominent city during the period in which Jonah lived. Archaeological findings confirm Nineveh's existence and its role as a significant Assyrian city. The city was indeed large enough to justify a three-day journey across it, as described in Jonah 3:3. The historical existence of Nineveh adds credibility to the text's claim of events.

Literary Coherence

The book has a unified message that focuses on themes of divine mercy, repentance, and obedience. Contrary to claims that the book is a conglomeration of different stories or traditions, its singular thematic focus supports its unity. The book is internally consistent and doesn't contain anachronisms, theological contradictions, or disparate sources that would hint at multiple authorship or later interpolations.

The Nature of Miracles

Critics often question the plausibility of Jonah's survival inside the fish. However, these objections fundamentally rest on the presupposition against the possibility of miracles. This is a logical fallacy. If one accepts that God is the Creator and Sustainer of the universe, then by definition, He can perform actions that transcend natural laws.

Theological Consistency

Jonah's account is consistent with the rest of the Hebrew Scriptures in terms of its portrayal of God's attributes and man's moral obligations. For instance, Jehovah's willingness to forgive the repentant Ninevites aligns with His merciful character as depicted in other books like Psalms and Isaiah. Jonah's own struggle with obedience and eventual submission echoes the experiences of other prophets and figures in Scriptures, such as Moses and David. This theological consistency within the broader corpus of the Hebrew Bible lends further credence to the book's authenticity.

The Psalm of Thanksgiving

Jonah's psalm in chapter 2 has been a focal point of scrutiny. Detractors argue that it seems incongruent for Jonah to offer a prayer of thanksgiving before his deliverance is complete. However, such a perspective misses the broader spiritual understanding that thanksgiving is an integral part of Hebrew prayer life, as well evidenced in the Psalms. Moreover, the psalm reflects Jonah's thankfulness for being saved from drowning, not for being delivered from the fish. In other words, the context makes the content of the psalm entirely fitting. The lexical parallels between Jonah's psalm and the Psalms of David offer another layer of validation to its authenticity.

Critique of Source Criticism

Rationalistic scholars who dissect the book into various sources commit a methodological error. Their critiques rest on a flawed premise—the supposed impossibility of miracles—and they bring this bias to their reading of the text. Upon unbiased examination, no compelling case can be made for multiple sources underlying the book of Jonah. Moreover, if one begins to dissect the Hebrew Scriptures based on the criteria that anything miraculous must be considered inauthentic, then one would have to reject much of the Hebrew Bible, thereby undermining the foundation of these very critiques.

Conclusion

In summary, the book of Jonah stands as an authentic narrative when subjected to rigorous textual, historical, and literary scrutiny. Its language, thematic unity, historical backdrop, and theological coherence all attest to its authenticity. The objections raised against the book are often rooted in a priori assumptions that preclude a fair evaluation of the text. Thus, based on the objective historical-grammatical method of interpretation, the book of Jonah is an integral and authentic part of the Hebrew Bible. Its message and historicity should not be undermined by speculative theories that cannot stand up to serious academic scrutiny.

Authenticity, Authorship, and Date of Micah

Character of the Prophet Micah

Micah, whose name means "Who is like Jehovah?", was a prophet of deep moral and spiritual convictions. He hailed from the town of Moresheth, located in the Judean lowlands. Micah ministered during the reigns of Jotham, Ahaz, and Hezekiah, Kings of Judah, a period that can be roughly dated to the late 8th century B.C.E.

Prophet of Justice: Micah was deeply concerned with justice and ethical righteousness. He spoke against the corrupt practices of the leaders and the rich who exploited the poor and needy. His famous dictum, "He has told you, O man, what is good; and what does Jehovah require of you but to do justice, and to love kindness, and to walk humbly with your God?" (Micah 6:8), encapsulates his commitment to social ethics rooted in a relationship with Jehovah.

Unyielding Faith in Jehovah's Sovereignty: Micah's faith in Jehovah's ultimate reign was unshakeable. He believed that Zion would be the ultimate center of God's government, from which law and truth would emanate (Micah 4:1-3).

Candid and Fearless: Micah was not a man to sugarcoat the truth. He straightforwardly condemned the sins of both the northern kingdom of Israel and the southern kingdom of Judah. His oracles against the cities in Micah 1:10-16, for example, are notable for their poetic intensity and courageous forthrightness.

Compassionate yet Uncompromising: Even though Micah delivered harsh messages, his book reveals a man of compassion. He wept over the sins of his people and the judgment they would incur (Micah 1:8). However, his compassion did not lead him to compromise on delivering Jehovah's unaltered message.

Messianic Hope: Micah also brought a message of hope, notably the prophecy of the coming Messiah who would be born in Bethlehem (Micah 5:2). This not only underscores his role as a prophet but also reveals his orientation towards ultimate redemption and salvation through Jehovah's appointed servant.

Micah was a man of strong moral fiber, unwavering faith, and compassionate sternness. His prophecies remain deeply relevant, both as an indomitable call for social justice and a profound articulation of theological hope. His life and work stood as a testament to his unwavering commitment to Jehovah and His righteous standards.

Micah's Prophetic Ministry and Historical Context

Period of Prophesying: Micah's ministry can be definitively placed in the 8th century B.C.E., specifically during the reigns of Jotham, Ahaz, and Hezekiah, Kings of Judah. This is explicitly stated in the introduction to the book (Micah 1:1). The period would span approximately from 750 B.C.E. to around 686 B.C.E., overlapping with some of the darkest days for the northern kingdom of Israel, leading to its fall in 722 B.C.E., as well as a challenging time for the kingdom of Judah.

Historical Context: This was a period of significant geopolitical turmoil. The Assyrian empire was on the rise, and Israel and Judah were caught in the crosshairs. Israel ultimately fell to the Assyrian forces, while Judah barely survived due to Hezekiah's faith and Jehovah's miraculous intervention (Isaiah 37:36-37). Economic disparity was also widespread, and Micah's message frequently targeted social injustice and the abuse of the marginalized.

Assyrian Threat: During Micah's lifetime, the Assyrian empire was the dominant force in the Near East. The fall of Samaria in 722 B.C.E. to the Assyrians under Sargon II was a vivid backdrop to Micah's prophecies against the northern kingdom. This Assyrian menace was also felt in Judah, culminating in the siege of Jerusalem during Hezekiah's reign, which was miraculously lifted as prophesied by Isaiah and confirmed in historical accounts.

Religious Apostasy: Both Israel and Judah were steeped in idolatry and false religious practices during this period. King Ahaz of Judah even went to the extent of closing the temple and setting up idolatrous altars throughout the land (2 Chronicles 28:24-25). Micah staunchly opposed such religious declension and called the people to return to the worship of Jehovah alone.

Period of Injustice: The era was also marked by extreme economic disparity. The rich and powerful exploited the poor, a theme Micah constantly highlighted in his messages. Land-grabbing and judicial corruption were prevalent, and Micah condemned these practices without reservation (Micah 2:1-2; 3:9-11).

Notable Figures: Micah was contemporaneous with other prophets like Isaiah, Amos, and Hosea. However, his message was unique in its blend of stern warning and messianic hope. His voice added weight to the prophetic corpus that Jehovah was revealing through various channels during that critical period.

In summary, the prophet Micah lived and ministered in one of the most pivotal periods in Israelite history. His message was shaped by the turbulent times, but it was aimed at timeless issues: justice, righteousness, and obedience to Jehovah. His prophecies and exhortations were firmly rooted in the historical and social realities of his day, and they carry enduring theological significance.

Micah: The Textual Integrity Examined

The Book of Micah, like many other books of the Hebrew Bible, has had its fair share of scrutiny. Critics often question the authenticity of chapters 6 and 7, arguing that these chapters contain themes and ideas that align more closely with later periods in Israel's history. Despite these claims, evidence supports the integrity of these chapters as originating from Micah, an 8th-century prophet.

Later-Themed Motifs: Are They Really Anachronistic?

One of the criticisms is that chapters 6 and 7 in Micah discuss the *regathering of God's dispersed people* and *Israel's triumph over its enemies under the Messiah*. Critics such as Heinrich Ewald have attributed these chapters to an unknown author from the time of Manasseh (697–642 C.E.). Julius Wellhausen went further, suggesting that Micah 7:7–20 was written during the exile and was contemporary with Deutero-Isaiah.

However, these arguments rest on the premise that an 8th-century prophet like Micah could not have had the insight to make such predictions. This approach, however, limits the prophetic capabilities of biblical figures based on what we understand today and imposes a form of *antisupernatural bias*.

The Controversial Verse: Micah 4:10

Critics have particular issues with Micah 4:10, which mentions that Israel will come "even unto Babylon" where they will be rescued. They claim that this prediction could not have been possible without supernatural foresight, and therefore must be a later addition. But isn't the premise of prophecy based on divine revelation? If Micah were indeed a prophet, it stands to reason that he could have received such revelation from Jehovah.

The Problem of Antisupernatural Bias

The arguments against the genuineness of Micah 4:10—and by extension, chapters 6 and 7—are rooted in the same bias that critics apply to Isaiah 40–66. This bias is grounded in the idea that prophecy is not possible because it involves supernatural elements, thereby disqualifying it from authenticity in the eyes of these critics.

Comparisons with Other Scholarly Opinions

While some critics argue for a later date, moderate scholars like Driver question the necessity of doing so. If we apply the same *historical-grammatical method* of interpretation consistently, there is no compelling reason to separate these chapters from Micah's authorship.

In Defense of Textual Integrity

In sum, the doubts cast on the authenticity of Micah's later chapters often come from a standpoint that denies the possibility of supernatural elements in biblical texts. When scrutinized through an unbiased lens that takes into account the prophetic nature of these writings, these chapters align coherently with Micah's overarching themes and messages. Therefore, rather than being products of a different time, they appear to be genuine parts of Micah's prophetic message.

The Significant Times During Which Micah Served

A Period of National Crises

Micah served during the reigns of Jotham, Ahaz, and Hezekiah, Kings of Judah. This timeframe—specifically from about 750 B.C.E. to 686 B.C.E.—was a period rife with internal and external threats. The Assyrian empire was ascending to a new peak of power, having already conquered Israel in 722 B.C.E. Judah was on the brink of facing similar catastrophe, especially during the reign of Hezekiah when Assyria laid siege to Jerusalem. Thus, Micah's ministry was set against the backdrop of some of the most challenging years in Judah's history.

Era of Religious Apostasy

Micah also lived during an age of religious turmoil and apostasy. The kingdom of Judah, under the reign of Ahaz, had turned its back on Jehovah to worship other gods. This was a period when idolatrous practices were abundant, and the worship of Jehovah was in decline. The northern kingdom of Israel had already been subsumed by its idolatry, which led to its downfall. Micah's message, therefore, was especially pertinent, given the apostate condition of the religious landscape.

Why Jehovah Commissioned Micah as Prophet

A Call for Spiritual Renewal

Jehovah commissioned Micah as a prophet to serve as His mouthpiece during these turbulent times. The spiritual declension of the people, characterized by idolatry and corrupt practices, necessitated divine intervention. Micah was entrusted with the task of calling the people back to pure worship and adherence to the Law.

Social Justice and Ethical Righteousness

Exploitation of the weak, social injustice, and rampant corruption were societal norms that Micah had to address head-on. Jehovah used him to bring these issues to the forefront, condemning the people's actions and forewarning of the consequences of such behaviors.

Messiah and Future Hope

Apart from calling out the sins of his contemporaries, Micah was also commissioned to provide a message of hope. In Micah 5:2, he prophesied the birthplace of the Messiah, Bethlehem. This was a significant prophecy pointing to future redemption and the establishment of Jehovah's rule on earth.

A Testament to Divine Faithfulness

Jehovah used Micah to remind the people of His covenant promises. While the nation was to be punished for its unfaithfulness, Jehovah's commitment to His covenant would remain intact. This message underscored Jehovah's enduring faithfulness, even in the face of human disobedience.

Micah served in a pivotal era for the kingdom of Judah—an age filled with national and spiritual crises. Jehovah commissioned him to be a prophet to address these serious issues, to lead the people back to righteous living, and to point them toward future hope through the promised Messiah. His commission was not just a response to the spiritual, social, and political conditions of his day, but also a testament to Jehovah's enduring covenant faithfulness.

The Authenticity of the Book of Micah

Internal Consistency and Historical Reliability

The book of Micah demonstrates remarkable internal consistency in its style, message, and focus. Moreover, the historical elements in Micah align well with what is known about the period from external sources, providing a strong case for its authenticity. The geopolitical landscape and the spiritual apostasy described in the book fit into the era in which Micah was said to have prophesied, specifically during the reigns of Jotham, Ahaz, and Hezekiah.

The Testimony of Other Scriptures

One of the strongest validations of Micah's authenticity is its acknowledgment by other parts of the Scripture. Most notably, the prophet Jeremiah directly quotes from Micah in Jeremiah 26:18, referencing Micah's prophecy about the destruction of Jerusalem. This attestation from another canonical prophet lends significant weight to the book's authenticity.

Unity of Message and Purpose

The book maintains a consistent message throughout—condemning injustice, calling for repentance, and pointing towards the hope in the coming Messiah. This unified message is exactly what would be expected from a genuine prophetic work inspired by Jehovah.

Fulfillment of Prophecies

Many of Micah's prophecies have been fulfilled, further attesting to the book's authenticity. Most notably, Micah 5:2 predicts that the Messiah would be born in Bethlehem. This prophecy was fulfilled in the birth of Jesus, as recorded in the New Testament. The fulfillment of Micah's prophecies serves as a powerful validation of the book's divine origin.

Integrity of Textual Transmission

The book of Micah has been preserved well over the centuries, as evidenced by its presence in ancient manuscripts such as the Dead Sea Scrolls. The textual integrity and the lack of substantive variations across manuscripts contribute to the credibility of the book as an authentic prophetic work.

Language and Literary Style

The Hebrew language and literary style found in Micah are consistent with the period in which the prophet lived. These factors corroborate the traditional understanding of the book's origin and further substantiate its authenticity.

The authenticity of the book of Micah is supported by its internal consistency, historical reliability, prophetic fulfillments, and textual integrity. Furthermore, it is validated by other Scriptures and maintains a unity of message and purpose. All these factors combined provide compelling evidence that the book of Micah is a genuine and reliable prophetic work inspired by Jehovah.

Archaeological Evidence Confirming the Fulfillment of Micah's Prophecies

Evidence of Social Conditions

Micah's portrayal of the social and religious conditions in Judah and Israel is corroborated by various archaeological findings. For instance, Micah condemns the rampant idolatry and social injustice of his time (Micah 1:7; 6:10-12). Archaeological excavations have uncovered idols and Asherah poles that were commonly used in idol worship during the period, as well as inscriptions that give us insight into the social inequalities of the era.

Destruction Layers

One of Micah's key prophecies was the impending judgment upon Samaria and Jerusalem (Micah 1:6; 3:12). Archaeological excavations reveal destruction layers that correspond to the time of the Assyrian invasion for Samaria and the Babylonian invasion for Jerusalem, respectively. These physical layers of ash and burnt debris provide tangible evidence of the destruction foretold by Micah.

Bethlehem and the Messiah

Micah's prophecy that the Messiah would come from Bethlehem (Micah 5:2) is notably confirmed by the New Testament accounts of Jesus' birth. Bethlehem itself is an archaeological site that has been excavated and studied. Its existence and historical significance further affirm the accuracy of Micah's prophecy.

Moresheth-Gath

Micah's hometown, Moresheth-Gath, is mentioned in Micah 1:14. Archaeological discoveries confirm the existence of this town, situated in the Shephelah region of Judah. Knowing the location of Micah's hometown adds an additional layer of credibility to the historical context in which he prophesied.

Inscriptions and Records

While there are no specific inscriptions directly confirming Micah's individual prophecies, the broader historical records and inscriptions, such as the Assyrian Annals, confirm the geopolitical conditions described in the book. These external records corroborate the nations and cities mentioned in Micah as well as the kinds of judgments that befell them, thereby indirectly confirming the fulfillment of Micah's prophecies.

Archaeological findings provide powerful testimony to the fulfillment of Micah's prophecies. From confirming the social conditions and religious practices of the period to providing physical evidence of the destruction of cities, archaeology substantiates the divine origin and fulfillment of the prophecies made in the book of Micah.

Undeniable Evidence of Micah's Divine Inspiration

Fulfilled Prophecies

The most compelling evidence affirming the divine inspiration of the book of Micah lies in the fulfillment of its prophecies. Micah predicted the fall of Samaria to the Assyrians (Micah 1:6) and the destruction of Jerusalem by the Babylonians (Micah 3:12). Both these events occurred precisely as foretold, making a strong case for the divine origin of these prophetic utterances.

Harmony with Other Scriptures

Micah's teachings and prophecies are in complete harmony with other parts of the Hebrew Bible, further demonstrating its divine inspiration. The emphasis on justice, mercy, and humble walking with Jehovah (Micah 6:8) resonate well with other prophetic books as well as the Law and the Psalms.

Quotations in Later Scriptures

The New Testament also testifies to Micah's inspiration, as his prophecies are cited and fulfilled, notably the birth of the Messiah in Bethlehem (Micah 5:2; Matthew 2:4-6). The seamless integration of Micah's words into the broader canon confirms its divine origin.

Internal Consistency

The book of Micah presents a coherent and unified message, despite addressing multiple audiences, cities, and themes. This internal consistency is another indication that the book is not a mere product of human design but divinely inspired.

Credibility and Authenticity

Micah himself lived and prophesied during a critical period in Israel's history, overlapping with other prophets like Isaiah and Hosea. The historical accuracy and contextual relevance of Micah's book make a strong case for its divine inspiration.

Theological Depth

The theological teachings in Micah, including the nature of Jehovah, the requirements for true worship, and the future Messianic kingdom, exhibit a profound understanding that transcends mere human wisdom. The depth and intricacy of these teachings confirm that they originate from a source greater than human imagination.

The fulfilled prophecies, harmony with other Scriptures, internal consistency, quotations in later Scriptures, historical accuracy, and theological depth collectively put the inspiration of Micah beyond all doubt. The book stands as an enduring testament to the divine orchestration of history and the unwavering faithfulness of Jehovah to His purposes.

Micah's Exemplary Power of Expression

Vivid Imagery

Micah excels in the use of imagery to convey complex spiritual and moral truths. For instance, the metaphor of Jehovah pleading His case before the mountains and hills in a cosmic court of justice (Micah

6:1-2) is strikingly illustrative. This compelling visual representation magnifies the gravity of Israel's rebellion and Jehovah's justice.

Poetic Form

Micah's use of poetic form enhances the impact of his message. Parallelism and chiastic structures are frequent, helping the reader or listener to grasp the symmetry and balance in Jehovah's justice and mercy.

Clarity and Precision

Despite dealing with intricate themes such as social injustice, religious apostasy, and divine retribution, Micah's expressions remain remarkably clear and straightforward. His prophetic indictments are unequivocal, making it impossible for the recipients to misunderstand Jehovah's view.

Rhetorical Devices

Micah employs rhetorical questions to challenge his audience into introspection and to confront them with their own failings. An example can be found in Micah 6:3-5, where he asks, "O my people, what have I done to you? And how have I wearied you? Answer me!" This rhetorical device places the burden of proof on the people, compelling them to acknowledge their wrongdoing.

Emotional Resonance

Micah's language is imbued with a pathos that helps to engage the emotional and moral faculties of his audience. Phrases such as "you who hate good and love evil" (Micah 3:2) or "He has shown you, O man, what is good" (Micah 6:8) resonate deeply, moving the reader toward moral and spiritual reflection.

Consistency in Theme

Micah maintains a consistent thematic focus throughout his book. Whether admonishing the leaders of Israel for their corruption or painting the hopeful picture of a future Messianic kingdom, his power of expression remains aligned with the central message of Jehovah's sovereignty and Israel's accountability.

Micah's power of expression is both versatile and profound. He employs a range of literary devices, from vivid imagery and poetic forms to rhetorical questions, all aimed at conveying Jehovah's message with utmost impact. The clarity, emotional depth, and thematic consistency in his expressions make him a standout communicator among the prophets, affirming the divinely inspired nature of his writings.

Structure and Content of the Three Sections of the Book of Micah

The book of Micah can be neatly divided into three distinct sections, each starting with the imperative "Hear" and including a combination of rebukes, warnings of impending punishment, and promises of future blessing.

First Section: Micah 1-2

Rebukes: In the first section (Micah 1-2), Micah sternly rebukes the people for their idolatry and immorality. In particular, he calls out the southern kingdom of Judah and its capital, Jerusalem. Micah also identifies specific sins, such as coveting and seizing other people's land and houses.

Warnings of Punishment: The prophet outlines the consequences that Judah and Israel will face for their rebellion against Jehovah. These include military defeat and exile, represented in graphic terms, such as the melting of the Samaria's idols and the laying bare of her foundations.

Promises of Blessing: Despite the stern tone and warnings, this section also contains promises of Jehovah's deliverance for a remnant who would be gathered like "sheep in a fold" (Micah 2:12).

Second Section: Micah 3-5

Rebukes: Micah 3 opens with rebukes aimed at the leaders of Israel who "hate good and love evil" (Micah 3:2). He accuses them of exploiting the people and perverting justice.

Warnings of Punishment: The leaders are warned that because of their actions, "Zion shall be plowed as a field; Jerusalem shall become a heap of ruins" (Micah 3:12).

Promises of Blessing: Nevertheless, Micah speaks of a future time when the nations will come to Jerusalem to learn from Jehovah, and there will be universal peace under the Messianic King (Micah 4:1-4).

Third Section: Micah 6-7

Rebukes: Micah 6 features Jehovah's lawsuit against Israel. Jehovah recounts His past goodness and questions why the people have turned away from Him.

Warnings of Punishment: Micah outlines how Jehovah will make Israel "desolate" because of their ingratitude and rebellion (Micah 6:13-16).

Promises of Blessing: In a grand finale, Micah 7:18-20 magnifies Jehovah's mercy and faithfulness. Despite Israel's failure, Jehovah will show compassion, subduing their iniquities and casting their sins into the depths of the sea.

Each section serves as a cohesive unit that oscillates between rebuke, punishment, and blessing. This pattern reinforces the balance of Jehovah's justice and mercy, embodying the themes of divine retribution and ultimate restoration. The repeated use of "Hear" underscores the urgency and gravity of the prophet's message.

CHAPTER 12 Defending Nahum, Habakkuk, and Zephaniah

Authenticity, Authorship, and Date of Nahum

Ancient Nineveh: A City of Significance and Infamy

Geographical and Strategic Importance

Nineveh was situated on the eastern bank of the Tigris River, near the modern-day city of Mosul in Iraq. The city was strategically important due to its location, which allowed for easy control of trade routes that passed between the Mediterranean Sea and the lands to the east. This location also made it an effective military outpost for Assyria.

Architectural Grandeur

The city was famed for its architectural marvels, including its massive walls and the palace of its kings. The walls were reported to be wide enough for three chariots to ride abreast, an engineering feat that demonstrated the city's power and wealth. The palaces contained intricate stone reliefs and cuneiform inscriptions, revealing the artistic and literary accomplishments of the Assyrians.

Cultural and Religious Center

Nineveh was a hub of culture and religion. The city housed the famous library of Ashurbanipal, one of the world's earliest libraries, containing a vast collection of cuneiform texts. The Assyrians worshiped a multitude of gods and goddesses, with Ishtar and Ashur being among the most prominent. These deities were believed to grant military victories and prosperity, further reinforcing the aggressive expansionist policies of the Assyrian empire.

Brutal Military Campaigns

However, Nineveh was notorious for its cruelty and ruthless military campaigns. The Assyrian military was one of the most effective fighting forces of the ancient world and employed brutal tactics, including flaying and beheading, to intimidate their foes. The empire expanded through sheer force, subjugating various peoples and nations.

Decline and Fall

Despite its grandeur and power, Nineveh had a marked downfall. Nahum's prophecy was clear about the city's impending doom. The city was besieged by a coalition of Babylonians and Medes in 612 B.C.E. and was subsequently destroyed, fulfilling Nahum's prophetic words about its fall (Nahum 3:7).

Archaeological Evidence

Archaeological excavations have uncovered the ruins of Nineveh, providing empirical evidence that corroborates the biblical account. The remains of the city walls, palaces, and libraries all testify to its former glory and significance. The Assyrian reliefs and cuneiform inscriptions found in these excavations offer non-biblical historical records that align with the biblical depiction of Nineveh's wealth, power, and brutality.

In summary, Nineveh was a city of great significance in terms of geography, architecture, culture, and military might. Yet, it was also a city marked by extreme cruelty and hubris, characteristics that led to its downfall, just as foretold by the prophet Nahum. The archaeological evidence substantiates the biblical account, making the case for Nineveh's historicity and Nahum's prophetic accuracy incontrovertible.

Nineveh's Religion: A Pantheon of Deities and Rituals Rooted in Power

Multiplicity of Gods

Nineveh's religious system was polytheistic, entailing the worship of a multitude of gods and goddesses. Among these, the deity Ashur held a central place. Considered the national god of the Assyrian empire, Ashur embodied the ideals of kingship and military might. His worship was closely tied to the empire's expansionist ambitions.

Prominence of Ishtar

Another significant deity was Ishtar, the goddess of love and war. She was an embodiment of the dual nature of Assyrian power: at once beautiful and terrible. Ishtar was often invoked for success in battle, and her statues and symbols adorned both temples and military paraphernalia.

Ritual Practices

The religious rituals performed in Nineveh were intricate and highly ceremonial. They involved animal sacrifices, libations, and intricate hymns sung to honor the gods. Priests and religious officials held significant social and political power, often advising the king on matters of state and war through divination and other religious practices.

Military and Religion: An Inseparable Duo

Nineveh's religious practices were inseparably linked to its military endeavors. The gods were invoked for victory in battles, and spoils from conquered lands were used to adorn temples and fund religious ceremonies. The Assyrian kings often depicted themselves as the earthly representatives of Ashur, claiming divine authority for their military campaigns.

Religious Texts and Temples

Several temples and ziggurats were dedicated to these gods, and they were adorned with lavish decorations and offerings. Religious texts, often in the form of cuneiform tablets, described the myths, hymns, and rituals dedicated to these deities. The famous library of Ashurbanipal in Nineveh contained a multitude of such religious texts, which offer a deep insight into the complexity and richness of Nineveh's religious practices.

Contrast with the Monotheistic Faith of Israel

This polytheistic religious system stands in stark contrast to the monotheistic faith of Israel, emphasizing the one true God, Jehovah. The Book of Nahum emphasizes the judgment that would come upon Nineveh due to its wickedness, implicitly critiquing not just the city's political and military actions but also its religious practices, which stood in opposition to the worship of Jehovah.

In summary, Nineveh's religion was characterized by a pantheon of gods and goddesses, elaborate rituals, and a deep intertwining of religious practice with military conquest. These elements together formed a religious system that was not only divergent from but also antagonistic to the monotheistic worship of Jehovah as depicted in Scripture.

Nahum's Origin: Firmly Rooted in Elkosh

The Book of Nahum identifies the prophet as Nahum the Elkoshite. The term "Elkoshite" designates his place of origin, which is Elkosh. While the precise location of Elkosh remains a matter of scholarly debate, the most credible stance aligns it with a town in ancient Judah, based on Jewish tradition and also historical considerations.

Significance of Nahum's Judean Origin

Nahum's Judean origin holds significant implications for the prophetic message he delivered. Being from Judah, he would have had a vested interest in the events surrounding the Assyrian oppression and would have likely been familiar with the religious reforms happening in Judah. His Judean roots also serve to strengthen the authenticity of his prophecy against Nineveh, the Assyrian capital, given that Judah was directly impacted by Assyrian aggression.

Impact on the Message

Nahum's background gives his message a specific tone and intensity, shaped by the environment and religious climate he grew up in. As a Judean, Nahum would have been raised in the traditions of worshiping Jehovah, thereby contrasting the polytheistic religious system of the Assyrians. His Judean upbringing would have given him a deep sense of the religious, moral, and socio-political issues facing his people, and this, in turn, informs his prophecy against Nineveh.

The Appropriateness of Nahum's Name

The name "Nahum" is derived from the Hebrew root word "nacham," which means "to comfort" or "consolation." This is particularly fitting for the prophet's message. Nahum prophesies the fall of Nineveh, which was a source of terror and oppression for the Israelites. His prophecy brings comfort to his own people by foretelling the demise of their enemies. The name "Nahum" is, therefore, remarkably appropriate, as his words provide comfort to Judah by assuring them of divine justice against Nineveh.

Chronological Placement of Nahum's Prophecy

Nahum's prophecy can be firmly dated to the period leading up to the fall of Nineveh, which occurred in 612 B.C.E. This places Nahum as a contemporary of the prophet Zephaniah and likely the prophet Jeremiah. He prophesied during a time when Assyria was beginning to wane in power, but before its ultimate destruction. The historical and political circumstances that Nahum addresses—the immanent downfall of Nineveh—fit precisely within this time frame.

Nahum's specific chronological setting also interacts with the reigns of certain Judean kings. During this period, Manasseh's long reign had ended, and the godly King Josiah had initiated religious reforms. While the dating within Josiah's reign is a subject of discussion, the signs of Assyria's weakening power and the emerging influence of the Babylonians make this period the most plausible for Nahum's prophecy.

In summary, Nahum's name is extraordinarily appropriate, embodying the essence of comfort and consolation that his prophecies offered to Judah. Moreover, his prophecies belong to the period leading up to the fall of Nineveh in 612 B.C.E., making him a crucial voice during a pivotal time in the history of both Judah and Assyria.

Qualities of Writing in the Book of Nahum

The book of Nahum is a masterpiece of Hebrew poetry and prophetic literature. Its qualities of writing are outstanding in several ways:

Vivid Imagery

Nahum employs rich and vivid imagery to convey his messages. He describes the siege and downfall of Nineveh in almost cinematic detail, using metaphors and similes that are easily visualized. For example, in Nahum 2:4, the "chariots rage in the streets" and "jostle one against another in the broad ways." Such descriptions allow the reader to visualize the chaos and destruction that will befall Nineveh.

Lyrical Eloquence

The language of Nahum is not just functional but also beautiful, adhering to the conventions of Hebrew poetry such as parallelism and rhythm. This lyrical eloquence serves to elevate the message and engage the audience more deeply. The beauty of the language contrasts sharply with the grimness of the subject matter, creating a compelling tension in the text.

Precision and Economy of Words

Nahum is concise yet impactful. He doesn't waste words but gets straight to the point, making every sentence and phrase count. This precision is evident in how he describes the attributes of Jehovah, as in Nahum 1:2–3, where Jehovah is described as "a jealous and avenging God" whose "way is in the whirlwind and storm."

Theological Depth

Beyond its poetic and literary brilliance, the book also displays a deep theological understanding. Nahum articulates the complex balance between Jehovah's justice and mercy. While he focuses primarily on Jehovah's vengeance against Nineveh, he opens his book by acknowledging that Jehovah is "slow to anger but great in power."

Emotional Resonance

Nahum's words resonate emotionally, designed to instill fear in the enemies of Jehovah and comfort in the people of Judah. This emotional depth is not just a byproduct of his message but a carefully crafted element of his writing.

Structural Integrity

The book is well-structured, following a clear and logical flow from the declaration of Nineveh's sins to the prophetic judgments and, finally, to the pronounced destruction. This organization makes the book easy to follow and heightens its impact.

In summary, the book of Nahum is a remarkable piece of literary artistry, combining vivid imagery, lyrical eloquence, precision, theological depth, emotional resonance, and structural integrity to deliver a powerful message. It stands as one of the high points of prophetic literature in the Hebrew Scriptures.

Authenticity of Nahum's Prophecy

The authenticity of the book of Nahum rests on multiple grounds, ranging from its internal consistency to its prophetic accuracy and its placement within the canon of Scripture.

Internal Consistency and Theological Coherence

Firstly, the book is internally consistent both thematically and theologically. Nahum's description of Jehovah aligns perfectly with the depiction of Jehovah elsewhere in the Scriptures. His portrayal of Jehovah as a God of justice, who will not let the wicked go unpunished, echoes throughout other prophetic and historical books. This internal consistency strengthens the case for its authentic origin.

Historical Accuracy

Nahum prophesies the fall of Nineveh, which was a significant city of the Assyrian Empire. The book refers to specific details about the city and its defenses, details which have been corroborated by archeological findings. For example, Nahum mentions that the waters of the river will be the city's undoing (Nahum 2:6). Later historical accounts confirm that the Tigris River did indeed play a part in the fall of Nineveh in 612 B.C.E.

Prophetic Accuracy

The accuracy of Nahum's prophecies further attests to the book's authenticity. Nahum prophesied the utter destruction of Nineveh, which was fulfilled in precise detail. Nineveh was not only sacked but also so thoroughly destroyed that it was literally lost to history until its rediscovery by archeologists in the 19th century. This extreme level of destruction was precisely what Nahum had prophesied.

Canonical Acceptance

The book of Nahum has been part of the Hebrew Bible canon and has been accepted by both Jews and Christians as authoritative Scripture. This broad acceptance over millennia indicates that the communities that held to the Hebrew Scriptures considered it genuine and authentic.

Uniqueness of Content

Finally, the very nature of Nahum's prophecy—focused solely on the fall of a non-Israelite city—serves to substantiate its authenticity. It would be unlikely for a text with such a specific focus to have been fabricated or altered, especially given its harmony with the broader Scriptural messages regarding Jehovah's justice and sovereignty.

In summary, the book of Nahum stands as an authentic piece of prophetic literature, based on its internal consistency, historical and prophetic accuracy, canonical acceptance, and the unique nature of its content. These factors collectively serve to validate its authenticity as a genuine prophetic work in the canon of Hebrew Scripture.

Archaeological Vindication of Nahum's Prophecy Regarding Nineveh

The archaeological excavations at the site of ancient Nineveh offer compelling evidence that validates the accuracy of the book of Nahum. Multiple facets of Nahum's description of Nineveh and its downfall align closely with what has been uncovered through archaeology.

Architectural Features and Defensive Walls

Nahum describes Nineveh as a well-fortified city, alluding to its walls and gates (Nahum 3:13). Archaeological digs have confirmed the existence of massive walls and complex gate systems in Nineveh. These findings align perfectly with Nahum's depiction of the city as strongly fortified, corroborating the prophetic details.

Luxury and Opulence

Nahum mentions the luxury and opulence of Nineveh (Nahum 2:9). Archaeological discoveries, including intricate carvings, sculptures, and other artifacts, showcase the lavish lifestyle and prosperity of Nineveh. This supports Nahum's portrayal of a city engrossed in wealth.

Water Systems

Nahum predicts that the river gates would be opened and the palace would melt away (Nahum 2:6). Archaeologists have discovered evidence of a complex water system in Nineveh. Furthermore, historical accounts indicate that flooding was involved in the city's fall. The water defenses, once the city's strength, contributed to its downfall, thus validating Nahum's prophecy.

Signs of Destruction

Nahum prophesied the complete destruction of Nineveh (Nahum 3:7). The archaeological site reveals signs of violent destruction, including burn layers and collapsed structures. This aligns perfectly with Nahum's prophecy of utter ruin for the city.

Library of Ashurbanipal

One of the most significant finds at Nineveh was the Library of Ashurbanipal, which contained a vast number of cuneiform tablets. Although these tablets mainly contain Mesopotamian literature and administrative texts, they provide indirect support for Nahum's depiction by giving us a glimpse into the historical and cultural setting of Nineveh.

In summary, the archaeological evidence unearthed from the site of ancient Nineveh corroborates Nahum's descriptions and predictions in various respects, including its architecture, luxury, water systems, and its catastrophic end. This lends significant credence to the authenticity and historical accuracy of Nahum's prophecy.

The Canonicity of the Book of Nahum

The book of Nahum holds a firmly established position within the canon of the Hebrew Bible, and there are several compelling reasons for this that reflect both internal and external evidences.

Internal Consistency and Alignment with Established Theology

Firstly, Nahum is internally consistent and is coherent with the broader biblical narrative and theology. The book's central theme — the impending judgment upon Nineveh — dovetails perfectly with the rest of Scripture in presenting Jehovah as the righteous judge who would vindicate His people. The book neither contradicts nor strays from the established theology found in other biblical texts.

Recognition by Jewish Authorities

The Jewish tradition has always recognized the book of Nahum as canonical. It is part of the "Twelve Minor Prophets," a collection that holds authoritative status in the Tanakh. Nahum is found in every major manuscript tradition, including the Masoretic Text, which is critical to the Hebrew Bible.

Early Christian Acceptance

Early Christianity also affirmed the canonicity of Nahum. The book is included in the Septuagint, an ancient Greek translation of the Hebrew Bible, which further solidifies its canonical status. Nahum was accepted by early Church fathers and councils that affirmed the Old Testament canon, including the Council of Carthage in 397 C.E.

Presence in Historic Manuscripts and Lists

The presence of Nahum in significant historical manuscripts, such as the Codex Vaticanus and Codex Sinaiticus, indicates its recognized status as part of the biblical canon. Moreover, Nahum is listed in early Christian canonical lists, further affirming its accepted place in Scripture.

Historical Accuracy and Authenticity

As previously discussed, the historical accuracy and the fulfillment of the prophetic elements in Nahum provide further evidence of its divine inspiration and, thus, its rightful place in the canon. The book stands up to rigorous academic scrutiny and is supported by external evidence, including archaeological findings.

Purpose and Relevance

Lastly, the book of Nahum serves a significant theological purpose. It is not merely a record of past judgments but serves as a perpetual reminder of Jehovah's justice and the consequence of opposing His will. The relevance of its message for successive generations also supports its canonical status.

In summary, both internal and external factors overwhelmingly support the canonicity of the book of Nahum. Its internal consistency, recognition by religious authorities, presence in key historical manuscripts, historical accuracy, and enduring theological purpose all argue convincingly for its rightful place in the canon of Scripture.

Authenticity, Authorship, and Date of Habakkuk

Sublime Truths in the Prophecy of Habakkuk

The book of Habakkuk offers a rich tapestry of sublime truths that contribute significantly to our understanding of Jehovah's nature, human suffering, and the ultimate vindication of divine justice.

Jehovah's Sovereignty and Justice

One of the most sublime truths presented in Habakkuk is the unyielding sovereignty and justice of Jehovah. Despite the rampant iniquity in Judah and the impending threat of Babylonian invasion, Jehovah assures His prophet that He is fully in control and that justice will prevail. The opening dialogue between the prophet and Jehovah serves as a theodicy that offers profound insight into the administration of divine justice (Habakkuk 1:2-4, 12-17).

The Just Shall Live by Faith

The declaration in Habakkuk 2:4, "the righteous person will live by his faith," is a pivotal verse that has reverberating effects on later biblical literature and Christian theology. This statement encapsulates the essence of faithfulness and obedience in the life of the believer. It is cited in the New Testament multiple times, serving as a foundational text for understanding the principle of justification by faith (Romans 1:17; Galatians 3:11; Hebrews 10:38).

The Role of Questioning in Faith

Habakkuk stands unique among the prophetic books because it features the prophet questioning Jehovah openly about the problem of evil and suffering. This establishes the legitimacy of questioning and seeking understanding as a part of a robust faith life. However, the questioning leads to deeper understanding and resolute faith, as seen in the later chapters.

Universal Judgment and Restoration

While the prophecy is largely concerned with the impending Babylonian invasion, Habakkuk also points towards a broader, universal judgment. The five "woes" pronounced against the oppressors in Chapter 2 (vv. 6-20) establish that divine judgment is not arbitrary but based on clear moral and ethical grounds. It is a universal principle applicable to all nations and people who defy the divine standard.

Praise in the Midst of Calamity

Habakkuk 3 serves as a psalm of praise and a model of how to maintain faith in the midst of severe calamity. The prophet extols the power and glory of Jehovah even when faced with the prospect of utter devastation. His words reveal a mature faith that trusts in Jehovah's ultimate goodness and justice, irrespective of current circumstances.

God's Glory Filling the Earth

The text culminates with the sublime proclamation that "For the earth will be filled with the knowledge of the glory of Jehovah, as the waters cover the sea" (Habakkuk 2:14). This promises the future universal acknowledgment of Jehovah's glory, providing hope for the ultimate realization of divine justice and righteousness.

In sum, the book of Habakkuk articulates profound truths concerning the justice of Jehovah, the essence of true faith, the scope of divine judgment, and the triumph of divine glory. These truths serve as enduring principles that have significant bearing on both the Judeo-Christian tradition and individual faith journeys.

Information about the Writer, Habakkuk

The book of Habakkuk provides only limited direct information about its author. What we do know can be gleaned from the text and its immediate context. Habakkuk is identified as a prophet in the superscription of the book: "The pronouncement that the prophet Habakkuk saw" (Habakkuk 1:1). Unlike some other prophets, Habakkuk's lineage and the names of his family members are not mentioned. Thus, his social status and background remain unspecified.

Time Period of Habakkuk's Prophecy

As for the period to which Habakkuk's prophecy belongs, internal evidence suggests that he prophesied during the seventh century B.C.E., particularly in the decades leading up to the Babylonian invasion of Jerusalem in 586 B.C.E. The text indicates that the Babylonians, referred to as the Chaldeans, are on the rise as a threatening world power (Habakkuk 1:6). This context aligns well with the rise of the Neo-Babylonian Empire under Nabopolassar and his son Nebuchadnezzar II, which suggests a period of prophecy most likely between 612 B.C.E., when the Babylonians overthrew Nineveh, and 586 B.C.E., when they conquered Jerusalem.

Prophet of Deep Spiritual Insight

While biographical details are scant, the nature of Habakkuk's dialogue with Jehovah reveals him as a man of deep spiritual concern and intellectual engagement. His questioning and probing dialogue with God indicate a pursuit for understanding that is more intense and philosophical than typically found in prophetic literature. The kind of questions he raises about justice, suffering, and the nature of God's sovereignty show him to be a prophet who not only serves as a mouthpiece of Jehovah but also as a thinker engaging with the most profound questions of his time.

Significance of the Name

The name "Habakkuk" itself is believed to be derived from the Hebrew root "ḥābaq," which means "to embrace" or "to clasp." The name is apt, given that the central theme of the book is a wrestling with theological and existential questions, much as one might "embrace" or "wrestle with" a difficult problem or reality. It also reflects the prophet's ultimate stance of embracing faith in Jehovah, even in the face of troubling questions and future calamities.

Circumstances Affecting Judah Indicating the Time of Writing of Habakkuk

Habakkuk's prophecy is set against a backdrop of looming crisis and a volatile international stage that offers clues about its timing. The book makes specific mention of the Chaldeans, also known as the Babylonians, describing them as a "bitter and hasty nation" (Habakkuk 1:6). The description indicates that Babylon was on the rise as a dominant world power, threatening the existing geopolitical structures and particularly menacing for Judah. This accords with the late 7th century B.C.E., particularly the period after the fall of Nineveh in 612 B.C.E., when the Neo-Babylonian Empire emerged as a significant power in the ancient Near East.

Internal Evidence from Habakkuk

The internal issues within Judah also provide a temporal context for the book. Habakkuk begins his book by lamenting the violence, iniquity, and corruption he sees in Judah (Habakkuk 1:2-4). These circumstances correspond to the spiritual and moral decline that characterized the later years of the kingdom of Judah, leading up to its downfall.

The Theological Context

Habakkuk's theological concerns are centered on justice and the apparent triumph of wickedness, both within Judah and in the international arena. He openly questions Jehovah about why He allows evil to flourish, both among His own people and in the empires that oppress them (Habakkuk 1:13). This line of questioning suggests a time of significant existential crisis for the people of Judah, caught between their own internal failures and an external existential threat, which would be consistent with the decades leading up to the Babylonian exile.

Political Background

The political environment of Judah was marked by significant instability and fear of invasion during the period leading up to the Babylonian exile. After the death of Josiah at Megiddo in 609 B.C.E., Judah became increasingly subject to foreign powers, including Egypt and Babylon. This political vulnerability coincides with the moral and spiritual questions raised in the book, making it likely that Habakkuk was writing during this period of national decline and insecurity.

Evidence for the Divine Inspiration of the Book of Habakkuk

The book of Habakkuk carries multiple indicators that attest to its divine inspiration. Here are the key points:

Prophetic Accuracy

One of the most compelling indicators is the prophetic accuracy contained in the book. Habakkuk foretells the rise of the Babylonians and their role as an instrument of divine judgement (Habakkuk 1:6). This prophecy was fulfilled with historical precision when the Babylonians sacked Jerusalem in 586 B.C.E.

Theological Depth

The book of Habakkuk tackles some of the most profound theological questions that have puzzled humanity, particularly the problem of evil and why a just God would allow suffering. The answers given align with the broader scriptural teaching, demonstrating a consistency that goes beyond mere human wisdom. Habakkuk comes to recognize that the righteous shall live by faith (Habakkuk 2:4), a principle later cited by the Apostle Paul in Romans 1:17, Galatians 3:11, and Hebrews 10:38, thus tying both Testaments together in a coherent theological framework.

Internal Consistency

The book maintains an internal consistency, not only within its own text but also when compared to other prophetic writings and the wider corpus of Scripture. For instance, its description of the Babylonians and their role in divine judgment is congruent with the portrayal found in other prophetic books like Jeremiah and Isaiah.

The Principle of Harmony

The messages in the book of Habakkuk are in perfect harmony with other inspired writings. There is no contradiction in terms of doctrine, prophecy, or historical accounts when compared with other parts of Scripture. This harmonious interrelationship further validates its divine origin.

Presence in Canonical Lists and Early Manuscripts

The book of Habakkuk is included in all the ancient canonical lists, such as those by Josephus and the Councils of Hippo and Carthage, indicating its acceptance among the early Jews and the Christian community. It is also part of the Septuagint and was among the texts found in the Dead Sea Scrolls, adding to its historical credibility and acceptance as inspired text.

Liturgical and Scholarly Usage

Throughout history, Habakkuk has been cited and used in Jewish liturgical practices as well as by early church fathers. It was studied and commented upon as authoritative Scripture, further affirming its recognized inspiration and divine authority.

Existential and Moral Relevance

The book's lasting impact on ethical and existential queries attests to a wisdom beyond human capability. Its teachings have universal applicability, lending itself to the betterment of moral understanding and the human condition across different cultures and times.

Divine Judgment and Sovereignty

Finally, the book emphasizes Jehovah's sovereign control over nations and history for His purposes, including the raising up and putting down of empires. Such a high view of divine sovereignty aligns with the rest of Scripture and further supports its divine inspiration.

Contents of the Book of Habakkuk Summarized

The book of Habakkuk, comprising just three chapters, unfolds as a dialogue between the prophet and Jehovah. Written likely between 612-605 B.C.E., during the period leading up to the Babylonian captivity, the book addresses profound questions about divine justice and human suffering.

Chapter 1: Divine Justice Questioned

In the first chapter, Habakkuk opens with a lament, questioning why Jehovah allows wickedness and injustice to persist in Judah. He is deeply troubled by the rampant sin among his people. Jehovah responds by declaring that He will send the Babylonians, a fierce and swift nation, to execute judgment on Judah. This answer further perplexes Habakkuk, who then questions how a just God could use a wicked nation like Babylon as an instrument of judgment.

Chapter 2: Jehovah's Answer and Five Woes

Jehovah instructs Habakkuk to write down the vision, assuring him that its fulfillment is certain, though it may tarry. Jehovah responds to Habakkuk's inquiry by affirming that the just will live by faith. He also pronounces five "woes" against the Babylonians, warning that they, too, will face divine judgment for their wickedness. This includes their greed, injustice, violence, and idolatry.

Chapter 3: A Prayer and Hymn of Faith

The final chapter is a psalm where Habakkuk praises Jehovah for His majesty and might as displayed in His past acts of salvation for His people. Although the prophet acknowledges the looming judgment, he expresses unwavering faith in Jehovah's plan and sovereignty. The book concludes with Habakkuk affirming his trust in Jehovah, even if calamity should strike and provisions should fail.

Authenticity, Authorship, and Date of Zephaniah

Zephaniah's Message and Its Timeliness

The prophetic message of Zephaniah was exceedingly appropriate to his time. Written during the reign of King Josiah of Judah, around 640-609 B.C.E., Zephaniah spoke against the pervasive idolatry and social injustice that plagued the Kingdom of Judah. Despite the spiritual revival led by King Josiah, it was evident that the corruption and apostasy had deep roots, requiring stern divine correction. Zephaniah's prophecy served as a grim warning to Judah of the impending judgment, known as the "Day of Jehovah," and a call to repentance. This message resonated powerfully at a time when moral and spiritual decay had reached critical levels, and the Babylonian threat was looming larger on the horizon.

Significance of Zephaniah's Name

The meaning of the name Zephaniah is "Jehovah Hides" or "Jehovah Has Hidden," which poignantly fits the situation. In the climate of impending judgment, the name could imply that Jehovah would hide or protect a remnant during the period of chastisement, consistent with Zephaniah 2:3. Alternatively, the name could be seen as a warning: that Jehovah, who had been patient, would soon hide His face and execute judgment, in accord with divine justice. In either interpretation, Zephaniah's name encapsulated the essence of his message and the impending dynamics between Jehovah and His covenant people.

Zephaniah's message and the meaning of his name synergistically acted to stress the urgency and gravity of the time, thus making his prophecy highly pertinent to the sociopolitical and spiritual conditions of Judah. It was a call for self-examination, repentance, and a return to Jehovah to avert total disaster, precisely what was needed given the state of decay in which Judah found itself.

Zephaniah's Impact and Its Temporary Nature

Zephaniah's prophetic efforts did bear significant fruit, particularly when considered within the larger context of King Josiah's reign. Josiah initiated a spiritual revival in Judah, which involved a series of religious reforms aimed at removing idolatry and reestablishing the worship of Jehovah (2 Kings 22-23). Zephaniah's messages would have reinforced these reforms by providing divine urgency and substantiating the call for immediate change. We can observe the synchronization of Zephaniah's core messages with Josiah's actions, especially in the removal of idols, Baals, and Asherah poles. The message of impending doom unless repentance was enacted would have provided a powerful moral and theological underpinning for Josiah's reforms.

Temporary Nature of the Impact

However, the positive impact was sadly short-lived. Despite Josiah's efforts and the warnings issued through prophets like Zephaniah, the deep-seated corruption and apostasy were not entirely eradicated. After Josiah's untimely death in battle at Megiddo in 609 B.C.E., his successors quickly reverted to idolatrous practices and ignored the covenantal relationship with Jehovah. Kings like Jehoahaz, Jehoiakim, and Zedekiah led the nation back into the kinds of practices that Zephaniah had vehemently condemned.

This rapid decline culminated in the Babylonian invasion and the eventual destruction of Jerusalem in 586 B.C.E., effectively fulfilling the prophecies concerning Judah's judgment. It underscores the temporary nature of the reform; although there was a surface-level compliance during Josiah's reign, the heart of the nation had not fully turned back to Jehovah. The reforms did not achieve a lasting transformation, proving that the people's repentance and commitment were not deeply rooted.

Time and Location of Zephaniah's Prophecy

Zephaniah prophesied during the reign of King Josiah of Judah, specifically between 640 and 609 B.C.E. His ministry likely occurred in the early part of Josiah's reign, before the king initiated his well-known religious reforms. As a prophet in Judah, the focus of Zephaniah's ministry was Jerusalem and the surrounding areas, which were the center of political and religious activities at the time.

Twofold Message of the Book

The Book of Zephaniah contains a twofold message: one of impending judgment and another of future restoration.

1. **Impending Judgment**: The initial chapters of the book outline the dire judgments that are to come upon Judah and Jerusalem if they continue in their ways of idolatry and disobedience to Jehovah. Zephaniah describes this coming time as a "day of Jehovah's wrath" where not only Judah but also surrounding nations will be punished for their wickedness (Zephaniah 1:14-18; 2:4-15). His message serves as a divine wake-up call for the nation to turn from its sin.

2. **Future Restoration**: As with many of the Minor Prophets, the book doesn't end on a note of utter despair. The final portion of Zephaniah's prophecy (Chapter 3:9-20) shifts to a message of hope, highlighting Jehovah's plans for the restoration of His people. This is not just spiritual restoration but also involves returning from captivity and having their fortunes restored. Zephaniah reveals that after the period of judgment, Jehovah will purify His people and create a righteous remnant.

The twofold message is crucial for understanding the complexity of Jehovah's relationship with His people. On the one hand, there is the unyielding justice of God who cannot tolerate sin; on the other, there is the unfailing love of God who promises to restore and bless those who return to Him. This balance exemplifies the multifaceted character of Jehovah, blending justice with mercy, and judgment with restoration.

Internal Consistency and Prophetic Accuracy

One of the first indicators of Zephaniah's authenticity and divine inspiration is the internal consistency of the text. The message flows logically from judgment to redemption, congruent with the overall message of the Scriptures. The prophecy aligns well with historical events and religious practices of the time, lending credibility to its claims.

Archaeological Corroborations

Archaeological findings, including those that corroborate the existence of King Josiah, add another layer of verification to the book's authenticity. The social and religious context in which Zephaniah prophesied is confirmed through these historical artifacts, strengthening the book's position as a genuine document from that era.

Canonical Acceptance

The Book of Zephaniah has been universally accepted into the canon of the Hebrew Bible, and later, the Christian Old Testament. The Jews, who were meticulous in their preservation of Scripture, recognized this book as carrying the weight of divine inspiration. Furthermore, the early church fathers cited Zephaniah, and it has been included in the various lists and codices that form our current Old Testament.

Harmony with Broader Scriptural Themes

The book is in complete harmony with broader Scriptural teachings, particularly those concerning Jehovah's justice and mercy. It doesn't introduce any new or contradictory doctrine but rather supplements what is already understood about God's character and His covenant relationship with His people. This unity of teaching confirms its place within the inspired texts.

Theological Depth and Timelessness

The theology presented in Zephaniah is neither shallow nor bound by time. While its immediate context is Judah in the 7th century B.C.E., the themes are applicable universally and across time. The judgments announced and the salvation promised are echoed in later prophetic literature and are ultimately fulfilled in various ways throughout Biblical history. The timelessness of the message serves as a testament to its divine origin.

Fulfilled Prophecies

The accuracy of the prophecies concerning the judgment of Judah and the surrounding nations, many of which have been historically fulfilled, further substantiates the book's divine inspiration. The unfolding of events, as foretold by Zephaniah, showcases the reliability of the text and its divine origin.

Historical Fulfillment of Zephaniah's Prophecies

Zephaniah prophesied during a time of religious decline in Judah, setting the stage for the divine judgments that were to follow. His prophecies can be broadly categorized into those concerning Judah and Jerusalem and those concerning foreign nations. In both categories, we find evidence of accurate fulfillment.

Judgment on Judah and Jerusalem

Zephaniah predicted severe judgment upon Judah and Jerusalem because of their idolatry, injustice, and moral degradation. His prophecies came to pass when Nebuchadnezzar, king of Babylon, conquered Jerusalem in 587/586 B.C.E. The city was razed, the Temple was destroyed, and the people were led into exile. This catastrophic event was a direct fulfillment of Zephaniah's predictions about divine wrath against Judah for its apostasy and sins.

Judgment on Foreign Nations

The book also contains prophecies against foreign nations such as Philistia, Moab, Ammon, Assyria, and Cush. Subsequent to Zephaniah's time, these nations indeed experienced judgment and downfall. Assyria, one of the world's most formidable powers at the time, was conquered by the Babylonians in 612 B.C.E., fulfilling Zephaniah's prophecies concerning its demise. Philistia, Moab, and Ammon were also subdued and absorbed into larger empires, as foretold.

Restoration and Hope

Amidst the pronouncements of judgment, Zephaniah also spoke of a future restoration for the faithful remnant. Historically, this prophecy was partially fulfilled when the exiles returned from Babylon and rebuilt Jerusalem and the Temple. This period of restoration provided an initial, partial fulfillment of Zephaniah's prophecy and can also be seen as a foreshadowing of the ultimate restoration through the Messiah.

Theological Harmony

It is worth mentioning that Zephaniah's prophecies are theologically harmonious with the wider Scriptural message. The pattern of sin, judgment, and divine intervention that he describes is consistent with the historical pattern demonstrated throughout the Scriptures. His words not only came true but also served as a typology for divine patterns of judgment and redemption.

Corroborating Historical Records

Extra-Biblical historical records and archaeological discoveries provide independent verification of the conditions and events described in Zephaniah. For example, cuneiform texts and archaeological evidence support the accounts of the fall of Assyria and Babylon.

Zephaniah's Rightful Place in the Canon of Scripture

Zephaniah's book unquestionably takes its rightful place in the canon of Scripture for several compelling reasons:

Historical Accuracy

First and foremost, the book of Zephaniah accurately portrays the socio-religious context of its time. Its detailed account of the conditions in Judah, as well as the fates of surrounding nations, aligns with historical data. The book's prophecies were also precisely fulfilled, as mentioned in the previous discussion.

Theological Consistency

Zephaniah is theologically consistent with the rest of Scripture. The book presents Jehovah as the one true God who will judge sin but will also provide redemption for His faithful remnant. This dual focus on divine justice and mercy resonates with the larger Scriptural narrative, thereby validating its canonicity.

Prophetic Authenticity

Zephaniah himself stands as a true prophet of Jehovah. His prophecies were not just general or vague utterances but specific declarations that were subsequently fulfilled. This fulfills the biblical test for prophethood laid out in Deuteronomy 18:22, which states that a prophecy must come true for a prophet to be considered genuine.

Early Recognition and Acceptance

The book of Zephaniah was recognized early on by the religious community as an authoritative work. The Hebrew Bible includes Zephaniah in its collection of the Twelve Minor Prophets, a placement that signals its acceptance as canonical by the Jewish community of the time.

Inspired Writing

The literary and theological depth of the book indicates divine inspiration. Zephaniah uses vivid imagery and language to describe the divine judgments and future hope. His language echoes the divine attributes of justice and mercy, qualities that are found throughout the Scriptures.

Contribution to the Full Counsel of God

Finally, Zephaniah contributes to the "full counsel of God" (Acts 20:27). It serves as an indispensable component of Biblical eschatology, helping to round out our understanding of end-time events and the ultimate fulfillment of divine justice and redemption.

Given these substantial reasons—historical accuracy, theological consistency, prophetic authenticity, early recognition and acceptance, inspired writing, and its contribution to the full counsel of God—Zephaniah takes its rightful and unassailable place in the canon of Scripture.

Edward D. Andrews

CHAPTER 13 Defending Haggai, Zechariah, and Malachi

Authenticity, Authorship, and Date of Haggai

Prophet Haggai and His Twofold Message

Biographical Information About Haggai

Haggai is one of the post-exilic prophets who lived and ministered during the time when the Israelites had returned to Judah from Babylonian exile. The book itself provides specific dates for his prophecies, the first of which was given in the sixth month of the second year of King Darius (Haggai 1:1), around 520 B.C.E. Though little is known about Haggai's personal life, his timely messages played a critical role in the rebuilding of the temple in Jerusalem, which had languished incomplete due to various obstacles and the lethargy of the people.

Haggai's Twofold Message

Haggai had a focused, twofold message:

1. **Rebuild the Temple:** Haggai's primary message was a call to the returned exiles to prioritize the rebuilding of Jehovah's temple in Jerusalem. The people had been neglectful, attending to their own houses while the house of God lay in ruins (Haggai 1:4). Haggai condemned this negligence, equating the people's lack of blessings with their failure to rebuild the temple (Haggai 1:5–11).

2. **Divine Blessing Follows Obedience:** The second part of Haggai's message was a promise of divine blessings that would

follow the people's obedience. Once the people resumed work on the temple, Haggai assured them that Jehovah was with them (Haggai 1:13). Moreover, the glory of the second temple would surpass that of Solomon's temple, and it would become a place filled with divine peace (Haggai 2:9).

The brilliance of Haggai's message lay in its urgent simplicity. He minced no words in calling out the misplaced priorities of the people and used pointed questions to stir their conscience. Through a combination of rebuke and promise, Haggai successfully motivated the people to resume the temple's construction, thus fulfilling their religious and national responsibility.

Historical Background of the Prophet Haggai

The Context of the Babylonian Exile and Return

To fully comprehend the significance of Haggai's prophetic ministry, it is essential to understand the historical context in which he operated. Haggai was a post-exilic prophet, meaning he prophesied after the Babylonian exile. The Israelites had been in Babylonian captivity for about 70 years, as foretold by the prophet Jeremiah (Jeremiah 25:11). In 539 B.C.E., Babylon fell to the Persians under Cyrus the Great, who subsequently issued a decree allowing the Jews to return to Judah and rebuild the temple (Ezra 1:1-4).

Initial Enthusiasm and Subsequent Apathy

When the first group of exiles returned under the leadership of Zerubbabel and Joshua the High Priest, initial efforts were made to rebuild the temple. They even laid the foundation. However, due to opposition from surrounding peoples and a sense of complacency among the returnees, the work halted. The temple lay unfinished, and the people focused instead on their personal affairs, building their own homes and neglecting the house of Jehovah.

The Time of Haggai's Ministry

Haggai began his ministry in the second year of King Darius, specifically in the sixth month of that year (Haggai 1:1). This places his prophetic activity around 520 B.C.E. The dating is precise and allows us to situate Haggai in a very specific historical context, making his message even more pointed.

Political and Religious Atmosphere

During Haggai's time, the Persian Empire was stable under the rule of Darius I, yet the Jews in Jerusalem faced internal and external challenges. Externally, they had to contend with opposition from neighboring peoples. Internally, they were suffering from a spiritual malaise, having grown complacent and self-focused.

Convergence with Other Prophets

Haggai wasn't alone in his prophetic ministry during this period. Zechariah was his contemporary, and both prophets worked in tandem to encourage the Jews to complete the temple's rebuilding. Their ministries are complementary, and their messages were aimed at galvanizing the Jewish community toward fulfilling their religious responsibilities.

Failure to Grasp the Purpose of Return from Exile

Diverted Priorities

Upon their return from Babylonian exile, the Jews began rebuilding their lives in the land of Judah. The initial enthusiasm for rebuilding the temple, however, was quickly replaced by personal pursuits. In this period, the people prioritized their own homes and well-being over the reconstruction of the temple. This is evident in Haggai 1:4, which says, "Is it a time for you yourselves to dwell in your paneled houses, while this house lies in ruins?"

Misunderstanding of the Divine Mandate

The returnees failed to recognize that their return from exile was not merely a chance to rebuild their own lives but was, in fact, a divine mandate to first and foremost rebuild the temple of Jehovah. This was the primary reason Jehovah had permitted their return; they were to reestablish true worship in Jerusalem by reconstructing the temple.

Spiritual Apathy

A lack of urgency in reconstructing the temple was symptomatic of a deeper spiritual apathy. The people had not fully grasped that the state of the temple was a reflection of their relationship with Jehovah. This spiritual lethargy had material consequences, which Haggai points out in Haggai 1:5–6: "Now, therefore, thus says Jehovah of hosts: Consider your ways. You have sown much, and harvested little. You eat, but you never have enough; you drink, but you never have your fill. You clothe yourselves, but no one is warm. And he who earns wages does so to put them into a bag with holes."

Misalignment with Prophetic Guidance

The prophets Haggai and Zechariah were sent to correct this misunderstanding and guide the people toward fulfilling the divine mandate. They were not merely social reformers but spiritual leaders who were urging the people to align themselves with Jehovah's purposes. Ignoring this prophetic guidance indicated a misalignment of priorities and a disregard for the reason Jehovah had permitted their return.

Failure to Recognize Covenantal Responsibilities

The Jews had a covenantal responsibility to Jehovah, which included the proper worship of Him in a temple that served as the spiritual center of the nation. By neglecting this duty, they had essentially forgotten the conditions under which Jehovah had restored them to their land.

Factors Hindering the Temple Building

Political Interference and Opposition

The Jews encountered considerable opposition from their neighbors when they initially returned to rebuild the temple. According to Ezra 4:1–5, the adversaries managed to "frustrate their purpose" during the entire reign of Cyrus and into the reign of Darius. Various political maneuvers, including false reports sent to the Persian court, halted the temple's construction.

Economic Hardship

Economic challenges also served as a deterrent to building the temple. Resources were scarce, and the people found themselves struggling to maintain even their own households. This economic hardship was exploited as a justification for not prioritizing the temple.

Spiritual Lethargy and Misplaced Priorities

As I have previously noted, the primary impediment to rebuilding the temple was the spiritual lethargy of the people themselves. Their attention had turned to their own affairs—building their own homes and tending to their own fields—while neglecting the temple of Jehovah.

Impact of Haggai's Prophecy on Temple Building

Immediate Response to the Prophetic Message

Haggai's arrival on the prophetic scene was a catalyst for change. When he began to prophesy in the second year of Darius the king, 520 B.C.E., there was an immediate shift in the people's attitudes and priorities. Haggai 1:12 records the reaction: "Then Zerubbabel the son of Shealtiel, and Joshua the son of Jehozadak, the high priest, with all the remnant of the people, obeyed the voice of Jehovah their God, and the words of Haggai the prophet, as Jehovah their God had sent him. And the people feared Jehovah."

Restarting the Construction

Haggai's words had an electrifying effect on the leadership and the people. The Scripture records that construction resumed just 23 days after Haggai's first prophetic message. This is evident from the dating given in Haggai 1:15: "In the twenty-fourth day of the month, in the sixth month." This implies that the people responded swiftly to the prophetic call to resume work.

Divine Blessing and Encouragement

With the resumption of construction came divine encouragement and blessings. Haggai's subsequent prophecies assured the people that

Jehovah was with them (Haggai 1:13). He promised to fill the temple with glory and to bring peace to the land (Haggai 2:7–9).

The Role of Leadership

The leadership, especially Zerubbabel and Joshua, played a pivotal role in this turnaround. Their obedience to the prophetic word galvanized the community into action, highlighting the importance of godly leadership in achieving divine objectives.

The Canonical Status of the Book of Haggai

Divine Authority and Prophecy

One of the most compelling proofs of Haggai's canonical status is the claim within the text that the messages are directly from Jehovah. The frequent phrase "the word of Jehovah came by Haggai the prophet" (Haggai 1:1; 2:1, 10) strongly indicates divine origin. Furthermore, the book details prophecies that were fulfilled in a manner consistent with Jehovah's actions, thereby confirming divine authority.

Historical Accuracy

The book of Haggai is precise in its historical details, including its dating, which aligns with known historical events. Haggai prophesied during the reign of Darius, who ruled from 522 to 486 B.C.E., fitting into the historical framework and proving its authenticity. The accurate rendering of historical facts lends credence to its canonical status.

Consistency with Established Canon

The messages and themes of Haggai are in harmony with the theological and ethical norms presented in the established canonical books. The centrality of the temple, the call for obedience to Jehovah, and the promise of divine blessing upon compliance are consistent with the teachings found in the Torah and the other prophetic writings.

Recognition by Later Scripture and Writers

The prophetic ministry of Haggai is acknowledged in other parts of the Bible. Ezra 5:1 and 6:14 confirm Haggai's role, along with

Zechariah, in the rebuilding of the temple. These external references to Haggai within the corpus of the Scriptures validate its canonical status.

Preservation and Transmission

The book of Haggai has been meticulously preserved and transmitted as part of the Hebrew Bible. Its presence in the Septuagint, the ancient Greek translation of the Hebrew Scriptures, also attests to its acceptance in early Judaism as a part of the sacred canon.

Acceptance by the Community of Faith

Finally, the book of Haggai has been universally accepted by both the Jewish and the Christian communities as a divinely inspired text. This long-standing consensus confirms the book's place within the canon of Scripture.

Content and Emphasis on Jehovah's Name in Haggai's Prophecy

Prophecy's Core Content

The prophecy of Haggai comprises four distinct messages, each aimed at the rebuilding of the temple in Jerusalem. These messages were delivered within a span of approximately four months, from the sixth to the ninth month of the second year of King Darius, which corresponds to the year 520 B.C.E.

1. **The Call to Rebuild the Temple**: The first message (Haggai 1:1-15) emphasizes that the people should put Jehovah first and cease neglecting the temple's construction. They had prioritized their own homes while the temple lay in ruins. This neglect had resulted in divine disfavor, manifesting as crop failures and economic hardships.

2. **Assurance of Jehovah's Presence**: In the second message (Haggai 2:1-9), Jehovah assures the people that although the new temple might appear inferior to Solomon's temple, He would still be present among them. Moreover, the future glory of the temple would exceed its former glory.

3. **Purification and Blessing**: The third message (Haggai 2:10-19) addresses ritual purity and teaches that holiness is not transferable whereas uncleanness is. Jehovah promises to bless them from that day forward if they are obedient.

4. **Zerubbabel, the Signet Ring**: The fourth and final message (Haggai 2:20-23) promises divine judgment on the nations and establishes Zerubbabel as Jehovah's "signet ring," denoting him as a chosen servant through whom Jehovah will accomplish His purposes.

Emphasis on Jehovah's Name

The emphasis on Jehovah's name is highly conspicuous throughout the prophecy. The name is invoked repeatedly as the source of the prophecy and the commands therein. Haggai serves merely as a messenger, with statements such as "the word of Jehovah came by Haggai the prophet" making it clear that the directives are not human but divine in origin (Haggai 1:1; 2:1, 10, 20). The constant invocation of Jehovah's name emphasizes His role in the events being described and underscores that the temple building isn't a mere architectural project but a task with profound spiritual implications. Jehovah's name being emphasized serves as an indicator of divine authority, sanctioning the prophecy and commands.

Therefore, the content of Haggai's prophecy is structured around the urgent need to rebuild the temple and return to spiritual priorities. This focus is intricately bound to the name of Jehovah, affirming His sovereignty, presence, and intentions for His people.

Haggai's Encouragement and the Tenor of His Message

Call to Action

Haggai's core encouragement to the Jews was straightforward: **Rebuild the Temple**. He presented this directive as an immediate obligation, not just a religious duty but a divine mandate. The people had been dwelling in their paneled houses while the house of Jehovah remained in ruins (Haggai 1:4). This was unacceptable. In failing to rebuild the temple, the Jews were essentially sidelining Jehovah and, as a result, were suffering from His withdrawal of blessing, which manifested in various forms such as crop failure and economic downturn (Haggai 1:6, 9-11).

Promises and Warnings

Haggai didn't just command; he also promised. He assured the Jews that upon their obedience, Jehovah would bless them (Haggai 2:19). This positive reinforcement would have served as a strong motivational factor for the people. But Haggai also balanced the promises with warnings: failure to heed Jehovah's command would lead to continued hardship and divine displeasure (Haggai 1:6, 9-11).

Divine Affirmation

In the second message, Haggai seeks to uplift the disheartened Jews by reminding them that Jehovah is with them (Haggai 2:4). Although they were discouraged due to the temple's diminished grandeur compared to Solomon's temple, Jehovah assures them that the glory of the latter house would be greater than the former (Haggai 2:9).

Tenor of the Message

The tenor of Haggai's message is one of **urgent exhortation** but also of **reassurance**. He employs a rhetorical style that is confrontational but not condemning, authoritative yet uplifting. It is as if Haggai is shaking the Jews from a spiritual stupor, urging them to recognize their misplaced priorities and to rectify them immediately. While he does pinpoint their shortcomings, he also ensures to convey Jehovah's promises, thereby injecting hope into what might otherwise seem like a bleak exhortation.

Haggai is consistently concrete, tangible, and practical in his messaging. There are no abstract theological dissertations; it's all about action, outcomes, and Jehovah's direct response. Jehovah is presented as intimately involved in the affairs of His people, actively shaping their conditions based on their obedience or lack thereof.

Authenticity, Authorship, and Date of Zechariah

Temple Situation When Zechariah Began to Prophesy

Stalled Construction and Spiritual Apathy

When Zechariah began his prophetic ministry around 520 B.C.E., the Second Temple's construction in Jerusalem had come to a standstill. It had been nearly two decades since the Jews returned from the Babylonian exile in 538 B.C.E., and despite initial enthusiasm and partial construction (Ezra 3:8-13), the work had been halted.

This cessation was due to a variety of factors, including external opposition from surrounding nations and internal discouragement among the Jewish people themselves. Many Jews who had seen the first temple lamented the diminished grandeur of what was being built (Ezra 3:12). As a result, they had shifted their focus from rebuilding Jehovah's house to attending to their own homes and well-being (Haggai 1:4). This led to a form of spiritual apathy and lethargy, where the mandate to rebuild the temple was marginalized.

Political Context

Further complicating the situation was the political landscape. The decree of Cyrus had initially permitted the Jews to return and rebuild (Ezra 1:2-4), but the subsequent rulers were not as favorable. Opposition came in various forms, including letters to King Artaxerxes that led to a formal order to stop the construction (Ezra 4:6-24).

Zechariah's Entry

Thus, when Zechariah arrived on the prophetic scene, he entered into a context of physical inaction, spiritual despondency, and external antagonism. His ministry closely paralleled that of Haggai, both prophets sharing the objective of galvanizing the Jews towards resuming the temple construction.

The Mountainous Task and Zechariah's Response

Perceived Insurmountable Challenges

The task of rebuilding the temple seemed mountainous to the Jewish returnees for several reasons. First, the resources were limited, as many of the Jews had returned with only modest means. Second, there was significant local opposition, manifesting both politically and socially, which discouraged the Jews and led to the cessation of work. Third, the spirit of the people was dampened due to the lack of progress and the seemingly unsurmountable obstacles. Those who had seen the glory of Solomon's temple doubted that the new temple could ever compare (Ezra 3:12).

Zechariah's Visionary Focus

In this context, Zechariah employed vivid imagery and direct divine communication to refocus the people's attention. In Zechariah 4:6-10, he relayed Jehovah's message to Zerubbabel, stating, "*Not by power, nor by might, but by my Spirit, says Jehovah of hosts.*" The message clarified that human inadequacy was not an obstacle for Jehovah. Furthermore, Zechariah drew attention to the finishing of the foundation by Zerubbabel and used the metaphor of the plumb line (Zechariah 4:10) as a symbol of accuracy, justice, and the imminent completion of the temple.

The Great Mountain and the Capstone

Importantly, Zechariah likened the challenges to a "great mountain" but stated unequivocally that this mountain would become a "plain" before Zerubbabel (Zechariah 4:7). By this, Zechariah drew their attention to the omnipotence of Jehovah, who could flatten mountains and elevate valleys. The laying of the capstone amid shouts of "Grace, grace to it!" (Zechariah 4:7) was not merely an optimistic future event but a sure promise anchored in Jehovah's faithfulness.

Zechariah's prophetic ministry was pivotal in shifting the focus from what seemed like a mountainous task to the limitless power and faithfulness of Jehovah. He used vivid imagery and prophetic assurance to ignite a renewed sense of purpose, underscoring that with

Jehovah's backing, no obstacle was insurmountable. The ultimate aim was to assure the people that Jehovah was fully invested in the completion of His temple and that they were instruments in fulfilling His divine purpose.

Identification of Zechariah and the Appropriateness of His Name

Zechariah is identified as the son of Berechiah, the son of Iddo the prophet. He is explicitly called a prophet, setting him apart as a divinely ordained messenger (Zechariah 1:1). His lineage indicates that he comes from a family steeped in spiritual service; his grandfather Iddo was among those who returned from the Babylonian exile with Zerubbabel (Nehemiah 12:4).

The name "Zechariah" means "Jehovah Remembers," which is exceedingly fitting for the role he assumes and the period in which he prophesies. At a time when the Israelites could feel forgotten due to their hardships and the delayed temple construction, Zechariah's name alone was a message of hope. The name underscored that Jehovah had not forgotten His promises nor His people.

Chronological Context of Zechariah's Prophecy

Zechariah's prophecies were spoken and recorded during a specific period following the return from the Babylonian exile. The book opens with a clear chronological marker: "*In the eighth month, in the second year of Darius, the word of Jehovah came to Zechariah the prophet, the son of Berechiah, son of Iddo*" (Zechariah 1:1). Utilizing a conservative Bible chronology, the second year of Darius can be dated to approximately **520 B.C.E.** This date places Zechariah's prophetic activities in the same period as Haggai, specifically during the rebuilding phase of the temple in Jerusalem.

Zechariah's prophecies are both timely and timeless. They addressed immediate concerns, namely, the rebuilding of the temple, but they also spoke of future events involving the messianic kingdom. The dating of the book adds to the legitimacy and significance of his message. His words come at a time when the Jewish community was in dire need of both physical and spiritual rejuvenation, and his prophecies served to encourage, correct, and motivate the Jews in their divine mission.

Challenging the Disunity of Zechariah: A Rebuttal to Pre-Exilic and Post-Alexandrian Theories

The Pre-Exilic Theory: A Misreading of the Text?

1. **Matthew's Citation and Jeremiah:** The claim that Zechariah 11:12–13 should be attributed to the time of Jeremiah due to its mention in Matthew 27:9–10 misunderstands Matthew's composite quoting. Matthew synthesizes elements from both Jeremiah and Zechariah, an approach not uncommon in New Testament quoting practices. To pin the date of Zechariah 11 solely based on this would be a misinterpretation.

2. **Geopolitical Evidence and Syria:** The argument that Zechariah 9:1–2 necessarily precedes the conquest of Syria by Tiglath-pileser in 732 B.C.E. is flawed. These places could have had significant future roles even while under Persian rule. They indeed faced judgment during Alexander the Great's invasion in 332 B.C.E., supporting a later dating.

3. **Judah and Israel Reunification:** Claims that Zechariah 11:14 was written before the fall of Samaria due to its focus on Judah and Israel's possible reunification are weak. Postexilic texts, like Ezra 6:17 and 8:35, reveal that a conceptual reunification was already considered at the time of the Second Temple's dedication.

4. **The Assyrian Misconception:** Interpreting Zechariah 10:10–11 as pre-exilic due to its mention of Assyria is unwarranted. Assyria, in this context, serves as a geographical marker for future world powers, not a current political entity.

5. **The Issue of Idolatry:** Arguments that Zechariah 10:1–4 must be pre-exilic because of its reference to idols and diviners miss the point. The text recalls Israel's past follies, serving as a warning against future transgressions.

The Post-Alexandrian Theory: A Slew of Assumptions

1. **The Greek Connection**: Zechariah 9:13's mention of the "sons of Greece" may not necessarily indicate a post-Alexander era. This can be viewed as predictive prophecy, especially given the historical context where Greece had defeated Xerxes in 480–479 B.C.E.

2. **Provinces and Alexander**: Just because Zechariah 9:1–2 refers to places conquered by Alexander doesn't mean the text is post-Alexandrian. Predictive prophecy, again, offers a more plausible explanation.

3. **The 'Good Shepherd'**: Post-Alexandrian dating based on identifying the "good shepherd" with historical figures such as Onias III or Onias IV hinges on speculative identifications and assumes linguistic uniformity between fifth-century and second-century B.C.E. Hebrew.

4. **Apocalyptic Tendencies**: Dating these chapters as late due to their apocalyptic elements leans on the problematic evolutionary scheme, which regards apocalypticism as a late stage in Jewish religion.

5. **Stylistic Differences**: Variations in language and style between Zechariah 9–14 and 1–8 may simply reflect the diverse literary forms and thematic focuses within a single book, not necessarily different authorship.

Conclusions

In sum, neither the pre-exilic nor the post-Alexandrian theories present compelling evidence for the disunity of Zechariah. Whether scrutinized through the lens of biblical citations, geopolitical contexts, or even stylistic elements, these theories operate on either shaky assumptions or misinterpretations. Therefore, a unity of authorship and a postexilic dating for the entire book remains the most plausible explanation.

Prediction of Tyre's Fall Post-Nebuchadnezzar's Siege

Zechariah's prophecy concerning Tyre is indeed noteworthy because it comes long after the city had already been besieged by Nebuchadnezzar. One might question why a prophecy would be given for an event that, on the surface, appeared to be past. However, it's essential to understand the historical and theological contexts. Nebuchadnezzar's siege did not result in the complete annihilation or irreversible downfall of Tyre. The city rebounded and continued to be a significant power in the region.

Zechariah's prophecy about Tyre (Zechariah 9:3-4) should be seen in the broader context of Jehovah's judgment on the nations that opposed His purposes for Israel. By prophesying Tyre's downfall long after Nebuchadnezzar's initial attack, Zechariah demonstrated that divine judgment was not a one-time event but an ongoing process. Tyre's resurgence as a power and its interactions with the post-exilic Israelite community would have made it a subject of concern and a fitting target for prophetic utterance.

Fulfilled Prophecies Confirming Inspiration

The proof of the inspiration of the book of Zechariah is most convincingly found in the accurate fulfillment of its prophecies. One of the most compelling is the prediction of the coming of the Messiah. Zechariah foretells that the King will come, "humble and mounted on a donkey" (Zechariah 9:9). This prophecy was precisely fulfilled in the triumphal entry of Jesus into Jerusalem, as accounted in all four Gospels (Matthew 21:1-11; Mark 11:1-11; Luke 19:28-44; John 12:12-19).

Another prophecy of note is the betrayal of Jesus for thirty pieces of silver (Zechariah 11:12-13). The Gospel accounts confirm that Judas Iscariot betrayed Jesus for this exact amount (Matthew 26:15). Moreover, the prophecy foretells the fate of this betrayal money: it was thrown into the house of Jehovah, to the potter. The fulfillment is seen in the Gospels when Judas throws the money into the temple, and it's used to buy a potter's field (Matthew 27:3-10).

Furthermore, Zechariah predicts the piercing of the Messiah: "*And I will pour out on the house of David and the inhabitants of Jerusalem a spirit of grace and pleas for mercy, so that, when they look on me, on him whom they have pierced, they shall mourn for him, as one mourns for an only child*" (Zechariah 12:10). This finds its fulfillment in the crucifixion of Jesus, where he is indeed pierced (John 19:34-37).

Change of Style in Zechariah from Chapter 9 Onward

The book of Zechariah displays a noticeable change in style and focus from chapter 9 onward. The first eight chapters are characterized by a series of eight visions and deal predominantly with immediate post-exilic issues, while chapters 9–14 lack these visions and turn their focus more squarely on the coming of the Messiah and the eschatological future of Israel.

This change can be attributed to the difference in subject matter and audience needs. The early chapters are primarily aimed at encouraging the people of Israel during their immediate post-exilic challenges. The visions are meant to assure them that Jehovah is on their side and will help them rebuild Jerusalem and the temple. In contrast, chapters 9–14 aim to provide a broader eschatological perspective that goes beyond immediate concerns. They offer an extended view of Israel's future under the Messiah and the ultimate triumph of Jehovah's people.

Matthew's Reference to "Jeremiah" Instead of Zechariah

In the New Testament, Matthew 27:9-10 cites a prophecy about thirty pieces of silver that, in content, resembles Zechariah 11:12-13 more closely than anything in the book of Jeremiah. However, Matthew attributes this prophecy to Jeremiah. There have been several scholarly theories proposed to account for this discrepancy.

One likely explanation is that in the Jewish arrangement of the Scriptures, the Book of Jeremiah comes first in the order of the Latter Prophets, followed by Ezekiel, Isaiah, and the Twelve Minor Prophets, including Zechariah. During this period, it was common to refer to the entire section of the Latter Prophets by the name of the book that was first in that collection. Therefore, when Matthew cites "Jeremiah," he may be referring to the section of the Hebrew Scriptures known as the Latter Prophets.

Another suggestion is that both Zechariah and Jeremiah spoke concerning similar themes such as the rejection of the shepherd figure and the ensuing calamities. It's possible that Matthew was engaging in a composite citation, pulling together elements from both prophets to make his point but attributed it to Jeremiah due to his more substantial prophetic stature.

In Summary

The shift in style in Zechariah from chapter 9 is due to the change in focus from immediate post-exilic concerns to a broader eschatological outlook, indicating that different segments of the book address different needs of the audience. As for Matthew's reference to Jeremiah instead of Zechariah, this could be understood either as a reference to the entire collection of the Latter Prophets, or as a composite citation that draws from the themes of both prophets. Both instances underscore the book's integrity and its crucial role in the Scriptural canon.

Structural Arrangement of the Book of Zechariah

The book of Zechariah is organized into two major sections. These two segments are distinguished not just by content but also by style, language, and focus, making for a complex yet unified composition.

1. **Chapters 1–8: Night Visions and Messages**
   - **1:1–6**: Introductory Call to Repentance
   - **1:7–6:15**: Eight Night Visions
     - Vision of the Horsemen (1:7–17)
     - Vision of the Horns and Craftsmen (1:18–21)
     - Vision of the Man with a Measuring Line (2:1–13)

- Vision of Joshua the High Priest (3:1–10)
- Vision of the Lampstand and Olive Trees (4:1–14)
- Vision of the Flying Scroll (5:1–4)
- Vision of the Woman in a Basket (5:5–11)
- Vision of the Four Chariots (6:1–8)
- **6:9–15**: Symbolic Crowning of Joshua
- **7:1–8:23**: Four Messages
  - Rebuke of Insincere Fasting (7:1–7)
  - Call to Justice and Mercy (7:8–14)
  - Promise of Restoration and Blessing (8:1–17)
  - Promise of Future Prosperity and Peace (8:18–23)

2. **Chapters 9–14: Oracles and Prophecies**
   - **9:1–11:17**: Judgment and Restoration Oracles
     - Judgment on Israel's Enemies (9:1–8)
     - Coming of Zion's King (9:9–17)
     - Jehovah as Shepherd (10:1–12)
     - Rejection of the Good Shepherd (11:1–17)
   - **12:1–14:21**: Eschatological Oracles
     - Jerusalem's Future Deliverance (12:1–9)
     - Mourning for the One Pierced (12:10–14)
     - Cleansing of Jerusalem (13:1–6)
     - Scattering and Regathering of the Flock (13:7–9)
     - The Day of Jehovah (14:1–21)

Each section serves a specific purpose. The first segment, including the night visions and four messages, focuses on the immediate context of the post-exilic community, urging them to rebuild the temple and re-establish their covenant relationship with Jehovah.

The second section, on the other hand, shifts its focus from the immediate concerns to future eschatological events. It provides a comprehensive eschatological framework, ranging from the judgment of the nations to the establishment of the Messianic Kingdom.

By scrutinizing the structure, one can see how Zechariah weaves together the immediate needs of the post-exilic community with the long-term eschatological promises. The book is intricately designed to address both immediate and future concerns, affirming Jehovah's sovereign control over history and the fulfillment of His promises.

Authenticity, Authorship, and Date of Malachi

Malachi's Zeal for Jehovah

The book of Malachi is infused with the prophet's intense zeal for Jehovah, a zeal that emanates from the text through various elements.

1. **Vehement Confrontation of Spiritual Laxity**
   - Malachi is unflinching in confronting the people and priests who were offering blemished sacrifices (Malachi 1:6–14). His criticism doesn't come from a place of contempt but rather from a profound concern for the sanctity of the worship of Jehovah.

2. **Unyielding Stand on Covenant Principles**
   - The prophet fervently admonishes the Israelites for marrying foreign women who serve other gods, thereby diluting the covenant community (Malachi 2:10–12).

3. **Defense of Jehovah's Character**
   - When the people question Jehovah's love, Malachi cites the historical narrative of Esau and Jacob to reaffirm Jehovah's unfailing love for Israel (Malachi 1:2–3).

4. **Robust Theology**
   - Malachi articulates a robust theology that includes the fear of Jehovah and the importance of the Law (Malachi 4:2–6). His declaration that "the sun of righteousness shall rise with healing in its wings" (Malachi 4:2) is an assertion of Jehovah's ultimate justice.

5. **Call to Return to Jehovah**
   - One of the most telling indicators of Malachi's zeal is his impassioned plea for the people to return to Jehovah (Malachi 3:7). Instead of writing off a wayward people, he extends Jehovah's own invitation for them to return.

6. **Focus on the Day of Jehovah**
   - Malachi ends his book with a vivid description of the coming "Day" when Jehovah will exercise judgment and purification (Malachi 4:1–3). This serves as a final warning to turn to Jehovah, underlining Malachi's zealous commitment to bringing his people into right relationship with their God.

7. **Exhortation for Proper Giving**
   - In challenging the Israelites to bring the full tithe into the storehouse, Malachi demonstrates a zealous desire for the people to trust Jehovah and to uphold His laws for their well-being (Malachi 3:10).

By challenging spiritual laxity, reaffirming the covenant, and exhorting the Israelites to honor Jehovah in all aspects of life, Malachi manifests a consuming zeal for Jehovah. This zeal is not mere emotional fervor but is deeply rooted in the Scripture, which makes it all the more compelling and convicting. His ardent desire is that Jehovah's name be honored and that His people live in a manner worthy of their calling.

Malachi's Name and Chronological Context

Meaning of Malachi's Name The name Malachi translates to "My Messenger" or "Messenger of Jehovah." This is remarkably fitting, given that the essential theme of his prophetic ministry was to act as Jehovah's messenger to call Israel back to faithfulness. The name itself speaks volumes about his prophetic role, primarily functioning as the intermediary between Jehovah and His wayward people.

Chronological Context of Malachi Malachi lived and prophesied during the post-exilic period, likely around the years 450–400 B.C.E. This time frame is deduced from several contextual indicators within the book itself as well as historical records.

1. **Post-Exilic Indicators**: Malachi addresses issues pertinent to a community that has returned from Babylonian exile. The Temple has been rebuilt, and the sacrifices have been resumed (Malachi 1:7–10), yet the spiritual apathy among both the leaders and the people indicates a significant time has elapsed since the initial zeal of restoration.

2. **Issues with the Priesthood**: The dilution of the priesthood and corrupt practices (Malachi 2:1–9) also suggest a lapse in time since the return from exile, giving further evidence for the approximate dating.

3. **Comparison with Other Prophets**: Malachi's ministry followed those of Haggai and Zechariah and dealt with issues that continued to plague the Israelite community. His messages bear similarities to those of Nehemiah, reinforcing the argument for a close chronological proximity to Nehemiah's reforms.

4. **Historical Corroboration**: The concerns that Malachi addresses about mixed marriages and neglect of tithes align well with the reforms initiated by Nehemiah, thereby placing Malachi in a similar timeframe as Nehemiah, who was active around 444 B.C.E.

Therefore, with these multiple lines of evidence, it is assertive to state that Malachi lived and prophesied in the latter part of the 5th century B.C.E. His ministry filled a critical role in sustaining and redirecting the covenant community's faithfulness in a complex and challenging post-exilic context.

Evidence for the Dating of Malachi's Prophecy to 435 B.C.E.

Determining the precise date of Malachi's prophetic activity requires a careful analysis of both internal and external evidence. While the book itself does not provide explicit chronological markers as found in other prophetic writings, various lines of evidence point convincingly toward a date around 435 B.C.E.

1. Post-Exilic Temple Activity: Malachi addresses the issues concerning the Temple offerings and sacrifices (Malachi 1:6–14; 3:8). These practices presume the Temple's reconstruction, which was completed in 516 B.C.E. Since Malachi is addressing lapses in Temple worship, this suggests that a considerable period has passed since the Temple's reconstruction, allowing time for corruption to set in.

2. Comparison with Ezra-Nehemiah: The situation depicted in Malachi closely parallels the challenges faced by Ezra and Nehemiah. Particularly, the issues of intermarriage with foreign women and the neglect of tithes (Malachi 2:10–16; 3:8–12) align well with the concerns raised by Nehemiah, who was active around 444 B.C.E. This makes it plausible to date Malachi's prophetic activity a few years after Nehemiah's reforms, pointing toward a date of approximately 435 B.C.E.

3. Absence of Persian Influence: Unlike some other post-exilic writings, the book of Malachi does not exhibit strong Persian influence in its language or concepts. This suggests that the book likely predates the intensified Persian control over Judah that occurred toward the end of the 5th century B.C.E.

4. Predecessor Prophets: Malachi's prophecies follow those of Haggai and Zechariah. Given that Zechariah's last dated prophecy is around 518 B.C.E., and considering the issues Malachi addresses—issues that require a significant lapse of time after the Temple's completion—a date around 435 B.C.E. fits well within this prophetic sequence.

5. Liturgical and Social Conditions: The religious laxity and social issues that Malachi addresses suggest a community that has settled into routine after the initial fervor of post-exilic restoration has faded. This comfortably places Malachi at least a generation after the completion of the Temple.

Therefore, the collective weight of these indicators aligns with the understanding that Malachi's prophetic activity occurred around 435 B.C.E.

Authenticity and Inspiration of the Book of Malachi

The book of Malachi stands as a divinely inspired work, its authenticity substantiated by multiple lines of evidence.

1. Canonical Acceptance: The inclusion of Malachi in the Hebrew Bible canon by the Jewish community testifies to its recognition as an authentic and inspired work. The canonization process was rigorous, aimed at ensuring that only texts divinely inspired would be accepted.

2. Internal Consistency: The book of Malachi maintains a high level of internal coherence in terms of its themes, vocabulary, and message. It consistently addresses the religious, social, and moral issues pertinent to the post-exilic community in Judah, thereby demonstrating the divine wisdom encapsulated in its teachings.

3. Doctrinal Harmony: Malachi aligns perfectly with the broader theological landscape of the Old Testament. It reinforces the covenantal relationship between Jehovah and His people and underlines the significance of purity in worship, matters that are recurrent throughout the Old Testament Scriptures.

4. Prophetic Foresight: The book contains prophetic elements that reveal knowledge beyond human capacity. One notable example is the prediction of the coming "messenger," fulfilled in the person of John the Baptist, who prepared the way for the Messiah (Malachi 3:1; 4:5–6). These fulfilled prophecies affirm the book's inspired nature.

5. The Voice of Jehovah: Throughout the book, Malachi claims to be delivering the word of Jehovah (e.g., Malachi 1:1; 3:1). The conviction and authority with which the message is delivered resonate with the tone and style of other divinely inspired prophetic books.

6. Influence and Quotation: The New Testament writers and early church fathers frequently quote or allude to Malachi, validating its influence and acceptance as inspired Scripture. For example, the Gospel of Matthew (11:10) and the Gospel of Mark (1:2) both cite Malachi when speaking of John the Baptist as the forerunner of Jesus.

7. Archeological Evidence: Although direct archaeological evidence for Malachi is limited, the circumstances described in the book fit well within the broader archaeological findings related to post-exilic Judah. This congruence lends further credence to the book's authenticity.

8. Thematic Unity with Other Prophets: The themes that Malachi discusses—such as the critique against corrupt priesthood, the call for social justice, and the emphasis on pure worship—are themes that other prophets also address. This thematic unity further underscores the book's authenticity and inspiration.

By scrutinizing these factors collectively, one can confidently assert that the book of Malachi is both authentic and divinely inspired. Its place in the canon, internal coherence, doctrinal harmony, prophetic foresight, and impact on subsequent religious writings all point unequivocally to its divine origin.

Low Spiritual Condition Prompting Malachi's Prophecy

The book of Malachi addresses a community in spiritual decline, characterized by flagrant disobedience, lack of reverence for Jehovah, and general moral laxity. This abysmal spiritual condition necessitated divine intervention through Malachi's prophecy. Let's delve into the key areas that were particularly compromised:

1. Polluted Offerings: Malachi criticizes the priests for offering defiled sacrifices on Jehovah's altar. The prophet describes how blind and lame animals were being offered as sacrifices, contrary to the Law's requirement for unblemished animals (Malachi 1:6-8).

2. Unfaithfulness in Marriage: The people had dealt treacherously against their wives, engaging in divorce and marital unfaithfulness. This was a breach of both covenantal and societal norms (Malachi 2:13-16).

3. Corrupt Priesthood: Malachi also focuses on the priesthood's failure to honor Jehovah and instruct the people in righteousness. They had deviated from their Levitical functions and were leading the people astray (Malachi 2:1-9).

4. Withholding Tithes: The prophecy includes a strong denunciation of the people for withholding tithes and offerings, which effectively robbed Jehovah (Malachi 3:8-10).

5. Questioning God's Justice: The people had grown skeptical, questioning the justice of Jehovah. They wondered why the wicked prospered while they, despite their service, were not experiencing divine blessings (Malachi 2:17; 3:13-15).

6. Lack of Reverence for Jehovah's Name: There was a significant decline in the reverence for Jehovah among the people. Malachi begins his book by addressing the people's doubt about Jehovah's love for them (Malachi 1:2-5).

Each of these symptoms indicated a serious moral and spiritual crisis that threatened the covenantal relationship between Jehovah and His people. The society Malachi addressed was slipping further away from the divine standards. The people were not only in violation of the Mosaic Law but also had hardened their hearts to the point where they no longer recognized their own sins. Thus, Malachi's prophecy served as a stern wake-up call to urge repentance and revival among Jehovah's covenant people.

Malachi's Distinctive Style of Writing

Malachi employs a unique rhetorical technique often referred to as the "disputation speech" or "covenant lawsuit." This style involves a series of declarations or accusations from Jehovah followed by anticipated questions or objections from the people, and finally Jehovah's rebuttal to those questions. This dialogical framework allows the text to present itself as an interactive discourse even though it's essentially a monologue from Jehovah through His prophet.

Examples of Disputation Speech

A clear example of this technique is found in Malachi 1:2-5. Jehovah initiates the dialogue with the statement, "I have loved you," to which the people's anticipated response is, "How have You loved us?" Jehovah then offers a detailed answer, contrasting Jacob and Esau to demonstrate His selective love for Israel.

Another instance is in Malachi 3:8, where Jehovah accuses the people of robbing Him. The people respond with, "How have we robbed You?" Jehovah's answer follows, specifying that they have robbed Him through tithes and offerings.

Language and Imagery

Malachi also employs vivid language and imagery to drive home his points. For instance, he uses the metaphor of a refiner's fire and launderer's soap to illustrate Jehovah's purifying judgement (Malachi 3:2). These images not only capture the essence of the divine actions but also make them relatable and easy to understand for the audience.

Purpose and Impact

This style serves a dual purpose: it underscores the gravity of the people's transgressions and their need for repentance, while simultaneously showcasing Jehovah's unwavering commitment to the covenant despite Israel's shortcomings. It creates an engaging narrative that invites the audience into self-examination, provokes questions, and provides divine answers.

APPENDIX A Bible Difficulties Explained

IT SEEMS THAT the charge that the Bible contradicts itself has been made more and more in the last 20 years. Generally, those making such claims are merely repeating what they have heard because most have not even read the Bible, let alone done an in-depth study of it. I do not wish, however, to set aside all concerns as though they have no merit. There are many who raise legitimate questions that seem, on the surface anyway, to be about well-founded contradiction. Sadly, these issues have caused many to lose their faith in God's Word, the Bible. The purpose of this chapter is, to help its readers to be able to defend the Bible against Bible critics (1 Pet. 3:15), to contend for the faith (Jude 1:3), and help those, who have begun to doubt. – Jude 1:22-23.

Before we begin explaining things, let us jump right in, getting our feet wet, and deal with two major Bible difficulties, so we can see that there are reasonable, logical answers. After that, we will delve deeper into explaining Bible difficulties.

Is God permitting Human Sacrifice?

Judges 11:29-34, 37-40? Updated American Standard Version (UASV)

²⁹ Then the Spirit of the Lord was upon Jephthah, and he passed through Gilead and Manasseh; and passed on to Mizpah of Gilead, and from Mizpah of Gilead he passed on to the sons of Ammon. ³⁰ And Jephthah **made a vow** to Jehovah and said, "If You will indeed give the sons of Ammon into my hand, ³¹ then it shall be that **whatever** comes out of the doors of my house to meet me when I return in peace from the sons of Ammon, it shall be Jehovah's, and I will offer it up as a burnt offering." ³² So Jephthah crossed over to the sons of Ammon to fight against them; and Jehovah gave them into his hand. ³³ He struck them with a very great slaughter from Aroer as far as Minnith, twenty cities, and as far as Abel-keramim. So the sons of Ammon were subdued before the sons of Israel.

³⁴ When Jephthah came to his house at Mizpah, behold, **his daughter was coming out to meet him** with tambourines and with dancing. Now she was his one and only child; besides her he had no son or daughter.

³⁷ And she said to her father, "Let this thing be done for me: leave me alone two months, that I may go up and down on the mountains and weep because of my virginity, I and my companions." ³⁸ And he said, "Go." So he sent her away for two months; and **she left with her companions, and wept on the mountains because of her virginity.** ³⁹ At the end of two months she returned to her father, who **did to her according to the vow that he had made**; and she never known a man.³ Thus it became a custom in Israel, ⁴⁰ that the daughters of Israel went year by year **to commemorate⁴ the daughter** of Jephthah the Gileadite four days in the year.

It is true; to infer that having the idea of an animal sacrifice would really have not been an impressive vow, which the context requires. Human sacrifice will be repugnant if we are talking about taking a life. Jephthah had no sons, so he likely knew it was the daughter, who would come to greet him.

First, the text does not say he killed his daughter. The idea of some that he did kill her is concluded only by inference. While it is not good policy to interpret backward, using Paul on Judges, he does say humans are to be **"as a living sacrifice."** Therefore, Jephthah could have offered his daughter at the temple, "as a living sacrifice" in service, like Samuel.

This is not to be taken dismissively, because, under Jewish backgrounds, it is no small thing to offer a **perpetual virginity** as a sacrifice. This would mean Jephthah's lineage would not be carried on, the family name, was no more.

Second, the context says she went out to weep for two months, not mourn her death. It says, "she left with her companions, and **wept on the mountains because of her virginity.**"

If she was facing imminent death, she could have married, and spent that last two months as a married woman. There would be absolutely no reason for her to mourn her virginity if she were not facing perpetual virginity. – Exodus 38:8; 1 Samuel 2:22

---

³ I.e., *never had relations with a man*

⁴ Or *lament*

Third, it was completely forbidden to offer a human sacrifice. – Leviticus 18:21; 20:2-5; Deuteronomy 12:31; 18:10

Imagine an Israelite believing that he could please God with a human sacrifice that was intended to offer up a human life. To do so would have been a rejection of Jehovah's Sovereignty (the very person you are asking for help), and a rejection of the Law that made them a special people. Worse still, this interpretation would have us believe that Jehovah knew this was coming, allowed the vow, and then aided this type of man to succeed over his enemies.

The last point is simple enough. If such a man as one who would make such a vow, in gross violation of the law, and then carry it out; there is no way he would be mentioned by Paul in Hebrews chapter 11 among the most faithful men and women in Israelite history.

In review, there is no way God would have granted and helped in Jephthah's initial success knowing the vow that was coming because both Jehovah and Jephthah would be as bad as the Canaanites. There is no way that God would accept such a vow and then go on to help Jephthah with his enemies yet again. Then, to allow such a vow to be carried out, to then put Jephthah on the wall of star witnesses for God in Hebrews chapter 11.

Does Isaiah 45:7 mean that God Is the Author of Evil?

Isaiah 45:7 King James Version (KJV)	Isaiah 45:7 English Standard Version (ESV)
⁷ I form the light, and create darkness: I make peace, and **create evil**: I the Lord do all these things.	⁷ I form light and create darkness, I make well-being and **create calamity**, I am the Lord, who does all these things.[5]

Encarta Dictionary: (Evil) (1) morally bad: profoundly immoral or wrong (2) deliberately causing great harm, pain, or upset

---

[5] See Jeremiah 18:11, Lamentations 3:18, and Amos 3:6

QUESTION: Is this view of evil always the case? No, as you will see below.

Some apologetic authors try to say, 'we do not understand Isaiah 45:7 correctly, because there are other verses that say God is not evil (1 John 1:5), cannot look approvingly on evil (Hab. 1:13), and cannot be tempted by evil. (James 1:13)' Well, while all of these things are Scripturally true, the question at hand is not: Is God evil, can God approvingly look on evil, or can God be tempted with evil? Those questions are not relevant to the one at hand, as God cannot be those things, and at the same time, he can be the yes to our question. The question is, is God the author, the creator of evil?

We would hardly argue that God was **not just** in his bringing "calamity" or "evil" down on Adam and Eve. Thus, we have Isaiah 45:7 saying that God is the creator of "calamity" or "evil."

Let us begin simple, without trying to be philosophical. When God removed Adam and Eve from the Garden of Eden, he sentenced them and humanity to sickness, old age, and death. (Rom. 5:8; i.e., enforce penalty for sin), which was to bring "calamity" or "evil" upon humankind. Therefore, as we can see "evil" does not always mean wrongdoing. Other examples of God bringing "calamity" or "evil" are Noah and the flood, the Ten Plagues of Egypt, and the destruction of the Canaanites. These acts of evil were not acts of wrongdoing. Rather, they were righteous and just, because God, the Creator of all things, was administering justice to wrongdoers, to sinners. He warned the perfect first couple what the penalty was for sin. He warned the people for a hundred years by Noah's preaching. He warned the Canaanites centuries before.

Nevertheless, there are times, when God extends mercy, refraining from the execution of his righteous judgment to one worthy of calamity. For example, he warned Nineveh, the city of blood, and they repented, so he pardoned them. (Jonah 3:10) God has made it a practice to warn persons of the results of sin, giving them undeservedly many opportunities to change their ways. – Ezekiel 33:11.

God cannot sin; it is impossible for him to do so. So, when did he create evil? Without getting into the eternity of his knowing what he was going to do, and when, let us just say, evil did not exist when he was the only person in existence. We might say the idea of evil existed because he knew what he was going to do. However, the moment he created creatures (spirit and human), the potential for evil came into existence because both have free will to sin (fall short of perfection). Evil became a reality the moment Satan entertained the idea of causing Adam to sin, to get humanity for himself, and then acted on it.

God has the right and is just to bring the *calamity of* or *evil* down on anyone that is an unrepentant sinner. God did not even have to give us the underserved kindness of offering us his Son. God is the author or agent of evil regardless of the source books that claim otherwise. If he had never created free will beings, evil would have never gone from the idea of evil to the potential of evil, to the existence of evil. However, God felt that it was better to get the sinful state out of angel and human existence, recover, and then any who would sin thereafter; he would be justified in handing out evil or calamity to only that person or angel alone.

Who among us would argue that he should have created humans and angels like robots, automatons with no free will? The moment he chose the free will, he moved evil from an idea to a potential, and Satan moved it to reality. God has a moral nature that does not bring about evil and sin when he is the only person in existence. However, the moment he created beings in his image, which had the potential to sin, he brought about evil. The moment we have a moral code of good and evil that is placed upon one's with free will; then, we have evil as a potential.

In English, the very comprehensive Hebrew word ra' is variously translated as "bad," "downcast (sad, NASB)," "ugly," "evil," "grievous (distressing, NASB)," "sore," "selfish (stingy, HCSB)," and "envious," depending upon the context. (Gen 2:9; 40:7; 41:3; Ex 33:4; Deut. 6:22; 28:35; Pro 23:6; 28:22)

Evil as an adjective **describes** the **quality of** a class of people, places, or things, or of a specific person, place, or thing

Evil as a noun, **defines** the **nature** of a class of people, places, or things, or of a specific person, place, or thing (e.g., the evil one, evil eye).

We can agree that "evil" is a thing. Create means to bring something into existence, be it people, places, or things, as well something abstract, for lack of a better word at the moment. We would agree that when God was alone evil was not a reality; it did not exist? We would agree that the moment that God created free will creatures (angels and humans), creating humans in his image, with his moral nature, he also brought the potential for evil into existence, and it was realized by Satan?

Inerrancy: Can the Bible Be trusted?

If the Bible is the Word of God, it should be in complete agreement throughout; there should be no contradictions. Yet, the rational mind must ask, why is it that some passages appear to be contradictions when compared with others? For example, Numbers 25:9 tells us that 24,000 died from the scourge, whereas at 1 Corinthians 10:8, the apostle Paul says it was 23,000. This would seem to be a clear error. Before addressing such matters, let us first look at some background information.

Full inerrancy in this book means that the original writings are fully without error in all that they state, as are the words. The words were not dictated (automaton), but the intended meaning is inspired, as are the words that convey that meaning. The Author allowed the writer to use his style of writing, yet controlled the meaning to the extent of not allowing the writer to choose a wrong word, which would not convey the intended meaning. Other more liberal-minded persons hold with *partial inerrancy*, which claims that as far as faith is concerned, this portion of God's Word is without error, but that there are historical, geographical, and scientific errors.

There are several different levels of inerrancy. *Absolute Inerrancy* is the belief that the Bible is fully true and exact in every way; including not only relationships and doctrine, but also science and history. In other words, all information is completely exact. *Full Inerrancy* is the belief that the Bible was not written as a science or historical textbook, but is phenomenological, in that it is written from the human perspective. In other words, speaking of such things as the sun rising, the four corners of the earth or the rounding off of number approximations are all from a human perspective. *Limited Inerrancy* is the belief that the Bible is meant only as a reflection of God's purposes and will, so the science and history is the understanding of the author's day, and is limited. Thus, the Bible is susceptible to errors in these areas. *Inerrancy of Purpose* is the belief that it is only inerrant in the purpose of bringing its readers to a saving faith. The Bible is not about facts, but about persons and relationships, thus, it is subject to error. *Inspired: Not Inerrant* is the belief that its authors are human and thus subject to human error. It should be noted that this author holds the position of full inerrancy.

For many today, the Bible is nothing more than a book written by men. The Bible critic believes the Bible to be full of myths and legends, contradictions, and geographical, historical, and scientific errors. University professor Gerald A. Larue had this to say, "The views of the writers as expressed in the Bible reflect the ideas, beliefs, and concepts current in their own times and are limited by the extent of knowledge in those times."[6] On the other hand, the Bible's authors claim that their writings were inspired of God, as Holy Spirit moved them along. We will discover shortly that the Bible critics have much to say, but it is inflated or empty.

2 Timothy 3:16-17 Updated American Standard Version (UASV)

[16] All Scripture is inspired by God and profitable for teaching, for reproof, for correction, for training in righteousness; [17] so that the man of God may be fully competent, equipped for every good work.

2 Peter 1:21 Updated American Standard Version (UASV)

---

[6] Gerald Larue, "The Bible as a Political Weapon," *Free Inquiry* (Summer 1983): 39.

²¹ for no prophecy was ever produced by the will of man, but men carried along by the Holy Spirit spoke from God.

The question remains as to whether the Bible is a book written by imperfect men and full of errors, or is written by imperfect men, but inspired by God. If the Bible is just another book by imperfect man, there is no hope for humankind. If it is inspired by God and without error, although penned by imperfect men, we have the hope of everything that it offers: a rich, happy life now by applying counsel that lies within and the real life that is to come, everlasting life. This author contends that the Bible is inspired of God and free of human error, although written by imperfect humans.

Before we take on the critics who seem to sift the Scriptures looking for problematic verses, let us take a moment to reflect on how we should approach these alleged problem texts. The critic's argument goes something like this: 'If God does not err and the Bible is the Word of God, then the Bible should not have one single error or contradiction, yet it is full of errors and contradictions.' If the Bible is riddled with nothing but contradictions and errors as the critics would have us believe, why, out of 31,173 verses in the Bible, should there be only 2-3 thousand Bible difficulties that are called into question, this being less than ten percent of the whole?

First, let it be said that it is every Christian's obligation to get a deeper understanding of God's Word, just as the apostle Paul told Timothy:

1 Timothy 4:15-16 Updated American Standard Version (UASV)

¹⁵ Practice these things, be absorbed in them, so that your progress will be evident to all. ¹⁶ Pay close attention to yourself and to your teaching; persevere in these things, for as you do this you will ensure salvation both for yourself and for those who hear you.

Paul also told the Corinthians:

2 Corinthians 10:4-5 Updated American Standard Version (UASV)

⁴For the weapons of our warfare are not of the flesh⁷ but powerful to God for destroying strongholds.⁸ ⁵We are destroying speculations and every lofty thing raised up against the knowledge of God, and we are taking every thought captive to the obedience of Christ,

Paul also told the Philippians:

Philippians 1:7 Updated American Standard Version (UASV)

⁷It is right for me to feel thus about you all, because I hold you in my heart, for you are all partakers with me of grace, both in my imprisonment and in the defense and confirmation of the gospel.

In being able to defend against the modern-day critic, one has to be able to reason from the Scriptures and overturn the critic's argument(s) with mildness. If someone were to approach us about an alleged error or contradiction, what should we do? We should be frank and honest. If we do not have an answer, we should admit such. If the text in question gives the appearance of difficulty, we should admit this as well. If we are unsure as to how we should answer, we can simply say that we will look into it and get back to them, returning with a reasonable answer.

However, we do not want to express disbelief and doubt to our critics, because they will be emboldened in their disbelief. It will put them on the offense and us on the defense. With great confidence, we can express that there is an answer. The Bible has withstood the test of 2,000 years of persecution and interrogation and yet it is the most printed book of all time, currently being translated into 2,287 languages. If these critical questions were so threatening, the Bible would not be the book that it is.

When we are pursuing the text in question, be unwavering in purpose, or resolved to find an answer. In some cases, it may take hours of digging to find the solution. Consider this: as we resolve these difficulties, we are also building our faith that God's Word is inerrant. Moreover, we will want to do preventative maintenance in our

---

⁷ That is *merely human*
⁸ That is *tearing down false arguments*

personal study. As we are doing our Bible reading, take note of these surface discrepancies and resolve them as we work our way through the Bible. We need to make this part of our prayers as well. I recommend the following program. Below are several books that deal with difficult passages. As we daily read and study our Bible from Genesis to Revelation, do not attempt it in one year; make it a four-year program. Use a good exegetical commentary like *The Holman Old/New Testament Commentary* (HOTC/HNTC) or *The New American Commentary* set, and *The Big Book of Bible Difficulties* by Norman L. Geisler, as well as *The Encyclopedia of Bible Difficulties* by Gleason Archer.

We should be aware that men under inspiration penned the originally written books. In fact, we do not have those originals, what textual scholars call autographs, but we do have thousands of copies. The copyists, however, were not inspired; therefore, as one might expect, throughout the first 1,400 years of copying, thousands of errors were transmitted into the texts that were being copied by imperfect hands that were not under inspiration when copying. Yet, the next 450 years saw a restoration of the text by textual scholars from around the world. Therefore, while many of our best literal translations today may not be inspired, they are a mirror-like reflection of the autographs by way of textual criticism.[9] Therefore, the fallacy could be with the copyist error that has simply not been weeded out. In addition, we must keep in mind that God's Word is without error, but our interpretation and understanding of that Word is not.

It should be noted that the Bible is made up of 66 smaller books that were hand-written over a period of 1,600 years, having some 40 writers of various trades such as shepherd, king, priest, tax collector, governor, physician, copyist, fisherman, and a tentmaker. Therefore, it should not surprise us that some difficulties are encountered as we casually read the Bible. Yet, if one were to take a deeper look, one would find that these difficulties are easily explained. Let us take a few pages to examine some passages that have been under attack.

---

[9] Textual criticism is the study of copies of any written work of which the autograph (original) is unknown, with the purpose of ascertaining the original text. Harold J. Green, Introduction to New Testament Textual Criticism (Peabody, MA: Hendrickson, 1995), 1.

This chapter's objective is not to be exhaustive, not even close. What we are looking to do is cover a few alleged contradictions and a couple of alleged mistakes. This is to give us a small sampling of the reasonable answers that we will find in the above recommended books. Remember, our Bible is a sword that we must use both offensively and defensively. One must wonder how long a warrior of ancient times would last who was not expertly trained in the use of his weapon. Let us look at a few scriptures that support our need to learn our Bible well so will be able to defend what we believe to be true.

When "false apostles, deceitful workmen, disguising themselves as apostles of Christ" were causing trouble in the congregation in Corinth, the apostle Paul wrote that under such circumstances, we are to *tear down their arguments* and *take every thought captive*. (2 Corinthians 10:4, 5; 11:13–15) All who present critical arguments against God's Word, or contrary to it, can have their arguments overturned by the Christian, who is able and ready to defend that Word in mildness. – 2 Timothy 2:24–26.

1 Peter 3:15 Updated American Standard Version (UASV)

[15] but sanctify Christ as Lord in your hearts, always being prepared to make a defense[10] to anyone who asks you for a reason for the hope that is in you; yet do it with gentleness and respect;

Peter says that we need to be prepared to make a *defense*. The Greek word behind the English 'defense' is *apologia*, which is actually a legal term that refers to the defense of a defendant in court. Our English apologetics is just what Peter spoke of, having the ability to give a reason to any who may challenge us, or to answer those who are not challenging us but who have honest questions that deserve to be answered.

2 Timothy 2:24-25 Updated American Standard Version (UASV)

[24] For a slave of the Lord does not need to fight, but needs to be kind to all, qualified to teach, showing restraint when wronged [25] with

---

[10] Or *argument*; or *explanation*

gentleness correcting those who are in opposition, if perhaps God may grant them repentance leading to accurate knowledge[11] of the truth,

Look at the Greek word (*epignosis*) behind the English "knowledge" in the above. "It is more intensive than *gnosis* (1108), knowledge because it expresses a more thorough participation in the acquiring of knowledge on the part of the learner."[12] The requirement of all of the Lord's servants is that they be able to teach, but not in a quarrelsome way, and in a way to correct his opponents with mildness. Why? Because the purpose of it all is that by God, and through the Christian teacher, one may come to repentance and begin taking in an accurate knowledge of the truth.

Inerrancy: Practical Principles to Overcoming Bible Difficulties

Below are several ways of looking at the Bible that enable the reader to see he is not dealing with an error or contradiction, but rather a Bible difficulty.

Different Points of View

At times, you may have two different writers who are writing from two different points of view.

Numbers 35:14 Updated American Standard Version (UASV)

¹⁴ You shall give three cities across the Jordan and three cities you shall give in the land of Canaan; they will be cities of refuge.

Joshua 22:4 Updated American Standard Version (UASV)

⁴ And now Jehovah your God has given rest to your brothers, as he spoke to them; therefore turn now and go to your tents, to the land

---

[11] *Epignosis* is a strengthened or intensified form of *gnosis* (*epi*, meaning "additional"), meaning, "true," "real," "full," "complete" or "accurate," depending upon the context. Paul and Peter alone use *epignosis*.

[12] Spiros Zodhiates, *The Complete Word Study Dictionary: New Testament*, Electronic ed. (Chattanooga, TN: AMG Publishers, 2000, c1992, c1993), S. G1922.

of your possession, which Moses the servant of Jehovah gave you beyond the Jordan. [on the other side of the Jordan, ESV]

Here we see that Moses is speaking about the east side of the Jordan when he says "on this side of the Jordan." Joshua, on the other hand, is also speaking about the east side of the Jordan when he says "on the other side of the Jordan." So, who is correct? Both are. When Moses was penning Numbers the Israelites had not yet crossed the Jordan River, so the east side was "this side," the side he was on. On the other hand, when Joshua penned his book, the Israelites had crossed the Jordan, so the east side was just as he had said, "on the other side of the Jordan." Thus, we should not assume that two different writers are writing from the same perspective.

A Careful Reading

At times, it may simply be a case of needing to slow down and carefully read the account, considering exactly what is being said.

Joshua 18:28 Updated American Standard Version (UASV)

28 and Zelah, Haeleph and the Jebusite (that is, Jerusalem), Gibeah, Kiriath; fourteen cities with their villages. This is the inheritance of the sons of Benjamin according to their families.

Judges 1:21 Updated American Standard Version (UASV)

21 But the sons of Benjamin did not drive out the Jebusites who lived in Jerusalem; so the Jebusites have lived with the sons of Benjamin in Jerusalem to this day.

Joshua 15:63 Updated American Standard Version (UASV)

63 But as for the Jebusites, the inhabitants of Jerusalem, the sons of Judah could not drive them out; so the Jebusites live with the sons of Judah at Jerusalem until this day.

Judges 1:8-9 Updated American Standard Version (UASV)

8 And then the sons of Judah fought against Jerusalem and captured it and struck it with the edge of the sword and set the city on fire. 9 And afterward the sons of Judah went down to fight against the

Canaanites living in the hill country and in the Negev[13] and in the Shephelah.[14]

2 Samuel 5:5-9 Updated American Standard Version (UASV)

⁵ At Hebron he reigned over Judah seven years and six months, and in Jerusalem he reigned thirty-three years over all Israel and Judah.

⁶ And the king and his men went to Jerusalem against the Jebusites, the inhabitants of the land, and they said to David, "You shall not come in here, but the blind and lame will turn you away"; thinking, "David cannot come in here." ⁷ Nevertheless, David captured the stronghold of Zion, that is the city of David. ⁸ And David said on that day, "Whoever would strike the Jebusites, let him get up the water shaft to attack 'the lame and the blind,' who are hated by David's soul." Therefore it is said, "The blind and the lame shall not come into the house." ⁹ And David lived in the stronghold and called it the city of David. And David built all around from the Millo and inward.

There is no doubt that even the advanced Bible reader of many years can come away confused because the above accounts seem to be contradictory. In Joshua 18:28 and Judges 1:21, we see that Jerusalem was an inheritance of the tribe of Benjamin, yet the Benjamites were unable to conquer Jerusalem. However, in Joshua 15:63 we see that the tribe of Judah could not conquer them either, with the reading giving the impression that it was a part of their inheritance. In Judges 1:8, however, Judah was eventually able to conquer Jerusalem and burn it with fire. Yet, to add even more to the confusion, we find at 2 Samuel 5:5–8 that David is said to have conquered Jerusalem hundreds of years later.

Now that we have the particulars let us look at it more clearly. The boundary between Benjamin's inheritances ran right through the middle of Jerusalem. Joshua 8:28 is correct, in that what would later be called the "city of David" was in the territory of Benjamin, but it also in part crossed over the line into the territory of Judah, causing both

---

[13] I.e. *South*

[14] I.e., lowland

tribes to go to war against this Jebusite city. It is also true that the tribe of Benjamin was unable to conquer the city and that the tribe of Judah eventually did. However, if you look at Judges 1:9 again, you will see that Judah did not finish the job entirely and moved on to conquer other areas. This allowed the remaining ones to regroup and form a resistance that neither Benjamin nor Judah could overcome, so these Jebusites remained until the time of David, hundreds of years later.

Intended Meaning of Writer

First, the Bible student needs to understand the level that the Bible intends to be exact in what is written. If Jim told a friend that 650 graduated with him from high school in 1984, it is not challenged, because it is all too clear that he is using rounded numbers and is not meaning to be exactly precise. This is how God's Word operates as well. Sometimes it means to be exact, at other times, it is simply rounding numbers, in other cases, the intention of the writer is a general reference, to give readers of that time and succeeding generations some perspective. Did Samuel, the author of judges, intend to pen a book on the chronology of Judges, or was his focus on the falling away, oppression, and the rescue by a judge, repeatedly. Now, it would seem that Jeremiah, the author of 1 Kings was more interested in giving his readers an exact number of years.

Acts 2:41 Updated American Standard Version (UASV)

[41] So those who received his word were baptized, and there were added that day about three thousand souls.

As you can see here, numbers within the Bible are often used with approximations. This is a frequent practice even today, in both written works and verbal conversation.

Acts 7:2-3 Updated American Standard Version (UASV)

[2] And Stephen said:

"Brothers and fathers, hear me. The God of glory appeared to our father Abraham when he was in Mesopotamia, before he lived in

Haran, ³ and said to him, 'Go out from your land and from your kindred and go into the land that I will show you.'

If you were to check the Hebrew Scriptures at Genesis 12:1, you would find that what is claimed to have been said by God to Abraham is not quoted word-for-word; it is simply a paraphrase. This is a normal practice within Scripture and in writing in general.

Numbers 34:15 Updated American Standard Version (UASV)

¹⁵ The two and a half tribes have received their inheritance beyond the Jordan opposite Jericho, eastward toward the sunrising."

Just as you would read in today's local newspaper, the Bible writer has written from the human standpoint, how it appeared to him. The Bible also speaks of "to the end of the earth" (Psalm 46:9), "from the four corners of the earth" (Isa 11:12), and "the four winds of the earth" (Revelation 7:1). These phrases are still used today.

Unexplained Does Not Mean Unexplainable

Considering that there are 31,173 verses in the Bible, encompassing 66 books written by about 40 writers, ranging from shepherds to kings, an army general, fishermen, tax collector, a physician and on and on, and being penned over a 1,600 year period, one does find a few hundred Bible difficulties (about one percent). However, 99 percent of those are explainable. Yet no one wants to be so arrogant to say that he can explain them all. It has nothing to do with the inadequacy of God's Word but is based on human understanding. In many cases, science or archaeology and the field of custom and culture of ancient peoples has helped explain difficulties in hundreds of passages. Therefore, there may be less than one percent left to be answered, yet our knowledge of God's Word continues to grow.

Guilty Until Proven Innocent

This is exactly the perception that the critic has of God's Word. The legal principle of being "innocent until proven guilty" afforded mankind in courts of justice is withheld from the very Word of God. What is ironic here is that this policy has contributed to these Bible critics looking foolish over and over again when something comes to light that vindicates the portion of Scripture they are challenging.

Daniel 5:1 Updated American Standard Version (UASV)

¹ Belshazzar the king made[15] a great feast for a thousand of his nobles, and he was drinking wine in the presence of the thousand.

Bible critics had long claimed that Belshazzar was not known outside of the book Daniel; therefore, they argue that Daniel was mistaken. Yet it hardly seems prudent to argue error from absence of outside evidence. Just because archaeology had not discovered such a person did not mean that Daniel was wrong, or that such a person did not exist. In 1854, some small clay cylinders were discovered in modern-day southern Iraq, which would have been the city of Ur in ancient Babylonia. The cuneiform documents were a prayer of King Nabonidus for "Bel-sar-ussur, my eldest son." These tablets also showed that this "Bel-sar-ussur" had secretaries as well as a household staff. Other tablets were discovered a short time later that showed that the kingship was entrusted to this eldest son as a coregent while his father was away.

He entrusted the 'Camp' to his oldest (son), the firstborn [Belshazzar], the troops everywhere in the country he ordered under his (command). He let (everything) go, entrusted the kingship to him and, himself, he [Nabonidus] started out for a long journey, the (military) forces of Akkad marching with him; he turned towards Tema (deep) in the west."[16]

Ignoring Literary Styles

The Bible is a diverse book when it comes to literary styles: narrative, poetic, prophetic, and apocalyptic; also containing parables, metaphors, similes, hyperbole, and other figures of speech. Too often,

---

[15] I.e., held

[16] J. Pritchard, ed., *Ancient Near Eastern Texts* (1974), 313.

these alleged errors are the result of a reader taking a figure of speech as literal, or reading a parable as though it is a narrative.

Matthew 24:35 Updated American Standard Version (UASV)

35 Heaven and earth will pass away, but my words will not pass away.

If some do not recognize that they are dealing with a figure of speech, they are bound to come away with the wrong meaning. Some have concluded from Matthew 24:35 that Jesus was speaking of an eventual destruction of the earth. This is hardly the case, as his listeners would not have understood it that way based on their understanding of the Old Testament. They would have understood that he was simply being emphatic about the words he spoke, using hyperbole. What he was conveying is that his words are more enduring than heaven and earth, and with heaven and earth being understood as eternal, this merely conveyed even more so that Jesus' words could be trusted.

Two Accounts of the Same Incident

If you were to speak to officers that take accident reports for their police department, you would find that there is cohesion in the accounts, but each person has merely witnessed aspects that have stood out to them. We will see that this is the case as well with the examples below, which is the same account in two different gospels:

Matthew 8:5 Updated American Standard Version (UASV)

5 When he[17] had entered Capernaum, a centurion came forward to him, imploring him,

Luke 7:2-3 Updated American Standard Version (UASV)

2 And a centurion's[18] slave, who was highly regarded[19] by him, was sick and about to die. 3 When he heard about Jesus, he sent some older

---

[17] That is *Jesus*
[18] I.e., army officer over a hundred solderiers
[19] Lit *to whom he was honorable*

men of the Jews[20] asking him to come and bring his slave safely through.[21]

Immediately we see the problem of whether the centurion or the elders of the Jews spoke with Jesus. The solution is not really hidden from us. Which of the two accounts is the most detailed account? You are correct if you said, Luke. The centurion sent the elders of the Jews to represent him to Jesus, so; that whatever response Jesus might give, it would be as though he were addressing the centurion; therefore, Matthew gave his readers the basic thought, not seeing the need of mentioning the elders of the Jews aspect. This is how a representative was viewed in the first century, just as some countries see ambassadors today as being the very person they represent. Therefore, both Matthew and Luke are correct.

Man's Fallible Interpretations

Inspiration by God is infallible, without error. Imperfect man and his interpretations over the centuries, as bad as many of them have been, should not cast a shadow over God's inspired Word. The entire Word of God has one meaning and one meaning only for every penned word, which is what God willed to be conveyed by the human writer he chose to use.

The Autograph Alone Is Inspired and Inerrant

It has been argued by conservative scholars that only the autograph manuscripts were inspired and inerrant, not the copying of those manuscripts over the next 3,000 years for the Old Testament and 1,500 years for the New Testament. While I would agree with this position as well, it should be noted that we do not possess the autographs, so to argue that they are inerrant is to speak of nonexistent documents. However, it should be further understood that through the science of textual criticism, we can establish a mirror reflection of the autograph manuscripts. B. F. Westcott, F. J. A. Hort, F. F. Bruce, and

---

[20] Or *Jewish elders*
[21] I.e., *save the life of his slave*

many other textual scholars would agree with Norman L Geisler's assessment: "The New Testament, then, has not only survived in more manuscripts than any other book from antiquity, but it has survived in a purer form than any other great book—*a form that is 99.5 percent pure.*"[22]

An example of a copyist error can be found in Luke's genealogy of Jesus at Luke 3:35–37. In verse 37 you will find a Cainan, and in verse 36 you will find a second Cainan between Arphaxad (Arpachshad) and Shelah. As one can see from most footnotes in different study Bibles, the Cainan in verse 36 is seen as a scribal error, and is not found in the Hebrew Old Testament, the Samaritan Pentateuch, or the Aramaic Targums, but is found in the Greek Septuagint. (Genesis 10:24; 11:12, 13; 1 Chronicles 1:18, but not 1 Chronicles 1:24) It seems quite unlikely that it was in the earlier copies of the Septuagint, because the first-century Jewish historian Josephus lists Shelah next as the son of Arphaxad, and Josephus normally followed the Septuagint.[23] So one might ask why this second Cainan is found in the translations at all if this is the case? The manuscripts that do contain this second Cainan are some of the best manuscripts that are used in establishing the original text: 01 B L A^1 33 (Kainam); A 038 044 0102 A^{13} (Kainan).

The Bible Was Miraculously Restored, not Miraculously Preserved

The Hebrew text was like the Greek NT; it had accumulated copyist errors, a few intentional, a good number accidental, between the Malachi days of 440 BCE and Rabbi Judah ha-Nasi (135 to 217 CE). The same thing happened to the Greek New Testament from about 400 CE to 1550 CE, a period of copyist errors. The good news is for the NT is fourfold: (1) the 144 NT papyri discovered in the early part of the 20th century, (2) a number of them dated within decades of the originals, and the great Codex Vaticanus (300-330 CE) and Codex

---

[22] Norman L. Geisler and William E. Nix: *A General Introduction to the Bible* (Chicago, Moody Press, 1980), 367. (Emphasis is mine.)

[23] *Jewish Antiquities*, I, 146 [vi, 4].

Sinaiticus (330-360 CE), (3) that we have 5,898 Greek NT MSS; (4) then, there was the era of many dozens of textual scholars, from 1550 to the present who restored the text to its original words.

So, the Hebrew OT corruption ran in earnest between 440 BCE to 220 CE. At that time, the Greek Septuagint, a translation of the Hebrew Scriptures, was produced between 280 – 150 BCE, which became favored by the Jews to the point that they claimed it was inspired. However, the fact that the lingua franca of the Roman Empire ran from 330 BCE to 330 CE, the Christians in the first century CE wisely used the Greek Septuagint to evangelize, to show that Jesus Christ was the long-awaited Messiah. Then, Jerusalem was destroyed by General Titus and the Roman army in 70 CE, killing one million one hundred thousand Jews and carrying another seventy thousand back to Rome as slaves. No temple led to the creation of the Mishnah, an authoritative collection of exegetical material embodying the oral tradition of Jewish law and forming the first part of the Talmud. During the 150 years in the wake of the temple's destruction in Jerusalem in 70 CE, rabbinic sages throughout Israel at once were quick to seek out a new source for preserving Jewish practice. They debated and combined various traditions of their oral law. Growing this foundation, they set new constraints, boundaries, and requirements for Judaism. This gave the Jewish people direction for their day-to-day life of holiness, even though they lacked a temple. This new spiritual structure was summarized in the Mishnah, which Judah ha-Nasi compiled by about 200-217 CE.

In addition, the Jewish scholars set about creating a corrected text of the Hebrew Old Testament because they realized it had some textual variants from the sopherim (scribes). But it was the greatest textual scholars who have ever lived, the Masoretes, who made corrected copies from 500 to 900 CE. Below is an article about them. The beauty is that they did not erase the manuscripts with the errors; they kept them, then simply put the corrections in the margin, called the Masorah. So, the Hebrew text was corrected just as the Greek text was. And then, in 1947, we found the Dead Sea Scrolls, which dated as early as the 3rd century BCE and validated the Masoretic text. And ironically at this same time, many of the **best** NT papyri were coming to light that validated the work of Johann Jakob Wettstein [1693-1754 A.D.], Karl Lachmann [1793-1851], Samuel Prideaux Tregelles [1813-1875], Friedrich Constantin von Tischendorf [1815-1874], and especially Westcott and Hort of 1881.

MIRACULOUS RESTORATION, NOT MIRACULOUS PRESERVATION

OLD TESTAMENT
Transmission: 1500 BCE – 440 BCE
Corruption: 440 BCE – 220 CE
Restoration: 500 – 900 CE – Present
Corroboration MSS (Dead Sea Scrolls): 1947

NEW TESTAMENT
Transmission: 45 CE – 98 CE
Corruption: 440 CE -1550 CE
Restoration: 1550 CE – Present
Corroboration MSS (NT Papyri): 1900s-1960s-Present

A Lack of <u>Preservation</u> Does Not Mean a Lack of <u>Inspiration</u>

- The Bible **was miraculously inspired** as men were moved along by the Holy Spirit (*Absolute Inerrancy*)

- The Bible **was not miraculously preserved** as men's human imperfection gave us corruption (*Limited Inerrancy*)

- The Bible **was restored** through tens of millions of hours by many hundreds of (men) textual scholars from the 16th to the 21st centuries. (*Absolute Inerrancy Restored*)

The **men who restored the text** are no more perfect than the **men who** intentionally and unintentionally **corrupted the text**. However, even hundreds of **imperfect men**, through dozens of lifetimes of sweat and toil, arrived at **a perfect text** that was lost but now is found. With the copyists, you have tens of thousands of men **focusing on their work as an individual** in reproducing a copy; with the textual scholars, it is teams of hundreds of men focusing on all of the manuscripts to ascertain the original words of the original texts.

Many of the above scholars gave their entire lives to God and the Hebrew and Greek text.[24] Each of these could have an entire book devoted to them and their work alone. The amount of work they accomplished before the era of computers is nothing short of astonishing. Rightly, the preceding history should serve to strengthen our faith in the authenticity and general integrity of the Hebrew Scriptures and the Greek New Testament. Unlike Bart D. Ehrman, men like Sir Frederic Kenyon have been moved to say that the books of the Greek New Testament have "come down to us substantially as they were written." And all this is especially true of the critical scholarship of the almost two hundred years since the days of Karl Lachmann. All today can feel confident that what they hold in their hands is a mirror reflection of the Word of God that was penned in twenty-seven books, some two thousand years ago.

It is true that the Jewish copyists and the later Christian copyists were not led along by the Holy Spirit, and therefore their manuscripts were not inerrant, infallible. Errors (textual variants) crept into the manuscripts unintentionally and intentionally. However, the vast majority of the Hebrew Old Testament and Greek New Testament has not been infected with textual errors. For the portions impacted with textual errors, it is the many tens of thousands of copies that we have to help us to weed out the errors. How? Well, not every copyist made the same textual errors. Hence, by comparing the work of different copyists and different manuscripts, textual scholars can identify the textual variants (errors) and remove those, leaving us with the original content.

Yes, it would be the greatest discovery of all time if we found the actual original five books that were penned by Moses himself, Genesis through Deuteronomy. However, there would be no way of establishing that they were the originals. The fact is, we do not need the originals. We do not need those original documents. What is so important about the documents? The documents are not important; it

---

[24] **The Climax of the Restored Text**

is the content on the original documents that we are after. And truly, miraculously, we have more copies than needed to do just that. We do not need miraculous preservation because we have miraculous restoration. We now know beyond a reasonable doubt that the Hebrew Old Testament and the Greek New Testament critical texts are a 99.99% reflection of the content that was in those ancient original manuscripts. Some textual scholars might say that I am exaggerating with the 99.99%. An example of how that is not so can be found in the 1881 Westcott and Hort critical Greek NT, which is 99.5% the same as the 2012 28th edition of the critical Greek NT. The discovery of the NT papyri from the 1900s to the 1960s and up to the present has validated Westcott and Hort's Greek NT and let us know that the 2012 Nestle-Aland Greek NT is a mirror-like reflection of the original. To be frank, there are about 100+ textual variants where Westcott and Hort were correct, and the Nestle-Aland text is likely not correct. This is because they took the textual eclecticism method of determining the original, which was to focus on both external and internal evidence. Still, they leaned heavily on internal evidence, which is a bit more subjective. Regardless, we have the apparatus in the 28th edition of the Nestle-Aland that gives the translator the variants, allowing him to make an objective determination. Therefore, the 100+ textual variants can be decided on a case-by-case basis. So, yes, what we have is 99.99% reflective of the original.

The critical text of Westcott and Hort of 1881 [(FENTON JOHN ANTHONY HORT (1828 – 1892) and BROOKE FOSS WESTCOTT (1825 – 1901)] has been commended by leading textual scholars over the last one hundred and forty years, and still stands as the standard. Numerous additional critical editions of the Greek text came after Westcott and Hort: Richard F. Weymouth (1886), Bernhard Weiss (1894–1900); the British and Foreign Bible Society (1904, 1958), Alexander Souter (1910), Hermann von Soden (1911–1913); and Eberhard Nestle's Greek text, *Novum Testamentum Graece*, published in 1898 by the Württemberg Bible Society, Stuttgart, Germany. The Nestle in twelve editions (1898–1923) to subsequently be taken over by his son, Erwin Nestle (13th–20th editions, 1927–1950), followed by Kurt Aland (21st–25th editions, 1952–1963), and lastly, it was coedited by Kurt Aland and Barbara Aland (26th–28th editions, 1979, 1993, 2012).

Look at the Context

Many alleged inconsistencies disappear by simply looking at the context. Taking words out of context can distort their meaning. *Merriam-Webster's Collegiate Dictionary* defines context as "the parts of a discourse that surround a word or passage and can throw light on its meaning."[25] Context can also be "the circumstances or events that form the environment within which something exists or takes place." If we were to look in a thesaurus for a synonym, we would find "background" for this second meaning. At 2 Timothy 2:15, the apostle Paul brings home the point of why context is so important: "Do your best to present yourself to God as one approved, a worker who has no need to be ashamed, rightly handling the word of truth."

Ephesians 2:8-9 Updated American Standard Version (UASV)

⁸ For by grace you have been saved through faith; and that not of yourselves, it is the gift of God; ⁹ not from works, so that no man may boast.

James 2:26 Updated American Standard Version (UASV)

²⁶ For as the body apart from the spirit[26] is dead, so also faith apart from works is dead.

So, which is it? Is salvation possible by faith alone as Paul wrote to the Ephesians, or is faith dead without works as James wrote to his readers? As our subtitle brings out, let us look at the context. In the letter to the Ephesians, the apostle Paul is speaking to the Jewish Christians who were looking to the works of the Mosaic Law as a means to salvation, a righteous standing before God. Paul was telling these legalistic Jewish Christians that this is not so. In fact, this would invalidate Christ's ransom because there would have been no need for

---

[25] Merriam-Webster, Inc: *Merriam-Webster's Collegiate Dictionary*. Eleventh ed. (Springfield, Mass.: Merriam-Webster, Inc. 2003).

[26] Or *breath*

it if one could achieve salvation by meticulously keeping the Mosaic Law. (Rom. 5:18) But James was writing to those in a congregation who were concerned with their status before other men, who were looking for prominent positions within the congregation, and not taking care of those that were in need. (Jam. 2:14–17) So, James is merely addressing those who call themselves Christian, but in name only. No person could truly be a Christian and not possess some good works, such as feeding the poor, helping the elderly. This type of work was an evident demonstration of one's Christian personality. Paul was in perfect harmony with James on this. – Romans 10:10; 1 Corinthians 15:58; Ephesians 5:15, 21–33; 6:15; 1 Timothy 4:16; 2 Timothy 4:5; Hebrews 10:23-25.

Inerrancy: Are There Contradictions?

Below I will follow this pattern. I will list the critic's argument first, followed by the text of difficulty, and conclude with an answer to the critic. What should be kept at the forefront of our mind is this: one is simply looking for the best answer, not absoluteness. If there is a reasonable answer to a Bible difficulty, why are the critics able to set them aside with ease? Because they start with the premise that this is not the Word of God, but only a book by imperfect men and full of contradictions; thus, the bias toward errors has blinded their judgment.

Critic: The critic would argue that there was an Adam and Eve, and an Abel who was now dead, so, where did Cain get his wife? This is one of the most common questions by Bible critics.

Genesis 4:17 Updated American Standard Version (UASV)

¹⁷ Cain had sexual relations[27] with his wife and she conceived, and gave birth to Enoch; and he built a city, and called the name of the city Enoch, after the name of his son, Enoch.

Answer: If one were to read a little further along, they would come to the realization that Adam had a son named Seth; it further

---

[27] Lit *knew*

adds that Adam "became father to sons *and daughters.*" (Genesis 5:4) Adam lived for a total of 800 years after fathering Seth, giving him ample opportunity to father many more sons and daughters. So it could be that Cain married one of his sisters. If he waited until one of his brothers and sisters had a daughter, he could have married one of his nieces once she was old enough. In the beginning, humans were closer to perfection; this explains why they lived longer and why at that time there was little health risk of genetic defects in the case of children born to closely related parents, in contrast to how it is today. As time passed, genetic defects increased and life spans decreased. Adam lived to see 930 years. Yet Shem, who lived after the Flood, died at 600 years, while Shem's son Arpachshad only lived 438 years, dying before his father died. Abraham saw an even greater decrease in that he only lived 175 years while his grandson Jacob was 147 years when he died. Thus, due to increasing imperfection, God prohibited the marriage of closely related people under the Mosaic Law because of the likelihood of genetic defects.—Leviticus 18:9.

Critic: If God is here hardening Pharaoh's heart, what exactly makes Pharaoh responsible for the decisions he makes?

Exodus 4:21 Updated American Standard Version (UASV)

[21] Jehovah said to Moses, "When you go and return to Egypt see that you perform before Pharaoh all the wonders which I have put in your hand; but I will harden his heart so that he will not let the people go.

Answer: This is actually a prophecy. God knew that what he was about to do would contribute to a stubborn and obstinate Pharaoh, who was going to be unwilling to change or give up the Israelites so they could go off to worship their God. Therefore, this is not stating what God is going to do; it is prophesying that Pharaoh's heart will harden because of the actions of God. The fact is, Pharaoh allowed his own heart to harden because he was determined not to agree with Moses' wishes or accept Jehovah's request to let the people go. Moses tells us at Exodus 7:13 (ESV) that "Pharaoh's heart was hardened, and he would not listen to them, as the Lord had said." Again, at 8:15 we read, "When Pharaoh saw that there was a respite, he hardened his heart and would not listen to them, as the Lord had said."

Critic: The Israelites had just received the Ten Commandments, with one commandment being: "You shall not make for yourself a carved image or any likeness of anything that is in heaven above, or that is in the earth beneath, or that is in the water under the earth." Therefore, how is the bronze serpent not a violation of this commandment?

Numbers 21:9 Updated American Standard Version (UASV)

⁹ And Moses made a bronze serpent and set it on the standard;[28] and it came about, that if a serpent bit any man, when he looked to the bronze serpent, he lived.

Answer: First, an idol is "a representation or symbol of an object of worship; *broadly*: a false god."[29] Second, it should be noted that not all images are idols. The bronze serpent was not made for the purpose of worship, or for some passionate devotion or veneration. There were times, however, when images were created with absolutely no intention of it receiving devotion, veneration, or worship, yet were later made into objects of veneration. That is exactly what happened with the copper serpent that Moses had formed in the wilderness. Many centuries later, "in the third year of Hoshea son of Elah, king of Israel, Hezekiah the son of Ahaz, king of Judah, began to reign. He removed the high places and broke the pillars and cut down the Asherah. And he broke in pieces the bronze serpent that Moses had made; for until those days the people of Israel had made offerings to it (it was called Nehushtan)."—2 Kings 18:1, 4.

Critic: Deuteronomy 15:11 (NET) says: *"There will never cease to be some poor people in the land;* therefore, I am commanding you to make sure you open your hand to your fellow Israelites who are needy and poor in your land." Is this not a contradiction of Deuteronomy 15:4?

---

[28] I.e., *pole*

[29] Merriam-Webster, Inc: *Merriam-Webster's Collegiate Dictionary*. Eleventh ed. (Springfield, Mass.: Merriam-Webster, Inc., 2003).

Will there be no poor among the Israelites, or will there be poor among them? Which is it?

Deuteronomy 15:4 Updated American Standard Version (UASV)

⁴ However, there will be no poor among you, since Jehovah will surely bless you in the land which Jehovah your God is giving you as an inheritance to possess,

Answer: If you look at the context, Deuteronomy 15:4 is stating that if the Israelites obey Jehovah's command to take care of the poor, "there should not be any poor among" them. Thus, for every poor person, there will be one to take care of that need. If an Israelite fell on hard times, there was to be a fellow Israelite ready to step in to help him through those hard times. Verse 11 stresses the truth of the imperfect world since the rebellion of Adam and inherited sin: there will always be poor among mankind, the Israelites being no different. However, the difference with God's people is that those who were well off financially were to offset conditions for those who fell on difficult times. This is not to be confused with the socialistic welfare systems in the world today. Those Jews were hard-working men, who labored from sunup to sundown to take care of their families. But if disease overtook their herd or unseasonal weather brought about failed crops, an Israelite could sell himself into the service of a fellow Israelite for a period of time; thereafter, he would be back on his feet. And many years down the road, he may very well do the same for another Israelite, who fell on difficult times.

Critic: Joshua 11:23 says that Joshua took the land according to what God had spoken to Moses and handed it on to the nation of Israel as planned. However, in Joshua 13:1, God is telling Joshua that he has grown old and much of the Promised Land has yet to be taken possession of. How can both be true? Is this not a contradiction?

Joshua 11:23 Updated American Standard Version (UASV)

²³ So Joshua took the whole land, according to all that Jehovah had spoken to Moses, and Joshua gave it for an inheritance to Israel

according to their divisions by their tribes, and the land had rest from war.

Joshua 13:1 Updated American Standard Version (UASV)

13 Now Joshua was old and advanced in years, and Jehovah said to him, "You are old and advanced in years, and there remains yet very much land to possess.

Answer: No, it is not a contradiction. When the Israelites were to take the land, it was to take place in two different stages: the nation as a whole was to go to war and defeat the 31 kings of this land; thereafter, each Israelite tribe was to take their part of the land based on their individual actions. (Joshua 17:14–18; 18:3) Joshua fulfilled his role, which is expressed in 11:23 while the individual tribes did not complete their campaigns, which is expressed in 13:1. Even though the individual tribes failed to live up to taking their portion, the remaining Canaanites posed no real threat. Joshua 21:44, *ASV*, reads: "Jehovah gave them rest round about."

Critic: The critic would point out that John 1:18 clearly says that *"no one has ever seen God,"* while Exodus 24:10 explicitly states that Moses and Aaron, Nadab and Abihu, and seventy of the elders of Israel *"saw the God of Israel."* Worse still, God informs them in Exodus 33:20: "You cannot see my face, for man shall not see me and live." The critic with his knowing smile says, 'This is a blatant contradiction.'

John 1:18 Updated American Standard Version (UASV)

^{18} No one has seen God at any time; the only begotten god[30] who is in the bosom of the Father,[31] that one has made him fully known.

Exodus 24:10 Updated American Standard Version (UASV)

^{10} and they saw the God of Israel; and under his feet was what seemed like a sapphire pavement, as clear as the sky itself.

Exodus 33:20 Updated American Standard Version (UASV)

---

[30] Jn 1:18: "only-begotten god", P^{66}ℵ*BC*Lsyr^{hmg,p}; **[V1]** "the only-begotten god," P^{75}33ℵcop^{bo}; **[V2]** "the only-begotten Son." AC^3(W^s)QYf1,13 MajVgSyr^c

[31] Or *at the Father's side*

²⁰ But he [God] said, "You cannot see my face, for no man can see me and live!"

Answer: Exodus 33:20 is one-hundred percent correct: No human could see Jehovah God and live. The apostle Paul at Colossians 1:15 tell us that Christ is the image of the invisible God, and the writer informs us at Hebrews 1:3 that Jesus is the "exact representation of His nature." Yet if you were to read the account of Saul of Tarsus (the apostle Paul), you would see that a mere partial manifestation of Christ's glory blinded Saul – Acts 9:1–18.

When the Bible says that Moses and others have seen God, it is not speaking of *literally* seeing him, because first of all He is an invisible spirit person. It is a *manifestation* of his glory, which is an act of showing or demonstrating his presence, making himself perceptible to the human mind. In fact, it is generally an angelic representative that stands in his place and not him personally. Exodus 24:16 informs us that "the glory of the Lord dwelt on Mount Sinai," not the Lord himself personally. When texts such as Exodus 24:10 explicitly state that Moses and Aaron, Nadab and Abihu, and seventy of the elders of Israel "*saw the God of Israel,*" it is this "glory of the Lord," an angelic representative. This is shown to be the case at Luke 2:9, which reads: "And *an angel of the Lord* appeared to them, and *the glory of the Lord shone around them* [the shepherds], and they were filled with fear."

Many Bible difficulties are cleared up elsewhere in Scripture; for example, in the New Testament, you will find a text clarifying a difficulty from the Old Testament, such as Acts 7:53, which refers to those "who received the law *as delivered by angels* and did not keep it." Support comes from Paul at Galatians 3:19: "Why then the law? It was added because of transgressions until the offspring should come to whom the promise had been made, and it was put in place through angels by an intermediary." The writer of Hebrews chimes in at 2:2 with "For since the message *declared by angels* proved to be reliable, and every transgression or disobedience received a just retribution. . . ." As we travel back to Exodus again, to 19:19 specifically, we find support that it was not God's own voice, which Moses heard; no, it was an angelic representative, for it reads: "Moses was speaking, and God was answering him with a voice." Exodus 33:22–23 also helps us to appreciate that it was the back of these angelic representatives of Jehovah that Moses saw: "While my glory passes by ... Then I will take away my hand, and you shall see my back, but my face shall not be seen."

Exodus 3:4 states: "God called to him out of the bush, 'Moses, Moses!' And he said, 'Here I am.'" Verse 6 informs us: "I am the God of your father, the God of Abraham, the God of Isaac, and the God of Jacob." Yet, in verse 2 we read: "And the angel of the Lord appeared to him in a flame of fire out of the midst of a bush." Here is another example of using God's Word to clear up what seems to be unclear or difficult to understand at first glance. Thus, while it speaks of the Lord making a direct appearance, it is really an angelic representative. Even today, we hear such comments, as 'the president of the United States is to visit the Middle East later this week.' However, later in the article it is made clear that he is not going personally, but it is one of his high-ranking representatives. Let us close with two examples, starting with,

Genesis 32:24-30 Updated American Standard Version (UASV)

[24] And Jacob was left alone, and a man wrestled with him until daybreak. [25] When he saw that he had not prevailed against him, he touched the socket of his thigh; so the socket of Jacob's thigh was dislocated as he wrestled with him. [26] Then he said, "Let me go, for the dawn is breaking." But he said, "I will not let you go unless you bless me." [27] And he said to him, "What is your name?" And he said, "Jacob." [28] And he said, "Your name shall no longer be called Jacob, but Israel,[32] for you have struggled with God and with men and have prevailed." [29] Then Jacob asked him and said, "Please tell me your name." But he said, "Why is it that you ask my name?" And he blessed him there. [30] So Jacob named the place Peniel,[33] for he said, "I have seen God face to face, yet my soul has been preserved."

It is all too obvious here that this man is simply a materialized angel in the form of a man, another angelic representative of Jehovah God. Moreover, the reader of this book should have taken in that the

---

[32] Meaning *he contends with God*
[33] Meaning *face of God*

Israelites as a whole saw these angelic representatives and spoke of them as though they were dealing directly with Jehovah God himself.

This proved to be the case in the second example found in the book of Judges where an angelic representative visited Manoah and his wife. Like the above mentioned account, Manoah and his wife treated this angelic representative as if he were Jehovah God himself: "And Manoah said to the angel of the Lord, 'What is your name, so that, when your words come true, we may honor you?' And the angel of the Lord said to him, 'Why do you ask my name, seeing it is wonderful?' Then Manoah knew that he was the angel of the Lord. And Manoah said to his wife, "We shall surely die, *for we have seen God.*" – Judges 13:3–22.

Inerrancy: Are There Mistakes?

I have addressed the alleged contradictions, so it would seem that our job is done here, right? Not hardly. Yes, there are just as many who claim that the Bible is full of mistakes.

Critic: Matthew 27:5 states that Judas hanged himself, whereas Acts 1:18 says, "Falling headlong, he burst open in the middle and all his intestines gushed out."

Matthew 27:5 Updated American Standard Version (UASV)

⁵ And he threw the pieces of silver into the temple and departed; and he went away and hanged himself.

Acts 1:18 Updated American Standard Version (UASV)

¹⁸ (Now this man acquired a field with the price of his wickedness, and falling headlong, he burst open in the middle and all his intestines gushed out.

Answer: Neither Matthew nor Luke made a mistake. What you have is Matthew giving the reader the manner in which Judas committed suicide. On the other hand, Luke is giving the reader of Acts, the result of that suicide. Therefore, instead of a mistake, we have two texts that complement each other, really giving the reader the full picture. Judas came to a tree alongside a cliff that had rocks below. He tied the rope to a branch and the other end around his neck and jumped over the edge of the cliff in an attempt at hanging himself. One of two things could have happened: (1) the limb broke plunging him to the rocks below, or (2) the rope broke with the same result, and he burst open onto the rocks below.

Critic: The apostle Paul made a mistake when he quotes how many people died.

Numbers 25:9 Updated American Standard Version (UASV)

⁹ The ones who died in the plague were twenty-four thousand.

1 Corinthians 10:8 Updated American Standard Version (UASV)

⁸ Neither let us commit sexual immorality, as some of them committed sexual immorality, only to fall, twenty-three thousand of them in one day.

Answer: We must keep in mind the above principle that we spoke of, the *Intended Meaning of the Writer*. We live in a far more precise age today, where specificity is highly important. However, we round large numbers off (even estimate) all the time: "there were 237,000 people in Time Square last night." The simplest answer is that the number of people slain was in between 23,000 and 24,000, and both writers rounded the number off. However, there is even another possibility, because the book of Numbers specifically speaks of "all the chiefs of the people" (25:4-5), which could account for the extra 1,000, which is mentioned in Numbers 24,000. Thus, you have the people killing the chiefs of the people and the plague killing the people. Therefore, both books are correct.

Critic: After 215 years in Egypt, the descendants of Jacob arrived at the Promised Land. As you recall they sinned against God and were sentenced to forty years in the wilderness. But once they entered the Promised Land, they buried Joseph's bones "at Shechem, in the piece of land that *Jacob bought* from the sons of Hamor the father of Shechem," as stated at Joshua 24:32. Yet, when Stephen had to defend himself before the Jewish religious leaders, he said that Joseph was buried "in the tomb that *Abraham had bought* for a sum of silver from the sons of Hamor." Therefore, at once it appears that we have a mistake on the part of Stephen.

Acts 7:15-16 Updated American Standard Version (UASV)

¹⁵ And Jacob went down to Egypt and died, he and our fathers. ¹⁶ And they were brought back to Shechem and buried in the tomb that Abraham had bought for a sum of silver from the sons of Hamor in Shechem.

Genesis 23:17-18 Updated American Standard Version (UASV)

¹⁷ So Ephron's field, which was in Machpelah, which faced Mamre, the field and cave which was in it, and all the trees which were in the field, that were in all its border around, were made over ¹⁸ to Abraham for a possession in the presence of the sons of Heth, before all who went in at the gate of his city.

Genesis 33:19 Updated American Standard Version (UASV)

¹⁹ And he bought the piece of land where he had pitched his tent from the hand of the sons of Hamor, Shechem's father, for one hundred qesitahs.[34]

Joshua 24:32 Updated American Standard Version (UASV)

³² As for the bones of Joseph, which the sons of Israel brought up from Egypt, they buried them at Shechem, in the piece of land that Jacob bought from the sons of Hamor the father of Shechem for one hundred qesitahs.[35] It became an inheritance of the sons of Joseph.

Answer: If we look back to Genesis 12:6-7, we will find that Abraham's first stop after entering Canaan from Haran was Shechem. It is here that Jehovah told Abraham: "To your offspring I will give this land." At this point Abraham built an altar to Jehovah. It seems reasonable that Abraham would need to purchase this land that had not yet been given to his offspring. While it is true that the Old Testament does not mention this purchase, it is likely that Stephen would be aware of such by way of oral tradition. As Acts chapter seven

---

[34] Or *pieces of money*; money of unknown value
[35] Or *pieces of money*; money of unknown value

demonstrates, Stephen had a wide-ranging knowledge of Old Testament history.

Later, Jacob would have had difficulty laying claim to the tract of land that his grandfather Abraham had purchased, because there would have been a new generation of inhabitants of Shechem. This would have been many years after Abraham moved further south and Isaac moved to Beersheba, and including Jacob's twenty years in Paddan-aram (Gen 28:6, 7). The simplest answer is that this land was not in use for about 120 years because of Abraham's extensive travels and Isaac's having moved away, leaving it unused; likely it was put to use by others. So, Jacob simply repurchased what Abraham had bought over a hundred years earlier. This is very similar to the time Isaac had to repurchase the well at Beersheba that Abraham had already purchased earlier. – Genesis 21:27–30; 26:26–32.

Genesis 33:18–20 tells us that 'Jacob bought this land for a hundred pieces of money, from the sons of Hamor.' This same transaction is also mentioned at Joshua 24:32, in reference to transporting Joseph's bones from Egypt, to be buried in Shechem.

We should also address the cave of Machpelah that Abraham had purchased in Hebron from Ephron the Hittite. The word "tomb" is not mentioned until Joshua 24:32, and is in reference to the tract of land in Shechem. Nowhere in the Old Testament does it say that Abraham bought a "tomb." The cave of Machpelah obtained by Abraham would eventually become a family tomb, receiving Sarah's body and, eventually, his own, and those of Isaac, Rebekah, Jacob, and Leah. (Genesis 23:14–19; 25:9; 49:30, 31; 50:13) Gleason L. Archer, Jr., concludes this Bible difficulty, saying:

> The reference to a *mnema* ("tomb") in connection with Shechem must either have been proleptic [to anticipate] for the later use of that shechemite tract for Joseph's tomb (i.e., 'the tomb that Abraham bought' was intended to imply 'the tomb location that Abraham bought"); or else conceivably the dative relative pronoun *ho* was intended elliptically [omission] for *en to topo ho onesato Abraam* ("in the place that Abraham bought") as describing the location of the *mnema*

near the Oak of Moreh right outside Shechem. Normally Greek would have used the relative-locative adverb *hou* to express 'in which' or 'where'; but this would have left o*nesato* ("bought") without an object in its own clause, and so *ho* was much more suitable in this context. (Archer 1982, 379–81)

Another solution could be that Jacob is being viewed as a representative of Abraham, for he is the grandson of Abraham. This was quite appropriate in Biblical times, to attribute the purchase to Abraham as the Patriarchal family head.

Critic: 2 Samuel 24:1 says that God moved David to count the Israelites, while 1 Chronicles 21:1 Satan, or a resister did. This would seem to be a clear mistake on the part of one of these authors.

2 Samuel 24:1 Updated American Standard Version (UASV)

[1] Now again the anger of Jehovah burned against Israel, and it incited David against them to say, "Go, number Israel and Judah."

1 Chronicles 21:1 Updated American Standard Version (UASV)

[1] Then Satan stood up against Israel and moved David to number Israel.

Answer: In this period of David's reign, Jehovah was very displeased with Israel, and therefore he did not prevent Satan from bringing this sin on them. Often in Scripture, it is spoken of as though God did something when he allowed an event to take place. For example, it is said that God 'hardened Pharaoh's heart' (Exodus 4:21), when he actually allowed the Pharaoh's heart to harden.

Inerrancy: Are There Scientific Errors?

Many truths about God are beyond the scope of science. Science and the Bible are not at odds. In fact, we can thank modern day science as it has helped us to better under the creation of God, from our solar system to the universes, to the human body and mind. What we find is a level of order, precision, design, and sophistication, which points to a Designer, the eyes of many Christians, to an Almighty God, with infinite intelligence and power. The apostle Paul makes this all too clear, when he writes, "For his invisible attributes, namely, his eternal power and divine nature, have been clearly perceived, ever since the creation of the world, in the things that have been made. So they are without excuse." – Romans 1:20.

Back in the seventeenth century, the world-renowned scientist Galileo proved beyond any doubt that the earth was not the center of the universe, nor did the sun orbit the earth. In fact, he proved it to be the other way around (no pun intended), with the earth revolving around the sun. However, he was brought up on charges of heresy by the Catholic Church and ordered to recant his position. Why? From the viewpoint of the Catholic Church, Galileo was contradicting God's Word, the Bible. As it turned out, Galileo and science were correct, and the Church was wrong, for which it issued a formal apology in 1992. However, the point we wish to make here is that in all the controversy, the Bible was never in the wrong. It was a misinterpretation on the part of the Catholic Church and not a fault with the Bible. One will find no place in the Bible that claims the sun orbits the earth. So where would the Church get such an idea? The Church got such an idea from Ptolemy (b. about 85 C.E.), an ancient astronomer, who argued for such an idea.

As it usually turns out, the so-called contradiction between science and God's Word lies at the feet of those who are interpreting Scripture incorrectly. To repeat the sentiments of Galileo when writing to a pupil–Galileo expressed the same sentiments: "Even though Scripture cannot err, its interpreters and expositors can, in various ways. One of these, very serious and very frequent, would be when they always want to stop at the purely literal sense."[36] I believe that today's scholars, in hindsight, would have no problem agreeing.

While the Bible is not a science textbook, it is scientifically accurate when it touches on matters of science.

The Circle of the Earth Hangs on Nothing

---

[36] Letter from Galileo to Benedetto Castelli, December 21, 1613.

Isaiah 40:22 Updated American Standard Version (UASV)

²² It is he who sits above **the circle of the earth**,
   and its inhabitants are like grasshoppers;
who stretches out the heavens like a curtain,
   and spreads them like a tent to dwell in.

More than 2,500 years ago, the prophet Isaiah wrote that the earth is a circle or sphere. First, how would it be possible for Isaiah to know the earth is a circle or sphere, if not from inspiration? Scientific America writes, "As countless photos from space can attest, Earth is round–the "Blue Marble," as astronauts have affectionately dubbed it. Appearances, however, can be deceiving. Planet Earth is not, in fact, perfectly round."[37] Scientifically speaking, the sun is not perfectly, absolutely 100 percent round but in everyday speech, this verse is both acceptable and accurate, when we keep in mind it is written from a human perspective, not from a scientific perspective. Moreover, Isaiah was not discussing astronomy; he was simply making an inspired observation that man came to realize once he was in space, looking back at the earth, it is round. See the section about title, "Intended Meaning of Writer."

Job 26:7 Updated American Standard Version (UASV)

⁷ "He stretches out the north over empty space
and hangs the earth on nothing.

Here the author describes the earth as hanging upon nothing. Many have never heard of the Greek mathematician and astronomer Eratosthenes. He was born in about 276 B.C.E. and received some of his education in Athens, Greece. In 240 B.C., the "Greek astronomer, geographer, mathematician and librarian Eratosthenes calculates the Earth's circumference. His data was rough, but he wasn't far off."[38] While man very early on used their God given intelligence to arrive at some outstanding conclusion that was actually very accurate, we learn

---

[37] Charles Q. Choi (April 12, 2007). Scientific America. Strange but True: Earth Is Not Round. Retrieved Monday, August 03, 2015.

http://www.scientificamerican.com/article/earth-is-not-round/

[38] Alfred, Randy (June 19, 2008). "June 19, 240 B.C.E: The Earth Is Round, and It's This Big". Wired. Retrieved Monday, August 03, 2015.

two points here. Eratosthenes was a very astute scientist, while Isaiah, who wrote some 500 years earlier, was no scientist at all. Moreover, Moses, who wrote the book of Job over 1,230 years before Eratosthenes, knew that the earth hung upon nothing.

How Is the Sun Standing Still Possible?

Joshua 10:13 Updated American Standard Version (UASV)

¹³ And the sun stood still, and the moon stopped,
until the nation avenged themselves of their enemies.
Is this not written in the Book of Jashar? The sun stopped in the midst of heaven and did not hurry to set for about a whole day.

The Canaanites had besieged the Gibeonites, a group of people that gained Jehovah God's backing because they had faith in Him. In this battle, Jehovah helped the Israelites continue their attack by causing "the sun [to stand] still, and the moon stopped, until the nation took vengeance on their enemies." (Jos 10:1-14) Those who accept God as the creator of the universe and life can accept that he would know a way of stopping the earth from rotating. However, there are other ways of understanding this account. We must keep in mind that the Bible speaks from an earthly observer point of view, so it need not be that he stopped the rotation. It could have been a refraction of solar and lunar light rays, which would have produced the same effect.

Psalm 136:6 Updated American Standard Version (UASV)

⁶ to him who spread out the earth above the waters,
for his lovingkindness is everlasting;

Hebrews 3:4 Updated American Standard Version (UASV)

⁴ For every house is built by someone, but the builder of all things is God.

2 Kings 20:8-11 Updated American Standard Version (UASV)

⁸ And Hezekiah said to Isaiah, "What shall be the sign that Jehovah will heal me, and that I shall go up to the house of Jehovah on the third day?" ⁹ And Isaiah said, "This shall be the sign to you from Jehovah, that Jehovah will do the thing that he has spoken: shall the shadow go forward ten steps or go back ten steps?" ¹⁰ And Hezekiah

answered, "It is an easy thing for the shadow to decline ten steps; no, but let the shadow turn backward ten steps." [11] And Isaiah the prophet cried to Jehovah, and he brought the shadow on the steps back ten steps, by which it had gone down on the steps of Ahaz.

How is it that the stars fought on behalf of Barak?

Judges 5:20 Updated American Standard Version (UASV)

[20] From heaven the stars fought, from their courses they fought against Sisera.

Judges 4:15 Updated American Standard Version (UASV)

[15] And Jehovah routed Sisera and all his chariots and all his army with the edge of the sword before Barak; and Sisera alighted from his chariot and fled away on foot.

In the Bible, you have Biblical prose, and Biblical poetry.

Prose: language that is not poetry: (1) writing or speech in its normal continuous form, without the rhythmic or visual line structure of poetry **(2)** ordinary style of expression: writing or speech that is ordinary or matter-of-fact, without embellishment.

Poetry: literature in verse: (1) literary works written in verse, in particular verse writing of high quality, great beauty, emotional sincerity or intensity, or profound insight **(2) beauty or grace:** something that resembles poetry in its beauty, rhythmic grace, or imaginative, elevated, or decorative style.

We have a beautiful example of both of these forms of writing communication in chapters four and five of the book of Judges. Judges, Chapter 4 is a prose account of Deborah and Barak, while Judges Chapter 5 is a poetic account. As we have learned from the above, poetry is less concerned with accuracy than evoking emotions. Poetry has a license to say things like what we find in of 5:20, which is in the poetry chapter: "from heaven the stars fought." This can be said, and the reader is expected not to take the language literally. What we can surmise from it though, is that God was acting against Sisera in some way, there was divine intervention.

Procedures for Handling Biblical Difficulties

1. You need to be completely convinced a reason or understanding exists.

2. You need to have total trust and conviction in the inerrancy of the Scripture as originally written down.

3. You need to study the context and framework of the verse carefully, to establish what the author meant by the words he used. In other words, find the beginning and the end of the context that your passage falls within.

4. You need to understand exegesis: find the historical setting, determine author intent, study key words, and note parallel passages. You need to slow down and carefully read the account, considering exactly what is being said

5. You need to find a reasonable harmonization of parallel passages.

6. You need to consider a variety of trusted Bible commentaries, dictionaries, lexical sources, encyclopedias, as well as books on Bible difficulties.

7. You should investigate as to whether the difficulty is a transmission error in the original text.

8. You must always keep in mind that the historical accuracy of the biblical text is unmatched; that thousands of extant manuscripts some of which date back to the second century B.C. support the transmitted text of Scripture.

9. We must keep in mind that the Bible is a diverse book when it comes to literary styles: narrative, poetic, prophetic, and apocalyptic; also containing parables, metaphors, similes, hyperbole, and other figures of speech. Too often, these alleged errors are the result of a reader taking a figure of speech as literal or reading a parable as though it is a narrative.

10. The Bible student needs to understand what level that the Bible intends to be exact in what is written. If Jim told a friend that 650 graduated with him from high school in 1984, it is not challenged, because it is all too clear that he is using rounded numbers and is not meaning to be precise.

Bibliography

Alden, R. L. (2001). *Job, The New American Commentary, vol. 11* . Nashville: Broadman & Holman Publishers.

Andrews, E. (2020). *FROM SPOKEN WORDS TO SACRED TEXTS: Introduction-Intermediate New Testament Textual Studies.* Cambridge: Christian Publishing House.

Andrews, E. D. (2016). *INTERPRETING THE BIBLE: Introduction to Biblical Hermeneutics.* Cambridge, OH: Christian Publishing House.

Andrews, E. D. (2023). *ARCHAEOLOGY & THE OLD TESTAMENT.* Cambridge, Ohio: Christian Publishing House.

Andrews, E. D. (2023). *CHRISTIAN APOLOGETICS: Answering the Tough Questions: Evidence and Reason in Defense of the Faith.* Cambridge, Ohio: Christian Publishing House.

Andrews, E. D. (2023). *HOW WE GOT THE BIBLE.* Cambridge, OH: Christian Publishing House.

Andrews, E. D. (2023). *INTRODUCTION TO THE TEXT OF THE OLD TESTAMENT: From the Authors and Scribes to the Modern Critical Text.* Cambridge, OH: Christian Publishing House.

Andrews, E. D. (2023). *THE BIBLE AS HISTORY: A Historical Journey Through the Bible.* Cambridge, Ohio: Christian Publishing House.

Andrews, E. D. (2023). *THE BIBLE ON TRIAL: Examining the Evidence for Being Inspired, Inerrant, Authentic, and True.* Cambridge, Ohio: Christian Publishing House.

Andrews, E. D. (2023). *THE BOOK OF PROVERBS Chapters 1-15: CPH Old Testament Commentary: Volume 17.* Cambridge, OH: Christian Publishing House.

Andrews, E. D. (2023). *THE BOOK OF PROVERBS Chapters 16-23: CPH Old Testament Commentary: Volume 18.* Cambridge, OH: Christian Publishing House.

Andrews, E. D. (2023). *THE EXPOSITORY DICTIONARY: A Companion Study Tool to the Updated American Standard Version.* Cambridge, OH: Christian Publishing House.

Andrews, E. D. (2023). *THE OLD TESTAMENT: Commentary, Background, & Bible Difficulties (Introduction to the Old Testament).* Cambridge, OH: Christian Publishing House.

Archer, G. L. (1982). *New International Encyclopedia of Bible Difficulties, Zondervan's Understand the Bible Reference Series.* Zondervan Publishing House: Grand Rapids, MI.

Archer, G. L. (1985). *The Expositor's Bible Commentary, Vol. 7: Daniel and the Minor Prophets.* Grand Rapids: Zondervan.

Archer, G. L. (2007). *A Survey of Old Testament Introduction. Revised and expanded ed.* Chicago: Moody.

Barker, K. L., & Bailey, W. (2001). *The New American Commentary: vol. 20, Micah, Nahum, Habakkuk, Zephaniah.* Nashville, TN: Broadman & Holman Publishers.

Bergen, R. D. (1996). *The New American Commentary: 1-2 Samuel.* Nashville: Broadman & Holman.

Block, D. I. (1999). *Judges, Ruth, vol. 6, The New American Commentary.* Nashville, TN: Broadman & Holman Publishers.

Brand, C., Draper, C., & Archie, E. (2003). *Holman Illustrated Bible Dictionary: Revised, Updated and Expanded.* Nashville, TN: Holman.

Breneman, M. (1993). *The New American Commentary, vol. 10, Ezra, Nehemiah, Esther.* Nashville: Broadman & Holman Publishers.

Bromiley, G. W. (1986). *The International Standard Bible Encyclopedia (Vol. 1-4).* Grand Rapids, MI: William B. Eerdmans Publishing Co.

Cole, R. D. (2000). *THE NEW AMERICAN COMMENTARY: Volume 3b Numbers.* Nashville: Broadman & Holman Publishers.

Cooper, L. E. (1994). *The New American Commentary, Ezekiel, vol. 17.* Nashville, TN: Broadman & Holman Publishers.

Elwell, W. A., & Beitzel, B. J. (1988). *Baker Encyclopedia of the Bible.* Grand Rapids, MI: Baker Book House.

Ernst Würthwein. (2014). *The Text of the Old Testament: An Introduction to the Biblia Hebraica, ed. Alexander Achilles Fischer, trans. Erroll F. Rhodes, Third Edition.* William B. Eerdmans Publishing Company: Grand Rapids, MI.

Garland, D. E., & Longman, T. I. (2008). *The Expositor's Bible Commentary: Proverbs-Isaiah.* Grand Rapids, MI: Zondervan.

Harrison, R. K. (1969). *Introduction to the Old Testament.* Grand Rapids, MI: Eerdmans.

House, P. R. (2001). *The New American Commentary: 2 Kings.* Nashville: Broadman & Holman Publishers.

Howard Jr., D. M. (1998). *Joshua, vol. 5, The New American Commentary.* Nashville, TN: Broadman & Holman Publishers.

Longman III, T. (1999). *The NIV Application Commentary : Daniel.* Grand Rapids: Zondervan Publishing House.

Longman III, T. (2006). *An Introduction to the Old Testament: Second Edition.* Grand Rapids, MI: Zondervan Academic.

Longman III, T. (2015). *Proverbs (Baker Commentary on the Old Testament Wisdom and Psalms).* Grand Rapids, MI: Baker Academic.

Mathews, K. A. (2001). *The New American Commentary vol. 1A, Genesis 1-11:26.* Nashville: Broadman & Holman Publishers.

Merrill, E. H. (1994). *Deuteronomy, vol. 4, The New American Commentary.* Nashville: Broadman & Holman Publishers.

Rooker, M. F. (2000). *The New American Commentary, vol. 3A, Leviticus.* Nashville: Broadman & Holman Publishers.

Stuart, D. K. (2006). *The New American Commentary: An Exegetical Theological Exposition of Holy Scripture EXODUS.* Nashville: Broadman & Holman.

Taylor, R. A., & Clendenen, R. E. (2007). *The New American Commentary: Haggai, Malachi, , vol. 21A* . Nashville, TN: Broadman & Holman Publishers.

Thompson, J. A. (1994). *1, 2 Chronicles, vol. 9, The New American Commentary.* Nashville, TN: Broadman & Holman Publishers.

Tremper, L. I. (2005). *How to Read Genesis (How to Read Series How to Read).* Grand Rapids: Intervarsity Press.

Vine, W. E., Unger, M. F., & White Jr., W. (1996). *Vine's Complete Expository Dictionary of Old and New Testament Words.* Nashville, TN: T. Nelson.

Walvoord, J. (2012). *Daniel (The John Walvoord Prophecy Commentaries)* . Chicago: Moody Publishers.

www.ingramcontent.com/pod-product-compliance
Lightning Source LLC
Chambersburg PA
CBHW050546160426
43199CB00015B/2555